9-11-94

Happy    Cooking

Laura & Alicia

with    love

Dopi Terzi

# ATHENIAN CUISINE

# ATHENIAN CUISINE

## OVER 600 RECIPES

*By*

POPI TERZI

JACKET DESIGN AND DRAWINGS
BY JOE NADZIEJKO

PUBLISHING

TARRYTOWN, NEW YORK
1987

(714) 840-8071

*Dedicated*
*to my children Sunday and George*
*"My best friends"*

# INTRODUCTION

This publication represents the realization of a dream that has existed in my heart for many years. As a young girl, I loved to watch and help my mother prepare her many tasteful dishes in our little kitchen in Greece, and after a while, I learned to prepare them myself.

When I came to the States and started cooking for my friends, I felt very proud when they continuously asked me for my recipes for their favorite dishes. Then, some of them came up with the idea of having me write a cookbook, so that they could have a collection of all my recipes instead of just a few. They said it so many times, that they finally convinced me into it. The collection of my recipes has been in my family for many years, but has been improved continuously to suit today's tastes and needs.

The traditional Easter dinner, for example, usually consists of a whole lamb and roasting it on a spit over red-hot coals. Although this fun-filled method is in my book, I've also added a less tedious method, which is prepared in the oven, fills the kitchen with such a delectable aroma, that one can't wait to sink his teeth in a piece of that juicy, golden brown meat, not to mention the stuffing and potatoes where all of those mouth-watering juices are collecting. All this, put together with a few finishing touches, makes a captivating feast fit for kings.

This is just one of the many delicious treasures found in this book. Just turn the pages one by one, and your tastebuds will travel a tasteful and most appealing journey through Greece!

*Popi Terzi*

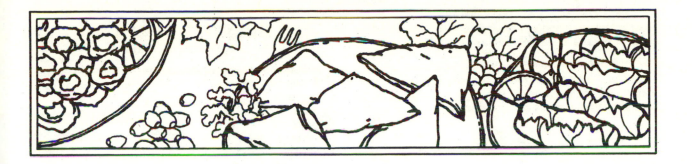

# APPETIZERS

## HOW TO PREPARE CANAPES
### Πῶς νὰ παρασκευάσης καναπὲ

Canapes are made from day-old white or dark slices of bread and then shaped with a cutter into circles, squares, stripes, triangles or other fancy shapes you desire. They are then ready to be covered with the mixture you prefer.

## ANCHOVY CANAPES
### Καναπὲ μὲ ἀντζούγιες

8 portions prepared bread
4 whole anchovies fillet
8 capers
Butter at room temperature

Spread butter on the prepared pieces of bread. Split anchovy lengthwise and curve around a circle of caper and lay on the canape.

## SHRIMP, LOBSTER, CRABMEAT, CANAPES
### Καναπὲ μὲ γαρίδες, ἀστακὸ ἢ καβοῦρι

8 portions prepared bread
8 teaspoons shrimp, cooked and finely chopped
1 tablespoon mayonnaise
1 hard-boiled egg, finely chopped
Salt and pepper to taste
Ketchup

Mix chopped shrimp if desired, egg, mayonnaise, salt and pepper together. Spread the prepared bread with the mixture and decorate the center of each canape with a little ketchup. Chill.

## BOMB
## BREAD FOR COCKTAIL SANDWICHES AND CANAPES

1½ cups scalding milk
½ cup warm water
⅓ cup butter or margarine
1 tablespoon sugar
2 teaspoons salt
1 package active dry yeast
1 egg plus 1 egg yolk, lightly beaten
5 cups all-purpose unbleached flour (about), sifted

Add butter, sugar, and salt to milk and water and cool to warm. Dissolve yeast in milk. Place milk mixture in a mixing bowl, add eggs and 2 cups of the flour and beat well. Add enough flour to make a soft dough. Turn out dough on floured board and knead until smooth and elastic. Place in greased bowl turning to greased top. Cover, let rise in warm place free from draft until doubled in bulk, about 60-70 minutes. Punch down dough and knead for few minutes. Divide into 2 equal pieces. Grease bottoms and sides of two coffee cans (the size of 1-lb.). Place dough in the cans and press down. Brush tops with butter. Cover with their covers; let rise in a warm place about 60 minutes or until double. Remove the covers. Bake in a preheated 350°F (180°C) oven for 30 minutes. Loosen edges of breads from sides of cans, turn onto wire rack to cool. Slice off rounded top portion of bread, set aside. Slice remaining bread crosswise into very thin slices. Starting at the bottom, take two slices of bread at a time, and spread with butter. Add ham, cheese spread, pate de foie gras or any other spread you like (see index for recipe) and form into sandwich. Put the sandwiches one on top the other. When you finish, the shape should look like what is was when you took it out of the can. Then cut crisscross, so for every sandwich you will make four sandwiches.

1

Make a bed of lettuce in a serving dish and place the bomb. Cover and refrigerate until ready to serve.

**For sandwich and canapes:**
Shape into loaves and place in greased bread pans. Brush with melted butter. Cover, let rise in a warm place about 60 minutes or until double.

❦❦❦

# PATE DE FOIE GRAS
Φουὰ γκρὰ

8 ounces chicken livers
8 tablespoons butter or margarine, at room
     temperature
½ cup chopped onion
Salt and pepper to taste
Dash Cayenne pepper
¼ teaspoon dry mustard

Carefully clean and rinse livers. In a skillet melt 4 tablespoons butter, add chopped onion and saute until it is transparent. Add the chicken livers and cook slowly for 10 minutes or until they are no longer pink, stirring occasionally. Add salt, pepper and mustard. Turn the liver mixture into a blender or food processor container and blend until smooth. Add the remaining 4 tablespoons butter to the liver mixture and blend until smooth and creamy. Pour into a bowl, cover and chill. This preparation makes excellent canapes or sandwiches.

❦❦❦

# CHEESE BALLS
Μπαλάκια τυριοῦ

¼ cup chilled butter or margarine
6 ounces grated kefalotyri or parmesan cheese
1 teaspoon salt
2 teaspoons baking powder
2 cups all-purpose flour
2 eggs, beaten

1 egg white, lightly beaten with 1 teaspoon water
In a large mixing bowl stir together flour, salt and baking powder, cut in butter until mixture resembles coarse crumbs. Add cheese and 2 eggs. Gently toss with your fingers, form dough into small balls 1-inch in diameter and place in a lightly greased baking sheet. Fllatten with a fork making a crisscross pattern. Brush with egg white. Bake in a preheated 350°F (180°C) oven for 15-20 minutes. Serve hot.

# CHEESE CROQUETTES
Κροκέττες ἀπὸ τυρὶ

4 tablespoons butter or margarine
6 tablespoons flour
1 cup milk
½ cup cream
Salt to taste
⅛ white pepper
½ teaspoon baking powder
3 egg yolks, beaten
1 cup cubed cheese, Kaseri or Swiss
Butter or oil for frying

Melt butter over medium heat, blend in flour until smooth using a whisk. Gradually add milk, stirring constantly until mixture is thick and smooth. Cook 3 minutes longer; add seasoning and blend. Add to egg yolks; when well mixed add cheese. Cool. Shape into small balls and fry in hot butter or oil until golden brown. Serve hot. Serves 10-14.

❦❦❦

# FRIED CHEESE CUBES
Τυράκια τηγανητὰ

1 beaten egg
½ cup cream
¾ cup flour
½ teaspoon baking powder
White pepper to taste
Salt to your taste
1 tablespoon melted butter or margarine
1 pound Kaseri cheese, cut into 1x½ inch cubes
Butter for frying

In a bowl blend egg, milk, flour, baking powder, pepper, salt and melted butter. Dip cheese cubes one at a time and fry in hot butter or margarine until golden brown. Serve immediately.

❦❦❦

# FRIED CHEESE ROUNDS
Μπαλάκια τυριοῦ τηγανητὰ

5 eggs, beaten
½ cup flour, sifted with
1½ teaspoons baking powder
1 teaspoon finely chopped parsley
1½ cups Kefalotyri cheese, grated
Butter for frying

Combine all ingredients together and mix well. Heat butter in a heavy frying pan over medium heat. With a damp teaspoon drop the batter in teaspoons into the hot butter. Fry until it becomes lightly golden on both sides. Remove from the butter and lay on an absorbent paper to drain. Serve hot.

⚜⚜⚜

# CHEESE AND HAM LOAF
## Κέϊκ μὲ τυρὶ

1 cup butter or margarine at room temperature
5 large eggs
1½ cups flour, sifted with
5 tablespoons baking powder
¾ cup shredded Kaseri cheese
½ cup shredded Cheddar cheese
¼ cup grater Parmesan cheese
¼ cup shredded Swiss cheese
¼ teaspoon pepper
8 ounces boiled chopped ham
⅓ cup milk

Cream butter until light. Add eggs one at a time, beating thoroughly after each addition. Add flour alternately with milk. Fold in cheeses, pepper and ham. Pour into buttered loaf pan. (10x6x3) inches. Bake in a preheated 350°F (180°C) oven for 45 minutes or until golden brown. Cool slightly before slicing. Serve warm.

⚜⚜⚜

# CHEESE TINY PIES WITH HOMEMADE PASTRY
## Τυροπιτάκια μὲ φύλλο σπιτικὸ

1 homemade pastry recipe A, B, or C (see index)
1 pound Feta cheese or 8 ounces Feta cheese and
8 ounces Farmers or Ricotta cheese
4 egg yolks
⅛ teaspoon pepper
3 egg whites, lightly beaten

Beat eggs. Add cheese and pepper, mix well to combine. Prepare homemade pastry. On a lightly floured surface, fold half of the pastry at a time to a 20-inch circle about ⅛-inch thick. With 4-inch round cookie cutter cut out circles of dough. Place 1 teaspoon of filling on one half of a circle. Brush edges with egg whites. Fold other half of circle making half-moon shape. Pinch edges together well to seal or seal by pressing with tines of fork. Place half-moon in a buttered baking sheet. Brush with egg white. Bake in a preheated 375°F (190°C) oven for 20-25 minutes. Serve hot. Makes 60-70 cheese pies.
Note: Cheese tiny pies may be frozen before or after baking, as in cheese puffs.

# CHEESE PUFFS
## Μπουρεκάκια μὲ τυρὶ

3½ tablespoons butter or margarine
4 tablespoons flour
1 cup milk
2 eggs plus 1 egg yolk, beaten
8 ounces Feta cheese, crumbled
4 ounces Swiss cheese, cut into cubes
8 ounces Ricotta or Farmers cheese
2 tablespoons grated Parmesan cheese
1 tablespoon finely chopped parsley (optional)
⅛ teaspoon pepper (optional)
1 pound phyllo pastry (thawed)
1½ cups clarified butter or margarine (see index)

In a saucepan melt butter over medium heat. Using a wire whisk, stir in flour and blend well. Gradually stir in milk, stirring constantly until sauce is thick and smooth. Stir little of the hot sauce into the eggs. Pour egg mixture into sauce and cook over low heat for 5 minutes, stirring constantly. Remove from heat. Add cheeses, the parsley and pepper if desired, in the egg mixture and mix well to combine. Let cool. Take the phyllo sheets from the package, cut into three strips about 6x13-inches each strip. Take one strip at a time, covering the remaining strips with a dry cloth, then with lightly dampened towel to prevent them from drying out. Every strip has 20-22 sheets. For each puff brush 1 sheet with melted butter and fold in half crosswise. Brush again with butter. Place 1 teaspoon cheese mixture at a narrow end and fold sides in toward the middle to enclose filling. Brush with melted butter and rollup into a tubeshape. Repeat with the remaining phyllo sheets. Place the puffs in a large buttered baking sheet and brush them with melted butter, again. Bake in a preheated 350°F (180°C) oven until golden, about 15-20 minutes. Makes 60-65 puffs. Cheese puffs may be frozen before or after baking. When ready to bake, bake in a preheated 350°F (180°C) oven until ready, about 30 minutes. Serve hot.

⚜⚜⚜

# CHEESE SPREAD
## Ἄλειμμα τυριοῦ

1 package (8 ounces) cream cheese
6 ounces Roquefort cheese
½ cup butter or margarine
¼ cup finely chopped walnuts or almonds (optional)
1 teaspoon Worcestershire sauce

All the ingredients have to be at room temperature. Mix all the ingredients together in a mixing bowl. Spoon in a serving bowl and refrigerate. When you are ready to use, let stay at room temperature and spread on crackers or canapes.

❈❈❈❈

## CHEESE TRIANGLES
### Τρίγωνα μὲ τυρὶ

Follow recipe as directed in Cheese Puffs. (See index). Prepare and bake them as directed in Spinach Triangles (see index).

❈❈❈❈

## CRACKERS
### Κρακεράκια

3  cups all-purpose unbleached flour
1  teaspoon salt
¾  cup butter or margarine, chilled
¾  cup grated Parmesan or Romano cheese
3  eggs plus 1 yolk, lightly beaten
1  egg white
¼  cup Ouzo (Greek liqueur)
½  cup or more chopped blanched almonds
Salt

In a mixing bowl stir together flour and salt. Cut in butter until mixture resembles coarse crumbs. Add grated cheese, the eggs and Ouzo. Gently toss with your finger. Roll dough to ⅛-inch thickness. With floured cutter, cut circles, squares, stripes, or other fancy shapes. Place on a lightly greased baking sheet. Brush with egg and sprinkle with chopped almonds and salt. Bake in a preheated 350°F (180°C) oven for 15-20 minutes. Serve with dip, spread or plain.

❈❈❈❈

## BATON SALE OR CRACKERS
### Μπατὸν σαλὲ ἢ κρακεράκια

5  cups all-purpose unbleached flour
½  teaspoon salt
1¼  cups butter or margarine
1¼  cups Kefalotyri or Parmesan cheese, grated
½  teaspoon dry mustard
⅛  teaspoon white pepper
2  eggs plus 2 egg yolks, lightly beaten
¼  cup cold water
2  teaspoons baking powder
2  egg whites

In a mixing bowl stir together flour, salt and baking powder. Cut in butter until mixture resembles coarse crumbs. Add cheese except ¼ cup, dry mustard, pepper, eggs and water; and gently toss with your

finger. Form dough into balls. On lightly floured surface, flatten one ball at a time with a rolling pin to ⅛-inch thickness. Cut with floured cutter, into circles, squares, strips or other fancy shapes. Place on a lightly greased baking sheet. Brush with egg white and sprinkle with Kefalotyri cheese. Bake in a preheated 400°F (205°C) oven for 10-12 minutes. Serve plain.

❈❈❈❈

## CODFISH CAVIAR SPREAD
### Ταραμοσαλάτα

2  medium peeled potatoes boiled or 9 ounces Italian
      day-old bread, crust removed
½  jar (5 ounces) tarama (codfish caviar)
Juice of ½ or more lemon
1½  cups salad oil
1  tablespoon finely grated onion (optional)

If you use bread, soak in cold water for 10 minutes. Squeeze it dry. In a food processor or blender, blend the tarama first for a few minutes. Add potatoes if desired and blend at high speed until smooth. While the machine is running, add onion, lemon juice, one teaspoon at a time, add oil in a slow thin stream until mixture is thick and smooth. Chill. Serve with crackers or spread on canapes.

❈❈❈❈

## CODFISH CROQUETTES
### Μπακαλιάρος κροκέττες

1  pound frozen or fresh cod or haddock fillet (thawed)
2½  cups mashed potatoes
3  egg yolks
3  tablespoons cream
1  small onion finely chopped
1  teaspoon salt
1  teaspoon pepper
1  cup flour
2  egg whites, lightly beaten
1½  cups fine bread crumbs
Oil for frying

Chop fish finely. In a mixing bowl, mix well, fish, mashed potatoes, egg yollks, cream, onion, salt and pepper. Chill for couple hours. Shape into small balls, each about 1-inch in diameter. Roll them lightly in flour, shake off excess flour, then in eggs whites and in crumbs. Fry croquettes in hot oil until golden brown on all sides. Lift out and drain on absorbent paper. Serve hot or cold.

# CUCUMBER AND YOGURT SPREAD
### Τζατζίκι

2  cups plain yogurt
2  tablespoons salad oil
2  cloves garlic, crushed
2  teaspoons wine vinegar
1  cucumber, peeled, seeded, grated and drained
Salt and pepper to taste
1  teaspoon finely chopped fresh dill

Gently blend yogurt, garlic and cucumber, add oil, vinegar, fresh dill, salt and pepper to taste, blend well to combine. Chill. Serve with carrot sticks, celery, cucumber slices, crackers or pieces of bread.

# DEVILED EGGS
### Αὐγὰ γεμιστὰ

6  hard-boiled eggs
Salt and pepper to taste
1  cup shrimp, or minced ham (optional)
4-5  teaspoons mayonnaise
½  teaspoon mustard
1  small finnely chopped dill pickled cucumber
Paprika or parsley for garnish

Cut hard-boiled eggs in half lengthwise. Mash the yolks, season with salt, pepper, shrimp if desired, mayonnaise, mustard and chopped picklle. Mix well to combine. Refill the whites with the mixture and garnish with paprika or parsley. Arrange on a platter. Chill.

# EGGPLANT SPREAD
### Μελιτζανοσαλάτα

1  large eggplant (about 1½ pounds)
1  clove minced garlic
1  tablespoon minced onion
2  tablespoons oil
½  cup ground blanched almonds or walnuts
Salt and pepper to taste
½  cup or more mayonnaise

Remove stem of the eggplant and wash well. Puncture with a fork to prevent it from exploding while it bakes. Place in a baking pan and bake in a pre-heated 400°F (205°C) oven for 60 minutes or until soft to the touch. While hot, remove skin. Cut into pieces. In a food processor combine all the ingredients except the mayonnaise and blend well. Add mayonnaise and blend for 1 second. Pour in a serving bowl and chill well. Serve with fresh bread or crackers. Makes 3 cups.

# RICE STUFFED GRAPEVINE LEAVES
### Ντολμαδάκια μὲ ρίζι

1  jar (16 ounces) grape leaves
4  cups finely chopped onion
1  cup olive oil
2  cups rice
1¾  cups boiling water
3  tablespoons finely chopped fresh dill or 1 teaspoon dried
2  tablespoons finely chopped fresh mint or ¾ teaspoons dried crushed
Salt and pepper to taste
½  cup or more chopped blanched almonds or ⅓ cup pine seeds
2¼  cups boiling water
Juice of 1 lemon or none

Rinse grape leaves thoroughly. Plunge grape leaves one by one into boiling water, few at a time and boil for 2 minutes. Rinse and drain. Cut off stems from leaves and reserve. Pick out few hard leaves and set aside. Line a Dutch oven with reserved stems and hard leaves. Saute onion with ½ cup oil until soft. Add rice and saute for few minutes. Add boiling water, dill, mint, salt and pepper. Cover and cook slowly for 5 minutes. Remove from heat. Cool. Add almonds if desired, mix thoroughly. Place 1 teaspoon filling on underside of each grape leaf. Fold base of leaf over filling, then fold in sides and drap into a roll. Place rolls in layers close together, seam-side down. Add remaining oil, lemon juice. Place an inverted heavy plate on top of stuffed grape leaves, add boiling water. Cover, cook slowly for approximately 45 minutes or until grape leaves are tender and pot juices have evaporated. Let stand for ½ hour to cool. Gently remove from pot and arrange into a serving platter. Decorate with thin lemon slices. Serve warm or cold with plain yogurt.

# HAM CHEESE LOG 'A'
### Ζαμπὸν μὲ τυρὶ ρολλὸ

7  slices of ham, cut into half (optional)
½  cup butter or margarine
5  ounces Roquefort cheese
2  hard-boiled eggs, using only the yolks
2  drops Worcestershire sauce

5

Mix all the ingredients, except the ham (have to be at room temperature), until smooth and creamy. Spread mixture on ham slices and roll up one by one. Makes 14 logs.
Note: You can spread the mixture on canapes or crackers instead of ham.

## HAM CHEESE LOG 'B'
### Ζαμπὸν μὲ τυρὶ ρολλὸ

5 ounces Roquefort cheese
5 ounces cream cheese
3 tablespoons butter or margarine
1 small finely chopped onion
1 teaspoon Worcestershire sauce
2 tablespoons dry white wine
8 ounces very thin sliced ham

Mix all the ingredients except the ham together (have to be at room temperature), until smooth and creamy. Spread the mixture on the slices of ham and roll. Place rolls on a serving plate and garnish with parsley if desired. Cover and chill.

## HAM LOG 'C'
### Ρολλὸ μὲ ζαμπὸν

8 slices ham
16 tablespoons Russian salad (see index)
1 tablespoon mustard

Cut ham slices in half, spread each one with mustard and place 1 tablespoon Russian salad on top and roll. Cover and chill. Makes 16 logs.

## COCKTAIL MEATBALLS
### Κεφτεδάκια μεζὲ

1 cup milk
1 egg plus 1 egg yolk, lightly beaten
2/3 cup dried bread crumbs (see index)
1½ tablespoons olive oil
½ cup minced onion
2 teaspoons salt
¼ teaspoon pepper
⅛ teaspoon Greek rigani (oregano)
1 tablespoon minced fresh mint or 1 teaspoon dried crushed
1 teaspoon red wine vinegar
1 pound lean ground beef
½ pound lean ground pork
Flour for rolling
¾ cup oil for frying

In a large bowl, mix milk, eggs and bread crumbs, let stay 15 minutes. In a small skillet heat the olive oil and saute the onion until soft. Add to the milk mixture and the rest of the ingredients. Mix well by hand until thoroughly blended. Cover and refrigerate for 2 hours or longer. Shape into 60 meatballs about 1-inch in diameter. Roll them lightly in flour. Shake off excess flour. Fry in hot oil until nicely browned. Lift out and drain on absorbent paper. Serve hot.

## MEAT PUFFS
### Μπουρεκάκια μὲ κιμᾶ

2 tablespoons butter or margarine
1 pound lean ground beef
1 medium onion, minced
1 medium tomato, skinned and chopped
Salt and pepper to taste
¼ cup grated Parmesan cheese
3 hard-boiled eggs and finely chopped
2 tablespoons bread crumbs (see index)
1 pound phyllo pastry (thawed)
1½ cups clarified butter (see index)

Heat butter and brown meat and onion together. Add wine, when the wine evaporates add tomato, salt and pepper. Cook slowly, covered for ½ hour. Remove from heat and let cool. Stir in cheese, eggs and bread crumbs. Cut, fill and fold, bake and freeze meat puffs as in Cheese Puffs. (See index). Makes 60-65 puffs.

## SWEDISH MEATBALLS
### Σουηδικὰ κεφτεδάκια

¾ cup milk
1 egg plus 1 egg yolk, lightly beaten
⅔ cup dry bread crumbs (see index)
½ cup butter or margarine
½ cup minced onion
1 pound lean ground beef
½ pound lean ground pork, lamb or veal
2 teaspoons salt
¼ teaspoon pepper
1 tablespoon minced parsley
1 teaspoon Worcestershire sauce
1 garlic clove, crushed
1½ tablespoons flour
1¼ cups dry white wine
½ cup water

In a large mixing bowl, mix milk, eggs and bread crumbs. Let stay 15 minutes. In a small skillet heat half of the butter and saute the onion until soft. In the milk mixture add onion, ground beef, pork if desired, 1½ teaspoons salt, pepper, parsley, Worcestershire sauce, and garlic. Mix well with your hand until thoroughly blended. Cover and refrigerate for 2 hours or longer. Shape into 60-70 meatballs, each about 1-inch in diameter. Heat remaining butter in a skillet over medium heat, add meatballs a few at a time and brown on all sides. Remove meatballs as browned and set aside. Drain fat from skillet into large saucepan. Stir in flour and blend well over low heat. Add wine, water and ½ teaspoon salt. Bring sauce to simmering point, gently add meatballs. Simmer covered for 25 minutes. Serve in a chafing dish.

## FRIED PEPPERS
### Πιπεριὲς τηγανητὲς

**12 small bell peppers**
**Oil for frying**
**1 tablespoon wine vinegar**
**Salt and pepper to taste**
**1 garlic clove, crushed (optional)**

Wash pepper well. Poke them in a few places with a fork. Heat oil in a medium heat, add peppers and cover. Fry for 5 minutes. Turn and fry 5 minutes longer. Place peppers in a platter and sprinkle with the vinegar and salt, add garlic if desired. Serves 4-6.

## ROASTED PEPPERS
### Πιπεριὲς ψητὲς

**⅓ cup olive oil**
**2 tablespoons wine vinegar**
**2 garlic cloves, crushed**
**Salt and pepper to taste**
**8 large green or red peppers**

Combine olive oil, vinegar, garlic and salt and pepper. Blend well. Set aside. Place peppers in a baking pan and broil in the oven or on the charcoal until the skins are blistered and peppers are soft. Let stay for 5 minutes. Peel them and remove seeds. Cut peppers into strips. In a serving bowl place peppers and pour over the olive oil mixture. Let cool. Serves 4-12.

## POTATO CROQUETTES
### Πατάτες κροκέττες

**⅔ cup grated Kefalotyri or Parmesan cheese**
**4 cups mashed potatoes**
**2 tablespoons cream**
**3 tablespoons butter or margarine**

**1 teaspoon minced parsley**
**Dash white pepper**
**3 egg yolks**
**1½ cups fine dried bread crumbs (see index)**
**3 eggs whites, slightly beaten**
**Oil for frying**

In a mixing bowl, combine cheese, potatoes, cream, butter, parsley, pepper and egg yolk. Beat until light. Shape into small cones, roll in crumbs, egg and again in crumbs. Fry croquettes in hot oil until golden brown on all sides. Lift out and drain on absorbent paper. Serve hot.

## SHRIMP COCKTAIL
### Γαρίδες κοκτέιλ

**3 cups cooked shrimp**
**Cocktail Sauce:**
**¼ cup tomato ketchup**
**1 cup mayonnaise**
**1½ tablespoons lemon juice**
**1½ teaspoons Worcestershire sauce**

Chill shrimp. Mix remaining ingredients well and chill. Place shrimp in chilled glasses and cover with sauce. Serves 12.
Note: Mix all the ingredients together and pour in serving bowl. This is excellent for buffet.

## BAKED SHRIMP WITH FETA CHEESE
### Γαρίδες μὲ φέτα στὸ σαγανάκι

**1 pound raw shrimp**
**¼ cup minced onion**
**¼ cup olive oil**
**¼ cup dry white wine**
**2 cups peeled, seeded and chopped tomatoes**
**1 tablespoon minced parsley**
**Salt and Pepper to taste**

**6 ounces feta cheese, cut into chunks**
Rinse shrimp and drain. Saute onion in oil until soft. Add wine, tomatoes, parsley, salt and pepper. Cover and simmer for 40 minutes or until mixture is very thick. Spoon half of the sauce into 2 individual oven dishes and arrange shrimp in each dish. Spoon remaining sauce over top with feta cheese. Bake in a preheated 350°F (180°C) oven for 20-30 minutes. Serve immediately. Serves 2.

# FRIED SHRIMP
Γαρίδες τηγανητὲς

1 pound raw shrimp
Salt
1 egg, lightly beaten
½ cup flour
Oil for frying
Juice of 1 lemon

Rinse shrimp and drain. Dry on paper towel. Sprinkle with salt. Dip shrimp into egg a few at a time and then in flour. Fry shrimp in hot oil on both sides until golden. Sprinkle with lemon juice and serve hot. Serves 2-4.

✿✿✿

# SPINACH TRIANGLES
Τρίγωνα μὲ σπανάκι

2 packages (10 ounces each) frozen leaf spinach
   (thawed well, drained and chopped)
1 cup chopped fresh scallions or ¼ cup onion
¼ cup olive oil
8 ounces Feta cheese, crumbled
4 ounces Farmers or Ricotta cheese
3 eggs, lightly beaten
1 tablespoon minced fresh parsley
1 tablespoon minced fresh dill
Salt and pepper to taste
1 pound phyllo pastry (thawed)
1½ cups clarified butter or olive oil (see index)

Gently fry scallions in oil until tender but not brown.

Add onion, cheese, eggs, parsley, dill, salt and pepper to the spinach and mix well to combine. Take the phyllo sheets from the package, cut into THREE strips lengthwise about, 4 inches each strip. Take one strip at a time covering the remaining strips with a dry cloth, then with lightly dampened towel to prevent them from drying out. For each triangle brush one sheet with melted butter if desired, fold in half lengthwise and brush again with butter. Place 1 teaspoon spinach mixture at one end of the folded strip. Lift a corner of the strip next to the filling and fold it over the filling so that it touches the opposite long side and forms a triangle enclosing the filling. Continue to fold up the pastry, keeping the triangular shape. Continue to fill and fold in triangles with the remaining strips. Place them in buttered baking sheets and brush with melted butter again. Bake in a preheated 350°F (180°C) oven until golden, about 20-25 minutes. Serve hot. Makes 70-80 triangles.

✿✿✿

# FRIED SQUID
Καλαμαράκια τηγανητὰ

2 pounds young squid
Salt
Flour for coating
Oil for frying
Lemon Juice

To clean squid, remove back bone, ink sac and pull off heads. Wash well in cold water. Pat dry. Slice in ½-inch rings, season with salt. Coat squid with flour, shake off excess flour. Fry in hot oil until light brown, no more than 3 minutes. Serve hot with lemon juice. Serves 6-10.

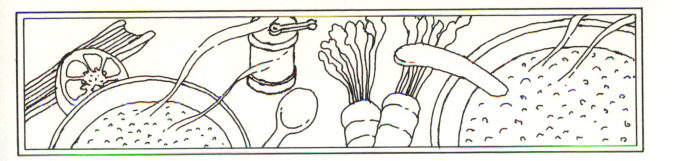

# SOUPS

## BOILED BEEF EGG-LEMON SOUP
### Βοδινὸ βραστὸ σούπα αὐγολέμονο

4 pounds beef shoulder, shank or brisket
4 small whole onions
3 carrots, cut in half
6 small whole potatoes
3 stalks celery, cut in half
1 tablespoon salt
9 tablespoons long grain rice
2 eggs
Juice of 1 or more lemons

Rinse meat and place in a large saucepan. Pour in cold water to cover the meat and bring to a boil. Skim the broth. Reduce heat, cover and simmer for 1 hour and 45 minutes. Add all the vegetables, salt and simmer for 60 minutes longer or until meat is tender. Remove meat and cut into slices. Place meat in a serving platter. With a straining spoon, remove the vegetables and arrange them around the meat. Strain the broth, measure it; add enough hot water to make 10 cups. Bring to a boil, add rice and stir. Reduce heat and simmer for 20 minutes. Remove from heat. In a medium bowl beat eggs until frothy, gradually beat in lemon juice. Add approximately a quarter of the hot broth, at first spoon by spoon and then a little more at a time beating constantly. Gradually add egg mixture to the soup, stirring gently to combine. Keep stirring for a few more minutes. Serve soup immediately, followed by the meat and the vegetables. Pass olive oil and vinegar dressing (see index). Serves 6.

## CHICKEN RICE EGG-LEMON SOUP
### Γαλόσουπα αὐγολέμονο

7 cups fresh chicken stock
7 tablespoons long grain rice

1 egg plus 1 egg yolk, at room temperature
Juice of ½ lemon, or more

Bring stock to a boil, add rice and stir until stock returns to boil. Simmer partially covered for 20 minutes. Remove soup from the heat. In a bowl beat eggs until frothy. Gradually beat in lemon juice. Add approximately a quarter of the hot broth, at first spoon by spoon and then a little more at a time, beating constantly. Gradually add egg mixture to the soup, stirring gently to combine. Keep stirring for 2 minutes longer after egg mixture is added. Serve immediately. Serves 3-4.

VARIATIONS:

## TURKEY RICE EGG-LEMON SOUP
### Γαλόσουπα αὐγολέμονο

Substitute turkey stock for the chicken.
Follow recipe and preparation as directed in chicken soup.

## EASTER SOUP
### Μαγερίτσα

1 milk-fed lamb head with the neck, the heart and the liver
2 tablespoons salt
1 tablespoon vinegar
¼ cup butter or margarine
2 cups finely chopped scallions
3 tablespoons flour
⅓ cup dry white wine
2 tablespoons fresh dill, minced
1 tablespoon parsley, minced
6 tablespoons long grain rice

Salt and pepper to taste
2 eggs
Juice of 1 lemon

Cut the nose from the lamb head, and wash the head and the neck. Place them in a large saucepan and cover with warm water, add 2 tablespoons salt and 1 tablespoon vinegar; let stay for 3 hours. Rinse well. In the same saucepan place lamb head and the neck, cover with cold water. Bring to a boil and boil for 2 minutes. Drain and rinse well. Cover again with hot water, add salt. Bring to a boil and simmer for 90 minutes. Rinse the lamb heart and the liver. Cut into very small pieces and set aside. In a medium saucepan, melt butter and saute the scallions until tender, add the heart and liver pieces and saute until tender and absorbs the liquids. Add flour and saute a few more minutes. Add wine and simmer until the wine has absorbed. Add dill and parsley. Measure the broth, add enough water to make 8 cups. Add to the liver mixture and simmer for half hour. Add rice and stir, simmer for 20 minutes longer. Remove from heat. Cut meat from the head and the neck, in small pieces and add to the soup; add salt and pepper to your taste. Beat eggs until frothy. Gradually beat in lemon juice. Add approximately a quarter of the hot broth, first spoon by spoon and then a little more at a time beating constantly. Gradually add egg mixture, stirring gently to combine. Keep stirring for 2 minutes. Serve immediately. Serves 6.

# FISH SOUP
Ψαρόσουπα

2 pounds whole or cut in half striped bass or sea bass,
       cod or pike
Salt
6 whole small potatoes, peeled
3 carrots cut in half
4 whole small onions
3 stalks celery, cut in half
2 whole tomatoes
8 cups water
¼ cup olive oil
6 tablespoons long grain rice
3 eggs yollks
Juice of 1 lemon
Pepper
Mayonnaise

Clean and rinse fish well. Sprinkle with 1 teaspoon salt, cover and keep in the refrigerator. Place vegetables, olive oil, salt and water in a large saucepan. Bring to a boil. Reduce heat and simmer for 40 minutes. Add fish and boil slowly, uncovered, for approximately 20 minutes. Remove fish and place on a serving platter.

With a straining spoon, remove the vegetables and arrange them around the fish. Keep warm. Strain the fish stock through a strainer, using the back of the spoon, press the tomatoes through. Make sure no fish bones or scale go into the stock. Return stock to the heat, bring to a boil, add rice and simmer for 20 minutes. Beat egg yolks well, add lemon juice beating all the while. Add approximately a quarter of the hot stock at first spoon by spoon and then a little more at a time, beating constantly. Gradually add avgolemono mixture into the soup and stir gently to combine. Serve immediately, followed by the fish and vegetables. Pass mayonnaise or lemon-oil dressing (see index), at the table. Serves 4.

Note: for a beautiful fish platter for a buffet or dinner party, gently remove skin and bones from the cooked fish. Re-form fish pieces into the shape of a fish. Cover with mayonnaise and decorate with slices of hard-boiled eggs, dill pickles and capers.

# BOILED FRESH HAM WITH EGG-LEMON SOUP
Χοιρινό μπούτι βραστό μέ σούπα αὐγολέμονο

3 pounds fresh ham
10 cups boiling water
Salt
10 black peppercorns
1 whole carrot, cut in half
2 stalks celery, cut in half
3 whole small onions
3 whole medium size potatoes, peeled and cut in half
8 tablespoons long grain rice
2 eggs
Juice of ½ lemon or more

Add ham to boiling water. Cover and bring to a boil; skim the broth. Half-cover the pot and simmer for 1 hour. Add salt, whole peppercorns, carrots, celery, onions and potatoes. Bring to a boil and simmer for 1 hour or until meat is tender. Remove meat and let cool. Slice the meat and place in a serving platter, with a straining spoon remove vegetables and arrange them around the sliced meat. Cover and keep warm. Strain the broth and measure it; add enough hot water to make 8 cups. Bring to a boil; add rice, stir and simmer for 20 minutes. Beat eggs until frothy. Gradually beat in lemon juice. Add approximately a quarter of the hot broth, at first spoon by spoon and then a little more at a time beating constantly. Gradually add egg mixture into the soup, stirring gently to combine. Keep stirring for 2 more minutes. Serve immediately. Serves 4-5.

# LAMB HEAD EGG-LEMON SOUP
### Κεφαλάκι ἀρνιοῦ σούπα αὐγολέμονο

1 milk-fed lamb head with the neck
1 tablespoon vinegar
1 tablespoon salt
5 black peppercorns
2 whole small onions
2 carrots, cut in half
2 stalks celery, cut in half
2 sprigs parsley
Salt
6 tablespoons long grain rice
2 eggs
Juice of ½ lemon or more

Prepare lamb head and neck as directed in Easter Soup (see index). In the same saucepan place lamb head and the neck, cover with cold water. Bring to a boil and boil for 2 minutes. Drain and rinse well. Cover again with hot water, add salt, peppercorns, onions, carrots, celery and parsley. Bring to a boil. Reduce heat, cover and simmer for 1½ hours. Remove from heat. Place head on a plate and remove the meat. Place meat and vegetables on a plate. Strain the broth and measure it. Add enough hot water to make 6 cups. Bring to a boil, add rice and stir. Reduce heat and simmer for 20 minutes. Beat eggs until frothy. Gradually beat in lemon juice. Add approximately a quarter of the hot broth, at first spoon by spoon and then a little more at a time beating constantly. Gradually add egg mixture into the soup and stir gently to combine. Serve immediately. Serves 4.

# MEATBALLS EGG-LEMON SOUP
### Γιουβαρελάκια σούπα αὐγολέμονο

1 pound ground lean beef
1 small minced onion
1 tablespoon minced parsley
Salt and pepper to taste
½ cup long grain rice
3 eggs
8 cups beef stock or water
2 tablespoons or more butter or margarine
Juice of 1 lemon

Combine meat, onion, parsley, salt, pepper, half of the rice and 1 egg. Mix well by hand. Shape into tiny balls. Boil stock. Remove from heat and drop in the meatballs. Return saucepan to heat and bring to a boil, add rice and butter, stir slowly. Simmer partially covered for 30 minutes. In a bowl beat eggs until frothy. Gradually beat in lemon juice. Add approximately a quarter of the hot broth, at first spoon by spoon and then a little more at a time beating con-

stantly. Gradually add egg mixture to the soup, stirring gently to combine. Keep stirring for a few more minutes after egg mixture is added. Serve immediately. Serves 5-6.

# LAMB TRIPE SOUP AVGOLEMONO
### Πατσάς ἀρνιοῦ αὐγολέμονο

2 pounds baby lamb tripe
2 pounds baby lamb feet
3 medium onions, quartered
3 cloves garlic, chopped
3 stalks celery, cut in half
Salt to your taste
12 black peppercorns
3 tablespoons corn starch
3 eggs
Juice of 1 lemon

Wash tripe and scrape well. Wash feet in warm water. In a large pot place water and bring to a boil. Add tripe and feet. Boil for 5 minutes. Drain. Rinse well in cold water. Return tripe and feet to the pot, add onions, celery, garlic, salt and peppercorns. Cover with water and bring to a boil. Skim the broth. Cook slowly covered for approximately 3 hours. Strain. Measure broth, add water to make 10 cups. Cut tripe into 1-inch cubes and return to the broth. Bring to a boil. Mix corn starch with ¼ cup cold water to a thin paste. Slowly add to the soup, stirring constantly. Cook slowly for 5 minutes. Remove from heat. Beat eggs in a large bowl, until frothy. Gradually beat in lemon juice. Add approximately a quarter of the hot broth, at first spoon by spoon, and then a little more at a time, beating constantly. Slowly add egg mixture to the soup, stirring gently to combine. Keep stirring for a few more minutes. Serve soup immediately. Serves 4-6.

# CREAM OF ONION AND POTATO SOUP
### Κρέμα σούπα ἀπὸ κρεμμύδι καὶ πατάτα

4 medium potatoes, chopped
3 leeks, chopped
1 medium onion, chopped
5 cups fresh beef stock
2 tablespoons butter or margarine
2 tablespoons flour
2 cups scalding milk
Salt and pepper to taste

Boil the potatoes, leeks, and onion together with the beef stock until tender. Drain. Save the broth, mash the vegetables through a sieve or blend until smooth in the blender or food processor. In a medium sauce-pan melt butter, using a wire whisk blend in flour until smooth. Gradually add milk and stock, stirring constantly until boiling point is reached. Reduce heat and cook for 3 minutes longer. Add seasonings and blend. Add vegetables; bring to a boil and simmer for 5 minutes, stirring constantly. Serve hot topped with croutons. Serves 4-5.

## CREAM OF SPINACH SOUP

Σούπα κρέμα σπανάκι

2 pounds fresh spinach
2 cups fresh chicken stock
2 tablespoons butter or margarine
2 tablespoons flour
2 cups milk
Salt and pepper to taste

Cook spinach with chicken stock until tender. Drain. Prepare cream of spinach soup as directed in cream of onion and potato soup. Serve hot topped with croutons. Serves 4-5.

## CREAM OF VEGETABLE SOUP

Σούπα κρέμα λαχανικῶν

1 small onion, chopped
2 carrots, chopped
1 medium potato, chopped
1 celery heart, chopped
2 small zucchini, chopped
1 leek, chopped
½ cup fresh or frozen peas
½ cup fresh or frozen peas
½ cup fresh or frozen beans
2 ripe tomatoes, peeled and chopped
2 cups fresh beef stock
2½ tablespoons butter or margarine
2½ tablespoons flour
2 cups scalding milk
Salt and pepper to taste

In a medium saucepan, place all the vegetables and the stock, cover. Bring to a boil, reduce the heat and simmer for 1 hour or until vegetables are tender. Drain. Prepare cream of vegetable soup as directed in cream of onion and potato soup (see index). Serve hot topped with croutons. Serves 4-6.

## SEMOLINA SOUP

Σούπα μὲ σιμιγδάλι

6 cups chicken or beef stock (fresh)

½ cup semolina
2 egg yolks
1 tablespoon melted butter or margarine
½ cup cream
Juice of ½ lemon

Bring fresh stock to a boil, sprinkle semolina in the stock, stirring constantly until it is cooked, approxi-mately 8-10 minutes, on low heat. In a large bowl place egg yolks, melted butter, cream and lemon juice; beat well. Add soup little by litttle stirring con-stantly. Serve hot. Serves 4.

## TOMATO SMALL PASTA SOUP

Σούπα ντομάτα μὲ πάστα

8 cups fresh chicken, beef or fish stock
1 cup ripe, peeled and chopped tomatoes or ½ cup
   tomato juice
½ cup small pasta
Salt and pepper to taste

Bring stock and tomato to a boil, add pasta and stir well. Reduce heat and simmer partially covered for 30 minuntes. Serve hot. Serves 4.

## TRAHANA SOUP

Σούπα τραχανᾶς

7 cups fresh chicken or beef broth
½ cup tomato juice
½ cup trahana
Salt and pepper to taste

Bring stock and tomato juice to a boil. Sprinkle tra-hana to the stock and stir well. Reduce heat and simmer partially covered, stirring once in a while. Simmer for 25 minutes. Serve hot. Serves 3-4.

## VEGETABLE SOUP

Χορτόσουπα

1 cup chopped celery
1 cup chopped carrots
1 cup chopped cabbage
1 cup chopped zucchini
1 cup chopped green beans, fresh or frozen
1 cup peas, fresh or frozen
2 cups ripe, peeled and chopped tomatoes
½ cup chopped onion
Salt and pepper to taste
12 cups fresh beef stock

In a large pot, place all the ingredients, add stock. Bring to a boil. Reduce heat, cover and simmer for 1 hour or until vegetables are tender. If soup is too thick add hot stock or water and simmer for 5 minutes longer. Serve hot. Serves 6-8.

## BEAN SOUP
Φασολάδα

1 pound dried white beans
1 large onion, minced
3 medium carrots, diced
1 celery heart, finely chopped
3 cups peeled and chopped tomatoes or ⅓ cup tomato puree or 8 ounces whole tomatoes chopped
⅔ cup or more olive oil
Salt and pepper to taste

Pick over beans, rinse well. Place beans in a large saucepan, cover with cold water. Bring to a boil, reduce heat, cover and simmer for 20 minutes. Drain well and cover with hot water. Cover saucepan, bring to a boil, reduce heat and simmer for 40 minutes. Add the remaining ingredients except the oil and salt, simmer for 1 hour. Add oil and salt and hot water if soup is too thick. Simmer until beans are tender. Serve hot or cold. Serves 6-8.

## CHICK PEA SOUP
Ρεβύθια σούπα

1 pound chick peas
10 cups hot water
1 minced onion
⅔ cup olive oil or more
Salt to taste
Juice of 1 lemon

Pick over chick peas. Rinse well and place in a medium saucepan, add hot water and bring to a boil. Skim froth, add onion. Reduce heat, cover and simmer for 1½ hours. Add salt and oil and simmer for 20 minutes or until peas are tender. Thin with boiling water if too thick. Serve hot with lemon juice. Serves 6.

## LENTIL SOUP
Φακὲς σούπα

1½ cups lentils
8 cups hot water
1 large onion, minced
3 garlic cloves, sliced
4 tablespoons tomato puree
2 small bay leaves
¼ teaspoon Greek rigani (oregano)
Salt and pepper to taste
½ cup or more olive oil
2 tablespoons wine vinegar

Pick over lentils and rinse wel. Place a medium saucepan, cover with cold water. Bring to a boil; reduce heat, cover and simmer for 10 minutes. Drain well and add 8 cups hot water, onion, garlic, tomato, bay leaves and rigani. Bring to a boil, reduce heat, cover and simmer for 45 minutes. Add olive oil, salt, pepper and vinegar; simmer for 30 minutes or until lentils are tender. Add more water if needed. Serve hot or cold. Serves 4-5.

## SPLIT PEA SOUP
Φάβα σούπα

2 cups yellow or green split peas
8 cups cold water
1 large onion, minced
⅔ cup or more olive oil
Salt
Lemon juice

Pick over split peas. Rinse well and place in a medium saucepan, add cold water and bring to a boil. Skim off the froth and add onion. Reduce heat, cover and simmer for 1½ hours. Add salt and oil. Thin with boiling water if too thick. Serve hot topped with croutons and lemon juice.

Note: You can add boiled or baked ham, ham bone or beef stock. Subtract the olive oil.

# SALADS

## BOILED BEEF SALAD
Βοδινὸ βραστὸ σαλάτα

2 pounds sliced boiled beef (see index)
1 medium cubed boiled potato
1 cup cooked peas
1 cup cubed cooked carrots
2 hard-boiled eggs, cut in half
¼ cup olive oil
1 tablespoon wine vinegar
Salt and pepper to taste
⅔ cup tartar sauce (see index)

Place meat in the center of a serving platter. Arrange vegetables and eggs around the meat. Combine oil, vinegar, salt and pepper, and blend well. Pour oil mixture over the meat and vegetables. Pass tartar sauce. Serve hot or cold. Serves 4-6.

❈ ❈ ❈ ❈

## CHICKEN RICE SALAD
Κόττα ρίζι σαλάτα

½ recipe Rice Pilaf B (see index)
2 cups cooked breast of chicken, cut into small cubes
1 cup finely chopped celery
1½ teaspoons curry powder or
½ teaspoon crushed tarragon
1 cup toasted slivered blanched almonds
¼ cup finely chopped onion
1 tablespoon lemon juice
1¼ cups mayonnaise or more
Pepper to taste
¾ cup or less Kefalotyri or Parmesan cheese, grated

Cook rice as directed in Rice Pilaf. Combine all the ingredients (except half of the cheese) together, toss well with two forks. Spoon in a greased casserole. Sprinkle with the remaining cheese and bake in a preheated 450°F (230°C) oven for 15 minutes. Serve hot. Serves 6.

❈ ❈ ❈ ❈

## CRAB OR LOBSTER SALAD
Καβουροσαλάτα

2 cups fresh cooked ham or can flaked crab or lobster meat
5 hard-boiled eggs, finely chopped
⅔ cup finely chopped pickles
½ cup chopped celery
1 tablespoon capers
2 medium cubed boiled potatoes
1 tablespoon minced onion
1 cup mayonnaise
Salt and pepper to taste
3 cups finely shredded lettuce
½ cup finely chopped scallions
1 tablespoon fresh minced dill or ½ teaspoon dried
¼ cup olive oil
2 tablespoons wine vinegar

Combine first seven ingredients together, add salt, pepper and toss well. Add mayonnaise and mix well. Set aside. In a bowl toss the rest of the ingredients together. In a serving platter, make bed with lettuce mixture and place crab mixture on top. Garnish with celery tops. Serves 6.

❈ ❈ ❈ ❈

## FISH SALAD
Ψάρι σαλάτα

1 pound fresh or frozen (thawed) skinlelss fillets of flounder or sole
¾ cup water

1 cup mayonnaise
½ teaspoon dry mustard
Salt and pepper to taste
1 small thin pickle, sliced
1 tablespoon capers
2 hard-boiled sliced eggs

Place water in a fry pan. Bring to a boil. Add fish and poach for 15 minutes. Drain well and flake. Set aside. Combine mayonnaise, mustard, salt and pepper together. Blend well. In a bowl mix the fish with ¾ cup of the mayonnaise mixture. In an oval serving platter, place fish and cover with the remaining mayonnaise.Decorate with pickles and capers. Arrange eggs around the fish. Chill. Serves 3-4.

## MEAT SALAD MOLD
Σαλάτα ζελὲ μὲ κρέας

3 tablespoons gelatin
2 cups boiling fresh beef stock
2 cups cold fresh beef stock
1 teaspoon lemon juice
Salt and pepper to taste
4 cups boiled beef or chicken (see index) cut in cubes
1 cup finely chopped celery
⅓ cup finely chopped pickles
⅓ cup chopped roasted red peppers
4 hard-boiled sliced eggs
½ cup cubed cooked carrots
1 cup asparagus tips
1 tablespoon capers
Lettuce

Dissolve gelatin in boiling stock, add cold stock, lemon juice, salt and pepper, and mix well. Set aside to cool. Mix all the ingredients in a large bowl. Add gelatin and mix well to combine. Pour into mold. Chill until firm. Make a bed of lettuce in a serving platter and place the salad mold. Serves 6-8.

## SHRIMP SALAD
Γαρίδες σαλάτα

1 pound cooked shrimp
⅓ cup mayonnaise
1 tablespoon ketchup
Lettuce

Mix mayonnaise with ketchup, add shrimp and mix well to combine. Place shrimp salad on a serving platter on a bed of lettuce. Serves 2-4.

## SHRIMP OR LOBSTER SALAD
Γαριδοσαλάτα

¾ cup mayonnaise
2 tablespoons ketchup
½ teaspoon Worcestershire sauce
3 cups cooked shrimp or lobster meat

Combine first three ingredients together and blend well. Add shrimp if desired and mix well. Chill until you are ready to serve. Place shrimp salad in a serving bowl. Sprinkle with paprika. Serves 6-10.

## TOMATO SURPRISE SALAD
Ντομάτα σαρπράϊζ

8 medium ripe firm round tomatoes
1¼ cups diced cooked chicken
¼ cup slivered roasted blanched almonds
⅛ teaspoon crushed tarragon
⅓ cup finely chopped celery
Salt and pepper to taste
½ cup mayonnaise

Carefully scoop the inside out of the tomatoes. Remove the seeds from the pulp. Chill the ingredients and when ready to serve mix the chicken, tomato pulp, almonds, tarragon, celery, salt and pepper with mayonnaise. Fill the tomatoes. Arrange on lettuce leaves. Decorate each tomato with parsley. Serves 8.

## TOMATO JELLY WITH SHRIMP SALAD
Ντομάτα ζελὲ μὲ γαρίδες σαλάτα

2 cups diced shrimp or lobster meat, cooked
1 tablespoon capers
½ thinly sliced onion
¼ cup salad oil
2 tablespoons wine vinegar
4½ cups tomato juice
1 medium chopped onion
3 stalks chopped celery
1 bay leaf
2 cloves
1 small chopped green pepper
Salt and pepper to taste
1½ teaspoons sugar
2 tablespoons gelatin
½ cup water
⅔ cup mayonnaise
½ cup finely chopped celery
Lettuce

In a bowl combine first five ingredients and mix well. Chill overnight to marinade. Cook tomato juice with other seven ingredients for 10 minutes. Soak gelatin in cold water, add to boiling tomato mixture. Bring to a boil. Strain, and pour into ring mold. Set aside to cool. Drain shrimp mixture from oil and vinegar well; add celery, mayonnaise and mix well. Fill center of the mold with shrimp mixture. Chill until firm. In a serving platter, make bed of lettuce and place salad mold. Serves 6-8.

## MACARONI SALAD
Μακαρόνι σαλάτα

1 pound elbow macaroni, cooked
1 can (7 ounces) white tuna in water
4 hard-boiled eggs, shelled and chopped
½ cup chopped celery
½ cup chopped pickles
⅓ cup minced onion
¼ cup small capers
2 tablespoons olive or salad oil
Pepper to taste
1 cup mayonnaise

In a large bowl combine all the ingredients and toss gently. Cover bowl and chill. At serving time, line bowl with lettuce leaves and mound macaroni salad. Serves 4-6.

## BEET SALAD
Πατζάρια σαλάτα

10-12 young beets with tops
½ tablespoon salt
½ cup olive oil
2 tablespoons wine vinegar

Remove the leaves and stalks from the beets. Retain tender leaves and stalks. Cut off leaves from the stalks and cut stalks in half and wash them well. Scrub beets well under cold runnning water to remove all dirt. In a large saucepan place beets and stalks. Cover with cold water, add salt. Bring to a boil, reduce heat, cover and boil for 30 minutes. Add leaves and boil until tender. Drain. Skin beets while hot and slice into a bowl. Add leaves and toss with olive oil and vinegar. Serve with garlic sauce (see index).

## BOILED WILD VEGETABLE SALAD
Βραστὰ χόρτα σαλάτα

3 pounds dandelion greens, mustard greens or chicory

Salt to your taste
⅓ cup olive oil
Juice of 1½ lemons

Remove the roots of each plant. Retain tender leaves. Cut in half. Wash the greens very thoroughly in plenty of water. Drain. In a large pot add water and salt. Bring to a boil. Add greens and boil uncovered until tender. Drain. Serve hot or cold with olive oil and lemon juice. Serves 4-5.

## CABBAGE APPLE SALAD
Λάχανο μῆλο σαλάτα

3 cups finely shredded cabbage, rinse well and drain
1 cup finely grated carrots
2 tart apples, clean and cut into small cubes
1 cup chopped walnuts or pecans
1½ cups mayonnaise

Mix all the ingredients together. Place into a serving bowl and chill until ready to serve.

## CABBAGE SALAD
Λάχανο σαλάτα

1 small head cabbage, finely shredded
2 medium peeled and grated raw carrots
Salt to taste
⅓ cup olive oil or less
Juice of 1 lemon

Rinse cabbage well. Drain well. When ready to serve, toss cabbage with 4 tablespoons olive oil, ⅔ of the lemon juice and salt. Place cabbage in a serving bowl. In a separate bowl, toss grated carrots, remaining olive oil and lemon juice, add salt. Decorate cabbage by placing carrots in the center of the bowl. Servies 6.

## DRIED BEAN SALAD
Φασόλια σαλάτα

½ pound dried white beans
⅓ cup more or less olive oil
1 small onion, minced
2 tablespoons minced parsley
Salt and Pepper to taste
Juice of ½ or more lemon

Pick over beans and rinse well. Place beans in a saucepan and cover with cold water. Bring to a boil; reduce heat, cover and simmer for 2 hours. Add salt to taste and simmer until tender. Drain, add cold water and drain again well. Placc beans in a serving bowl. Add oil, onion, parsley, lemon and pepper to taste, toss well to combine. Serve hot or cold. Serves 6.

## POTATO SALAD A
### Πατατοσαλάτα

6 medium cubed boiled potatoes (see index)
1 small onion, thinly sliced
¼ cup olive oil
1 tablespoon minced parsley
Juice of ½ lemon
Salt and pepper to taste

In a bowl combine all the ingredients and toss gently. Serve hot. Serves 4.

## POTATO SALAD B

6 medium cubed boiled potatoes (see index)
1 small finely chopped onion
4 hard-boiled eggs, finely chopped
4 tablespoons finely chopped pickles
1 tablespoon olive oil
1 tablespoon capers
Salt and pepper to taste
¾ cup mayonnaise
1 teaspoon mustard
1 ripe tomato, thinly sliced
Lettuce

In a bowl combine first seven ingredients. Add mayonnaise and mustard; toss gently. In a serving platter make a bed of lettuce and place potato salad. Garnish around salad with sliced tomatoes. Chill. Serves 6.

## RUSSIAN SALAD
### Ρωσσικὴ σαλάτα

3 cups cubed boiled potatoes (see index)
1 cup cooked small white dried beans
1 cup cooked peas
1 cup cubed cooked carrots
5 hard-boiled eggs, finely chopped
½ cup or more finely chopped pickles
2 tablespoons capers
1¼ cups mayonnaise

1½ teaspoons mustard
Salt and pepper to taste
1 hard-boiled egg, thinly sliced
12 Kalamata Greek olives
Lettuce

Chill all vegetables. In a large bowl, combine first six ingredients, add 1 tablespoon capers, 1 cup mayonnaise, salt, pepper and mustard; toss well. Place in a serving bowl, or make bed of lettuce on a serving platter and place salad. Spread the reserved mayonnaise over the salad. Garnish with sliced hard-boiled egg, olives and capers. Chill. Serves 10-12

Note: Add 2 cups cooked lobster, cut into cubes and increase mayonnaise from 1¼ to 1¾ cups, if desired.

## SPRING SALAD
### ᾿Ανοιξιάτικη σαλάτα

1 large finely shredded romaine lettuce
4 finely sliced scallions
1 tablespoon finely chopped fresh dill or ½ teaspoon dried
¼ cup olive oil
1½ tablespoons wine vinegar
Salt and pepper to taste

Combine all ingredients in a serving bowl and toss well. Serve immediately. Serves 4.

## SUMMER COUNTRY STYLE SALAD
### Καλοκαιρινὴ χωριάτικη σαλάτα

3 medium tomatoes, sliced
1 thin cucumber, peeled and sliced
1 medium onion, thinly sliced
1 medium green pepper, seeded and thinly cut into rings
2 tablespoons capers
¼ cup or more olive oil
1 tablespoon wine vinegar
½ pound Feta cheese, cut into small chunks
12 Greek Kalamata olives
Salt and pepper to taste

Chill all vegetables before cutting. Place vegetables and capers in a bowl. When ready to serve, add olive oil, vinegar, salt and pepper, toss gently. Add cheese and olives. Serves 4-6.

# TOMATO SALAD
### Ντοματοσαλάτα

3  medium tomatoes, sliced
1  small onion, thinly sliced
1  thin cucumber, peeled, seeded and thinly cut
        into rings
¼  cup olive oil
1½  teaspoons wine vinegar
**Salt to taste**

Chill all vegetables before slicing. Place sliced vegetables in a bowl. When ready to serve; add salt, olive oil and vinegar. Toss gently to combine. Serves 3.

# ZUCCHINI SALAD
### Κολοκυθάκια σαλάτα

12  small zucchini (4-5 inches long)
1  tablespoon salt
½  cup olive oil
**Juice of 1 small lemon**

Trim off stems and scrub the zucchini. Rinse well. Leave whole. Place zucchini in boiling salted water. reduce heat and boil partially covered for 30-45 minutes or until tender. Drain well. Slice and place in a serving bowl. Pour over olive oil and lemon juice. Serve hot or cold. Serves 6.

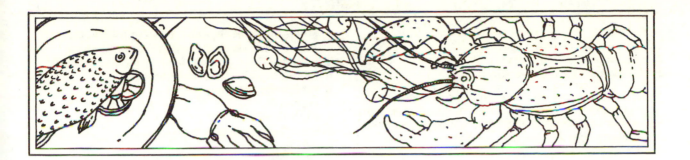

# FISH

## FRIED CODFISH
Μπακαλιάρος τηγανητὸς

2  pounds fresh or frozen (thawed) codfish or haddock
1⅔  cups flour
½  teaspoon baking powder
1½  teaspoons salt
⅛  teaspoon pepper
1  tablespoon olive oil
1  beaten egg (optional)
⅔  cup milk or water
Oil for frying

Rinse codfish well, and dry on a paper towel, let stand. Combine flour, baking powder, salt, pepper, egg if desired, oil and milk if desired. Blend until smooth. Dip fish into batter. Deep fry few pieces at a time in hot oil until golden brown and crisp. Drain on absorbent paper. Serve hot with garlic sauce (see index) and beet salad (see index) or any other salad you desire. Serves 6.

## CODFISH RAGOUT
Μπακαλιάρος ραγοῦ

1  pound fresh or frozen (thawed) codish or haddock
    fillets
1½  teaspoons salt
1  large sliced onion
2  cloves garlic, sliced
½  cup or more olive oil
4  whole ripe, peeled, seeded and chopped tomatoes
⅛  teaspoon pepper
2  tablespoons chopped parsley
5  medium potatoes, cut into fourths
1  cup water

Rinse fish well. Sprinkle with salt. Cover; let stay in the refrigerator. Saute onion and garlic in oil until soft. Add tomatoes, parsley, potatoes, salt, pepper and water. Bring to a boil. Reduce heat, cover and cook slowly for 20 minutes. Add fish and cook slowly for 20 minutes or until fish flakes easily when tested with a fork. Serve hot or cold. Serves 3-4.

## CODFISH PANCAKES
Μπακαλιάρος τηγανητὸς

1  pound codfish or haddock fresh or frozen (thawed)
    chopped
⅓  cup milk
1  beaten egg
1  cup flour
2  teaspoons baking powder
1  tablespoon olive oil
Salt and pepper to taste
1  tablespoon minced parsley
Oil for frying

Combine milk, egg, flour, baking powder, oil, salt, pepper and parsley. Blend until smooth. Add fish and mix well. Drop from tablespoon into hot oil and fry until brown on both sides. Serve with any salad. Serves 4-6.

## BAKED EEL
Χέλι τοῦ φούρνου

3  medium onions, minced
½  cup olive oil, or more
3  cloves garlic, sliced
1  cup dry white wine
4  medium ripe tomatoes, peeled, seeded and chopped
    or ½ cup tomato puree

1 bay leaf
Salt and pepper to taste
2 tablespoons minced parsley
3 pounds eel, skinned and sliced

Saute onion with the oil until soft and tender. Add garlic and saute few more minutes. Add wine and cook until evaporated. Add tomatoes, bay leaf, salt, pepper, parsley and 1 cup water. Cook slowly for 15 minutes. Pour half of the sauce in a baking dish, place fish on top and pour over the remaining sauce. Bake in a preheated 350°F (180°C) oven for about 30 minutes. Serve with salad and fresh bread and feta cheese. Serves 6.

# BROILED EEL
### Χέλι τῆς σχάρας

3 pounds eel, skinned and sliced
Juice of 1 lemon
Salt
½ cup oil
Lemon-oil dressing (see index)
2 tablespoons finely chopped parsley

Sprinkle fish with lemon juice and salt. Cover and marinate in the refrigerator for 2 hours or longer. Brush with oil and broil for 12-15 minutes on each side, depending on thickness. Serve with lemon-oil dressing and parsley, salad and french fries (see index). Serves 6.

# FRIED EEL
### Χέλι τηγανητὸ

3 pounds eel, skinned and sliced
Juice of 1 lemon
Salt
Flour for coating
Oil for frying

Sprinkle fish with lemon juice and salt. Cover and marinate in refrigerator for 2 hours, shake off excess flour. Fry in hot oil until golden brown. Serve hot with Garlic Sauce (see index) or mayonnaise, Wild Green vegetables (see index). Serves 6.

# FISH AU-GRATIN
### Ψάρι ὀγκρατὲν

2 cups water
Salt
5 peppercorns
1 bay leaf

1 pound fillets of flounder, fresh or frozen (thawed)
1 pound crab, shelled, fresh or frozen (thawed)
1 pound shrimp, shelled, fresh or frozen (thawed)
6 tablespoons butter or margarine
6 tablespoons flour
2 cups milk
1 cup fish stock
Salt and pepper to taste
2 tablespoons lemon juice
½ cup grated Kefalotyri or Parmesan cheese
¼ cup dried bread crumbs (see index)
3 tablespoons melted butter or margarine

In a saucepan place 2 cups water, salt, peppercorns and bay leaf. Bring to a boil. Add fish and boil, for 10 minutes. Drain and cut into 1 inch cubes. Reserve 1 cup from the stock. Melt butter; add flour and blend well. Add milk and fish stock, cook slowly until thickened, stirring constantly. Add salt and pepper. Cook slowly for 7 minutes longer. Add lemon juice and fish. Mix well. Fill a greased baking dish with the mixture. Top with cheese and then sprinkle with bread crumbs and melted butter. Brown in a preheated 425°F (205°C) oven for approximately 20 minutes. Serve immediately. Serves 6-8.

# FILET OF FLOUNDER AU-GRATIN
### Φιλέττα γλῶσσας ὀγκρατὲν

2 pounds flounder fillets, cut into serving pieces
6 tablespoons butter or margarine
6 tablespoons flour
1 tablespoon minced onion
1 cup milk
1 cup chicken stock
Salt and pepper to taste
2 tablespoons lemon juice
½ cup grated Kefalotyri or Parmesan cheese
½ cup dried bread crumbs (see index)

Place fish fillets in an oiled baking dish. Melt butter, add flour and onions, blend well. Add milk and chicken stock and simmer for 20 minutes, stirring until thickened. Add salt and pepper, lemon juice and mix well. Pour sauce over fish. Combine cheese and bread crumbs; mix well. Sprinkle over fish. Bake in a hot oven 400°F (205°C) oven for 30-35 minutes. Serve hot. Serves 6.

# BREADED FLOUNDER
### Ψάρι πανὲ

2 pounds fillet of flounder
Salt
1 cup dried bread crumbs (see index)

2 tablespoons grated Parmesan cheese
2 eggs, beaten with 1 tablespoon water
Clarified butter or margarine for frying

Wash and dry fish. Cut into serving pieces. Sprinkle with salt. Mix bread crumbs with grated cheese. Dip fish in egg and then roll in bread crumbs. Fry in hot butter until golden brown on both sides. Serve hot with Tartar Sauce (see index), salad and french fries (see index). Serves 6.

## BAKED FLOUNDER
Γλῶσσες φούρνου

6 whole medium size flounder, headless or 2 pounds fillets
3 cups water
⅔ cup dry white wine
8 tablespoons butter or margarine
4 egg yolks
Salt and pepper to taste
⅔ cup grated Parmesan cheese
1¼ cups bread crumbs (see index)
⅓ cup melted butter or margarine

Clean and wash fish well. In a large saucepan place water and wine. Bring to a boil, add fish and boil for 10 minutes. Remove fish from the saucepan, let stay, cover to keep warm. Strain fish stock through a strainer and measure it; add enough water to make 3 cups. In a small saucepan, melt butter over low heat. Using a wire whisk stir in flour and blend well. Gradually stir in fish stock. Cook, stirring constantly until sauce is very thick and smooth. Remove from heat. Add salt and pepper to taste and ⅓ cup of the cheese, mix well. Add egg yolks one at a time, stirring vigorously. Sprinkle ⅓ of the bread crumbs in a buttered baking dish and place fish neatly side by side. Sprinkle them again with ⅓ cup bread crumbs. Spoon sauce over fish. Sprinkle again with ⅓ cup bread crumbs. Spoon sauce over fish. Sprinkle them with remaining cheese and the bread crumbs. Pour on melted butter. Bake in a preheated 400°F (205°C) oven until the top is golden, for approximately 15-20 minutes. Let stand for 10 minutes before serving. Serve hot with Spring Salad (see index). Serves 6.

## FLOUNDER CROQUETTES
Κροκέττες ψαριοῦ

2 cups flaked cooked flounder or any other fish
1 cup thick white sauce (see index)
1 teaspoon Worcestershire sauce
2 tablespoons minced onion, saute in

1 tablespoon butter or margarine
Salt and pepper to taste
1 teaspoon lemon juice
1 tablespoon minced parsley
1 egg
2 tablespoons grated Parmesan or Kefalotyri cheese
2 eggs, beaten with 1 tablespoon water
Fine dried bread crumbs
Clarified butter, margarine or fine oil for frying
    (see index)

Combine all the ingredients except cheese, bread crumbs and the 2 eggs. Mix well. Chill and shape into cylinders. Mix bread crumbs with cheese. Roll fish cylinders in crumbs then in eggs and into crumbs again. Chill. Fry in hot oil or butter for 4-6 minutes or until golden. Drain on absorbent paper. Serve hot. Serves 4-5.

## BRAISED FISH
Ψάρι γιαχνί

¾ cup olive oil
2 large onions, sliced
¾ cup dry white wine
1 can (20 ounces) whole tomatoes, chopped
Salt and pepper to taste
2 tablespoons chopped parsley
6 medium potatoes, peeled and cut in fourths
2 cloves garlic, minced
2 pounds codfish, haddock, pollack or any other fish fresh or frozen (thawed) cut into pieces

Heat oil and saute onions, add wine, tomatoes, garlic, parsley, salt, pepper, potatoes and 1 cup water; cook slowly for 20 minutes. Add fish and cook slowly for 20-30 minutes longer. Serve hot or cold, with salad, feta cheese and fresh bread. Serves 6.

## FISH CREOLE
Ψάρι κρεόλ

2 pounds halibut, haddock, pollack or any other fish fillets, fresh or frozen (thawed)
3 tablespoons butter or margarine
Salt and pepper to taste
1½ tablespoons flour
1 small minced green pepper
2 tablespoons minced onion
1 can (16 ounces) whole tomatoes, finely chopped

Season fish fillets with salt annd pepper. Place in a greased baking dish. Melt butter and blend in flour. Add minced onion and green pepper; cook slowly for 5 minutes. Add chopped tomato, salt and pepper to taste and cook 15 minutes longer. Pour sauce over fish. Bake in a preheated 350°F (180°C) oven for approximately 35-45 minutes. Serves 6.

✠✠✠✠

# BAKED MACKEREL
### Σκουμπρὶ πλακὶ

2  mackerels (about 3 pounds)
Salt and pepepr to taste
2  cups sliced onions
3  cloves garlic, sliced
¼  cup olive oil
½  cup dry white wine
2  tablespoons chopped parsley
1  pound ripe tomatoes, peeled, seeded and chopped

Clean fish and pull off head, rinse well. Slice into 1½ inch rings. Place fish in an oiled baking dish, sprinkle with salt. Let stand. Cook onions slowly in olive oil until tender. Do not brown. Add wine, garlic, parsley, tomatoes and salt and pepper. Cook for 30 minutes. Pour over fish. Bake in a preheated 350°F (180°C) oven for approximatelyl 30-40 minutes. Serves 4-5.

✠✠✠✠

# FISH ORIENTAL
### Ψάρι ὀριεντὰλ

3  pounds whole trout, pike or white fish
Juice of ½ lemon
Salt
¾  cup olive oil
2  cups thinly sliced onions
1  cup dry white wine
1  clove garlic, crushed
2  tablespoons flour
½  cup tomato puree or 4 large ripe, peeled,
       seeded and chopped tomatoes
¼  cup chopped parsley
1  teaspoon sugar
Salt and pepper to taste
½  cup bread crumbs, dried (see index)

Clean and wash fish well. Sprinkle with lemon juice and season with salt. Cover, let stay in the refrigerator while preparing sauce. In a saucepan heat olive oil and saute onion until soft. Add garlic, flour and wine, saute for 2 minutes longer. Add tomatoes, parsley, sugar, salt and pepper to taste. Cover and simmer for 10 minutes. Place fish in an oiled baking dish. Pour sauce over the fish and sprinkle with bread crumbs. Bake in a preheated 350°F (180°C) oven for 40-45 minutes, basting occasionally with the sauce. Serve hot. Serves 6.

# STEAMED FISH
### Ψάρι ἀτμοῦ

2  pounds fresh or frozen (thawed) flounder or perch
      fillets
4  teaspoons melted butter or margarine
Salt and pepper to taste
1  cup water
1  bay leaf
½  lemon, sliced
1  tablespoon chopped parsley
Lemon-oil dressing (see index)

Rinse fish well. Brush with butter and season with salt and pepper. In a frypan place water, bay leaf and lemon slices. Bring to a boil. Add fish; cover and steam on low until tender, for approximately 20 minutes. Serve hot with lemon-oil dressing and potato salad. Sprinkle fish with chopped parsley. Serves 4-5.

✠✠✠✠

# HOW TO BOIL AND CLEAN A LOBSTER
### Πῶς νὰ βράσης καὶ νὰ καθαρίσης ἀστακὸ

1  medium onion, cut in half
1  carrot, cut in half
2  Stalks celery, cut in half
3  sprigs parsley
1  small bay leaf
½  teaspoon peppercorns
1  tablespoon salt
3  tablespoons white vinegar
3  quarts water
2  live lobsters, each about 2 pounds

In a large pot, put all the ingredients, except lobsters and boil for 30 minutes. Pick up live lobsters back of claws and plunge it into boiling water, head first. Cover and boil for 15 minutes. Reduce heat and simmer for 10 minutes longer. Leave lobster in the pot to cool. When cool enough to handle, take the meat from the shell in the following order. Chop off the claws. Split the body lengthwise and remove and discard the stomach, a small sac just back of the head. Also remove the gills and the intestine which runs down the center of the tail. Take out the meat from the body, the siver, and the coral found in female losters. Crack the claws and remove the meat. Serve with mayonnaise. Serves 2-3.

✠✠✠✠

# LOBSTER AU-GRATIN
### Ἀστακὸς ὀγκρατὲν

2  boiled lobsters (each about 2 pounds (see index)

4 medium boiled potatoes (see index)
¼ cup tomato puree
4 tablespoons water
¼ teaspoon sugar
6 tablespoon butter or margarine
8 tablespoons flour
1½ cups chicken stock
⅔ cup cream
Salt and pepper to taste
½ cup grated Kefalotyri or Parmesan cheese
¼ cup bread crumbs (see index)
¼ cup melted butter or margarine

Remove meat from lobster and cut into dice. Peel potatoes and dice. Boil tomato puree with the water and sugar, covered on low heat for 20 minutes. Melt butter, blend in flour, add chicken stock and cream, cook until thickened, stirring constantly. Add salt and pepper and cook slowly for 7 minutes longer. Add tomato and blend well. Add diced lobster and potatoes, mix well to combine. Fill greased scallop shells or shallow baking dish with the mixture. Top with Kefalotyri if desired and then with bread crumbs and sprinkle with butter. Brown in very hot oven 425°F (220°C) oven for approximately 15 minutes. Serve immediately. Garnish with the coral if desired.

## LOBSTER MAYONNAISE
Ἀστακὸς μαγιονέζα

2 cups Russian Salad (see index)
Lettuce
2 lobsters, boiled, cleaned and sliced (see index) chilled
½ cup mayonnaise
1½ teaspoons mustard
Lobster coral (optional)

Arrange Russian Salad in the center of a serving platter on a bed of lettuce. Place cold sliced lobster around salad. Mix mayonnaise with mustard and color red with lobster coral if desired and place on lobster. Serves 4.

VARIATION:

## CRAWFISH
Καραβίδα

Crawfish look like lobster but smaller. They may be prepared and served in the same way as lobster.

## BAKED FISH WITH LEMON
Ψάρι τοῦ φούρνου λεμονάτο

3-4 pounds red snapper, porgies or bluefish (whole)
¼ cup or more olive oil
¼ teaspoon crushed Greek rigani (oregano)
Juice of 1 lemon or more
⅛ teaspoon pepper
½ cup water

Clean and rinse fish well. Place in an oiled baking dish. Sprinkle with oil, lemon juice, salt, pepper and rigani. Add water in the pan and bake in a preheated 350°F (180°C) oven for approximately 45-60 minutes depending on the size of the fish. Occasionally baste with the sauce. Serve hot. Serves 4.

## BAKED FISH
Ψάρι πλακὶ

2 pounds whole red snapper, bass, haddock, codfish or pollack, fresh or frozen (thawed)
Juice of ½ lemon
Salt and pepper to taste
½ cup or more olive oil
1 large thinly sliced onion
2 cloves garlic, sliced
4 medium ripe tomatoes, peeled, seeded and chopped
¼ cup finely chopped parsley
Salt and pepper to taste
4 medium potatoes, cut into fourths

Clean and rinse fish well. Sprinkle with lemon juice and season with salt and pepper. Cover; let stand in the refrigerator while preparing sauce. In a frypan heat olive oil and saute onion, garlic until soft. Add tomatoes, parsley, salt and pepper to taste. Cover and simmer for 25 minutes, stirring occasionally. Place fish in an oiled baking dish, and arrange potatoes around. Pour sauce over the fish and potatoes. Bake in a preheated 350°F (180°C) oven for 45-55 minutes. Serves 4-5.

## BAKED FISH A LA SPETSIOTA
Ψάρι ἀ λὰ σπετσώτα τοῦ φούρνου

3 pounds (sliced into steaks), swordfish, pollack or 4 medium size porgies
5 ripe tomatoes, peeled, seeded and cut up
5 cloves garlic, sliced
¾ cup dry white wine
¾ cup or less olive oil
Salt and pepper to taste
¼ cup finely chopped parsley

¾ cup bread crumbs, dried (see index)

Cook tomatoes, wine and garlic for 15 minutes; let stand. Clean and rinse fish well and place in an oiled baking dish. Pour boiling tomato mixture over fish, add oil, sprinkle with salt and pepper, parsley and last the bread crumbs. Bake in a preheated 350°F (180°C) oven for 40-45 minutes or until fish flakes easily when tested with a fork, basting occasionally with the sauce. Serves 6.

## OCTOPUS PILAF
'Οκταπόδι πιλάφι

3 pounds octopus, fresh or frozen (thawed)
1 cup olive oil
2 medium finely chopped onions
¾ cup tomato puree
Salt and pepper to taste
1½ cups water
4½ cups boiling water
2 cups converted rice

Wash octopus well and cut into 1 inch cubes. In a medium saucepan heat oil and saute onions until soft. Add octopus and saute for a few more minutes; add tomato, 1½ cups water, salt and pepper. Cover and simmer until octopus is tender. Remove octopus and 1 cup of the sauce. Cover and keep warm. Add in the remaining sauce, the 4½ cups boiling water. Bring to a boil; add rice after you have rinsed well, stir. Reduce heat, cover and cook slowly for 20 minutes. Spoon into a ring mold. Unmold on a serving platter and cover with octopus and sauce. Serve hot. Serves 6.

## OCTOPUS IN WINE
'Οκταπόδι κρασάτο

3 pounds octopus, fresh or frozen (thawed)
½ cup olive oil
1 cup finely chopped onion
2 cloves garlic, finely chopped
1 cup dry red wine
½ cup tomato puree or sauce
Salt and pepper to taste

Wash octopus well and cut into 1 inch cubes. Heat oil and saute onion and garlic until soft. Add octopus and saute for a few more minutes; add wine and cook until wine evaporates. Add tomato, salt and pepper and 1 cup water. Cover and cook slowly for 1 hour or until tender. Serve hot, plain or with rice pilaf (see index), and salad. Serves 6.

## SHRIMP WITH RICE
Γαρίδες πιλάφι

1 pound raw shrimp
3 tablespoons olive oil or butter
2 tablespoons chopped onion
1 pound ripe tomatoes, peeled, seeded and cut up or
     1 can (16 ounces) whole tomatoes chopped
Salt and pepper to taste
1 cup converted rice
¼ cup butter or margarine

Saute onion with oil if desired until transparent. Add chopped tomatoes, salt, pepper, 1 cup water. Cover and bring to a boil, reduce heat and simmer for 20 minutes, stirring occasionally. Add shrimp and simmer for 30 minutes or until tender. Place 3 cups water in a saucepan, add salt; bring to a boil. Add rice and stir well, cover, cook slowly for 20 minutes. Drain. Add butter and stir gently with a fork. Place rice in a ring mold. Unmold rice in a serving platter. Pour shrimp with sauce over rice. Serves 4.

## FRIED SMELTS
Μαρίδες τηγανητές

2 pounds fresh or frozen (thawed) smelts
Salt
Flour for coating
Oil for frying
Juice of 1½ lemons

Rinse smelts, remove heads and evincerate, rinse again. Sprinkle with salt and refrigerate for 2 hours. Coat fish with flour and fry in hot oil until golden and crisp on both sides. Drain on absorbent paper. Serve immediately. Serve with lemon juice and Boiled Wild Vegetable Salad (see index) and french fries. Serves 4.

## BROILED RED SNAPPER
## OR PORGY
Σιναγρίδα καὶ τσιπούρα στὴ σχάρα

3 pounds whole snapper or porgies
¼ cup salad oil
Salt
Juice of ½ lemon
1 large thinly sliced onion
⅓ cup olive oil
Juice of 1 lemon
Salt
Parsley, finely chopped

Clean and rinse fish well, sprinkle with salt, cover;

let stand in the refrigerator for 2 hours. Mix salad oil with the juice of half lemon. Brush fish with the mixture and place on the grill. Broil fish for 15-20 minutes of each side depending on the thickness. Occasionally brush fish with oil-lemon mixture. Place fish on a serving platter. In a colander, place sliced onion and salt, rub well with your hand. Rinse off salt and pat on paper towel to absorb excess water. In a glass bowl blend olive oil and lemon juice, add onion and parsley, mix well to combine. Pour on top of the broiled fish. Serve fish with Spring Salad or Summer Country Style Salad (see index), and french fries. Serves 4-5.

## BAKED SWORDFISH WITH TOMATOES
Ξιφίας τοῦ φούρνου μὲ ντομάτες

2½ pounds swordfish, sliced into steaks
Salt
¼ cup olive oil
3 large thinly sliced onions
5 large ripe tomatoes, peeled, seeded and chopped
    or 1 cup tomato puree
½ cup chopped parsley
Salt and pepper to taste
2 large tomatoes, peeled and sliced into rounds
¾ cup bread crumbs dried (see index)

Rinse fish well. Sprinkle with salt and let stay in the refrigerator while preparing sauce. Heat oil and saute onion until soft. Add chopped tomatoes, half of the parsley, 1 cup water, salt and pepper to taste. Cook for 20 minutes. Spoon half of the tomato sauce into a baking dish. Place fish steaks in the dish and top with sliced tomatoes. Mix bread crumbs, remaining parsley, and sprinkle onto the sliced tomatoes. Spoon in remaining sauce. Bake in a preheated 350°F (180°C) oven for 35-40 minutes or until golden crust will form on the fish. Serves 4-5.

## SWORDFISH SHISHKEBAB
Ξιφίας σουβλάκι

⅓ cup olive oil

½ cup lemon juice
¼ teaspoon onion powder
3 bay leaves
Salt and pepper to taste
3 pounds swordfish, cut into 1 inch cubes
18 cherry tomatoes
12 bay leaves
½ cup olive oil
½ cup lemon juice
½ cup minced onion
2 tablespoons minced parsley
Salt and pepper to taste

In a bowl, combine the first 6 ingredients, mix well. Add fish cubes and toss well. Cover and marinate in the refrigerator for 5 hours. Thread fish cubes, cherry tomatoes and bay leaves, alternately on 12 skewers. Broil under a hot grill or over charcoal turning and basting frequently with remaining marinade. In a serving bowl combine oil, lemon juice, minced onion, parsley, salt and pepper. Mix well and serve with the shishkebab. Serves 6.

## STUFFED SQUID
Καλαμαράκια γεμιστὰ

2 pounds squid
½ cup finely chopped onion
½ cup olive oil
1 tablespoon finely chopped parsley
Salt and pepper to taste
½ cup dry white wine
½ cup rice
1 pound ripe tomatoes, peeled, seeded and chopped
    or 1 can (16 ounce) whole tomatoes, chopped

Wash and clean squid as directed in Fried Squid (see index). Cut off the tentacles and finely chop, reserve them. In a medium saucepan saute onion with ¼ cup oil until transparent. Add chopped squid tentacles, parsley, salt and pepper, wine, rice and ½ cup boiling water. Simmer for 15 minutes. Fill sacs of squids with rice mixture and arrange in a greased baking dish. Add ¼ cup olive oil, tomatoes and salt. Cover and bake in a preheated 350°F (180°C) oven for approximatelly 60 minutes. Serves 6.

# MEATS: BEEF, LAMB, PORK

## BEEF WITH CABBAGE
### Μοσχάρι μὲ λάχανο

2½ pounds lean boneless beef, chuck or round
     cut into serving pieces
½ cup butter, or less
4 tablespoons olive oil
1 large onion, chopped
½ cup tomato sauce
3 cups water
Salt and pepper to taste
1 pound cut up carrots
4 pounds cut up cabbage
4 cups boiling water
1 cup converted rice
Juice of 1 lemon

Brown meat with butter and oil, add onion and saute until soft. Add tomato, 3 cups water, salt and pepper. Cover and cook slowly for 1 hour. Add carrots and cabbage and cook for 45 minutes longer. Add boiling water and rice, cook slowly for 20 minutes. This casserole will look soupy. When it is cooked, add lemon juice. Serves 6.

## BASIC BEEF KAPAMA
### Μοσχάρι κοκκινιστὸ

2½ pounds lean boneless chuck, round or rump of
     beef cut into serving pieces
2 tablespoons butter
2 tablespoons olive oil
½ cup minced onion
1 cup tomato sauce
1 cinnamon stick ½-inch long (optional)

Place butter and oil in a Dutch oven and brown beef pieces. Add onion and saute until soft. Add tomato, salt, pepper, cinnamon if desired, and 2 cups water; stir well. Bring to a boil. Reduce heat, cover and cook slowly until tender for approximately 2 hours. As the liquid cooks away add more water as needed. Serve with pasta, rice pilaf or mashed potatoes and salad. Serves 4-6.

Variation:

## LAMB KAPAMA
### Ἀρνὶ κοκκινιστὸ

Follow recipe and preparation as directed in Beef Kapama.

## BEEF KAPAMA WITH POTATOES
### Μοσχάρι κοκκινιστὸ μὲ πατάτες

1 basic recipe for beef kapama (see index)
4 pounds potatoes, peeled and cut into fourths
¼ cup butter or margarine
Salt and pepper to taste

Follow preparation as directed in basic recipe. Add butter and cook beef for only 1 hour. Add potatoes, 1 cup hot water, salt and pepper. Cover and cook slowly for approximately 1 hour longer. As the liquid cooks away add more water as needed. Serve hot with salad, feta cheese and fresh bread. Serves 4-6.

Variation:

## LAMB KAPAMA WITH POTATOES
### Ἀρνὶ κοκκινιστὸ μὲ πατάτες

Substitute lamb for beef
Follow recipe and preparation as directed in beef kapamo with potatoes (see index).

26

## BEEF KAPAMA WITH RICE
### Μοσχάρι κοκκινιστὸ μὲ πιλάφι

1 basic recipe for beef kapama (see index)
2 cups converted rice
Salt
¼ cup butter or margarine
½ cup grated Kefalotyri, Parmesan or Romano cheese

Follow preparation as directed in basic recipe. Remove meat from pot to a plate, keep warm. Measure sauce, add water to make 4½ cups. Bring to a boil. Pick over rice and rinse in a strainer under cold running water (to get rid of the starch). Saute rice with butter for 5 minutes. Add rice to the boiling sauce and cook slowly partially covered for 20 minutes. Pack the rice into 1 6-cup ring mold. Unmold on a platter. Arrange meat pieces around rice. Serve hot with grated cheese and salad. Serves 6.

**Variation:**
## LAMB KAPAMA WITH RICE
### Ἀρνὶ κοκκινιστὸ μὲ πιλάφι

Substitute lamb for the beef.
Follow recipe and preparation as directed in beef kapama with rice (see index).

## BEEF KAPAMA WITH SPAGHETTI
### Μοσχάρι κοκκινιστὸ μὲ σπαγέττο

1 basic recipe for beef kapama (see index)
1 pound spaghetti
1 tablespoon salt
4 quarts boiling water
¼ cup butter or margarine, melted
½ cup or more grated Kefalotyri, Parmesan or
    Romano cheese

Follow preparation as directed in Basic recipe. Break spaghetti in half, drop into rapidly boiling salted water, cook uncovered for 20 minutes or until tender. Keep boiling and stir occasionally with a fork. Pour into a colander and rinse with warm water. Drain spaghetti and arange half of it on a large platter. Sprinkle with half of the cheese, cover with remaining spaghetti and top with remaining cheese. Pour hot butter over spaghetti and spoon pan sauce and beef kapama over. Serve immediately with salad. Serves 4-6.

**Variation:**
## LAMB KAPAMA WITH SPAGHETTI
### Ἀρνὶ κοκκινιστὸ μὲ σπαγέττο

Substitute lamb for the beef.
Follow recipe and preparation as directed in Beef kapama with spaghetti (see index).

**Variation:**
## DEER KAPAMA WITH SPAGHETTI
### Ἐλάφι κοκκινιστὸ μὲ σπαγέττο

Substitute deer for the beef.
Follow recipe and preparation as directed in Beef kapama with spaghetti (see index).

## BEEF WITH ONIONS
### Μοσχάρι στιφάδο

2½ pounds lean bonelss chuck of beef, cut into
    serving pieces
½ cup olive oil
1 large chopped onion
½ cup dry red wine
2 tablespoons wine vinegar
⅔ cup tomato sauce
2 bay leaves
3 cloves garlic, sliced
1 teaspoon rosemary
1 cinnamon stock, ½ -inch long
Salt and pepper to taste
3-4 pounds small white onions

Brown meat slowly in oil. Add onion and saute until soft. Add wine and vinegar; stir. Add tomato sauce, garlic, bay leaves, rosemary, cinnamon, pepper and salt. Cover and cook slowly for 40 minutes. As the liquid cooks away, add water as needed. While meat cooks, peel onions. Cross-cut root ends to prevent centers popping out during cooking. Boil the onions in a large amount of water for 5 minutes; drain. Add onions to the meat and spoon pot juices over them to coat them well. Do not stir. Cover and cook slowly for approximately 1½ hours or until meat and onions arc tender and sauce is thick, shaking the pot occasionally. Add water as needed. Serve hot. Serves 4-5.

**Variations:**
## VEAL WITH ONIONS
### Μοσχαράκι στιφάδο

Substitute veal for the beef.
Follow recipe and preparation as directed in Beef with onions (see index).

## BEEF HEART WITH ONIONS
### Καρδιὰ βοδινοῦ στιφάδο

Substitute 2½ small beef hearts for the beef, cut into 1-inch cubes.
Follow recipe and preparation as directed in Beef with onions (see index).

## VEAL HEART WITH ONIONS
### Καρδιὰ μοσχαριοῦ στιφάδο

Substitute veal hearts for the beef hearts.
Follow recipe and preparation as directed in Beef heart with onions (see index).

## BEEF TONGUE WITH ONIONS
### Γλῶσσα βοδινοῦ στιφάδο

Substitute 1 beef tonque for the beef (see index).
Follow recipe as directed in Beef with onions.

Place tonque in a large saucepan and cover with cold water, soak overnight. Wash and scrape tongue well. Cover with cold water and bring to a boil, boil for 5 minutes. Drain and rinse well. Cover tongue again with hot water. Bring to a boil; reduce heat, cover and simmer for 30 minutes, or until easy to peel. Remove tongue from stock and peel skin off when it is still very warm. Slice meat into 1-inch thick slices. Saute meat slices with oil, add onion and saute until soft. Follow preparation as directed in Beef with onions. Serve hot. Serves 4-6.

## VEAL TONGUE WITH ONIONS
### Γλῶσσα μοσχαριοῦ στιφάδο

Substitute veal tongue for the beef tongue.
Follow recipe and preparation as directed in Beef tongue with onions (see index).

## BEEF RAGOUT
### Μοσχαράκι ἐντράδα

**Basic recipe:**

3  pounds lean boneless chuck, round or rump of
    beef cut into serving pieces
4  tablespoons flour
1  teaspoon salt
¼  teaspoon pepper

2  tablespoons butter
3  tablespoons olive oil
1  cup finely chopped onion
1  cup tomato sauce or 6 medium ripe tomatoes,
    peeled, seeded and chopped
2  cups water

Mix flour, salt and pepper together. Coat meat pieces with flour mixture. Brown well in butter and oil. Add onion and saute until onion is soft. Add tomato sauce of fresh chopped tomatoes and water. Cover; bring to a boil. Reduce heat and simmer for approximately 1½ hours or until meat is tender and sauce is thick. As the liquid cooks away add more as needed. Serve hot with vegetables. Serves 4-5.

Variations:

## LAMB RAGOUT
### Ἀρνὶ ἐντράδα

Substitute lamb for the beef.
Follow recipe and preparation as directed in Beef ragout (see index).

## BEEF RAGOUT WITH EGGPLANT
### Μοσχάρι ἐντράδα μὲ μελιτζάνες

Basic recipe for Beef ragout (see index).

4  pounds small narrow eggplants (3-4-inches long)
½  cup olive oil for frying
Salt

Follow preparation as directed in Basic recipe. While meat is cooking prepare eggplants. Cut eggplants into fourths forming a cross. Sprinkle with salt and let stand for half hour. The salt will draw out the disagreeably bitter flavor. Rinse well under cold running water. Squeeze out excess moisture and saute in hot oil until tender. Add eggplants to beef ragout and spoon pot juices over them to coat them well. Do not stir. Simmer for 10 minutes. Serve hot. Serves 4-5.

Variation:

## LAMB RAGOUT WITH EGGPLANT
### Ἀρνὶ ἐντράδα μὲ μελιτζάνες

Substitute lamb for the beef.
Follow recipe and preparation as directed in Beef ragout with eggplants (see index).

# BEEF RAGOUT WITH OKRA
Μοσχάρι ἐντράδα μὲ μπάμιες

Basic recipe for Beef ragout (see index).

**2 pounds fresh or frozen okra**
**1 tablespoon salt**
**¼ cup wine vinegar**
**¼ cup butter, margarine or olive oil**

Follow recipe and preparation as directed in Basic recipe. Add ¼ cup butter and cook beef ½ hour less. While meat is cooking prepare okra. The pods of okra are so sticky that special care is needed to avoid breaking them during the cleaning. Wash them well and remove the stems. Place in one layer in a cookie sheet, sprinkle with vinegar and salt, let stand under the sun if possible for 1 hour. Gently rinse the okra well. Drain and add to the meat neatly. Cover and simmer for approximately 45 minutes depending on size of okra, until tender. Occasionally shake the pot but do not stir. Place meat and okra in the serving platter and serve hot. Serves 4-5.

**Variation:**

## LAMB RAGOUT WITH OKRA
’Ἀρνὶ ἐντράδα μὲ μπάμιες

Substitute lamb for the beef.
Follow recipe and preparation as directed in Beef ragout with okra (see index).

## BEEF RAGOUT WITH PEAS
Μοσχάρι ἐντράδα μὲ ἀρακά

**2 pounds grozen peas or fresh**
**¼ cup butter or margarine**
**Salt**

Basic recipe for Beef ragout (see index).
Follow preparation as directed in basic recipe.
While meat is cooking prepare peas. Place frozen peas in a saucepan, add 1 cup salted boiling water; cover and cook gently for 20 minutes. Add butter and cook until tender and liquid evaporates. Add peas to meat and simmer for 10 minutes. Serve hot. Serves 4-5.

**Variation:**

## LAMB RAGOUT WITH PEAS
’Ἀρνὶ ἐντράδα μὲ ἀρακά

Substitute lamb for the beef.

Follow recipe and preparation as directed in Beef ragout with peas (see index).

# BEEF RAGOUT WITH STRING BEANS
Μοσχάρι ἐντράδα μὲ φασολάκια

Basic recipe for Beef ragout (see index).

**3 pounds string beans fresh or frozen, cut them french style**
**¼ cup butter or margarine**
**1 teaspoon salt**

Follow preparation as directed in Basic recipe. While meat is cooking prepare string beans. Cover with least possible amount of boiling salted water, cook gently for 30 minutes. Add butter and cook until tender and liquid evaporates. Add string beans to beef ragout and simmer for 10 minutes. Serve hot. Serves 4-5.

**Variation:**

## LAMB RAGOUT WITH STRING BEANS
’Ἀρνὶ ἐντράδα μὲ φασολάκια

Substitute lamb for the beef.
Follow recipe and preparation as directed in Beef ragout with string beans (see index).

## LAYERED RUMP OF BEEF
Οὐρά μοσχαριοῦ

**4 pounds rolled rump of beef**
**2 stalks celery, whole**
**3 whole carrots**
**1 medium whole onion**
**Salt to taste**
**10 slices ham**
**20 slices Swiss or Provolone cheese**
**10 slices ripe tomato**
**10 slices white sandwich bread**
**Butter or margarine at room temperature**

Place meat in a pot, cover with boiling water, boil for 1 hour. Add celery, carrots, onion and salt. Cook slowly for 1 hour longer or until meat is tender. Let stand in the liquid until meat is completely cold. Cut into 10 slices. Spread the bread slices with butter and place them in a greased baking sheet. Ham and cheese slices must be the size of the bread. Top bread slices starting first with the meat, then with 1 slice cheese, ham, cheese again and finish with the tomato. Bake in a preheated 400°F (205°C) oven for 15 minutes or until cheese is melted. Serve immediately with vegeables and salad. Serves 10.

Note: This recipe is excellent for buffet.
With the stock you make avgolemono soup (see index).

🐝🐝🐝

## POT ROAST OF BEEF WITH LEMON
Μοσχάρι ψητὸ κατσαρόλας μὲ λεμόνι

**4 pounds rump or eye of the round**
**3 tablespoons olive oil**
**Salt and pepper to taste**
**¼ teaspoon garlic powder or 1 clove garlic, crushed (optional)**
**Juice of ½ lemon**

Brown meat on all sides in hot oil. Add lemon juice, season with salt, pepper and garlic if desired, add ¼ cup water to the pot, cover and simmer until tender for approximately 2 hours. As the liquid cooks away add more as needed. Serve with gravy, mashed potatoes, sauteed spinach and salad. Serves 4-6.

🐝🐝🐝

## POT ROAST OF BEEF WITH TOMATO
Μοσχάρι ψητὸ κατσαρόλας μὲ ντομάτα

**3 pounds top round or rump roast of beef**
**¼ cup olive oil, or 2 tablespoons olive oil and 2 tablespoons butter**
**1 cup chopped onion**
**1 cup chopped celery**
**1 cup chopped carrots**
**⅔ cup tomato sauce**
**Salt and pepper to taste**

Brown meat on all sides in a frying pan with hot oil. Remove the meat to a Dutch oven; let stand. In the same frying pan saute onion, celery and carrots. Add tomato. Heat thoroughly. Add salt and pepper. Pour the sauce over the meat, add 1 cup boiling water; cover, cook slowly for approximately 2½ hours or until meat is tender. As the liquid cooks away add water as needed. Remove meat from sauce, slice and place into a deep serving plate. Press the sauce through a sieve or mash in a food processor. Bring to a boil and pour over meat. Serve hot with spaghetti, mashed potatoes or french fries and salad. Serves 4-5.

## ROAST BEEF
Μοσχάρι ψητὸ φούρνου

**4 pounds rump, eye of the round or chuck of beef**
**Juice of ½ lemon**
**Salt and pepper to taste**
**6 artichokes, cleaned and cut into halves (see index for Artichoke Mousaka)**

Rub meat with lemon juice and season with salt, pepper. Place fat side up in an open roasting pan and roast in a preheated 400°F (205°C) oven for 30 minutes. Arrange artichokes around meat, add 1 cup water. Reduce heat and roast approximately 1½ hours longer. Serve with gravy, mashed, roast or baked potatoes, peas and salad. Serves 6.

🐝🐝🐝

## BEEF ROLL A
Ρολλὸ μὲ κρέας

**2 pounds whole round or flank steak**
**4 whole hard-boiled eggs, shelled**
**¼ cup butter or margarine**
**¼ cup dry white wine**
**½ cup finely chopped onion**
**1 cup tomato sauce**
**Salt and pepper to taste**

Place steak flat on a cutting board. Begin to halve the steak thickness, but do not cut through to other side; keep meat in one piece that can be opened. This makes it easier to stuff and roll up. Flatten with a mallet until meat is ½-inch thick. Place whole hard-boiled eggs down the center of the flattened meat 1-inch from edges. Then very carefully fold up meat lengthwise, around the edges like a jelly roll. To keep the roll closed, tie meat sides and ends with string. Melt butter and brown meat roll on all sides in a frying pan, remove to a Dutch oven. Saute onion until transparent, add to the meat, add wine and cook for 2 minutes. Add tomato, salt, pepper and 1 cup water; cover and cook slowly for 1 to 1½ hours or until meat is tender and sauce is thick. As the liquid cooks away, add water as needed. Slice roll and arrange on a serving platter. Serve hot with mashed or french fried potatoes. Serves 4-6.

🐝🐝🐝

## BEEF ROLL B
Ρολλὸ μὲ κρέας

**¼ cup finely chopped onion**
**6 tablespoons butter or margarine**
**½ cup chopped chicken livers**
**½ cup chopped mushrooms**

½  cup chopped ham
2  chopped hard- boiled eggs
1  beaten egg
½  cup cooked peas
1  cup soft bread crumbs (see index)
Salt and pepper to taste
2  pounds whole round or flank steak
½  cup dry white wine
1  cup tomato sauce

Saute onion in 4 tablespoons butter if desired until transparent. Add chicken livers and mushrooms, saute a few minutes longer. Remove from heat. Add all the ingredients except wine and tomato. Stir to blend. Let stand. Place steak flat on a cutting board. Begin to halve steaks thickness but do not cut through to other side; keep meat in one piece that can be opened. This makes it easier to stuff and rollup. Flatten with mallet until meat is ½-inch thick. Spread stuffing over meat up to 1-inch from edges. Then very carefully roll up meat lengthwise, tucking in stuffing like jelly roll.To keep the roll closed tie meat sides and ends with string. In a Dutch oven melt the remaining butter and brown meat roll on all sides. Add wine, tomato sauce and 1 cup water, salt and pepper to taste. Cover and cook slowly 1½ hours or until meat is tender and sauce is thick. Add water as needed. Place meat roll on serving platter and slice, spoon pot juices over and serve with mashed potatoes or spaghetti. Serves 4-5.

# ROLL WITH GROUND MEAT
Ρολλό μὲ κιμᾶ

¾  cup finely chopped onion
¼  cup butter or margarine
2  cups soft bread crumbs (see index)
2  lightly beaten eggs
¼  cup dry white wine
1  pound lean ground beef
½  pound lean ground pork
½  pound lean ground lamb
Salt and pepper to taste
1  tablespoon fresh finely chopped mint or ½
      teaspoon dried crushed
⅛  teaspoon crushed Greek rigani (oregano)
6  hard-boiled eggs, shelled
1½  cups tomato sauce
½  cup flour

Saute onion with 2 tablespoons butter if desired until transparent. In a large bowl mix bread crumbs, 2 eggs and wine. Add meat, salt, pepper, mint and rigani and mix well to combine. Divide the meat mixture in half. Roll out half of the mixture evenly on a 9x7-inch waxed paper sheet, which has been generously

sprinkled with flour. Place whole hard-boiled eggs down the center of the flattened meat mixture ½-inch from edges. Then very gently rollup waxed paper and meat lengthwise, around the eggs once. Seal the edges. Roll out second half the same way. Remove waxed paper. Place in a greased baking dish. Boil tomato, 1½ cups water, salt and pepper in a small saucepan and boil for 5 minutes. Pour tomato sauce over meat and dot with the remaining butter. Bake in a preheated 350°F (180°C) oven for 45-55 minutes. Place meat rolls on a serving platter. Slice meat and pour sauce over. Serve hot with french fries or mashed potatoes and salad. Serves 6.

Note: Substitute beef for the pork and lamb if desired.

# BAKED GROUND MEAT AND RICE
Κιμᾶς μὲ ρίζι στὸ φοῦρνο

½  pound lean ground beef
½  pound lean ground pork
½  pound lean ground lamb
1  tablespoon olive oil
½  cup finely chopped onion
½  cup dry white wine
1  medium ripe tomato, peeled, seeded and chopped
1  cup water
Salt and pepper to taste
2  cups fresh chicken stock or beef
1  cup converted rice
½  cup grated Parmesan or Romano cheese
½  cup fine dried bread crumbs (see index)
3  tablespoons butter or margarine, melted
2  small cloves garlic, minced
2  tablespoons olive oil
1  can (20 ounces) whole tomatoes, pressed through
      a food mill

Heat oil and saute onion and meat, until onion is soft. Add wine, chopped tomato, water, salt and pepper. Cook slowly until meat is tender and the liquid evaporates. In a saucepan boil stock; add rice and salt. Cook slowly for 20 minutes. Place half of the rice in a greased tubepan. Add meat mixture and cover with the remaining rice. Mix bread crumbs with grated cheese. Sprinkle the meat-rice with cheese and melted butter. Bake in a preheated 350°F (180°C) oven for 20 minutes. While meat-rice is baking prepare sauce. Heat oil and saute garlic for a few minutes. Do not brown. Add tomato puree, salt and pepper. Cook slowly until thick. Unmold meat-rice in a serving platter; pour tomato sauce over and serve. Serve 4-6.

Note: Substitute beef for the pork and lamb if desired.

## BRAISED BEEF WITH LEMON
### Μοσχάρι μὲ λεμόνι

⅓ cup flour
1½ teaspoons salt
¼ teaspoon pepper
3 pounds lean boneless beef, cut into serving pieces
1 cup finely chopped onion
1 tablespoon butter
2 tablespoons olive oil
1 cup dry white wine
Juice of 1 or less lemon
2 cups water

Mix flour, salt and pepper together. Coat meat pieces, shake off the excess. Heat butter and oil, brown meat and onion until it is soft. Add wine and saute few minutes longer. Add lemon juice, water and cover. Cook slowly approximately 1½ hours or until meat is tender and sauce is thick. Serve with rice pilaf, spaghetti, french fries or mashed potatoes and salad. Serves 6.

**Variations:**

## BRAISED VEAL WITH LEMON
### Μοσχαράκι μὲ λεμόνι

Substitute veal for the beef.
Follow recipe and preparation as directed in Braised beef with lemon.

## BRAISED LAMB WITH LEMON
### Ἀρνὶ μὲ λεμόνι

Substitute lamb for the beef.
Follow recipe and preparation as directed in Braised beef with lemon.

## BRAISED BEEF WITH OREGANO
### Μοσχαράκι ριγανᾶτο

⅓ cup flour
1½ teaspoons salt
¼ teaspoon pepper
3 pounds lean bonelss beef, cut into serving pieces
1 cup finely chopped onion
2 tablespoons butter
2 tablespoons olive oil
½ teaspoon Greek rigani (oregano)
Juice of 1 lemon
2 cups water
3 pounds potatoes, peeled and cut into fourths

Mix flour, salt and pepper together. Coat meat pieces, shake off the excess. Heat butter and oil and brown meat and onion until it is soft. Add lemon juice, rigani, water and cover. Cook slowly for approximately 1½ hours. Add potatoes and enough water to barely cover. Cook slowly until meat and potatoes are tender. Serve hot. Serves 4-6.

## BRAISED RUMP OF BEEF WITH WINE
### Οὐρὰ κατσαρόλας μὲ κρασὶ

4 pounds rolled rump
3 tablespoons olive oil
1 cup finely chopped onion
1 cup dry white wine
½ cup chopped carrots
½ cup chopped celery
1 tablespoon chopped parsley
1 can (20-ounces) whole tomatoes chopped
Salt and pepper to taste

Heat oil and brown meat on all sides. Add onion and saute until it is tender. Add wine and cook until wine evaporates and saute few minutes longer. Add the rest of the ingredients. Cover and cook slowly for approximately 2 hours or until tender. Add water as needed. Remove meat from sauce and slice. Press sauce through a food mill. Add meat slices to the sauce and heat through. Serve with mashed potatoes, rice pilaf or spaghetti (see index) and salad. Serves 6.

## FILLET MIGNON OF BEEF
### Μπόν-φιλὲ βοδινοῦ

3 pounds beef tenderloin (fillet mignon)
½ cup butter or margarine, clarified (see index)
Salt and pepper to taste
2 tablespoons flour
½ cup dry white wine
1½ cups beef stock (fresh)

Clean tenderloin, by removing skin and fat with a sharp knife. Cut fillet mignon intto 1½-inch thick slices. Saute in frypan with butter for 5 minutes. Turn, season with salt and pepper. Saute on the other side for same length of time. Remove to a hot platter, keep warm. Strain pan fat. In a saucepan place strained fat, blend in flour. Add wine, stock, salt and pepper. Cook slowly for 5 minutes. Pour sauce over fillets. Serve with salad, mashed potatoes, peas and carrots or spinach sauteed see index). Serves 6.

**Variation:**

## FILLET MIGNON OF VEAL
Μπόν-φιλέ μοσχαριοῦ

Substitute veal fillet mignon for beef.
Follow recipe and preparation as directed in Fillet mignon of beef (see index).

## RIB ROAST
Μπριζολίκι ψητὸ

3 first ribs
1¼ cups dry white wine
Salt and pepper to taste
¼ teaspoon garlic powder
2 tablespoons lemon juice
1 cup water

Place meat on rack in pan. Sprinkle on all sides with wine and lemon juice, salt and pepper and garlic. Turn fat side up. Add 1 cup water in the pan. Bake in a preheated 450°F (230°C) oven for 30 minutes. Reduce heat to 350°F (180°C) oven and bake for approximately 1½ hours longer or until meat is ready to your taste. Skim off fat of the juice and serve with meat. Serves 3-6.

## BAKED MEATBALLS WITH POTATOES
Κεφτέδες φούρνου μὲ πατάτες

1 pound ground sirloin
½ pound lean ground pork
½ pound lean ground lamb
2 cups soft bread crumbs (see index)
½ cup dry white wine
1 cup finely chopped onion
1 tablespoon fresh finely chopped mint or
    ¼ teaspoon dried
2 lightly beaten eggs
Salt and pepper to taste
¼ teaspoon crushed Greek rigani (oregano)
1 can (29-ounces) whole tomatoes, press through a
    food mill
4 pounds potatoes, peeled and cut into fourths
⅓ cup or more butter or margarine, cut into small
    pieces

Soak bread crumbs in wine. Add all the ingredients except tomato puree, potatoes and butter. Mix well with your hand to combine. Shape mixture into balls and place in a greased baking pan. Sprinkle potatoes with salt and pepper. Arrange them between meat-

balls. Add butter. Dilute tomato puree with 1 cup water and pour over potatoes. Bake in a preheated 350°F (180°C) oven for approximately 1½ hours or until potatoes are tender. Serve hot with salad. Serves 6.

## FRIED MEATBALLS
Κεφτέδες τηγανητοὶ

1½ pounds lean ground round steak or sirloin
½ pound lean ground pork
2 cups soft bread crumbs (see index)
½ cup dry white wine
1 cup finely chopped onion
1 tablespoon fresh finely chopped mint or parsley
¼ teaspoon crushed Greek rigani (oregano)
2 lightly beaten eggs
Salt and pepper to taste
Flour for coating
Oil for frying

Soak bread crumbs in wine and combine with all ingredients together, except oil and flour. Mix well with your hand. Cover and place in the refrigerator for 2 hours or longer. Shape mixture into balls the size of a large walnut. Roll them in flour, shake off excess flour. Heat oil and fry meatballs until browned on both sides and cooked through. Served hot with Boiled Green Vegetables and french fries. Serves 6.

## MEATBALLS AVGOLEMONO
Γιουβαρελάκια αὐγολέμονο

½ pound lean ground beef
½ pound lean ground lamb, or veal
½ pound lean ground pork
½ cup rice
½ cup finely chopped onion
3 beaten egg whites
Salt and pepper to taste
1 tablespoon fresh chopped dill or parsley or both
2 tablespoons butter or margarine
4 cups fresh beef stock or water, boiling
⅓ cup dry white wine
2 tablespoons corn starch
¼ cup water
3 beaten egg yolks
Juice of 1 or more lemon

Combine first 8 ingredients together, mix well with your hand. Shape into meatballs the size of a small walnut. In a Dutch oven place meatballs, wine, stock and butter if desired. Simmer covered for 1 hour. Mix corn starch with ¼ cup water to a thin paste. Slowly add to the meatballs stirring constantly. Cook slowly for 5 minutes. Beat egg yolks with the lemon juice. Gradually spoon some of the meatball liquid, stirring constantly. Pour over meatballs, and stir gently to combine. Serve immediately. Serves 4-6.

## MEATBALLS WITH CHILI
### Κεφτέδες πικάντικοι

2  pounds lean ground beef
1  teaspoon onion powder
½  teaspoon garlic powder
¼  teaspoon crushed Greek rigani (oregano)
Salt and pepper to taste
2½  teaspoons chili powder
2  eggs
½  cup dried bread crumbs (see index)
½  cup milk or water
1  can (20-ounces) whole tomatoes, pressed through food mill or 1 cup tomato sauce
2  cups water
1  teaspoon onion powder
Pepper to taste
3  tablespoons olive oil or butter

In a large bowl soak bread crumbs with the milk or water, let stand for 2 minutes. Add ground meat, onion, garlic, rigani, salt, pepper, chili and eggs. Mix well with your hand to combine. Shape into 2-inch long cylinders. Let stand. In a large frying pan with cover, place oil if desired, tomato, water, pepper and onion. Bring to a boil, and cook slowly for 20 minutes. Add meatballs to the sauce neatly in one layer. Spoon sauce over meatballs; cover and simmer for 20-30 minutes, or until sauce is thick. Serve with white rice pilaf, mashed potatoes or spaghetti (see index) and salad. Serves 6.

## MEATBALLS WITH CUMIN
### Σουτζουκάκια

1½  pounds ground round steak or sirloin
½  pound lean ground pork or lamb
2  cloves garlic or less, minced
½  teaspoon or more ground cumin
Salt and pepper to taste
1½  cups soft bread crumbs (see index)
2  lightly beaten eggs
½  cup dry white wine
1  can (29-ounces) whole tomatoes, pressed through a food mill
2  tablespoons butter or olive oil

Soak bread crumbs with the wine; combine with meat,

garlic, cumin, salt, pepper and eggs. Mix well with your hand. Shape into 2-inch long cylinders. Place them in a baking dish in one layer. Cook tomato for 5 minutes. Pour over meatballs. Bake in a preheated 350°F (180°C) oven for 45-55 minutes. Serve with white rice pilaf (see index), mashed potatoes or spaghetti and salad. Serves 6.

## MEATBALLS WITH SAUCE
### Κεφτέδες μὲ σάλτσα

Follow recipe and preparation as directed in Frying meatballs.
¼  cup butter or margarine
½  cup finely chopped onion
2  cloves garlic, minced (optional)
2  cans (29-ounces each) whole tomatoes, pressed through a food mill

Fry meatballs as directed, let stand. Heat butter and saute onion; add garlic if desired and saute for few minutes longer. Add tomato and cook slowly for 1 hour or until almost thick. Add meatballs and cook slowly for 15-20 minutes. Serve on spaghetti (see index). Serves 6.

## SMALL MEATBALLS WITH PILAF
### Μικρὰ κεφτεδάκια μὲ πιλάφι

½  pound lean ground beef
½  pound lean ground lamb
½  pound lean ground pork
2  cups soft bread crumbs (see index)
¼  cup water
2  eggs, beaten
1  teaspoon Worcestershire sauce
Salt and pepper to taste
1  tablespoon fresh chopped mint or dill (optional)
1  medium finely chopped onion
¼  cup butter or margarine
1  tablespoon flour
½  cup dry white wine
2  cups fresh beef stock
Salt and pepper to taste

Combine first 10 ingredients together, mix well with your hand. Shape into meatballs, the size of a small walnut. Saute with the butter if desired. Remove meatballs to a platter. Strain pan fat. In a sauce pan place strained fat, blend in flour. Add wine, stock, salt and pepper. Add meatballs, cover and cook slowly for 15 minutes. Serve with rice pilaf (see index). Serves 4-6.

## HAMBURGERS A
Μπιφτέκια

2 pounds lean ground sirloin or round steak
1 cup soft bread crumbs (see index) soaked in
¼ cup milk or water
1 clove garlic, finely chopped (optional)
¼ teaspoon crushed Greek rigani (oregano)
Salt and pepper to taste

Combine all ingredients together. Mix well with your hand. Press into a flat cake ½-inch thick. Broil. Spread with butter if desired and serve hot. Serves 6.

## HAMBURGERS B
Μπιφτέκια

2 pounds lean ground sirloin or round steak
1 cup soft bread crumbs, soaked in
¼ cup milk or water
2 beaten eggs
Salt and pepper to taste
¼ teaspoon crushed Greek rigani (oregano)
2 cloves garlic, minced or ¼ teaspoon minced onion

Combine all the ingredients together. Mix well with your hand. Press into flat round cakes ½-inch thick. Broil. Spread with butter if desired and serve hot. Serves 6.

## HAMBURGERS C
Μπιφτέκια

1½ pounds lean ground sirloin or round steak
½ pound lean ground lamb
1 cup soft bread crumbs (see index) soaked in
⅓ cup dry white wine
2 cloves garlic, minced (optional)
Salt and pepper to taste
¼ teaspoon crushed Greek rigani (oregano)

Combine all the ingredients together. Mix well with your hand. Press into a flat round cake ½-inch thick. Broil or fry with clarified butter (see index) or oil. Serve hot. Serves 6.

## BAKED STUFFED BREAST OF VEAL
Στῆθος μοσχαριοῦ γεμιστὸ

1½ pounds lean ground beef
1 medium onion, finely chopped
1 tablespoon olive oil
½ cup dry white wine

¾ cup converted rice
⅓ cup pine nuts or slivered blanched almonds
Salt and pepper to taste
6 pounds breast of veal
Juice of ½ lemon
2 tablespoons melted butter

Saute ground meat and onion with the oil until it is soft and meat juices have evaporated. Add wine and cook until wine evaporates. Rinse rice under cold running water, (to get rid of the starch), add to the meat mixture and saute all together for 2 minutes. Add ¾ cup hot water, pine nuts if desired, salt and pepper. Cover and cook slowly for 5 minutes. Remove from heat. Season breast inside and outside the pocket with salt and pepper. Pack stuffing into pocket and sew edges together. Place breast in a roasting pan. Brush top with melted butter and sprinkle with lemon juice. Bake in a preheated 400°F (205°C) oven for 30 minutes. Add 1 cup water to the pan, cover, reduce heat to 350°F (180°C) oven and bake for approximately 2 hours. Serves 6-8.

Variation:

## BAKED STUFFED BREAST OF LAMB
Στῆθος ἀρνιοῦ γεμιστὸ

Substitute lamb for the veal.
Follow recipe and preparation as directed in Baked stuffed breast of veal (see index).

## VEAL CUTLETS
Σνήτσελ πανὲ

3 pounds rump of veal, cut into ⅓-inch slices
Salt and pepper to taste
1½ cups fine bread crumbs, dried (see index)
⅓ cup or less grated Kefalotyri, Parmesan or
    Romano cheese
2 eggs, beaten with 1 tablespoon water
Clarified butter (see index) or fine quality oil for frying

Sprinkle cutlets with salt and pepper. Mix bread crumbs with cheese. Dip cutlets into eggs, then into bread mixture. Brown in hot butter if desired, on both sides on medium heat. Serve hot with french fries, pasta or rice pilaf. Serves 6.

## VEAL CUTLETS WITH CHEESE
Σνήτσελ πανὲ μὲ τυρὶ

3 pounds rump veal, cut into ⅓-inch slices

Salt and pepper to taste
1½ cups fine dried bread crumbs (see index)
⅓ cup or less grated Kefalotyri, Parmesan or
    Romano cheese
Clarified butter (see index) or fine quality oil
Equal slices Kaseri or Swiss cheese

Sprinkle cutlets with salt and pepper. Mix bread crumbs with cheese. Dip cutlets into eggs, then into bread mixture. Brown in hot butter or oil on both sides. When you turn the other side, place a slice of cheese on each cutlet and fry until cheese is melted. Serve immediately with french fries, pasta or rice pilaf. Serves 6.

❦❦❦❦

## FILLET MIGNON AU-GRATIN
Μπόν-φιλὲ ὀγκραντὲν

3 pounds veal fillet mignon (tenderloin)
Salt and pepper to taste
Flour for coating
Clarified butter or margarine for frying (see index)
1½ cups thick white sauce (see index)
½ cup grated Parmesan or Romano cheese
¼ cup ham, finely chopped
¼ cup fine dried bread crumbs (see index)
¼ cup butter or margarine, melted

Clean fillet mignon by removing skin and fat with a sharp knife. Cut fillet into ½-inch thick slices. Season with salt and pepper. Coat with flour and shake off the excess. Saute in hot butter if desired for 5 minutes. Turn and saute on other side for same length of time. Prepare white sauce as directed, add half of the grated cheese, the chopped ham and blend well to combine. Place fillets in a greased baking dish. Top each fillet with 1 tablespoon sauce. Sprinkle first with remaining cheese, then bread crumbs and lastly with melted butter. Place baking dish on the middle rack in the oven and broil until it has a golden crust. Serve immediately. Serve with Boiled Artichokes (see index) and peas. Serves 6.

❦❦❦❦

## BROILED CALF LIVER
Σηκώτι μοσχαριοῦ σχάρας

3 pounds calf liver, sliced
Salt and pepper to taste
Butter for spreading
Juice of 1 lemon

Wash liver thoroughly and dry. Place liver slices on a baking sheet. Season with salt and pepper. Broil under the broiler for 3-5 minutes on each side. Place on a platter, spread with butter and sprinkle with lemon juice. Serves 6.

## FRIED CALF LIVER PIQUANTE
Σηκώτι μοσχαριοῦ τηγανιτὸ πικάτικο

2 pounds calf liver, cut into 2x4-inch slices
Clarified butter (see index) or fine quality oil
Sauce Piquante (see index)

Wash liver thoroughly and dry. Fry quickly in hot butter if desired on both sides for 2-3 minutes on each side. Place on a platter. Pour Piquante Sauce over liver. Serve immediately. Serves 6.

❦❦❦❦

## HOW TO PREPARE CALF'S BRAINS
Προετοιμασία μυαλῶν μοσχαριοῦ

2 pairs calf's brains
2 tablespoons wine vinegar
1 teaspoon salt

Rinse brains with cold water. Cover them with warm water, soak for 30 minutes. Then very carefully remove the thick membrane covering them, and see that they are white and bloodless. Rinse with cold water. Put them into a saucepan and cover with boiling water, add 2 tablespoons vinegar and salt, bring to a boil, cover and simmer for 15 minutes. Drain. When they are cool, cut into ½-inch slices. They are then ready to be prepared as you desire.

❦❦❦❦

## BOILED CALF'S BRAINS
## WITH OIL-LEMON DRESSING
Μυαλὰ μοσχαριοῦ βραστὰ μὲ λαδολέμονο

2 pairs calf's brains
Oil-lemon dressing (see index)

Follow recipe and preparation as directed in How To Prepare Calf's Brains (see index). Drain and cool. Cut into ½-inch slices and sprinkle with Oil-Lemon Dressing. Let stand for 1 hour in the refrigerator. Serves 4.

❦❦❦❦

## BREADED CALF'S BRAINS
Μυαλὰ μοσχαριοῦ πανὲ

2 pairs calf's brains
1 cup fine dried bread crumbs (see index) mixed with
1 tablespoon grated Parmesan or Romano cheese
Pepper to taste
2 eggs, beaten with 1 tablespoon water
Clarified butter or margarine for frying (see index)
Juice of 1 lemon (optional)

Follow recipe and preparation as directed in How To Prepare Calf's Brains (see index). Dip into beaten eggs, then into bread crumb mixture. Fry in hot butter on both sides until golden brown. Serve immediately with lemon juice if desired and french fries or mashed potatoes and sauteed spinach and salad (see index). Serves 4.

✄✄✄✄

# LAMB WITH ARTICHOKES AVGOLEMONO
'Αρνὶ μὲ ἀγγινάρες αὐγολέμονο

3 pounds lean lamb (shoulder), cut into 6 serving
   pieces
1 bunch scallions, chopped
3 tablespoons butter
3 tablespoons olive oil
⅔ cup dry white wine
Salt and pepper to taste
9 artichokes, fresh or 3 boxes artichoke hearts
   frozen (thawed)
Juice of 1 lemon
3 tablespoons butter or margarine
3 tablespoons flour
3 egg yolks

Place butter and oil in a Dutch oven and saute lamb and scallions until onions are soft. Add wine, salt, pepper and 2 cups boiling water. Cover and simmer for 1½ hours or until meat is tender. While the meat is cooking, prepare artichokes as directed in How To Prepare Artichokes (see index). Drain and save 3 cups of the liquid. In a serving casserole place boiled artichokes and lamb with the sauce. Cover and bake in a preheated 350°F (180°C) oven for 30 minutes. Melt butter and blend in flour until smooth. Gradually add reserved artichoke liquid, stirring constantly until boiling point is reached. Reduce heat and cook for 5 minutes longer. Beat egg yolks lightly, slowly dilute with 1 cup of the hot sauce, then beat into the remaining sauce. Add salt and pepper if needed. Pour over casserole. Serve immediately. Serves 6.

✄✄✄✄

Variation:

# VEAL WITH ARTICHOKES AVGOLEMONO
Μοσχαράκι μὲ ἀγγινάρες αὐγολέμονο

Substitute veal for the lamb.
Follow recipe and preparation as directed in Lamb with artichokes avgolemono (see index).

# BRAISED LAMB
'Αρνὶ γιαχνὶ

4 pounds lean lamb (shoulder), cut into serving pieces
2 tablespoons butter
2 tablespoons olive oil
1 cup finely chopped onion
1 cup finely chopped carrots
1 tablespoon chopped parsley
1 cup tomato sauce
½ cup dry white wine
Salt and pepper to taste

In a frying pan brown meat in hot butter and oil. Remove the meat to a Dutch oven, add wine. In the same frying pan brown onions and carrots. Add celery, tomato, parsley and 2 cups hot water; bring to a boil. Pour the sauce over the lamb. Add salt and pepper to taste. Cover and simmer for 2 hours or until meat is tender. Serve with rice pilaf, spaghetti or mashed potatoes and salad (see index). Serves 6.

✄✄✄✄

# BROILED LAMB CHOPS
Παϊδάκια ἀρνιοῦ στὴ σχάρα

12 lamb chops or (4 pounds leg, cut into ½-inch
   slices)
1 teaspoon Greek rigani (oregano)
½ teaspoon salt
¼ teaspoon pepper
Juice of ½ lemon
¼ cup oil

Mix lemon juice and oil together. Combine oregano, salt and pepper together. Season chops with rigani mixture. Baste them with lemon and oil mixture on both sides and broil. Broil chops on both sides, basting frequently. Serve hot with french fries and salad (see index). Serves 4.

✄✄✄✄

# BREADED LAMB CHOPS
Κοτολέτες ἀρνιοῦ πανὲ

2 pounds boneless lamb chops
2 eggs, beaten with 1 tablespoon water
1½ cups dried bread crumbs (see index)
⅓ cup grated Parmesan or Romano cheese
Clarified butter or margarine (see index)
Salt and pepper to taste

Combine bread crumbs, cheese, salt and pepper together. Dip chops one at a time in egg and then into bread mixture until completely covered. Fry in hot butter, on both sides. Serve hot with Au-Gratin

Potatoes, french fries or or buttered macaroni and salad (see index). Serves 4.

✦✦✦✦

**Variation:**

## BREADED VEAL CHOPS
### Κοτολέτες μοσχαριοῦ πανὲ

Substitute veal for the lamb.
Follow recipe and preparation as directed in Breaded Lamb Chops (see index).

✦✦✦✦

## BREADED PORK CHOPS
### Κοτολέτες χοιρινοῦ πανὲ

Substitute pork for the lamb.
Follow recipe and preparation as directed in Breaded Lamb Chops (see index).

✦✦✦✦

## FRIED LAMB CHOPS
### Παϊδάκια ἀρνιοῦ τηγανητὰ

8 lamb chops
3 tablespoons olive oil or salad oil for frying
Salt and pepper to taste
¼ teaspoon crushed Greek rigani (oregano)
Juice of 1 lemon

Heat oil in a frying pan. Place chops in the frying pan and fry until brown on both sides. Reduce heat, cover pan and cook slowly until chops are tender for approximately 10 minutes. Turn chops occasionally. Sprinkle with lemon juice and season with salt and pepper and rigani. Cook slowly for 10 minutes longer. Serve immediately. Serves 4.

✦✦✦✦

**Variation:**

## FRIED PORK CHOPS
### Παϊδάκια χοιρινοῦ τηγανητὰ

Substitute pork chops for the lamb chops.
Follow recipe and preparation as directed in Fried Lamb Chops (see index).

✦✦✦✦

## LEG OF LAMB COUNTRY STYLE
### ᾿Αρνὶ ἐξοχικὸ

1 leg of lamb (6-8 pounds)
Juice of 1 lemon

2 cloves garlic, slivered or ¼ teaspoon garlic powder
½ teaspoon Greek rigani (oregano), crushed
Salt and pepper to taste
3 sheets of oiled paper and
2 grocery paper bags or
2 sheets heavy duty aluminum foil

Mix salt, pepper and rigani together. Make 8 deep slits in the meat and insert some salt mixture and garlic slivers. (Remove before serving if desired.) Rub meat with lemon juice and sprinkle with salt mixture. Wrap first tightly with oiled paper, if you don't use foil), closing the ends as you would a parcel to keep the juices in. Wrap again tightly with grocery paper bag. Tie with string. Place in baking pan and brush the surface of the paper with oil to keep from burning. Bake in a preheated 350°F (180°C) oven for 2½ hours. Serve hot with baked potatoes, carrots sauteed and spring salad (see index). Serves 6.

✦✦✦✦

## LAMB CROQUETTES
### Κροκέττες μὲ κιμᾶ ἀρνιοῦ

2 tablespoons finely chopped onion
1 tablespoon butter or margarine
2 cups finely ground cooked lamb
Salt and pepper to taste
1 teaspoon Worcestershire sauce
1 beaten egg
1 tablespoon finely chopped parsley
1 cup mashed potatoes
2 tablespoons grated Parmesan cheese
Fine dried bread crumbs (see index)
2 eggs, beaten with 1 tablespoon water
Clarified butter or margarine (see index) or oil for
    frying

Heat butter and saute onion until transparent. Combine first 8 ingredients together and mix well with your hand. Chill thoroughly. Shape into cylinders. Mix bread crumbs with cheese. Roll croquettes in crumbs, then into eggs and into crumbs again. Chill. Fry in hot butter until golden brown. Drain on absorbent paper. Serve hot. Serves 4-6.

✦✦✦✦

## MEAT CROQUETTES
### Κροκέττες μὲ κιμᾶ ἀνάμικτο

½ pound lean ground lamb
½ pound lean ground beef
½ pound lean ground pork
¼ cup finely chopped onion
1 tablespoon butter or margarine
1 teaspoon Worcestershire sauce

2 cups mashed potatoes
3 egg yolks
1 tablespoon finely chopped parsley
Salt and pepper to taste
3 tablespoons grated Parmesan or Romano cheese
Fine dried bread crumbs (see index)
3 beaten egg whites with 1 tablespoon water
Clarified butter or margarine (see index) or oil for
    frying

Saute onion with butter until transparent. Combine all the ingredients except cheese, bread crumbs and egg whites. Mix well with your hand. Shape into cylinders. Mix bread crumbs with cheese. Roll croquettes into crumbs, the into eggs and into crumbs again. Chill. Fry in hot butter if desired until golden brown. Drain on an absorbent paper. Serve hot. Serves 4-6.

❦❦❦❦

# MEAT STUFFED PITA BREAD
Πίττες μὲ κιμᾶ

6-8 pita breads (see index)
2 pounds lean ground lamb
1 clove garlic, finely chopped
1 tablespoon olive oil
½ teaspoon or less crushed Greek rigani (oregano)
Salt and pepper to taste
2 tomatoes, cut into thin slices
1 medium onion, thinly sliced
1½ cups cucumber and yogurt dip (see index)

Saute ground meat and garlic with oil. Add rigani, salt, pepper and ¾ cup water. Cook slowly for 45-55 minutes, or until it is cooked and dry. Cut a slit at one end of the pita bread and fill with the meat mixture, tomato slices, onion and cucumber yogurt dip. Serves 6-8.

❦❦❦❦

# LAMB FRICASSEE
Ἀρνὶ φρικασσὲ

2 pounds lean boneless lamb, cut into chunks
1 bunch scallions, chopped
¼ cup butter or margarine
4 tablespoons olive oil
2 tablespoons finely chopped fresh dill or ½ teaspoon
    dried
Salt and pepper to taste
2 cups hot water
3-4 heads endive or romaine lettuce
2 eggs
Juice of 1 lemon
3 teaspoons corn starch

In a Dutch oven saute onion and lamb in butter and oil until onion is soft. Add 1 cup water, dill, salt and pepper. Cover and cook slowly for 1 hour. While meat is simmering wash the vegetables and cut into small pieces about 2-inches long. Add prepared vegetables to the meat and continue to cook until meat and vegetables are tender. Remove from heat. Carefully drain liquid from pan into a measuring cup, add water to make 1¼ cups. Transfer liquid to a small saucepan, bring to a boil. Mix corn starch with ¼ cup cold water to a smooth paste. Gradually add to liquid, stirring until boiling and thickened. Let it boil for 3 minutes. In a bowl beat eggs until frothy, add lemon juice, beating constantly. Slowly add approximately 1 cup of the hot broth at first spoon by spoon, and then a little more at a time beating constantly. Gradually add egg mixture to the sauce. Pour avgolemono sauce into the lamb and stir gently with a fork to combine. Serve immediately. Serves 4-6.

❦❦❦❦

**Variation:**

# VEAL FRICASSEE
Μοσχαράκι φρικασσὲ

Substitute veal for the lamb.
Follow recipe and preparation as directed in Lamb Fricassee (see index).

## LAMB RAGOUT WITH LEEKS
Ἀρνὶ ἐντράδα μὲ πράσα

Substitute lamb for the beef in basic recipe for Beef Ragout (see index).
9 large leeks, cut into 2-inches long
2 tablespoons butter
2 tablespoons olive oil
Salt

Follow recipe and preparation as directed in basic recipe. Add butter and oil and cook lamb only 1 hour. Add cut up leeks to lamb ragout and simmer for approximately 50 minutes or until meat and leeks are tender. Occasionally shake the pot but do not stir. Place meat and leeks in the serving platter and serve hot. Serves 4.

❦❦❦❦

## LAMB WITH ZUCCHINI
Ἀρνὶ μὲ κολοκυθάκια

2½ pounds lean lamb (shoulder), cut into serving
    pieces
3 tablespoons flour
1 teaspoon salt
¼ teaspoon pepper
3 tablespoons butter or margarine
½ cup finely chopped onion

⅓ cup dry white wine (optional)
⅔ cup tomato sauce or puree
1 cup water
2½ pounds small zucchini
¼ cup olive oil

Mix flour, salt and pepper. Coat meat pieces with flour mixture. Heat butter in a Dutch oven and brown lamb pieces. Add onion and saute until soft. Add wine if desired and stir, cook until wine evaporates. Add tomato sauce, 1 cup water; cover and cook slowly for 1 hour. While meat is simmering, trim ends from zucchini, wash and cut them into fourths crosswise. Heat oil and saute zucchini just until lightly browned. Add zucchini to the lamb and cook slowly for 20 minutes or until meat and zucchini are tender. As the liquid cooks away, add more as needed. Serve hot. Serves 4-5.

❦❦❦❦

# LAMB WITH PASTA
'Αρνὶ γιουβέτσι

2½ pounds lean boneless lamb (shoulder or leg), cut into serving pieces
4 large ripe tomatoes, pass through a food mill or 1 cup tomato sauce
3 tablespoons butter
3 tablespoons olive oil
Salt and pepper to taste
1 pound Kritharaki (Greek pasta), home made noodles or tiny elbow macaroni
1 cinnamon stick ½-inch long (optional)
Grated Parmesan or Romano cheese

In a Dutch oven saute meat with butter and oil. Add tomato, 2 cups water, cinnamon, salt and pepper. Cover and cook slowly for 1½ hours. Add 8 cups water, bring to a boil. Transfer to a earthen dish if possible; add pasta, stir well and bake in a preheated 350°F (180°C) oven for 30 minutes or until pasta is tender, stir once in a while. The pasta will look moist and creamy. Serve hot with grated cheese. Serves 4-5.

❦❦❦❦

**Variation:**

# VEAL WITH PASTA
Μοσχαράκι γιουβέτσι

Substitute veal for the lamb.
Follow recipe and preparation as directed in Lamb with pasta (see index).

❦❦❦❦

# LAMB WITH PEAS AVGOLEMONO
'Αρνὶ μὲ ἀρακὰ αὐγολέμονο

2½ pounds lean boneless lamb, cut into serving pieces
1 bunch scallions, chopped
¼ cup butter
1 tablespoon olive oil
1 tablespoon fresh finely chopped dill or ¼ teaspoon dried
Salt and pepper to taste
1 bag (20-ounces) frozen peas
1 cup water
2 eggs
Juice of 1 lemon

In a Dutch oven saute onions and lamb in butter and oil, until onion is soft. Add 1 cup water, dill, salt and pepper; cover and cook slowly for 1½ hours. Add peas and simmer until meat and peas are tender. Add more water if needed. Remove from heat. In a bowl beat eggs until frothy. Add lemon juice. Gradually add hot sauce from the pot, beating constantly. Slowly pour avgolemon sauce into the pot and stir gently with a fork to combine. Serve immediately. Serves 4.

Note: 2 cups ripe tomatoes, peeled, seeded and finely chopped or ½ cup tomato puree may be used in place of the eggs and lemon juice. After you saute the onions and the meat, add tomatoes and the rest of the ingredients and cook slowly.

❦❦❦❦

# ROAST LEG OF LAMB WITH POTATOES
'Αρνὶ ψητὸ μὲ πατάτες

1 leg of lamb approximately (8 pounds)
5 pounds red or white potatoes, peeled and cut into fourths
Salt and pepper to taste
¼ teaspoon or more garlic powder (optional)
2 cloves garlic, slivered or ¼ teaspoon garlic powder
Juice of 1 or more lemon

Place potatoes in a large roasting pan. Sprinkle with salt, pepper and garlic if desired and toss well. Place slivers of garlic into deep narrow gashes cut in meat (remove before serving if desired). Place meat on top of the potatoes (fat side down), sprinkle with half of the lemon juice, salt and pepper; turn upside down (fat side up), sprinkle with remaining lemon juice, salt and pepper; add 2 cups water to the pan. Roast uncovered in a preheated 400°F (205°C) oven for 30 minutes. Reduce temperature to 350°F (180°C) oven and bake for 2½ hours longer or until meat and potatoes are tender. Baste the meat and potatoes occasionally. Add water if needed. Slice the meat and serve with the potatoes and salad. Serve hot. Serves 6-8.

## BAKED MIXED VEGETABLES WITH LAMB
'Αρνὶ τουρλοῦ στὸ φούρνο

6 lamb shanks or 3 pounds any piece of lamb, cut into serving pieces
1 pound fresh string beans, trim off the ends and cut into 1½-inch long
1 pound okra, remove the stem
1 pound zucchini, cut into ½-inch slices crosswise
1 eggplant peeled and cut into 1-inch cubes
3 medium potatoes, peeled and cut into fourths
2 medium onions, thinly sliced
1 can (16 ounces) whole tomatoes, chopped
2 tablespoons chopped parsley
Salt and pepper to taste
¼ cup butter
⅓ cup olive oil

Place vegetables in a deep 11x13x3 inch baking pan. Season with salt and pepper; toss well. Arrange meat between the vegetables, add butter, oil and 1 cup water. Cover. Bake in a preheated 350°F (180°C) oven for 60 minutes. Uncover and bake for approximately 1½ hours longer or until vegetables are tender. Serve hot. Serves 6-8.

## LAMB SHISHKEBAB
Σουβλάκια ἀρνιοῦ

1 leg of lamb (5-6 pounds) boned and cubed 1-inch
2 teaspoons crushed Greek rigani (oregano)
2 teaspoons salt
½ teaspoon pepper
1 cup salad oil
Juice of 1 lemon

Mix lemon juice and oil together. Combine rigani, salt and pepper together. Coat lamb cubes with the rigani mixture. Thread lamb cubes of 14 skewers. broil on hot grill or over charcoal, turning and basting frequently with lemon and oil mixture. Place on a platter and serve with french fries and summer country style salad (see index). Serve hot. Serves 4-6.

Variation:
## PORK SHISHKEBAB
Σουβλάκια χοιρινοῦ

Substitute pork for the lamb.
Follow recipe and preparation as directed in Lamb Shishkebab (see index).

## EASTER BAKED STUFFED SUCKLING LAMB
Πασχαλινὸ ἀρνὶ ψητὸ γεμιστὸ

1 whole lamb, approximately 20 pounds cut in half
4 pounds lean ground beef
1½ cups finely chopped onion
¼ cup butter or margarine
1 cup dry white wine
2 cups converted rice
¾ cup or more pine nuts or slivered blanched almonds
Salt and pepper to taste
Juice of 2 lemons
½ cup melted butter or margarine
6 pounds red or white potatoes, peeled and cut into fourths

Remove liver, heart, kidney and spleen from the cavity. Reserve for Easter Soup (see index). Rinse lamb innside and out with cold water. Cut and separate body from the legs. Sprinkle cavity with little salt. Saute ground meat and onion with the butter until meat juices evaporate. Saute 5 more minutes stirring constantly. Add wine and cook until wine evaporates. Add rice and saute all together for 3 minutes. Add 2 cups hot water, pine nuts, salt and pepper; cover and simmer for 5 minutes. Stuff lamb cavity with meat mixture. Close cavity by sewing with heavy thread. Place on rack in large roasting pan. Add cups water to pan. Rub outer surfaces with lemon juice. Brush with melted butter and sprinkle with salt and pepper. Roast in a preheated 350°F (180°C) oven for approximately 3-4 hours. Turn the meat once. Serve hot with baked hours. Turn the meat once. Serve hot with baked potatoes, artichokes and peas, and salad (see index). Serves 10-12.

Note: To the pan juices add 3 cups hot water, the potatoes, sprinkle with salt and pepper. Roast in a preheated 400°F (205°C) oven for 1 hour. Or place potatoes in the pan and place lamb on top of the potatoes.

## STUFFED CROWN OF LAMB
Ἄκοπα παϊδάκια ἀρνιοῦ γεμιστὰ

1 crown of lamb (12 chops) prepared
1 pound lean ground beef
¼ cup finely chopped onion
2 tablespoons butter or margarine
½ cup converted rice
⅓ cup pine nuts or slivered blanched almonds
¼ cup dry white wine
Salt and pepper to taste
Juice of ½ lemon

Saute ground meat and onion with the butter until

meat juices evaporate. Saute 5 more minutes, stirring constantly. Add wine and cook until wine evaporates. Rinse rice under cold running water, add to the mixture and saute all together for 2 minutes. Add ½ cup hot water, pine nuts, salt and pepper. Cover and cook slowly for 5 minutes. Place crown in an open roasting pan. Wrap rib ends with foil. Bake in a preheated 400°F (205°C) oven for 20 minutes. Reduce heat to 350°F (180°C) oven. Remove roast from oven and fill crown center with stuffing. Return to oven and bake for 1 hour longer or until meat is tender. Serve hot with sauteed peas, salad (see index) and feta cheese. Serves 4-6.

## SUCKLING LAMB ON A SPIT
### 'Αρνάκι στὴ σούβλα

1  whole lamb, approximately 20 pounds
Salt and pepper to taste
1  whole lemon, cut in half
Juice of 1 lemon, mixed with
1  cup butter, margarine or olive oil

Pull liver, heart and spleen from the cavity leave the kidneys. Wipe lamb inside and out with a damp cloth. Sprinkle cavity with salt and pepper; close with strong thread or stuff (see index for Easter stuffed suckling lamb) and close cavity with strong thread. Place lamb on the spit. Push spit through center from between the back legs, along the spine and through the neck. Tie the spine with spit every 3 inches with wire. Pull forelegs forwards and tie securely onto the spit with wire. Press back legs along the spit and cross them above it, again securing with wire. Rub outer surfaces with lemon and sprinkle with salt and pepper. Set a fire in a pit. When the charcoal is glowing; put spitted lamb in position and start cooking. Turn lamb slowly ovr fire. Begin with spit well away from fire if possible, basting occasionally with melted butter-lemon mixture. When the lamb is evenly browned move closer to the fire and move most of the charcoal to the areas of the legs and shoulders. The total cooking time depends on the size of the lamb, for approximately 6 hours. The lamb is ready when the meat begins to crack on the legs, shoulder blade, and when the fork goes through the meat easily. Serve hot with roasted potatoes, artichokes with peas, cheese pie, salad, Easter bread, red eggs, and wine (see index). Serves 10-12.

**Variation:**

## SUCKLING PIG ON A SPIT
### Γουρουνόπουλο στὴ σούβλα

Substitute suckling pig for the lamb.

Follow recipe and preparation as directed in Suckling Lamb on a spit (see index).

## LAMB LIVER FRICASSEE
### Σηκωταριά ἀρνιοῦ φρικασσὲ

1  whole baby lamb liver
1  whole baby lamb heart
1  whole baby lamb spleen
1  bunch scallions, chopped
½  cup butter or margarine
1  tablespoon fresh dill, finely chopped or ½ teaspoon
      dried
2  ripe large tomatoes, peeled, seeded and chopped or
      1 can (16-ounces) whole tomatoes, chopped
Salt and pepper to taste
2  cups converted rice
4½  cups boiling fresh beef stock or water
4  tablespoons butter or margarine
Salt

Rinse meat under cold running water and cut into 1-inch cubes. Heat butter in a Dutch ov  en and saute scallions and the meat until scallions are soft. Add chopped tomatoes, dill, salt and pepper and ½ cup water; cover. Cook slowly for 1 hour or until meat is tender and sauce is thick.While meat is cooking, prepare rice. Pick over rice and rinse in a strainer under cold running water (to get rid of the starch). Saute rice with butter for 5 minutes. Add boiling stock to the rice, stir and cook slowly, partially covered for 20 minutes. Pack the rice into a 6-cup ring mold. Unmold in a pllatter. Pour liver fricassee over rice. Serve hot with salad. Serves 6.

## LAMB LIVER WITH OREGANO
### Σηκωταριά ἀρνιοῦ ρηγανάτη

1  whole baby lamb liver
1  whole baby lamb heart
1  whole baby lamb spleen
1  bunch chopped scallions
½  cup olive oil
½  teaspoon or less crushed Greek rigani (oregano)
2  large ripe tomatoes, peeled, seeded and chopped
      or 1 can (16-ounces) whole tomatoes, chopped
Salt and pepper to taste
4½  cups boiling fresh beef stock
¼  cup butter or margarine
2  cups converted rice
Salt

Rinse meat well under cold running water. Cut into 1-inch cubes. Heat oil in a Dutch oven and saute scallions and meat until scallions are soft. Add chopped tomatoes, rigani, salt, pepper and ½ cup water. Cover and cook slowly for 1 hour or until meat is tender and sauce is thick. While meat is cooking prepare rice. Pick over rice and rinse in a strainer under cold running water (to get rid of the starch). Saute rice with the butter for 5 minutes. Add boiling stock to the rice, stir and cook slowly partially covered for 20 minutes. Pack the rice into a 6-cup ring mold. Unmold in a platter. Pour liver with oregano over rice. Serve hot with salad. Serves 6.

## FRIED LAMB LIVER
Σηκωτάκια ἀρνιοῦ τηγανητά

**2  pounds baby beef liver**
**Salt and pepper to taste**
**Flour for coating**
**Oil for frying**
**Juice of 1 lemon**

Rinse liver thoroughly and dry. Cut into 1x2-inch slices. Coat with flour and fry quickly in hot oil, on both sides. Place liver on a platter, season with salt and pepper and sprinkle with lemon juice. Serve with french fries and salad (see index). Serves 6.

**Variation:**

## FRIED CALF LIVER
Σηκωτάκια μοσχαριοῦ τηγανητά

Substitute calf liver for the lamb liver.
Follow recipe and preparation as directed in Fried Lamb Liver (see index).

## BOILED FRESH HAM
Χοιρινὸ βραστὸ

**4  pounds fresh ham**
**4  stalks celery, cut in half**
**3  carrots, cut in half**
**6  whole small onions**
**12  black peppercorns**
**Salt**

Wash ham thoroughly, cover with boiling water. Boil for 10 minutes. Skim off the froth. Add the rest of the ingredients. Cover and cook slowly for approximately 2 hours, allowing to cook 30 minutes per pound. Remove from heat, let stand in stock to cool. Drain, peel off rind and slice. Serve ham slices with Tartar Sauce (see index). Serves 6-8.

Note: With the stock you can make delicious Avgolemono Soup (see index).

## BREADED PORK TENDERLOIN
Φιλέτο χοιρινοῦ κοτολέτες

**2  pounds pork tenderloin**
**2  eggs, beaten with 1 tablespoon water**
**1½  cups fine dried bread crumbs (see index)**
**¼  cup grated Parmesan or Romano cheese**
**Salt and pepper to taste**

Clean tenderloin by removing skin and fat with a sharp knife. Cut into 1-inch thick slices. Flatten out. Combine bread crumbs, cheese, salt and pepper together. Mix well. Dip slices one at a time in egg and then into bread mixture until completely covered. Place in greased baking sheet. Bake in a preheated 350°F (180°C) oven for 30-40 minutes or until golden, turn and bake 30 more minutes or until golden again. Serves 6.

## PORK WITH BEANS
Χοιρινὸ μὲ φασόλια

**2½  pounds lean boneless pork, cut into serving portions**
**2  medium onions, finely chopped**
**⅓  cup olive oil**
**1  can (16 ounces) whole tomatoes, finely chopped**
**1  tablespoon finely chopped parsley (optional)**
**2  cups water**
**1  pound large white beans or lima beans**
**Salt and pepper to taste**

Saute pork pieces and onions in olive oil until they are soft. Add chopped tomatoes, parsley if desired, salt, pepper and water. Cover and cook slowly for 1 hour, stirring occasionally. While meat is simmering, prepare beans. Pick over beans, place in a colander and rinse well under cold running water. Place beans in a medium saucepan and 14 cups water. Bring to a boil, cover and boil for 1 hour. Drain. Add beans to the meat, stir gently, cover and simmer for 30 minutes or until meat and beans are tender, stirring occasionally to prevent from scorching. As the liquid cooks away add more as needed. Add more salt if needed. The dish will look moist and creamy. Serve hot. Serves 6.

## PORK WITH CABBAGE
Χοιρινὸ μὲ λάχανο

43

2½  pounds lean boneless pork, cut into serving
      pieces
2 medium onions, finely chopped
⅓  cup olive oil or butter
1 can (16-ounces) whole tomatoes finely chopped
2 tablespoons red wine vinegar
2 cups water
1 medium size white cabbage
Salt and pepper to taste

Saute meat and onions in olive oil until onions are
soft. Add chopped tomatoes, vinegar, salt, pepper
and water. Cover and cook slowly for 1 hour, stirring
occasionally. While meat is simmering prepare cabbage. Discard disclored or torn outside leaves of
cabbage. Cut cabbage into small pieces, place in a
colander and rinse well under running water. Drain
well. Plunge into boiling water to cover and boil for
5 minutes. Drain and add to the meat, stir gently,
cover. Simmer for approximately 45 minutes, or until
meat and cabbage are tender and sauce is thick. Add
more salt if needed. Serve hot. Serves 4-6.

## PORK WITH CELERY AVGOLEMONO
Χοιρινὸ μὲ σέλινο αὐγολέμονο

2½  pounds lean boneless pork, cut into serving
      pieces
2 medium onions, finely chopped
3 tablespoons butter
¼  cup olive oil
Salt and pepper to taste
2 cups water
3 pounds Italian celery
2 tablespoons corn starch
3 egg yolks
Juice of ½ or more lemon

Saute meat and onions in butter and oil until onions
are soft. Add salt, pepper and water. Cover and cook

slowly for 1 hour, stirring occasionally. While meat
is simmering, prepare celery by removing the roots of
each plant. Retain tender leaves. Cut in fourths. Wash
the celery very thoroughly in plenty of water. Drain.
In a large saucepan add water. Bring to a boil. Add
celery and boil for 5 minutes. Drain, add to the meat.
Stir gently, add 2 cups water, cover and simmer until
meat and celery are tender. Add salt if needed. Remove the liquid from pot, add water to make 2 cups.
Transfer liquid to a small saucepan. Bring to a boil.
Mix corn starch with ¼ cup cold water to make a
paste. Slowly add to the liquid stirring constantly.
Cook slowly for 5 minutes. Beat egg yolks with the
lemon juice. Gradually add some of the boiling sauce,
stirring vigorously. Add egg mixture to the sauce and
cook over very llow heat for 2-3 minutes, stirring
constantly. Pour avgolemono sauce into the pot and
stir gently to combine. Serve immediately. Serves 4-6.

## ROAST PORK WITH POTATOES
Χοιρινὸ ψητὸ μὲ πατάτες

4 pounds loin, center cut
½  cup olive oil
½  teaspoon crushed Greek rigani (oregano)
3 cloves garlic, crushed
Salt and pepper to taste
Juice of 1 lemon
3 cups water
4 pounds red potatoes, peeled and cut into fourths
Salt and pepper to taste

Place meat in a roasting pan, season with salt, pepper,
rigani and garlic. Pour oil over, cover and bake in a
preheated 350°F (180°C) oven for 1 hour. Season
potatoes and arrange around and under the meat.
Sprinkle with lemon juice. Add water in the pan,
cover and bake 1 hour longer. Uncover pan and continue cooking until meat and potatoes are tender.
Serve hot. Serves 6.

# POULTRY AND GAME

## BAKED CHICKEN WITH POTATOES
### Κοτόπουλο ψητὸ μὲ πατάτες

1 broiler chicken (about 3 pounds), cut in half
¼ cup melted butter or margarine
1 teaspoon mustard
1 tablespoon wine vinegar
1½ teaspoons Worcestershire sauce
Salt and pepper to taste
3 pounds red potatoes, peeled and cut into fourths
Juice of 1 lemon
Salt and pepper to taste
¼ cup butter or margarine, cut into small pieces
    (optional)

Place chicken halves in a roasting pan, skin side down. Blend together butter, mustard, vinegar, Worcestershire sauce, salt and pepper well and brush the chicken. Arrange potatoes around chicken. Sprinkle potatoes with lemon juice, salt and pepper; add butter pieces if desired. Pour 1 cup water in the pan. Bake in a preheated 350°F (180°C) oven for approximately 1 hour and 20 minutes or until chicken and potatoes are tender and golden, turning chicken once and brush with butter mixture. Serve hot with potatoes and salad. Serves 4-5.

❧❧❧

## BAKED STUFFED CHICKEN
### Κοτόπουλο γεμιστὸ

1 whole chicken (5-6 pounds)
1 pound lean ground beef
2 tablespoons olive oil
1 small onion, finely chopped
¼ cup dry white wine
½ cup converted rice
¼ cup pine nuts or slivered blanched almonds

Salt and pepper to taste
3 pounds red potatoes, peeled and cut into fourths
Juice of 1 lemon
Saltl and pepper to taste
2 cups water
¼ cup butter or margarine, cut into small pieces

Wash chicken well. Drain, set aside. Saute ground meat and onion with oil until onion is soft and meat juices have evaporated. Add wine and cook until wine evaporates. Pick over rice and rinse under cold running water (to get rid of the starch), add to the meat mixture and saute all together for 2 minutes. Add ½ cup hot water, pine nuts, salt and pepper. Cover and cook slowly for 5 minutes. Remove from heat. Pack stuffing into chicken's cavity and sew edges together. Place chicken in a roasting pan. Add potatoes around chicken. Sprinkle chicken and potatoes with lemon juice, salt and pepper, add butter and water to the pan. Bake in a preheated 350°F (180°C) oven for approximately 2 hours or until chicken and potatoes are golden and tender. Serve chicken with stuffing, potatoes and salad. Serves 4-5.

❧❧❧

**Variation:**

## BAKED STUFFED GUINEA-HEN
### Φραγκόκοτα γεμιστὴ φούρνου

Substitute guinea-hen for the chicken.
Follow recipe and preparation as directed in Baked Stuffed Chicken (see index).

❧❧❧

## BOILED CHICKEN
### Κοτόπουλο βραστὸ

1 whole chicken (about 3 pounds)

2 carrots, cut in half
3 stalks celery, cut in half
2 whole small onions
1 tablespoon salt

Clean and rinse chicken well. Place in a large pot and cover with cold water. Add salt and bring to a boil. Skim off the froth. Reduce heat and cook slowly half-covered for ½ hour. Add vegetables and cook 1 hour longer. Let stay in the broth for ½ hour. Remove chicken from broth and arrange on a platter with vegetables around if desired. With the broth you can make delicious soup or rice pilaf (see index).

Note: After chicken is boiled, cut into serving portions and saute with butter. Serve with french fries and salad (see index). Serves 4.

✾✾✾✾

# BREADED BREAST OF CHICKEN
Στῆθος κότας πανὲ

3 whole chicken breasts, boned and skinned
2 eggs, beaten with 1 tablespoon water
1½ cups fine dried bread crumbs (see index)
⅓ cup grated Parmesan or Romano cheese
Salt and pepper to taste
Clarified butter, or margarine (see index) or oil
    for frying

Place breast of chicken between two pieces of plastic wrap or waxed paper, and lightly pound to a thickness of ¼ of an inch. Combine bread crumbs, cheese, salt and pepper together. Dip chicken breasts one at a time in egg and then into bread mixture until completely covered. Fry in hot butter if desired until golden brown then turn and fry other side of cutlets. Repeat with remaining cutlets, adding more butter as needed. Serve hot. Serves 6.

✾✾✾✾

# BREADED CHICKEN
Κοτόπουλο πανὲ

6 chicken legs
1½ cups fine dried bread crumbs (see index)
⅓ cup grated Parmesan or Romano cheese
Salt and pepper to taste
1 teaspoon dried crushed parsley (optional)
2 eggs, beaten with 1 tablespoon water

Remove skin and fat from chicken, cut in half. Combine bread crumbs, cheese, salt, pepper and parsley if desired together. Dip chicken legs one at a time in egg and then into bread mixture until completely covered. Place chicken legs in a greased baking sheet. Bake in a preheated 350°F (180°C) oven for 1 hour,

turn and bake for approximately 25 minutes longer or until golden brown. Serve immediately. Serves 4-6.

✾✾✾✾

# BRAISED CHICKEN WITH WINE
Κοτόπουλο κρασάτο

1 frying chicken (about 3 pounds), cut into serving
    pieces
¼ cup oil
⅓ cup butter or margarine
2 tablespoons flour
1¼ cups white wine
1 tablespoon brandy
Salt and pepper to taste
1 clove garlic, minced
12 small white onions
1 pound fresh mushrooms, cut in half or 1 can
    (16 ounces) whole mushrooms
2 carrots, cut into small pieces
1 bay leaf
1 tablespoon fresh minced parsley

Heat oil in a frying pan and brown chicken pieces. Remove chicken pieces to a Dutch oven without the oil. Wash frying pan and melt butter, blend in flour, stir well and cook 2 minutes, add wine, brandy, garlic bay leaf, parsley, salt, pepper, carrots and 1 cup water. Bring to a boil and cook slowly for 5 minutes. Add to the chicken. Peel onions. Cross-cut root ends to prevent centers popping out during cooking. Boil the onions for 5 minutes. Drain. Add onion to the chicken. Saute fresh mushrooms with 2 tablespoons butter or margarine. Add to the chicken. Cover and cook slowly for 45-55 minutes or until chicken and vegetables are tender. Serves 4-5.

✾✾✾✾

# BROILED CHICKEN
# AND RICE PILAF
Κοτόπουλο σχάρας μὲ ρίζι πιλάφι

9 chicken legs (you may use breast if desired)
Juice of 1 lemon
¼ teaspoon garlic powder or ¼ teaspoon crushed
    rigani or both
Salt and pepper to taste
½ cup water
4½ cups boiling water
1 beef bouillon and 1 chicken (if desired)
2 cups converted rice
¼ cup butter or margarine

Rinse chicken legs. Place in a baking sheet, skin side down. Sprinkle with lemon juice, garlic, salt and pepper; add ½ cup water to the pan. Place baking sheet in the lower rack of the oven. Broil for 20 minutes. Turn off the broiler, let chicken stay in the oven. Turn chicken and broil for 15 minutes or until it is golden brown, turn off broiler again, let chicken stay in the oven for 15 minutes. While chicken is in the oven prepare rice. In a saucepan place boiling water, boulllions and butter. Bring to a boil. Pick over rice and rinse in a strainer under cold running water (to get rid of the starch). Add rice to the boiling water, stir and cook slowly partially covered for 20 minutes. Arrange chicken in a serving platter. Skim off the fat from the pan juices and pour over rice, stir well to combine; place in a serving bowl. Serve chicken with rice, vegetables and salad (see index). Serves 6.

## CHICKEN ATZEM PILAF
### Κοτόπουλο ἀτζὲμ πιλάφι

1 frying chicken (about 3 pounds), cut into serving
   pieces
¼ cup oil for sauteeing
1 medium onion, finely chopped
1 can (16 ounces) whole tomatoes, pressed through
   a sieve or food mill
1 cinnamon stick ½-inch long
Salt and pepper to taste
¼ cup butter or margarine
2 cups converted rice

In a frying pan heat oil and brown chicken pieces. Transfer to a Dutch oven. Set aside. Add onion in the frying pan and saute until soft and tender. Remove onion with a slotted spoon. Add onion, tomato, cinnamon, salt, pepper and 1 cup water to the chicken. Bring to a boil; cover and simmer for 50-60 minutes or until chicken is tender. Remove chicken from the pot to a serving platter, keep warm. Measure sauce, add water to make 5 cups. Bring to a boil. Pick over rice and rinse in a strainer under cold running water (to get rid of the starch). Saute rice with the butter for 5 minutes. Add rice to the boiling sauce, stir and cook slowly partially covered for 20 minutes. Place rice into a serving bowl. Serve chicken and rice hot with grated cheese if desired and salad. Serves 4-5.

Note: Substitute cracked wheat for the rice if desired.

**Variation:**
## QUAILS WITH RICE PILAF
### 'Ορτύκια πιλάφι

Substitute 4 quails for the chicken.
Follow recipe and preparation as directed in Chicken Atzem Pilaf (see index).

## CHICKEN JELLY
### Κοτόπουλο πυκτὴ

2½ tablespoons unflavored gelatin
1 cup cold chicken stock (fresh)
1 cup boiling chicken stock
3 cups boiled chicken breast, cut into very small
   cubes
1 cup celery, cut into thin slices
2 tablespoons capers
¼ cup finely chopped dill pickle
¾ cup mayonnaise
1 cup heavy cream, whipped
Freshly ground pepper to taste
2 hard-boiled eggs, sliced
Lettuce, carrots, parsley

Soften gelatin in one cup cold stock for 5 minutes. Add gelatin to boiling stock and stir untill dissolved, chill until firm. Mix chicken, celery, capers, pickle and mayonnaise. Fold in whipped cream. Season to your taste. Fold in the gelatin. Arrange sliced eggs in the bottom of the ring. Spoon chicken mixture gently into the ring mold and chill until firm. Make bed of lettuce in a serving dish and unmold the chicken jelly. Garnish with carrots and parsley. Serves 6-12. Note: This recipe is excellent for buffet.

## CHICKEN KAPAMA WITH POTATOES
### Κοτόπουλο καπαμὰ μὲ πατάτες

1 frying chicken (about 3 pounds), cut into serving
   pieces
½ cup olive oil
1 can (20 ounces) whole tomatoes pressed through
   a sieve or a food mill
Salt and pepper to taste
1 cinnamon stick, ½-inch long
3 pounds potatoes, peeled and cut into ½-inch slices
1 cup water

Heat oil and saute chicken pieces until golden brown on all sides. Transfer to a Dutch oven. Drain oil and saute potatoes on both sides; add to the chicken. Add tomato, salt, pepper, cinnamon and water. Cover and simmer for approximately 45 minutes or until chicken and potatoes are tender. Serve hot with salad and feta cheese. Serves 4-5.

## CHICKEN KAPAMA WITH NOODLES
### Κοτόπουλο καπαμὰ μὲ χυλοπίτες

1 **frying chicken (about 3 pounds) cut into serving
  pieces**
¼ **cup oil**
1 **can (20 ounces) whole tomatoes, pressed through
  a sieve or a food mill**
¼ **cup butter or margarine**
12 **ounces home made noodles (see index) or
  1 pound kritharaki (Greek pasta)**
**Salt and pepper to taste**
1 **cinnamon stick ½-inch long (optional)**
**Grated Parmesan cheese**

In a frying pan heat oil and brown chicken pieces. Transfer chicken to a Dutch oven without the oil. Add tomato, 1 cup water, cinnamon, salt, pepper and butter. Bring to a boil. Cover and cook slowly for 1 hour or until chicken is tender. Add more water if needed. Remove chicken pieces from the pot to a serving platter, keep warm. Measure sauce, add water to make 6 cups. Bring to a boil. Add noodles and stir well, simmer until pasta is tender, for approximately 20 minutes, stir once in a while. The pasta will look moist and creamy. Serve chicken and pasta hot with grated cheese and salad. Serves 4-6.

## CHICKEN MILANEZA
### Κοτόπουλο μιλανέζα

1 **whole chicken (about 4 pounds)**
2 **cups converted rice**
4½ **cups chicken stock**
½ **cup or more toasted slivered almonds**
5 **tablespoons butter or margarine**
5 **tablespoons flour**
3 **cups chicken stock**
1½ **cups milk**
4 **egg yolks, beaten**
½ **cup or more grated Parmesan cheese**
2 **cups frozen or fresh peas, cooked**
**Salt and pepper to taste**

Follow recipe and preparation as directed in Boiled Chicken (see index). Drain chicken. Remove bones and skin, cut into small pieces. Set aside. In a saucepan place 4½ cups chicken stock. Bring to a boil. Pick over rice and rinse in a strainer under cold running water (to get rid of the starch), add rice to the boiling stock and cook slowly partially covered for 20 minutes. Add toasted almonds and toss well. Pack the rice into 6-cup ring mold. Unmold in a large round platter. Arrange chicken pieces around rice. While rice is cooking prepare sauce. In a saucepan, melt butter over medium heat, blend in flour until smooth using a wire whisk. Gradually add chicken stock and milk, stirring constantly until mixture is thick and smooth. Cook 3 minutes longer. Remove

from heat. Spoon, little by little of the hot sauce into egg yolks stirring constantly. Add egg mixture to the sauce and cook over very low heat for 4-5 minutes, stirring constantly. Add cheese and stir well to combine; add salt and pepper. Pour half of the sauce over chicken and pilaf. Place the other half in a sauce dish. Fill the center of the rice mold with cooked peas. Serve hot with salad and pita (see index). Serves 6-8. Note: This dish is excellent for buffet.

**Variation:**
## TURKEY MILANEZA
### Γαλόπουλο μιλανέζα

Substitute ½ breast of turkey for the chicken.
Follow recipe and preparation as directed in Chicken Milaneza (see index). Serves 6-8

## CHICKEN WITH LEMON
### Κοτόπουλο λεμονάτο

1 **frying chicken (about 3 pounds), cut into serving
  pieces**
¼ **cup olive oil or butter**
2 **cloves garlic, minced or ½ teaspoon dried minced
  garlic**
**Salt and pepper to taste**
**Juice of 1 lemon**

In a Dutch oven heat oil if desired and saute chicken pieces. Add garlic, salt, pepper, lemon juice and 1 cup water. Bring to a boil; cover and simmer for approximately 1 hour or until chicken is tender. Serve with pasta, rice pilaf, french fries or mashed potatoes and salad (see index). Serves 4-5.

## CHICKEN WITH CREAM SAUCE
### Κοτόπουλο μὲ κρέμα

3 **whole breasts of chicken cut into half**
½ **lemon**
6 **fresh artichokes or 2 packages frozen artichoke
  hearts**
4 **whole medium potatoes, cut into half**
**Salt and pepper to taste**
1 **teaspoon onion 1 teaspoon onion powder**
2 **tablespoons corn starch**
**Juice of ½ lemon**
3 **tablespoons grated Parmesan cheese**

If artichokes are fresh, clean as directed in Artichokes Mousaka (see index). Remove skin and fat from chicken breasts. Rinse well and place in a Dutch oven. Add artichokes, potatoes, lemon juice, onion powder, salt, pepper and 2 cups water. Cover and cook slowly for approximately 1 hour or until chicken is tender. Remove from heat, let stand for 15 minutes. Remove the pot juices; bring to a boil. Blend corn starch in cold milk, add slowly to the boiling sauce, stirring constantly for a few minutes. Add cheese, blend well and pour over chicken. Serve hot. Serves 4-5.

## CURRY OF CHICKEN WITH RICE
### Κοτόπουλο πιλάφι μὲ κάρυ

1 chicken (about 3 pounds), cut into serving pieces
1 teaspoon salt
3 tablespoons butter or margarine
1 finely chopped onion
¾ teaspoon or more curry powder
2 tablespoons flour
Salt and pepper to taste
1 tablespoon tomato paste
2 cups converted rice

Place chicken in a saucepan with salt and cover with boiling water. Cover and cook slowly until chicken is tender. Heat butter and saute onion in a saucepan until soft and tender. Add flour and stir constantly for a few minutes. Gradually add 2 cups chicken stock, stir until thickened; add curry power, tomato paste, pepper and salt. Simmer for 2 minutes longer. Add chicken and simmer for 8 minutes. Measure chicken liquid, add water to make 4½ cups. Bring to a boil. Pick over rice and rinse in a strainer under cold running water (to get rid of the starch) and add to the boiling stock; stir and cook slowly partially covered for 20 minutes. Pack the rice into 6-cup ring mold. Unmold in a large platter. Arrange chicken pieces around rice. Pour sauce over rice and chicken. Serve hot. Serves 4-6.

**Variation:**
## CURRY OF TURKEY WITH RICE
### Γαλόπουλο πιλάφι μὲ κάρυ

Substitute ½ breast of turkey for the chicken.
Follow recipe and preparation as directed in Curry of Chicken with Rice (see index). Serves 4-5.

## CHICKEN WITH OKRA
### Κοτόπουλο μὲ μπάμιες

1 frying chicken (about 3 pounds), cut into serving
pieces
¼ cup olive oil
1 can (20 ounces) whole tomatoes, pressed through
a sieve or food mill
Salt and pepper to taste
2 pounds fresh or frozen baby okra

Clean and prepare okra as directed in Beef Ragout with Okra (see index). In a Dutch oven heat oil and saute chicken pieces. Add tomatoes, salt, pepper and 1 cup water. Cover and cook slowly for 30 minutes. Add okra to the chicken neatly. Cover and cook slowly for approximately 45 minutes depending on the size of okra until tender. Do not overcook. Occasionally shake the pot but do not stir. Arrange chicken and okra in the serving platter and serve hot. Serves 4-5.

## FRIED CHICKEN
### Κοτόπουλο τηγανιτὸ

2 broilers, cut each chicken into 6 pieces
1½ cups milk
1½ cups flour
½ teaspoon garlic powder
Salt and pepper to taste
½ teaspoon Greek rigani (oregano), crushed
½ cup clarified butter or margarine (see index) or
oil for frying

Dip each chicken piece into cold milk, drain. Combine flour, garlic powder, salt and pepper and rigani together. Roll in flour mixture to make a thick coating. Fry the chicken in butter if desired until each piece is tender and brown on both sides. Drain pieces well on absorbent paper. Serve with french fries and salad (see index). Serves 4-6.

## CHICKEN WITH RIGANI
### Κοτόπουλο ρηγανάτο

1 frying chicken (about 3 pounds), cut into serving
pieces
¼ cup olive oil
1 clove garlic, sliced
½ cup dry white wine
Juice of ½ lemon
Salt and pepper to taste
1 teaspoon crushed Greek rigani (oregano)
1 cup water

Heat oil and saute chicken pieces. Add garlic and saute few minutes longer. Add wine, lemon juice and stir, add salt and pepper, rigani and water. Cover and simmer for approximately 1 hour or until chicken is tender. Serve with home made noodles, rice pilaf or french fries and salad (see index). Serves 4.

✘✘✘

# CHICKEN CROQUETTES
### Κοτόπουλο κροκέττες

2 cups cooked chicken, minced
1 cup thick white sauce (see index)
2 egg yolks, beaten
Salt and pepper to taste
1 tablespoon grated Parmesan cheese
¼ teaspoon onion powder
1½ cups dry fine bread crumbs (see index)
1 egg plus 2 egg whites, beaten with 1 tablespoon
    water
Clarified butter or margarine (see index) or oil for
    frying

Combine chicken, white sauce, egg yolks, salt, pepper, cheese and onion. Shape and roll in fine crumbs. Dip croquettes in egg, then in crumbs and fry in hot butter on both sides, until golden brown. Drain on absorbent paper. Serve hot. Serves 4.

✘✘✘

# BREADED BREAST OF TURKEY
### Στῆθος γαλοπούλας πανὲ

½ breast of turkey, skinned and cut into
    ½-inch slices
2 eggs, beaten with 1 tablespoon water
2½ cups fine dried bread crumbs (see index)
⅓ cup grated Parmesan or Romano cheese
Salt and pepper to taste
Clarified butter or margarine (see index) or oil for
    frying

Place turkey cutlet between two pieces of plastic wrap or waxed paper and lightly pound to a thickness of ¼-inch. Combine bread crumbs, cheese, salt and pepper together and mix well. Dip cutlets one at a time in egg and then into bread mixture until completely covered. Fry in hot butter if desired until golden brown, then turn and fry other side of cutlets. Repeat with remaining cutlets, adding more butter as needed. Serve immediately with french fries, salad and feta cheese. Serves 6.

✘✘✘

# BRAISED TURKEY WITH WINE
### Γαλοπούλα κρασάτη

½ turkey (about 4 pounds), cut into serving pieces
½ cup butter or margarine

2 tablespoons flour
1 cup dry white wine
2 tablespoons brandy
Salt and pepper to taste
2 cloves garlic, minced
½ cup tomato sauce

Heat butter and brown turkey pieces. Remove to a Dutch oven. Add flour to the butter, stir well and cook 2 minutes; add wine, brandy, garlic, salt, pepper, tomato and 1 cup water. Bring to a boil and cook slowly for 2 minutes. Pour over turkey. Cover and cook slowly for 1½ hours or until turkey is tender. Serve over spaghetti, rice pilaf or mashed potatoes and salad (see index). Serves 4-6.

✘✘✘

# ROAST STUFFED TURKEY
### Γαλόπουλο γεμιστὸ

1 turkey (about 12-16 pounds)
3 tablespoons olive oil, butter or margarine
1 medium finely chopped onion
2 pounds lean ground beef
½ cup dry white wine
1 cup converted rice
½ cup pine nuts or slivered blanched almonds
1 pound roasted chestnuts
Salt and pepper to taste
Juice of ½ lemon
4 tablespoons corn starch

The night before, roast chestnuts. With a knife, cut two crisscross slashes on each chestnut shell. Place in a baking pan and broil for 10 minutes or until the shells are open. Remove shells and peel inner skins, cut into fourths. Cover turkey with water and add 4 tablespoons salt and soak for 3 hours. Rinse well and set aside. Saute onion and ground meat with the oil if desired until meat juices evaporate. Saute 2 more minutes stirring constantly. Add wine and cook until wine evaporates. Add rice and saute all together for 2 minutes. Add 1 cup water; cover and simmer for 5 minutes. Add pine nuts, chestnuts, salt and pepper. Stuff turkey cavity with the mixture and close up opening. Place turkey in a roasting pan. Sprinkle with the lemon juice, salt and pepper. Add 2 cups water to the pan. Roast turkey in a preheated 325°F (165°C) oven for 1½ hours. Cover with aluminum foil and roast for approximately 1½ hours longer or until turkey is golden and tender. Remove turkey from roasting pan. Place stuffing in a serving bowl. Carve turkey and arrange in a serving platter. Strain pan juices in a small saucepan. Pour off fat. Measure and add water to make 3½ cups. Bring to a boil; mix corn starch with ¼ cup cold water to a paste. Slowly

50

add to the stock stirring constantly. Cook slowly for 5 minutes. Serve turkey with stuffing, mashed potatoes and salad. Serves 6-8.

Note: With the neck and giblets make delicious soup for first dish if desired.

**Variation:**

## ROAST STUFFED GOOSE

Χῆνα γεμιστὴ ψητὴ

Substitute goose for the turkey.
Follow recipe and preparation as directed in Roast Stuffed Turkey (see index).

## ROAST TURKEY WITH POTATOES

Γαλόπουλο ψητὸ μὲ πατάτες

**½ half turkey (about 6 pounds)**
**4 pounds potatoes, peeled and cut into fourths**
**Juice of 1 lemon**
**Salt and pepper to taste**

In a roasting pan place potatoes; sprinkle with salt and pepper. Place turkey on top of potatoes, sprinkle with lemon juice, salt and pepper. Place cut side down. Add 2 cups water to the pan and bake in a preheated 350°C (180°C) oven for approximately 2 hours or until turkey is tender. Add water as needed. Remove turkey from pan. Return potatoes in the oven and turn on the broiler. Broil for 15 minutes. Carve turkey into slices and place in a serving platter. Arrange potatoes around. Serve hot with salad. Serves 4-6.

## CAPONS

Καπόνια

Capons are prepared for cooking in the same way as chickens and turkey.

## BRAISED DUCK

Πάπια γιαχνὶ

**2 ducks (about 2 pounds each)**
**¼ cup butter, margarine or olive oil**
**1 cup dry white wine**
**Salt and pepper to taste**
**1 medium onion, finely chopped**
**2 carrots, thinly sliced**
**1 cup thinly sliced celery**
**1 bay leaf**
**½ cup tomato sauce**
**2 tablespoons flour**

Clean, singe and wash the ducks. Heat butter if desired and saute until golden brown. Add wine, salt, pepper, onion, carrots, celery, bay leaf, tomato and 2 cups water. Bring to a boil, cover and cook very slow until ducks are tender. Remove ducks from sauce. Press sauce through a sieve or food mill. Bring sauce to a boil. Blend flour with ½ cup cold water until smooth; add gradually to sauce, stirring constantly. Cut ducks in half and serve with the sauce, french fries or mashed potatoes (see index). Serves 4.

## DUCK WITH OKRA

Πάπια μὲ μπάμιες

**2 ducks (about 2 pounds each)**
**¼ cup olive oil or butter**
**Salt and pepper to taste**
**½ cup tomato paste**
**2 pounds fresh or frozen baby okra**

Clean and prepare okra as directed in Beef Ragout with Okra (see index). Clean, singe and wash the ducks, cut in half. Heat oil if desired and saute duck halves until golden brown. Add tomato, salt, pepper and 2 cups water. Cover and cook slowly for 30 minutes. Add okra to the duck neatly. Cover and cook slowly for approximately 45 minutes, depending on the size of okra, or until tender. Do not over-cook. Occasionally shake the pot but do not stir. Arrange duck halves and okra in the serving platter and serve hot. Serves 4.

## ROAST DUCK

Πάπια ψητὴ

**1 duck (about 4 pounds)**
**Juice of ½ lemon**
**Salt and pepper to taste**
**¼ teaspoon garlic powder**

Clean, singe and wash the duck. Sprinkle with lemon juice and season with salt, pepper and garlic powder. Roast in a preheated 325°F (165°C) oven for approximately 2 hours or until tender. Baste every 20 minutes. Add water if needed. Serve with Artichokes with Peas Sauteed (see index) and potato Croquettes (see index) and salad. Serves 4-5.

# ROAST GUINEA-HEN
Φραγκόκοτα ψητή

**1 guinea-hen, cleaned, singed and washed**
**Juice of 1 lemon**
**3 tablespoons melted butter or margarine**
**Salt and pepper to taste**

Sprinkle bird with lemon juice. Brush with melted butter if desired and season with salt and pepper. Roast uncovered in a preheated 325°F (165°C) oven until tender. Allow 20 minutes per pound. Baste frequently. Serves 4.

# PARTRIDGES SALMI
Πέρδικες σαλμὶ

**2 partridges, cleaned, singed and washed**
**½ cup butter**
**1 small onion, finely chopped**
**1 clove garlic, crushed**
**2 tablespoons flour**
**1 cup dry white wine**
**2 tablespoons brandy**
**2 cups hot water**
**1 bay leaf**
**1 stalk celery, finely chopped**
**Salt and pepper to taste**

In a Dutch oven heat butter and brown birds. Remove from pot, let cool and cut into 4 pieces. Add onion and garlic and saute until onion is soft. Add flour and stir until golden brown. Add wine, brandy, water, bay leaf, celery, salt and pepper; cover and cook slowly for 20 minutes. Add bird pieces, cover and cook slowly for 1 hour or until meat is tender. Add water if necessary. Arrange bird pieces in a serving platter and pour sauce over. Serve immediately. Serve with Noodles or Rice Pilaf (see index). Serves 4.

# PARTRIDGES WITH WINE
Πέρδικες κρασάτες

**2 partridges, cleaned, singed and washed, cut into**
    **serving pieces**
**3 tablespoons butter or margarine**
**3 tablespoons olive oil**
**1 clove garlic, crushed**
**1 cup white wine**
**2 tablespoons brandy**
**Salt and pepper to taste**
**1 cup water**

Heat butter and oil, saute bird pieces, add garlic and saute few minutes longer. Add wine, brandy, salt, pepper and water; cover and simmer for approximately 1 hour or until meat is tender. Add water if necessary. Serve with rice pilaf, noodles or french fries (see index). Serves 4.

# PHEASANT WITH WINE
Φασιανὸς κρασάτος

**1 pheasant, cleaned, singed and washed**
**½ cup butter or margarine**
**1 cup dry white wine**
**2 tablespoons brandy**
**2 tablespoons lemon juice**
**1 pound small white onions**
**1 pound fresh mushrooms, cut in half**
**Salt and pepper to taste**
**1 cup chicken, beef stock or water**

Truss pheasant. Heat half of the butter and brown the bird. Add wine, brandy and lemon juice; cover and simmer for 20 minutes. While bird is simmering, peel onions, (cross-cut root ends to prevent centers popping out during cooking). Boil the onions in a large amount of water for 5 minutes, drain. Set aside. Saute mushrooms with the remaining butter. Add onions and mushrooms with the butter in the pot, add 1 cup water, salt and pepper. Cover and simmer for 1 hour or until meat and vegetables are tender. Serves 4.

# ROAST PHEASANT
Φασιανὸς ψητὸς

**1 pheasant, cleaned, singed and washed**
**Juice of 1 lemon**
**3 tablespoons melted butter**
**Salt and pepper to taste**

Truss pheasant. Sprinkle with lemon juice. Brush with butter and season with salt and pepper. Roast uncovered in a preheated 350°F (180°C) oven for 80 minutes or until bird is tender. Serves 4.

# BREADED PIGEON OR SQUAB
Περιστεράκια ἢ πιτσούνια πανὲ

**4 pigeons or squabs, cleaned, singed, washed and**
    **cut in half**
**1¼ cups fine dried bread crumbs (see index)**
**3 tablespoons grated Parmesan or Romano cheese**
**2 eggs, beaten with 2 tablespoons water**
**Salt and pepper to taste**

Place squab pieces between two pieces of plastic wrap

or waxed paper and lightly pound. Combine bread crumbs, cheese, salt and pepper together. Dip squab pieces one at a time in egg then into bread crumb mixture until completely covered. Place squab pieces in a greased baking sheet. Bake in a preheated 350°F (180°C) oven for 30 minutes, turn and bake for approximately 15 minutes longer or until golden brown. Serve hot. Serves 4.

❦❦❦

**Variation:**

# BREADED QUAILS
### Όρτύκια πανέ

Substitute quails for the squabs.
Follow recipe and preparation as directed in Breaded Squabs (see index).

❦❦❦

# PIGEONS OR SQUABS PILAF
### Περιστεράκια ἤ πιτσούνια πιλάφι

4  pigeons or squabs, cleaned, singed, washed and
    cut in half
½  cup butter or maragrine
1  small onion, finely chopped
½  cup dry white wine
1  can (16 ounces) whole tomatoes, pressed through
    food mill
Salt and pepper to taste
1  cinnamon stick ¼-inch long
2  cups converted rice

Heat butter and saute squabs and onion, until onion is soft. Add wine and cook for 2 minutes. Add tomato, salt, pepper, cinnamon and 1 cup water. Cover and simmer until squabs are tender. Remove squabs from sauce to a serving platter, keep warm. Measure sauce, add water to make 5 cups. Bring to a boil. Pick over rice and rinse in a strainer under cold running water (to get rid of the starch). Add rice to the boiling sauce, stir and cook slowly partially covered for 20 minutes. Place rice into a serving bowl. Serve squabs and rice hot with grated cheese if desired and salad. Serves 5.

❦❦❦

# STUFFED PIGEONS OR SQUABS
### Περιστεράκια ἤ πιτσούνια γεμιστά

1  pound lean ground beef
2  tablespoons butter or margarine
1  small onion, minced
¼  cup dry white wine
½  cup converted rice
¼  cup pine nuts or slivered blanched almonds

Salt and pepper to taste
4  pigeons or squabs, cleaned, singed and washed
¼  cup butter or margarine
½  cup dry white wine
Salt and pepper to taste
1  tablespoon tomato paste, mixed with 1 cup water

Saute ground meat and onion with the butter until onion is soft, and meat juices have evaporated. Add wine and cook until wine evaporates. Pick over rice and rinse under cold running water (to get rid of the starch) add ½ cup hot water, pine nuts, salt and pepper. Pack stuffing into squabs cavities and sew edges together. Heat butter and saute squabs. Add wine, salt, pepper and tomato. Cover and cook slowly until squabs are tender. Serves 4.

❦❦❦

# QUAILS SALMI
### Όρτύκια σαλμί

4  quails, cleaned, singed and washed
¼  cup butter or margarine
1  small onion, minced
2  tablespoons flour
1  clove garlic, minced
1  cup dry white wine
2  tablespoons brandy
1  stalk celery, finely chopped
1  carrot, finely chopped
Salt and pepper to taste
4  slices white bread, fried in butter or margarine

In a Dutch oven heat butter and brown the birds. Add onion and garlic. Saute a few minutes longer. Add flour and stir until golden brown. Add wine, brandy, celery, carrot, salt, pepper and 1 cup hot water. Cover and simmer until birds are tender. Arrange slices of bread on a serving platter. Place each bird on a slice of bread. Pour sauce over birds. Serve immediately with rice pilaf (see index). Serves 4.

❦❦❦

# ROAST WOODCOCK
### Μπεκάτσες ψητές

4  woodcocks, cleaned, singed and washed
½  cup red wine
4  strips of salt pork
Salt and pepper to taste
2  tablespoons flour

Tuck back the wings and truss. Sprinkle birds with the wine, and season with salt and pepper. Lard by laying strips of salt pork across breasts. Roast uncovered in a preheated 350°F (180°C) oven for approximately 55 minutes or until meat is tender and well browned. Arrange in a serving platter. Keep warm. Thicken gravy with the flour and 1 cup water. Add salt and pepper if necessary and pour over the birds. Serve with artichokes and peas sauteed and potato croquettes and salad (see index). Serves 4-8.

🌿🌿🌿

**Variation:**

## ROAST PARTRIDGES
### Πέρδικες ψητές

Substitute 2 partridges for the woodcocks.
Follow recipe and preparation as directed in Roast Woodcocks (see index). Serves 4.

🌿🌿🌿

## WOODCOCK SALMI
### Μπεκάτσες σαλμί

4 woodcocks, cleaned, singed and washed
3 tablespoons butter or margarine
3 tablespoons olive oil
2 medium onions, finely chopped
2 cloves garlic, crushed
1¼ cups dry red wine
1 bay leaf (optional)
Salt and pepper to taste
1 stalk celery, finely chopped
1 carrot, finely chopped
1 tablespoon flour

Heat butter and oil and saute the birds, add ½ cup water; cover and cook slowly for 45 minutes. Remove the birds and cut in half. Keep warm. Add onion and garlic in the pot and saute until onion is soft. Add wine, bay leaf if desired, celery, carrot, salt, pepper and 2 cups water; cook slowly for 30 minutes. Add the birds, cover and simmer until they are tender. Arrange birds in a serving platter, keep warm. Thicken sauce with 1 tablespoon flour and stir well. Add salt if necessary and cook slowly until thick. Pour over the birds and serve immediately with rice pilaf and salad (see index). Serves 4-6.

🌿🌿🌿

**Variation:**

## WILD DUCK SALMI
### Ἀγριόπαπια σαλμί

Substitute 2 wild ducks for the woodcock.
Follow recipe and preparation as directed in Woodcock Salmi (see index). Serve with rice pilaf. Serves 3-6.

## WOODCOCK WITH WINE
### Μπεκάτσες κρασάτες

4 woodcocks, cleaned, singed and washed
⅓ cup butter or margarine
¾ cup dry red wine
2 tablespoons brandy
Salt and pepper to taste
2 tablespoons flour
1 cup cream or milk
8 slices white bread, fried in butter

Heat butter in a Dutch oven and brown woodcocks. Add wine, brandy, salt and pepper, cover and cook slowly until tender. Remove birds from the pot. Cut in half, keep warm. Blend flour in the pot juices, gradually add cream stirring constantly until thick and smooth. Arrange fried bread slices in a large serving platter. Place half birds inside down on each slice of bread. Pour the hot sauce over it and serve immediately. Serves 4-8.

🌿🌿🌿

## BROILED DEER STEAKS
### Μπριζόλες ἐλαφιοῦ στὴ σχάρα

6 deer steaks
1 recipe for marinate as directed in Hare or Rabbit with onions (see index)
Salt and pepper to taste
½ cup olive oil or salad oil

Follow recipe and preparation for marinate. Dip steaks in marinate, cover and leave to marinate for 48 hours in the refrigerator. Lift out of marinate and dry with paper towels. Brush generously with oil. Place in a preheated broiler rack and broil for 8-10 minutes on each side. Season with salt and pepper. Serve immediately with lemon juice if desired. Serves 6.

🌿🌿🌿

## ROAST LEG OF DEER
### Μπούτι ἐλαφιοῦ ψητὸ

1 leg of deer
1 recipe for marinate as directed in Hare or Rabbit with Onions (see index)
1½ cups dry red wine
½ cup melted butter or margarine
Salt and pepper to taste

Follow recipe and preparation for marinate. Make 12 deep slits in the meat. Place meat in marinate, cover and leave for 48 hours in the refrigerator. Lift meat out of marinate. Lay the leg on rack of roaster. Sprinkle with wine, brush with butter and season with salt and pepper. Add 1 cup water to the pan. Roast uncovered in a preheated 325°F (165°C) oven allowing 20 minutes per pound. Baste meat frequently, add water in the pan as often as necessary. Make gravy from the pan juices if desired. Serves 6-8 depending on the size of the leg.

✠✠✠✠

# HARE OR RABBIT KAPAMA WITH PASTA

Κουνέλι ἢ λαγὸς καπαμὰ μὲ ζυμαρικὸ

1 hare or rabbit fresh frozen (thawed), cut into
    serving pieces
3 tablespoons butter
3 tablespoons olive oil
1 can (20 ounces) whole tomatoes, pressed through
    a food mill
Salt and pepper to taste
1 cinnamon stick ¼-inch long
1 pound spaghetti or any other kind of pasta
4 quarts boiling water and
1 tablespoon salt
¼ cup butter, melted
½ cup or more grated cheese, Parmesan or Romano

Marinate rabbit as directed in Hare or Rabbit with Onions (see index) for recipe. Lift meat pieces of marinate and dry with paper towels. Drain marinate and reserve ½ cup of the liquid. Heat butter and oil, saute meat pieces. Add the reserved liquid, tomato, salt, pepper and cinnamon stick; cover, bring to a boil and cook slowly for approximately 1½ hours. Add water if necessary. Break spaghetti in half, drop into rapidly boiling salted water and cook uncovered for 20 minutes or until tender. Keep boiling and stir occasionally with a fork. Pour into a colander and rinse with warm water. Drain spaghetti and arrange half of it on a large platter. Sprinkle with half of the cheese, cover with remaining spaghetti and top with remaining cheese. Pour hot butter over spaghetti and spoon sauce and rabbit kapama over. Serve immediately with salad. Serves 4-6.

✠✠✠✠

# HARE OR RABBIT SALMI

Κουνέλι ἢ λαγὸς σαλμὶ

1 hare or rabbit fresh or frozen (thawed), cut into
    cut into serving pieces
1 recipe for marinate as directed in Hare or Rabbit
    with Onion (see index).
3 tablespoons butter
3 tablespoons olive oil
1 medium onion, finely chopped

2 cloves garlic, crushed
1 bay leaf
Salt and pepper to taste
1 stalk celery, finely chopped
1 carrot, finely chopped
1 tablespoon flour

Follow recipe and preparation for marinate. Heat butter and oil and saute the meat pieces. Add onion and garlic and saute until onion is soft. Add 1½ cups from marinate liquid, bay leaf, carrot, salt, pepper and 1 cup water; cover and cook slowly for approximately 1½ hours or until meat is tender. Arrange meat pieces in a serving platter, keep warm. Thicken sauce with flour. Add salt if necessary and cook slowly until thick. Pour over the meat and serve immediately. Serves 4-6. Serve with rice pilaf if desired.

✠✠✠✠

Variation:

# DEER SALMI

Ἐλάφι σαλμὶ

Substittute 3 pounds, any piece of deer, cut into serving pieces for the Hare or Rabbit Salmi (see index). Follow recipe and preparation as directed in Hare or Rabbit Salmi.

✠✠✠✠

# HARE OR RABBIT WITH ONIONS

Κουνέλι ἢ λαγὸς στυφάδο

Marinate:
3 stalks celery, finely chopped
2 carrots, finely chopped
1 medium onion, finely chopped
2 cloves garlic, crushed
2 tablespoons parsley, finely chopped
3 whole cloves
2 bay leaves, crushed
12 black peppercorns
¼ cup olive oil
2½ cups dry red wine
¼ cup wine vinegar
1 hare or rabbit, fresh or frozen (thawed), cut into
    serving pieces
Other Ingredients:
½ cup olive oil
3 tablespoons butter
½ cup tomato sauce
1 bay leaf
1 teaspoon rosemary
12 black peppercorns
Salt and pepper to taste
1 cinnamon stick ½-inch long
5 whole allspice
2 pounds small white onions

55

Mix marinate ingredients in a large pyrex casserole. Dip meat in marinate; cover and leave to marinate for 48 hours in refrigerator. Lift meat out of marinate and dry with paper towel. Drain marinate and reserve the liquid. Heat oil and brown meat. Add the reserved liquid, tomato, bay leaf, rosemary, peppercorns, salt, pepper, cinnamon, allspice and 1 cup water; cover. Bring to a boil and cook for approximately one hour. While meat is simmering, prepare onions as directed in Beef with Onions (see index). Add onions and cook 1½ hours longer or until meat and onions are tender. Serve hot. Serves 4-6.

## DEER WITH ONIONS
Ἐλάφι στυφάδο

Substitute 3 pounds, any piece of deer, cut into serving pieces, for the Hare or Rabbit.
Follow recipe and preparation as directed in Hare or Rabbit with Onions (see index).

# HARE OR RABBIT WITH WINE
Κουνέλι ἢ λαγὸς κρασάτο

1  hare or rabbit, fresh or frozen (thawed), cut into serving pieces
1  recipe for marinate as directed in Hare or Rabbit with Onions (see index).
¼  cup butter
¼  cup olive oil
1  small onion, finely chopped
1  clove garlic, crushed
2  tablespoons flour
1  cup dry red wine
2  tablespoons brandy
Salt and pepper to taste
1  tablespoon tomato paste, mixed with
1  cup water

Follow recipe and preparation for marinate. Lift meat pieces out of marinate and dry with paper towels. Heat butter and oil and saute rabbit. Add onion and garlic and saute a few more minutes. Add wine, brandy, salt, pepper and tomato. Cover and cook slowly for approximately 1½ hours or until meat is tender. Add water if necessary. Serve with french fries or noodles and salad (see index). Serves 4-6.

# HOMEMADE PASTRY AND PITTES

## HOMEMADE PASTRY A
### Φύλλο σπιτικό

⅔ cup butter or margarine, chilled
1½ cups cream or evaporated milk
4½ cups all-purpose unbleached flour, sifted with
3 teaspoons baking powder
1½ teaspoons salt, or less

In a mixing bowl stir together flour, salt and baking powder. Cut in butter if desired until mixture resembles coarse crumbs. Add milk and gently toss with your fingers. Form dough into a ball. Use according to recipe directions.

❈❈❈

## HOMEMADE PASTRY B
### Φύλλο σπιτικό

1 cup salad oil
1 cup evaporated milk
1 cup grated Kefalotyri, Parmesan or Romano cheese
5 eggs, lightly beaten
5 teaspoons baking power, sifted with
6 cups all-purpose unbleached flour

In a large mixing bowl combine the oil, milk and eggs. Mix at high speed in an electric mixer for 5 minutes. Add cheese, 3 cups of the flour. Mix at low speed for 2 minutes, scraping sides of bowl constantly. Mix at high speed 3 more minutes. By hand, stir in all the remaining flour to make a soft smooth dough. Cover, let stand ½ hour. Use according to recipe directions.

❈❈❈

## HOMEMADE PASTRY C
### Φύλλο σπιτικό

1 cup butter or margarine, at room temperature

1 cup salad oil
1 cup plain yogurt
3 teaspoons baking powder, sifted with
1½ teaspoons salt, and
6 cups all-purpose unbleached flour

In a large mixing bowl combine the butter, oil and yogurt. Mix at high speed in an electric mixer for 5 minutes. Add 3 cups of the flour mixture to the butter mixture. Mix at low speed for 3 minutes, scraping sides of bowl constantly. By hand, stir in all the remaining flour to make a soft, smooth dough. Let stand ½ hour. Use according to recipe directions.

❈❈❈

## CLARIFIED BUTTER OR MARGARINE
### Διϋλισμένο βούτυρο ἢ μαργαρίνη

Melt butter or margarine in a heavy saucepan over medium-low heat until it foams. Watch it carefully, avoid browning or burning. Remove from heat and let stand until cool. Chill over night. Using a spoon, skim off the foam and discard. Use the same method with the unsalted butter and margarine. Slowly spoon clarified butter into a jar, being careful not to disturb the unwanted milk which have sunk to the bottom. Store clarified butter in refrigerator until you are ready to use.

❈❈❈

## CHEESE PITTA A
### Τυρόπιττα

1½ cups Thick White Sauce (see index). Do not add salt
6 large eggs, lightly beaten
1 pound feta cheese, crumbled

¼ cup grated Parmesan, Kefalotyri or Romano cheese
1 package (7½ ounces) farmer's cheese
Pepper to taste
1 cup melted clarified butter or margarine (see index)
1 pound Phyllo pastry (thawed)

Prepare white sauce as directed. Spoon little by little of the hot sauce into eggs, stirring constantly. Add egg mixture to the sauce and stir well. Add cheeses and pepper; mix well to combine. Prepare and bake as directed in Spinach Pitta A (see index). Serves 12 as a first course or 6 as a main course.

❈ ❈ ❈ ❈

## CHEESE PITTA B
Τυρόπιττα

3 ounces grated Parmesan, Kefalotyri or Romano cheese
7 ounces shredded Kaseri cheese
6 ounces shredded Swiss cheese
½ teaspoon white pepper
6 large eggs, lightly beaten
3½ cups milk
1 cup melted clarified butter or margarine (see index)

❈ ❈ ❈ ❈

## CHEESE PITTA C
Τυρόπιττα

1 pound crumbled feta cheese
8 lightly beaten eggs
1 cup milk
½ cup salad oil
½ cup melted clarified butter or margarine
Pepper to taste
1 pound phyllo pastry (thawed)

Mix cheese, eggs, milk, oil and pepper. Grease a 13x11x3-inch baking pan. Line pan with 4 sheets of the phyllo, brushing every other sheet with the melted butter if desired. Sprinkle evenly with a ladelful of the cheese mixture. Place two more phyllo sheets on the cheese mixture (do not brush with butter). Sprinkle evenly with another ladelful of the cheese mixture. Repeat and continue until all the cheese is used. Then layer the remaining phyllo sheets, brushing every other sheet with melted butter. Score top eight layers of phyllo sheets with a sharp knife into 3x3-inch squares or rectangles. Bake in a preheated 350°F (180°C) oven for 50-60 minutes or until crisp and golden color. Cut scored lines when you are ready to serve. Serve hot. Serves 12 as a first course or 6 as a main course.

## ROLLED CHEESE PITTA
Τυρόπιττα ρολλὸ

8 ounces grated Pecorino-Romano cheese
8 ounces shredded Kaseri cheese
1 pound crumbled feta cheese
1¼ cups sour cream
4 large eggs, lightly beaten
White pepper to your taste
1 pound phyllo pastry (thawed)

1½ cups melted clarified butter or margarine

Divide Pecorino-Romano cheese into two parts, set aside. Mix Kaseri cheese, feta, sour cream, eggs and pepper well to combine. Divide into two parts, set aside. Divide phyllo pastry into two parts. Use one part at a time. Fold other part and place back on the plastic bag and in the box, refrigerate until you need it. Place one phyllo sheet on a 20x14-inch heavy duty foil. Gently brush pastry with the warm melted butter if desired without brushing the foil. Place one more phyllo sheet on top of the first, brush again with the melted butter. Sprinkle evenly with a handful of the grated Pecorino-Romano cheese. Place on another phyllo sheet on the cheese, brush with melted butter. Sprinkle evenly with another handful of the cheese. Repeat and continue until all the cheese and phyllo is used. Take one part of the cheese egg mixture and spread evenly over the phyllo. Gently lift layered pitta from the wide side without the foil and roll. Wrap in with the foil, seal and freeze. Continue with the second part. Follow preparation as the first. When you are ready to use the rolled pitta, thaw for 60-90 minutes and slice into 1-inch slices. Place slices on a well greased baking sheet and bake in a preheated 350°F (180°C) oven for 45 minutes. Serve hot. Makes two rolls.

❈ ❈ ❈ ❈

## CHICKEN PITTA
Κοτόπιττα

2 cups medium white sauce (see index)
¼ cup grated Parmesan or Romano cheese
4 ounces Kaseri or Swiss cheese, cut into very small cubes
3 cups chopped cooked chicken breast
8 beaten eggs
Pepper to taste
½ cup chopped blanched almonds
1 pound phyllo pastry (thawed)
1 cup melted clarified butter or marmargine (see index)

Prepare white sauce as directed. Spoon little by little of the hot sauce into eggs, stirring constantly. Add egg mixture to the sauce and stir well. Add chicken, pepper, salt if needed, cheese and almonds, mix well to combine. Prepare and bake as directed in Veal Pitta (sec index). Serve hot. Serves 12 as a first course or 6 as a main dish.

Variation:

## TURKEY PITTA
### Γαλόπιττα

Substitute turkey for the chicken.
Follow recipe and preparation as directed in Chicken Pitta (see index). Serves 12 as a first course or 6 as a main dish.

## BEEF PITTA
### Κρεατόπιττα

2½ pounds lelan ground beef
½ cup finely chopped onion
1 tablespoon olive oil
3 beaten eggs
Salt and pepper to taste
4 ounces Kaseri or Swiss cheese, cut into very
    small cubes the size of a dime
1 pound phyllo pastry (thawed)
1 cup clarified butter or margarine (see index),
    melted

Saute meat and onion with butter until onion is soft and liquid has evaporated. Add ½ cup water, salt and pepper. Cover and cook slowly for 20 minutes. Remove from heat. Set aside to cool for 15 minutes. Add cheese cubes and the beaten eggs. Stir to combine. Grease with butter a 13x11x3-inch baking pan. Line pan with 10 sheets of the phyllo, brushing every other one with melted butter. The sheets will extend up the sides of the pan. Spoon in the meat mixture and spread evenly. Cover meat mixture with 2 phyllo sheets and brush with butter. Fold overhanging phyllo sheets over the filling to enclose it. Top with the rest of phyllo sheets, brush every other one with melted butter and tuck in overhanging sheets inside the pan. Brush top with butter. Score top eight layers of phyllo sheets with a sharp knife into 3x3-inch squares or rectangles. Bake in a preheated 350°F (180°C) oven for 50-60 minutes or until it has a golden color. Cut through scored lines when you are ready to serve. Serve hot. Serves 12 as a first course or 6 as a main dish.

## VEAL PITTA
### Μοσχαράκι πίττα

3 pounds lean boneless veal, cut into very small
    cubes the size of a dime

¼ cup finely chopped onion
3 tablespoons butter or margarine
4 beaten eggs
Salt and pepper to taste
4 ounces Kaseri or Swiss cheese, cut into very
    small cubes the size of a dime
1 pound phyllo pastry (thawed)
1 cup clarified butter or margarine (see index)
    melted

Follow preparation as directed in Beef Pitta (see index). Serves 12 as a first course or 6 as a main dish.

Variation:

## LAMB PITTA
### Ἀρνάκι πίττα

Substitute lamb for the veal.
Follow recipe and preparation as directed in Veal Pitta (see index).

## PORK PITTA
### Χοιρινὸ πίττα

2½ pounds ground boiled fresh ham (see index)
4 beaten eggs
Pepper to taste
4 ounces Kaseri or Swiss cheese, cut into very small
    cubes the size of a dime
1 pound phyllo pastry (thawed)
1 cup melted clarified butter or margarine (see index)

Mix ground ham, eggs, cheese and pepper well to combine. Add salt if you use Swiss cheese. Prepare and bake as directed in Beef Pitta (see index).

## LEEK CHEESE PITTA
### Πρασοτυρόπιττα

3 medium leeks, finely chopped (about 3 cups)
3 tablespoons butter or margarine
1½ pounds Ricotta or Farmer's cheese
8 ounces feta cheese( crumbled
¼ cup grated Kefalotyri, Parmesan or Romano
    cheese
6 large beaten eggs
Salt and pepper to taste
1 cup Thick White Sauce (see index)
1 pound phyllo pastry (thawed)
1 cup melted clarified butter or margarine (see index)

Clean and wash leeks well. Chop finely and rinse again in a strainer under cold running water. Drain well. Saute leeks in butter on medium heat until soft.

Remove from heat. Set aside. Prepare white sauce as directed. In a large bowl combine Ricotta, feta, Kefalotyri cheese, eggs, pepper and leeks, mix well. Prepare and bake as directed in Beef Pitta (see index).

**Variation:**

## SCALLION CHEESE PITTA
Κρεμυδοτυρόπιττα

Substitute 3 cups of scallions for the leeks.
Follow recipe and preparation as directed in Leek Cheese Pitta (see index).

## SPINACH PITTA A
Σπανακόπιττα

3  pounds fresh spinach or 4 packages (10- ounces each frozen cut leaf spinach (thawed), well drained and chopped
2  bunches scallions, chopped
⅓  cup olive oil
2  tablespoons chopped parsley
¼  cup chopped fresh dill or ½ teaspoon dried
5  large beaten eggs
¼  teaspoon pepper
Salt to your taste
1  pound feta cheese, crumbled, or 8 ounces feta cheese and 1 pound Farmer's or Ricotta cheese
¼  cup grated Kefalotyri, Parmesan or Romano cheese
1  pound phyllo pastry (thawed)
1  cup melted clarified butter or margarine (see index) or olive oil, or ½ cup butter and ½ cup oil

If spinach is fresh, remove roots and coarse leaves. Wash in several waters. Place spinach in 1 cup boiling water and bring to a boil. Remove from heat and drain in a strainer. Drain off all moisture and chop. Place in a large bowl to cool. Gently saute scallions in ⅓ cup oil until tender but not brown. Add sauteed scallions, cheeses, eggs, parsley, dill, salt and pepper to the spinach and mix well to combine. Grease a 13x11x3- inch baking pan. Line pan with 10 sheets of the phyllo, brushing every other sheet with butter if desired. The sheets will extend up the sides of the pan. Spoon in the spinach mixture and spread evenly. Cover spinach mixture with 2 phyllos and brush with butter. Fold overhanging phyllo over the filling to enclose it. Top with the rest of phyllo brushing every other one with butter, and tuck in overhanging sheets inside the pan. Brush top with butter. Score top eight layers of phyllo with a sharp knife into 3x3- inch squares or rectangles. Bake in a preheated 350°F 180°C) oven for 50-60 minutes or until golden in color. Cut through scored lines when you are ready to serve. Serve hot if you use butter. Hot or cold if you use oil. Serves 12 as a first course or 6 as a main course.

## SPINACH PITTA B
Σπανακόπιττα

3  pounds fresh spinach or 4 packages (10- ounces each) frozen cut leaf spinach (thawed), well drained and chopped
1  cup Thick White Sauce (see index)
5  large beaten eggs
1  pound feta cheese, crumbled or 8 ounces feta and 1 pound Farmer's or Ricotta cheese
¼  cup grated Kefalotyri, Parmesan or Romano cheese
1  tablespoon finely chopped parsley (optional)
4  tablespoons melted butter or margarine
Salt and pepper to taste
1  pound phyllo pastry (thawed)
1  cup melted clarified butter or margarine (see index)

Prepare spinach if it is fresh as directed in Spinach Pitta A (see index). Follow recipe and preparation for white sauce as directed. Combine spinach, white sauce, eggs, cheeses, pepper, salt, parsley if desired and the 4 tablespoons butter; mix well. Prepare and bake as directed in Spinach Pitta A (see index).

## BUTTERNUT SQUASH PITTA
Κολοκυθόπιττα

1  large butternut squash (4 cups cooked and mashed)
2  teaspoons salt
5  large eggs
⅓  cup heavy cream or evaporated milk
¼  teaspoon cinnamon
Pinch of nutmeg (optional)
¼  cup clarified butter, melted
3  tablespoons or more sugar
1  pound phyllo pastry (thawed)
1  cup melted clarified butter or margarine (see index)

Wash the squash and cut into large pieces, peel, remove the seeds and the soft mesh surrounding them. Boil in 3 cups of boiling water with the 2 teaspoons salt until tender. Do not over boil it. Drain in a strainer very well and press to remove excess liquid. Place in a medium mixing bowl, mash on a low speed for a few minutes. Fold in eggs one at a time. Add cream, sugar, butter, cinnamon and nutmeg if desired and mix slowly to combine. Prepare and bake as directed in Spinach Pitta A (see index). Serves 12 as a first course and 6 as a main course. Serve hot or at room temperature.

Variation:

## BUTTERNUT AND PUMPKIN PITTA
### Κολοκυθόπιττα

Substitute one half of the butternut with pumpkin. Follow recipe and preparation as directed in Butternut Squash Pitta (see index).

✻✻✻✻

## PUMPKIN PITTA
### Κολοκυθόπιττα

Subustitute 4 cups pumpkin for the butternut squash. Follow recipe and preparation as directed in Butternut Squash Pitta (see index).

✻✻✻✻

## ZUCCHINI PITTA
### Κολοκυθόπιττα

3 medium-sized zucchini, trimmed, washed and grated (4 cups)
¼ cup heavy cream or evaporated milk
5 large eggs, lightly beaten
½ teaspoon salt
3 tablespoons or more sugar
¼ cup melted clarified butter or margarine
1 pound phyllo pastry (thawed)
1 cup melted clarified butter or margarine (see index)

Place grated zucchini in a strainer to drain. Combine zucchini, cream, eggs, salt, sugar and butter; mix thoroughly. Prepare and bake as directed in Spinach Pitta A. (see index).

## ZUCCHINI CHESSE PITTA A
### Κολοκυθοτυρόπιττα

3 pounds small zucchini, trimmed, washed and grated
5 large beaten eggs
8 ounces feta cheese, crumbled
1 package 7½-ounces) Farmer's cheese
⅓ cup grated Kefalotyri, Parmesan or Romano cheese
Salt and pepper to taste
1 tablespoon finely chopped parsley
1 tablespoon finely chopped fresh dill (optional)
4 tablespoons melted butter or margarine
1 pound phyllo pastry (thawed)
1 cup melted clarified butter or margarine (see index)

Place grated zucchini in a strainer to drain. Combine zucchini( eggs, cheeses, salt and pepper, parsley, butter and mix well. Prepare and bake as directed in Spinach Pitta A (see index).

✻✻✻✻

## ZUCCHINI CHEESE PITTA B
### Κολοκυθοτυρόπιττα

½ cup finely chopped onion
2 tablespoons salad oil
1 tablespoon butter
4 medium sized zucchini, trimmed, washed and cut into cubes
Salt and pepper to taste
3 large eggs, beaten
⅓ cup heavy cream or evaporated milk
1½ cups grated Kefalotyri, Parmesan or Romano cheese
1 pound phyllo pastry (thawed)
1 cup melted clarified butter or margarine (see index)

Saute onion with oil and butter until onion is soft. Add zucchini and saute until tender. Combine onion-zucchini mixture, salt, pepper, eggs, cream and grated cheese and mix thoroughly. Prepare and bake as directed in Spinach Pitta A (see index).

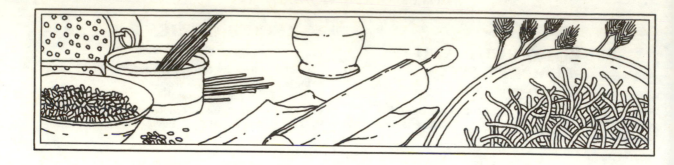

# PASTA AND RICE

## HOMEMADE CANNELLONI
### Κανελλόνι σπιτικὸ

3¼ cups all-purpose unbleached flour
3 beaten large eggs
¼ cup heavy cream or milk
1 teaspoon salt
2 tablespoons olive oil

In a large mixing bowl stir together flour and salt. Make a well in the center, add the beaten eggs, the cream if desired, and the oil; stir to make a stiff dough. Turn out onto unfloured kneading surface. With oiled hands kneed 8-10 minutes or until smooth. Divide dough into two parts. Shape into balls. Cover; let rest at room temperature for 60 minutes or longer. Roll one ball at a time to ⅛-inch thickness. Cut into 4-4-inch squares. Cover. Repeat with the remaining dough. Cover. At this point the cannelloni are ready to use.

Note: You can prepare the dough in a food processor and form the cannelloni with a pasta maker.

❦❦❦❦

## HOMEMADE NOODLES
### Χυλοπίττες σπιτικὲς

Follow recipe and preparation for the dough as directed in Homemade Cannelloni (see index).
Divide dough into 6 parts. Shape into balls. Cover; let rest at room temperature for 60 minutes or longer. Prepare noodles as directed in pasta maker.

❦❦❦❦

## MEAT STUFFED CANNELLONI
### Κανελλόνια

Meat Filling:
1¼ pounds lean ground sirloin or round steak

1 tablespoon olive oil
½ cup finely chopped onion
¼ cup dry white wine
2 medium ripe tomatoes, peeled, seeded and chopped
Salt and pepper to taste
1 beaten egg

Heat oil and saute onion and ground meat until onion is soft and meat juices have evaporated. Add wine and saute few minutes longer. Add tomatoes, salt, pepper and ½ cup water. Cover; cook slowly for 45- 55 minutes. Set aside. When cool add beaten egg and mix well to combine.

Tomato Sauce:
1 teaspoon onion powder
¼ teaspoon garlic powder
3 tablespoons butter or margarine
1 can (29-ounces) whole tomatoes, pressed through a
    sieve or food mill
Salt and pepper to taste

Combine all the ingredients together, add 2 cups water. Cover; cook slowly for 30 minutes.

1 box cannelloni manicotti shells
½ cup or more grated Parmesan or Romano cheese

Follow cooking according to package direction. Cover the bottom of a baking dish with tomato sauce. Fill cannelloni with meat filling. Place in a baking dish, in one layer only. Cover with tomato sauce. Sprinkle with grated cheese and cover with foil. Bake in a pre-heated 350°F (180°C) oven for 30-40 minutes. Serve hot with salad. Serves 6.

❦❦❦❦

## MEAT STUFFED HOMEMADE CANNELLONI
### Κανελλόνια σπιτικὰ

1 recipe for homemade cannelloni (see index)
1 recipe for meat filling and tomato sauce (see index)
   in Meat Stuffed Cannelloni

Follow preparation for Homemade Cannelloni as directed. Prepare meat filling and tomato sauce as directed. Decrease cooking time for tomato sauce from 30 minutes to 15. Cover the bottom of a baking dish with tomato sauce. Divide the filling among the 30 cannelloni. Fill and roll them. Place cannelloni in one layer only. Cover with tomato sauce. Sprinkle with grated cheese. Cover with foil and bake in a preheated 350°F (180°C) oven for 55-60 minutes. Serve hot with salad. Serves 6.

Note: With the scraps of dough you can make noodles. Follow preparation as directed in Homemade Noodles (see index)..

## HOMEMADE CANNELLONI WITH WHITE SAUCE
Κανελλόνια σπιτικά μὲ μπεσαμὲλ

1 recipe for Homemade Cannelloni (see index)
1 recipe for Meat Filling (see index) in Meat Stuffed Cannelloni
Melted butter or margarine
1 recipe for Thin White Sauce (see index)
½ cup or more grated Parmesan or Romano cheese
½ cup or more toasted blanched slivered almonds

Follow preparation as directed for Homemade Cannelloni. Prepare meat filling as directed. Follow preparation as directed in Meat Stuffed Homemade Cannelloni. Place cannelloni in one layer only. Brush with melted butter. Add enough hot water to cover the cannelloni. Cover with foil and bake in a preheated 350°F (180°C) oven for 55-60 minutes or until cannelloni are tender. While cannelloni are baking, prepare white sauce as directed. Arrange cannelloni in a serving platter. Pour hot sauce over and sprinkle with grated cheese and almonds. Serve hot. Serves 6.

## BAKED MACARONI WITH HAM AND CHEESE
Μακαρόνια μὲ ζαμπὸν καὶ τυρὶ στὸ φοῦρνο

1 pound elbow macaroni, boiled (see index)
¼ cup butter or margarine
3 cups milk
3 ounces grated Swiss cheese
2 ounces Velveeta cheese, cut into small cubes
1 cup grated Kefalotyri, Parmesan or Romano cheese
½ pound ham, cut into cubes

Pepper to taste

Boil macaroni as directed in boiled macaroni, reduce cooking time from 20 minutes to 12. Drain. While macaroni is cooking prepare cheese sauce. Melt butter on medium heat, add milk, cheese, except ¼ cup grated, and pepper. When cheese is melted, remove from heat. Add macaroni and stir well to combine. Pour in a greased casserole. Sprinkle with remaining cheese and bake in a preheated 350°F (180°C) oven for 15-20 minutes. Serve hot. Serves 6-8.

## BAKED MACARONI WITH MEAT SAUCE AND CHEESE
Μακαρόνια μὲ κυμὰ στὸ φοῦρνο

⅔ recipe meat sauce A, B, or C (see index)
1 pound ziti or elbow macaroni boiled (see index)
¼ cup melted butter
½ cup grated Parmesan or Romano cheese
¾ pound Mozzarella cheese, shredded

Follow recipe and preparation as directed in Meat Sauce. Boil macaroni as directed in Boiled Macaroni (see index), reduce cooking time from 20 minutes to 12. Drain. Add butter and stir well. Add cheese and meat sauce and toss well to combine. Cover and bake in a preheated 350°F (180°C) oven for 30 minutes. Serve immediately. Serves 4.

## BAKED MACARONI WITH MEAT SAUCE
Μακαρόνια μὲ κυμὰ καὶ τυρὶ στὸ φοῦρνο

1 recipe meat sauce A, B, or C (see index)
1 pound elbow macaroni, boiled
⅔ cup grated Parmesan or Romano cheese
¼ cup butter or margarine

Follow recipe and preparation as directed in Meat Sauce. Boil macaroni as directed in Boiled Macaroni (see index), reduce cooking time from 20 minutes to 12. Drain. Add butter and stir well. Place half of the macaroni in a greased casserole, cover with half of the meat sauce and sprinkle with half of the cheese. Continue with the remaining macaroni, meat sauce and top with cheese. Cover and bake in a preheated 350°F (180°C) oven for 30 minutes. Serve immediately. Serves 4-6.

## BOILED MACARONI
Μακαρόνια βραστὰ

1 pound spaghetti or any other kind of pasta
1 tablespoon salt (optional)
4 quarts boiling water
½ cup melted butter or margarine
½ cup or more grated Parmesan or Romano cheese

Break spaghetti in half, drop into rapidly boiling salted water and cook uncovered for 20 minutes or until tender. Keep boiling and stir occasionally with a fork. Pour into a colander and rinse well with warm water. Drain spaghetti and arrange half of it on a large platter; sprinkle with half of the cheese, cover with remaining spaghetti and top with remaining cheese. Pour hot butter over spaghetti. Serve hot, plain.

Note: If you use meat sauce or tomato sauce reduce butter to ¼ cup.

✻✻✻✻

# MACARONI AU GRATIN
### Μακαρόνια ὀ γκρατὲν

1 pound elbow macaroni, boiled (see index)
¼ cup melted butter or margarine
¾ cup grated Parmesan or Romano cheese
3 ounces shredded Swiss cheese
3 ounces shredded Kaseri cheese
2 recipes of medium white sauce (see index)
5 eggs, beaten
¼ teaspoon pepper

Boil macaroni as directed in Boiled Macaroni, reduce cooking time from 20 minutes to 12. Drain. Place in a greased baking dish. Add butter, Swiss and Kaseri cheese and ⅓ of the grated cheese and toss well to combine. Follow recipe and preparation as directed in medium white sauce. Spoon little by little of the hot sauce into beaten eggs stirring constantly. Add egg mixture to the sauce and cook over very low heat for 2-3 minutes, stirring constantly. Add ½ of the remaining Parmesan cheese and pepper, stir well. Pour sauce over macaroni, stir a little. Sprinkle with the remaining cheese. Bake in a preheated 350°F (180°C) oven for 30-40 minutes or until golden brown. Let it stand for 30 minutes before cutting. Serves 6 -8.

✻✻✻✻

# MACARONI AU GRATIN WITH TOMATO SAUCE
### Μακαρόνια ὀ γκρατὲν μὲ σάλτσα ντομάτας

1 recipe tomato sauce A, B, or C (see index)
1 pound elbow macaroni or any other kind, boiled
¼ cup melted butter or margarine
¾ cup grated Parmesan or Romano cheese

2 recipes of medium white sauce (see index)
5 beaten eggs
¼ teaspoon pepper

Follow recipe and preparation as directed in tomato sauce. Boil macaroni as directed in boiled macaroni (see index), reduce cooking time from 20 minutes to 12. Drain. Place macaroni in a greased baking dish. Add butter and ⅓ of the cheese, toss well to combine. Add tomato sauce and toss well. Follow recipe and preparation as directed in medium white sauce. Spoon little by little of the hot sauce into beaten eggs stirring constantly. Add egg mixture to the sauce and cook over very low heat for 2-3 minutes, stirring constantly. Add ½ of the remaining cheese and pepper, stir well. Pour sauce over macaroni. Sprinkle with the remaining cheese. Bake in a preheated 350°F (180°C) oven for 30-40 minutes or until golden brown. Let it stand for 30 minutes before cutting. Serves 6-8.

✻✻✻✻

# MACARONI WITH TOMATO
### Μακαρόνια μὲ ντομάτα

1 can (16-ounces) whole tomatoes, pressed through a sieve or food mill, or ½ cup tomato sauce
1 beef boullion
1 chicken boullion
5 cups water
Salt and pepper to taste
½ cup butter or margarine
2 cups Kritharaki (Greek pasta) or elbow macaroni
½ cup or more grated Parmesan or Romano cheese

In a pot put tomato, boullions, water, salt and pepper. Bring to a boil, cover and boil in medium heat for 20 minutes. While broth is boiling prepare macaroni. Heat butter if desired and saute pasta, stirring constantly for 5 minutes. The pasta must be nicely coated with butter. Add broth and simmer partially covered for 20 minutes or until pasta is tender, stir once in a while. The pasta will look moist and creamy. Serve hot with grated cheese. Serves 4.

✻✻✻✻

# PASTITSIO
### Παστίτσιο

2½ pounds lean ground beef
½ cup finely chopped onion
2 tablespoons olive oil
½ cup dry white wine
Salt and pepper to taste
1 can (16-ounces) whole tomatoes, pressed through a sieve or food mill
1 cinnamon stick ½-inch long

1 beaten egg
2 tablespoons dried bread crumbs (see index)
1½ pounds macaroni No. 5, or ⅛-inch thick
½ cup or less butter or margarine, melted
1⅓ cups grated Parmesan or Romano cheese
6 cups medium white sauce (see index)
6 large beaten eggs

Heat oil, saute onion and meat until onion is soft. Add wine and saute few minutes longer. Add tomato, cinnamon, salt, pepper and ½ cup water. Cover; cook slowly for 45 minutes. Remove from heat. Let stay 10 minutes. Then add bread crumbs and egg. Stir well to combine. Boil macaroni in boiling salted water for 10 minutes. Drain. Rinse and drain again, return to pot. Add melted butter if desired and ⅓ cup of the cheese. Toss well. Place half of the macaroni in a deep 11x13x5-inch greased baking pan. Top with meat mixture. Cover with remaining macaroni. Prepare white sauce as directed. Spoon little by little of the hot sauce into eggs, stirring constantly. Add egg mixture to the sauce and cook over very low heat for 2-3 minutes, stirring constantly. Do not boil. Add ½ of the remaining cheese and stir well to combine. Pour sauce over macaroni, and spread evenly. Sprinkle with the remaining cheese. Bake in a preheated 350°F (180°C) oven for 45 minutes or until golden. Let it stand for 30 minutes before cutting. Serve hot. Serves 6 for main course or 12 for first course.

## CRACKED WHEAT PILAF
### Πλιγοῦρι πιλάφι

4 cups fresh chicken or beef stock
¼ cup tomato puree
Salt and pepper to taste
3 tablespoons butter or margarine
1 cup cracked wheat

Combine stock, tomato, salt and pepper in a sauce pan and bring to a boil and boil for 5 minutes. While stock is boiling saute cracked wheat with the butter for 5 minutes in a three quart sauce pan, stirring constantly. Add boiling stock mixture, stir and cook slowly partially covered for 20 minutes or until wheat is tender and liquid has been absorbed. Serve and sprinkle with grated cheese. Serves 4 as a side dish or 2 as a main dish.

## RICE PILAF A
### Πιλάφι

3 quarts water
1 tablespoon salt
2 cups converted rice

½ cup butter or margarine, melted

Bring water to a boil, add salt. Pick over rice. Add rice to the boiling salted water, stir, and boil partially covered on medium heat for 20 minutes. Place in a strainer and pour hot water over to remove the loose starch and separate the grains. Drain well and transfer to the pot. Add hot butter and toss well with two forks. Serve with Lamb Liver with Rigani (see index) or any other kind of sauce you desire. Serves 6.

## RICE PILAF B
### Πιλάφι

¼ cup butter or margarine
2 cups converted rice
4½ cups boiling fresh chicken or beef stock
Salt and pepper to taste

Pick over rice and rinse in a strainer under cold running water (to get rid of the starch). Drain well. Lay rice on a cloth towel to allow the rice to dry out. Saute rice with the butter if desired for 5 minutes, stirring constantly. Add the boiling stock, salt and pepper, stir and cook in medium heat partially covered for 20 minutes. Serves 6.

## RICE PILAF C
### Πιλάφι

4½ cups boiling fresh chicken or beef stock
Salt and pepper to taste
2 cups converted rice
¼ cup butter or margarine, melted

Pick over rice and rinse in a strainer under cold running water (to get rid of the starch). Drain well. Add rice to boiling stock, stir and cook in medium heat partially covered for 20 minutes. Add hot butter and toss well with two forks. Serves 6.

## RICE AU GRATIN
### Ρίζι ὁ γκρατὲν

2 cups converted rice
4 cups boiling fresh chicken stock
2 cups medium white sauce (see index)
½ cup grated Parmesan or Romano cheese
3 beaten eggs
Pepper to taste
3 tablespoons dried bread crumbs (see index)
8 ounces ham, cut into small cubes (optional) or

**1 package (10-ounces) frozen artichoke hearts cooked, cut into fourths**

Prepare rice as directed in Rice Pilaf B, reduce cooking time from 20 minutes to 15 (see index). Follow recipe and preparation as directed in medium white sauce. Spoon little by little of the hot sauce into beaten eggs, stirring constantly. Add egg mixture to the sauce and cook over very low heat for 2-3 minutes, stirring constantly. Add half of the grated cheese and pepper, stir well. Combine rice, white sauce, ham or artichokes if desired, mix well. Place rice mixture in a greased baking dish. Mix the remaining cheese and bread crumbs and sprinkle over rice au gratin. Bake in a preheated 350°F (180°C) oven for approximately 30 minutes or until golden brown. Let stand for 20 minutes before cutting. Serves 6-8.

# RICE AND PASTA PILAF

Ρίζι καὶ κριθαράκι πιλάφι

¼  cup butter or margarine
1  cup converted rice
1  cup Kritharaki (Greek pasta)
5  cups boiling fresh chicken stock
Salt and pepper to taste
Grated Parmesan or Romano cheese

Pick over rice and rinse in a strainer under cold running water (to get rid of the starch). Drain well. Lay rice on a cloth towel to allow the rice to dry out. Saute rice and Kritharaki with the butter if desired for 5 minutes, stirring constantly. Add the boiling stock, salt and pepper. Stir and cook in medium-low heat covered for 20 minutes. Stir occasionally. Serve with grated cheese. Serves 6.

# RICE WITH CURRY

Ρύζι μὲ κάρυ

2  tablespoons butter or margarine
1  small finely chopped onion
1  can (16-ounces) whole tomatoes, finely chopped
Salt and Pepper to taste
3  cups fresh chicken stock
¼  cup butter or margarine
2  cups converted rice
1½  teaspoons or less curry powder

In a saucepan saute onion with butter until onion is soft. Add chopped tomatoes, salt, pepper, chicken stock and curry powder. Cover and cook slowly for 30 minutes. Pick over rice and rinse in a strainer under cold running water (to get rid of the starch),

drain well.  Lay rice on a cloth towel to allow the rice to dry out. Saute rice with the butter if desired for 5 minutes. Add rice to the boiling sauce, stir, and cook in medium heat partially covered for 20 minutes. Pack the rice into 6-cup ring mold. Unmold in a large serving platter. Serves 6.

# RICE CROQUETTES

Ρύζι κροκέτες

2  cups thick white sauce (see index)
1  cup grated Kefalotyri or Parmesan cheese
White pepper to taste
1  recipe Rice Pilaf A (see index)
2  eggs beaten with 2 tablespoons cold water
2  cups or more fine dried bread crumbs (see index)
Clarified butter or margarine (see index) for frying

Follow recipe and preparation as directed in Thick White Sauce. Set aside. Folow recipe and preparation as directed in Rice Pilaf. Add grated cheese to the sauce, stir until it is melted, add pepper. Add rice and chill. Shape into small cones, roll in crumbs, eggs and again in crumbs. Fry croquettes in hot butter until golden brown on all sides. Drain on absorbent paper. Serve hot. Makes 24.

**Variation:**

# RICE WITH CHILI

Ρίζι μὲ τσίλι

Substitute chili for the curry.
Follow recipe and preparation as directed in Rice with Curry (see index).

# RICE WITH HAM AND MUSHROOMS

Ρίζι μὲ ζαμπὸν καὶ μανιτάρια

2  cups converted rice
4½  cups fresh chicken stock
8  ounces ham, cut into small cubes
1  jar (8-ounces) mushrooms, drained, cut into pieces
Pepper to taste
½  cup grated Parmesan or Romano cheese

Bring chicken stock to a boil. Pick over rice and rinse in a strainer under cold running water (to get rid of the starch), add to the boiling stock, stir and cook slowly partially covered for 20 minutes. Remove from heat. Add ham, mushrooms, pepper and half of the cheese. Toss well with two forks. Pack rice mixture into a 8-cup ring mold. Unmold in a serving platter. Sprinkle with the remaining cheese and serve. Serves 6-8.

# RICE PILAF TAS-KEBAP
Ρίζι πιλάφι τὰς κεμπάμπ

**Basic recipe for Beef Ragout (see index**
**Rice Pilaf A (see index)**

Follow recipe and preparation as directed in Beef Ragout. Prepare rice. Follow recipe and preparation as directed. Pack rice in a 6-cup ring mold. Unmold in a serving platter. Spoon Beef Ragout over rice and serve immediately. Serves 6.

Note: Substitute lamb for the beef. Follow recipe and preparation as directed.

# RICE MILANEZA
Ρίζι μιλανέζα

4  cups fresh chicken stock
2  cups converted rice
3  tablespoons butter or margarine
3  tablespoons flour
2  cups fresh chicken stock
1  cup milk
3  eggs yolks, beaten
½  cup or more grated Parmesan, Kefalotyri or
        Romano cheese
Salt and pepper to taste
½  cup toasted slivered blanched almonds
2  cups frozen or fresh peas, cooked (optional)

Bring chicken stock to a boil. Pick over rice and rinse in a strainer under cold running water (to get rid of the starch), add rice to boiling stock, stir and

cook slowly partially covered for 20 minutes. Remove from heat. Add almonds and toss well with two forks to combine. Pack the rice into a 6-cup ring mold. Unmold in a large serving platter. While rice is cooking prepare sauce. In a saucepan melt butter if desired over medium heat, blend in flour until smooth using a whisk. Gradually add chicken stock and milk, stirring constantly until mixture is thick and smooth. Cook 3 minutes longer. Remove from heat. Spoon little by little of the hot sauce into egg yolk stirring constantly. Add egg mixture to the sauce and cook over very low heat for 4-5 minutes, stirring constantly. Add cheese and stir, add freshly ground pepper, add salt if needed. Pour sauce over rice pilaf. Fill the center of the rice mold with cooked peas if desired. Serve with any kind of meat or poultry. Serves 6.

# RICE WITH PEAS
Ρίζι μὲ ἀρακὰ

4½ cups fresh chicken stock
2  cups converted rice
Salt and pepper to taste
1½  cups fresh or frozen peas (cooked)

Bring chicken stock to a boil. Pick over the rice and rinse in a strainer under cold running water (to get rid of the starch), add to the boiling stock, stir and cook slowly partially covered for 20 minutes. While rice is cooking prepare peas. Drop peas into boiling salted water, cover and cook slowly for 20-30 minutes or until tender. Drain and rinse (to get rid of the green color). Add peas to the rice and toss gently with two forks. Pack the rice-pea mixture into a 8-cup ring mold. Unmold in a platter and serve. Serves 6.

# SAUCES

## WHITE SAUCE
### Σάλτσα μπεσαμελα

**Thin White Sauce:**
For gravies, sauces, scalloped and soups
2 tablespoons butter or margarine
2 tablespoons flour
2 cups milk
Salt and pepper to taste

**Medium White Sauce:**
For au-gratin, mousaka and pastitsio
5 tablespoons butter or margarine
5 tablespoons flour
2 cups milk
Salt and pepper to taste

**Thick White Sauce:**
For croquettes, pittes and souffles
7 tablespoons butter or margarine
8 tablespoons flour
2 cups milk
Salt and pepper to taste

Melt butter if desired over medium heat, blend in flour until smooth using a whisk. Gradually add milk, stirring constantly until mixture is thick and smooth. Cook 3 minutes longer; add seasoning and blend. Remove from heat. Makes 2 cups.

## WHITE SAUCE WITH EGGS
### Σάλτσα μπεσαμελα μὲ αὐγὰ

3 beaten eggs or less
1 recipe White Sauce (see index)

Follow recipe and preparation as directed in White Sauce. Spoon little by little of the hot sauce into eggs, stirring constantly. Gradually add egg mixture to the sauce and cook over very low heat for 2-3 minutes, stirring constantly. Remove from heat. Use as you desire.

**Variation:**

## VELOUTE SAUCE
### Σάλτσα βελουτὲ

Substitute chicken, beef or veal stock for the milk. Follow recipe and preparation as directed in Thin or Medium White Sauce (see index).

## SHRIMP SAUCE
### Σάλτσα γαρίδας

1 recipe Medium White Sauce (see index)
1 cup finely chopped cooked shrimp
1 teaspoon Worcestershire sauce
1 tablespoon ketchup

Combine white sauce, shrimp, Worcestershire sauce and ketchup. Blend well. Serve with fish. Makes 3 cups.

## POULETTE SAUCE
### Σάλτσα πουλὲ

2½ tablespoons butter or margarine
2 tablespoons flour
1 cup fresh chicken stock
2 egg yolks, beaten with
1 cup cream
2 tablespoons lemon juice

Follow preparation as White Sauce (see index). Gradually add egg-cream mixture to the sauce, stirring constantly. Cook over very low heat for 3 minutes, stirring constantly. Remove from heat.

※ ※ ※ ※

# OIL-LEMON DRESSING A
### Λαδολέμονο

**1 cup olive oil or salad oil**
**Juice of 1 lemon**
**Salt and pepper to taste (optional)**

Combine all the ingredients in a bowl. Beat with a fork until well blended. Serve with salads, boiled vegetables, broiled fish or boiled meat.

※ ※ ※ ※

# OIL-LEMON DRESSING B
### Λαδολέμονο

**1 cup olive oil or salad oil**
**Juice of 1 lemon**
**Salt and pepper to taste**
**1 large onion, cut into very thin slices**
**2 tablespoons chopped parsley**

Combine oil, lemon, salt and pepper in a bowl. Beat with a fork until well blended. Add onion slices and parsley, mix well. Serve on broiled fish or broiled meat.

※ ※ ※ ※

# OIL-VINEGAR DRESSING
### Λαδόξυδο

**1 cup olive oil or salad oil**
**¼ cup wine vinegar**
**1 teaspoon Greek rigani (oregano)**
**½ teaspoon garlic powder**
**2 tablespoons lemon juice**
**½ teaspoon salt**
**¼ teaspoon pepper**
**¼ teaspoon sugar**

Combine all the ingredients in a blender and blend well. Use the dressing with salads or boiled meat.

※ ※ ※ ※

# COCKTAIL SAUCE
### Σάλτσα κοκτέϊλ

**1 cup mayonnaise**
**¼ cup ketchup**
**¼ cup cream, whipped**
**1 teaspoon Worcestershire sauce**
**½ teaspoon mustard**

Mix all the ingredients well and chill until needed. Serve with crawfish, crab, lobster or shrimp.

※ ※ ※ ※

# MAITRE D'HOTEL SAUCE
### Σάλτσα μαίτρ-ντ'ότέλ

**1 cup butter or margarine**
**2 tablespoons lemon juice**
**1 tablespoon finely chopped parsley**
**Salt and pepper to taste**
**2 tablespoons mustard**
**2 egg yolks, beaten**

Melt butter if desired in a medium heat. All all the ingredients except egg yolks. Mix well. Remove from heat. Slowly add beaten yolks, stirring constantly. Simmer in very low heat for 2 minutes. Serve with meat, fish or vegetables.

※ ※ ※ ※

# SAUCE PIQUANTE
### Σάλτσα πικάντικη

**2 tablespoons butter or margarine**
**¼ cup finely chopped onion**
**1 clove garlic, finely chopped**
**1 tablespoons parsley, finely chopped**
**2 tablespoons flour**
**1 cup fresh beef stock**
**1 medium tomato, peeled, seeded and chopped**
**2 tablespoons wine vinegar**
**Salt and pepper to taste**
**1 teaspoon Worcestershire sauce**
**1 tablespoon chopped capers**
**1 cucumber pickle, finely chopped**

Melt butter if desired and saute onion on medium heat, add garlic and parsley, saute until onion is soft. Add flour and stir well, simmer for 4 minutes, stirring constantly. Gradually add beef stock, tomato, vinegar, salt and pepper. Simmer for 10 minutes. Press through a sieve or food mill. When it is cool add Worcestershire sauce, capers and pickles. Serve with boiled beef, veal or tonque.

※ ※ ※ ※

# TARTAR SAUCE
### Σάλτσα ταρτάρ

**1 cup mayonnaise**
**1½ tablespoons finely chopped cucumber pickle**
**1½ tablespoons finely chopped capers**
**1 teaspoon mustard**

1 tablespoon finely chopped onion (optional)

Combine all the ingredients and mix well. Chill until needed. Serve with fish, meat or tongue.

⚜⚜⚜

# CURRY SAUCE
### Σάλτσα κάρυ

2 tablespoons butter or margarine
1 tablespoon finely chopped onion
2 tablespoons flour
1 cup fresh chicken stock
1 cup milk
1 teaspoon curry powder
Salt and pepper to taste

Melt butter and saute onion until soft. Add flour and stir until smooth. Gradually add stock and milk, stirring constantly. Add curry, salt and pepper. Simmer for 15 minutes stirring constantly. Press through a sieve or food mill. Serve with cold meat or fish, hard-boiled eggs, lobster, shrimp and rice pilaf.

⚜⚜⚜

# CREOLE SAUCE
### Σάλτσα κρεόλ

3 tablespoons butter
3 tablespoons olive or salad oil
1 large finely chopped onion
1 tablespoon flour
Salt and pepper to taste
1 can (29-ounces) whole tomatoes, or fresh, pressed through a sieve or food mill
1 bay leaf
1 green pepper, minced
½ cup chopped mushrooms
1 tablespoon finely chopped parsley
1 cup fresh stock

Saute onion with oil and butter until onion is soft. Add flour and stir until browned. Add salt and pepper, tomatoes, bay leaf, green pepper, mushrooms, parsley and stock. Cover and simmer for 45-60 minutes or until sauce thickens, stirring frequently. Serve hot on eggs, pasta or rice. Serves 4-6.

⚜⚜⚜

# TOMATO SAUCE A
### Σάλτσα ντομάτας

3 tablespoons olive oil
3 tablespoons butter
1 medium finely chopped onion
2 cloves garlic, minced
1 can (29-ounces) whole tomatoes, or fresh, pressed through a sieve or food mill
Salt and pepper to taste
½ cup water or stock

Saute onion in oil and butter until soft. Add garlic, tomatoes, salt, pepper and water if desired. Cover and cook slowly for 60 minutes or until sauce thickens, stirring frequently. Serve hot on pasta or rice. Serves 4-6.

⚜⚜⚜

# TOMATO SAUCE B
### Σάλτσα ντομάτας

3 tablespoons olive oil
3 tablespoons butter
1 medium finely chopped onion
½ teaspoon garlic powder
1 can (29-ounces) whole tomatoes, or fresh, pressed through a sieve or food mill
1 tablespoon chili powder
½ cup water or fresh chicken or beef stock
Salt and pepper to taste

Saute onion in oil and butter until soft. Add the rest of the ingredients; cover and cook slowly for approximately 60 minutes or until sauce thickens, stirring frequently. Remove from heat and serve on pasta or rice. Serves 4-6.

⚜⚜⚜

# MEAT SAUCE A
### Σάλτσα μὲ κυμὰ

3 tablespoons olive oil
1 medium finely chopped onion
1½ pounds lean ground beef
½ cup dry white wine
1 can (16-ounces) whole tomatoes, or fresh, pressed through a sieve or food mill.
Salt and pepper to taste
1 cup water
1 cinnamon stick ½-inch long

Saute onion in oil until soft, add ground meat, stir breaking up clumps until brown. Add wine, tomatoes, salt, pepper, cinnamon and water. Cover and cook slowly for 75 minutes or until liquid is absorbed and meat is cooked, stirring occasionally. Remove cinnamon. Serve on pasta or rice. Serves 4-6.

## MEAT SAUCE B
### Σάλτσα μὲ κυμὰ

3 tablespoons olive oil
1 medium finely chopped onion
2 garlic cloves, minced
1½ pounds lean ground beef
½ cup dry red wine
1 can (16-ounces) whole tomatoes, or fresh, pressed
  through a sieve or food mill
Salt and pepper to taste
1 tablespoon finely chopped parsley
1 cup water

Saute onion in oil until soft, add garlic and ground meat, stir breaking up clumps until brown. Add wine, tomatoes, salt, pepper and water. Cover and cook slowly for 75 minutes or until all liquid is absorbed and meat is cooked, stirring occasionally. Serve hot on pasta or rice. Serves 4-6.

## MEAT SAUCE C
### Σάλτσα μὲ κυμὰ

3 tablespoons olive oil
1 medium finely chopped onion
2 cloves garlic
½ pound lean ground beef
½ pound lean ground pork
½ pound lean ground lamb
½ cup dry white wine
1 can (16-ounces) whole tomatoes, or fresh, pressed
  through a sieve or food mill
1 cup water
Salt and pepper to taste

Saute onion in oil until soft, add garlic and ground meat, stir, breaking up clumps until brown. Add wine, tomatoes, water, salt and pepper. Cover and cook slowly for 75 minutes or until all liquid is absorbed and meat is cooked, stirring occasionally. Add water if needed. Serve hot on pasta or rice. Serves 4-6.

## GARLIC SAUCE WITH BREAD
### Σκορδαλιὰ μὲ ψωμὶ

6 cloves garlic, chopped
1 pound stale Italian bread, crust removed and sliced
½ teaspoon salt
1½ cups olive or salad oil
3 tablespoons wine vinegar

Soak bread in cold water for 5 minutes. Squeeze dry as possible. Place garlic, salt and bread in a food processor or blender. Process about 1 minute. Remove the pusher from the feed tube and add oil and vinegar in a fine stream while the motor is running. When all the oil and vinegar is added and the garlic sauce is thick and smooth, turn off the motor. Transfer the sauce to a covered container for refrigeration storage. When you are ready to serve, place sauce in a serving bowl. Serve with Fried Codfish, Fried Eggplants, Fried Zucchini and Boiled Beets.

Variation:

## GARLIC SAUCE WITH POTATOES
### Σκορδαλιὰ μὲ πατάτα

Substitute bread with
4 medium potatoes, boiled in salted water, peeled
  and mashed

Follow recipe and preparation as directed in Garlic Sauce with Bread (see index). Serve as directed.

## GARLIC SAUCE WITH ALMONDS
### Σκορδαλιὰ μὲ ἀμύγδαλα

6 cloves garlic, chopped
½ pound stale Italian bread, crust removed and sliced
½ teaspoon salt
1 cup finely ground blanched almonds
1½ cups olive or salad oil
3 tablespoons wine vinegar

Follow preparation as directed in Garlic Sauce with Bread (see index). Serve as directed.

# VEGETABLES

## HOW TO PREPARE ARTICHOKES
### Προετοιμασία ἀγγινάρας

Clean artichokes by removing 5 layers of leaves and trim carefully around base with a sharp knife. Slice 1-inch off the tips and the stems. Cut in half lengthwise. Scoop out the spiny choke below the leaves and above the heart. Rub each one well with cut side of lemon and then immerse in a bowl of cold water (to prevent from darkening). Keep them in the water until you are ready to cook. Cook as you desire.

✤✤✤✤

## BOILED ARTICHOKES
### 'Αγγινάρες βραστὲς

12  fresh or frozen artichokes
Juice of half lemon
3  cups boiling water
1  teaspoon salt

Clean artichokes as directed in How to Prepare Artichokes (see index). Boil artichokes in boiling salted water and the juice of half lemon for 30 minutes or until they are tender. Drain. Serve with Maitre D Hotel Sauce or Oil-Lemon Dressing A (see index). Serves 6-12.

✤✤✤✤

## ARTICHOKES A LA POLITA
### 'Αγγινάρες ἀ λὰ πολίτα

12  fresh or frozen artichokes
1  bunch scallions, chopped
1  cup olive oil, or more
6  whole small white onions, peeled
12  whole small potatoes, peeled
6  small carrots, cut in half
1  celery heart, cut into 1-inch long pieces

¼  cup chopped fresh dill or 1 teaspoon dried
Salt and pepper to taste
3  cups water
Juice of 1 or more lemon

Clean artichokes as directed in How to Prepare Artichokes (see index). Saute onions with oil until soft. Arrange whole onions, potatoes, carrots, celery, artichokes, dill, salt and pepper in a large pot. Add lemon juice and water. Cover and cook slowly for approximately 1½ hours or until vegetables are tender. Add water as needed. Serve hot or cold. Serves 6.

✤✤✤✤

## ARTICHOKES AU GRATIN
### 'Αγγινάρες ὁ γκρατὲν

6  fresh or frozen artichokes, thawed, boiled (see index)
3  tablespoons butter or margarine
⅓  cup dried bread crumbs (see index)
1  cup grated Parmesan or Romano cheese
2  cups medium white sauce (see index)
3  beaten eggs

Clean and prepare artichokes as directed in Boiled Artichokes. Drain well. Lay on paper towels to absorb excess moisture. Generously grease a baking dish and sprinkle with bread crumbs. Cut artichokes in half again lengthwise and place in one layer in the prepared dish. Sprinkle with ⅓ of the cheese. Dot with butter. Follow recipe and preparation as directed in Medium White Sauce. Spoon little by little of the hot sauce into eggs, stirring constantly. Add egg mixture to the sauce and cook over very low heat for 2-3 minutes, stirring constantly. Remove from heat. Add half of the remaining cheese, salt and pepper, stir well to combine. Pour sauce over artichokes. Sprinkle with remaining cheese. Bake in a preheated

350°F (180°C) oven for approximately 40 minutes or until golden brown. Serve immediately. Serves 6.

# BREADED ARTICHOKES
## 'Αγγινάρες πανὲ

6 fresh or frozen boiled artichokes (see index)
1 cup fine dried bread crumbs (see index)
¼ cup grated Parmesan or Kefalotyri cheese
2 eggs, beaten with 1 tablespoon cold water
Clarified butter or margarine (see index)
Oil for frying

Clean and prepare artichokes as directed in Boiled Artichokes. Drain well. Lay on paper towels to absorb excess moisture. Combine bread crumbs, cheese and mix well. Dip artichoke pieces one at a time in egg and then into bread mixture until completely covered. Brown in hot butter if desired on both sides. Serve hot. Serves 4.

# FRIED ARTICHOKES
## 'Αγγινάρες τηγανιτὲς

6 fresh or frozen boiled artichokes (see index)
1 cup flour
1 teaspoon baking powder
¼ teaspoon salt
Pepper to taste
⅓ cup milk
1 tablespoon olive oil
1 beaten egg
Clarified butter or margarine (see index) or
Oil for frying

Clean and prepare artichokes as directed in Boiled Artichokes. Drain well, lay on paper towels to absorb excess moisture. Combine flour, baking powder, salt, pepper, egg, oil and milk. Blend until smooth. Dip artichokes one at a time into batter. Fry in hot butter if desired until golden brown and crisp. Drain on absorbent paper. Serve hot or cold. Serves 4.

# ARTICHOKES MOUSAKA
## 'Αγγινάρες μουσακὰ

12 large fresh artichokes
Juice of ½ lemon
½ pound lean ground beef
½ pound lean ground lamb
1 medium onion, finely chopped

2 tablespoons olive oil
½ cup dry white wine
1 ripe tomato, peeled, seeded and chopped
Salt and pepper to taste
1 tablespoon fresh chopped dill or ¼ teaspoon dried
4 cups medium white sauce (see index)
4 beaten eggs
1 cup grated Parmesan or Romano cheese
1 cup dried bread crumbs (see index)
¼ cup butter or margarine, melted

Clean artichokes as directed in How to Prepare Artichokes (see index). Boil artichokes in 2 cups boiling salted water and the juice of ½ lemon for 15 minutes. Drain. Heat oil and saute meat and onion until onion is soft. Add wine and cook until it evaporates. Add salt, pepper, tomato and ⅔ cup water. Cook slowly covered for approximately 60 minutes. Prepare white sauce as directed. Spoon little by little of the hot sauce into eggs, stirring constantly. Add egg mixture to the sauce and cook over very low heat for 2-3 minutes, stirring constantly. Remove from heat. Add half of the cheese and mix well to combine. Set aside. Generously brush a baking dish with melted butter if desired. Sprinkle with bread crumbs. Place artichokes in one layer. Cover with meat sauce. Spoon white sauce over meat and spread evenly. Sprinkle with the remaining cheese and melted butter. Bake in a preheated 350°F (180°C) oven for 40 minutes or until golden. Serves 12 as a first course or 6 as a main course.

# MEAT STUFFED ARTICHOKES
## 'Αγγινάρες γεμιστὲς

12 large fresh artichokes
½ pound lean ground beef
½ pound lean ground lamb
1 medium onion, finely chopped
2 tablespoons olive oil
½ cup dry white wine
1 ripe tomato, peeled, seeded and chopped
Salt and pepper to taste
1 tablespoon fresh chopped dill or ¼ teaspoon dried
1 cup medium white sauce (see index)
2 egg yolks, beaten
¼ cup grated Parmesan or Romano cheese
¼ cup butter or margarine, melted

Clean and prepare artichokes as directed in Boiled Artichokes (see index). Leave them whole. Drain well. Lay on paper towels up-side-down. Heat oil and saute meat and onion until onion is soft. Add wine and cook until it evaporates. Add salt, pepper, tomato and ⅔ cup water. Cover and cook slowly for approximately 60 minutes or until all the liquids have evaporated. Place artichokes in a greased baking dish right-side-up. Brush with melted butter, fill with the meat sauce. Prepare white sauce as directed. Spoon little by little of the hot sauce into egg yolks, stirring constantly. Add egg mixture to the sauce and cook over very low heat for 2-3 minutes, stirring constantly. Place 1 tablespoon sauce on each artichoke to cover the meat. Sprinkle with grated cheese and butter. Bake in a preheated 350°F (180°C) oven for 30 minutes or until crust has golden color. Serve immediately as a first course. Serves 6-12.

🌿🌿🌿

## ARTICHOKES WITH PEAS
'Αγγινάρες μὲ ἀρακὰ

6  fresh or frozen artichokes
3  pounds fresh peas, shelled or 20-ounces frozen
1  bunch scallions, chopped
¾  cup olive oil
¼  cup chopped fresh dill of 1 teaspoon dried
Juice of ½ lemon or more
Salt and pepper to taste
1½  cups water

Prepare artichokes as directed in How to Prepare Artichokes (see index). Heat oil and saute scallions until soft. Arrange artichokes in the pot, add peas, dill, lemon juice, salt, pepper and water. Cover and cook slowly for approximately 60 minutes or until artichokes and peas are tender. Add water as needed. Serve hot or cold. Serves 6.

🌿🌿🌿

## ARTICHOKES WITH FRESH FABA BEANS
'Αγγινάρες μὲ φρέσκα κουκιὰ

6  fresh or frozen artichokes
3  pounds fresh faba beans, shelled
1  bunch scallions, chopped
¾  cup olive oil
¼  cup fresh chopped dill or 1 teaspoon dried
Juice of ½ or more lemon
Salt and pepper to taste
1½  cups water

Prepare artichokes as directed in How to Prepare Artichokes (see index). Heat oil and saute scallions until soft. Arrange artichokes in the pot, add faba beans, dill, lemon juice, salt, pepper and water. Cover and cook slowly for approximately 60 minutes or until artichokes and faba beans are tender. Add water as needed. Serve hot or cold. Serves 6.

## ARTICHOKES SOUFFLE
'Αγγινάρες σουφλὲ

8  fresh or frozen artichokes, boiled
½  cup cream
8  thin slices Kaseri or Swiss cheese
8  thin slices boiled ham
2  cups thick white sauce (see index)
7  eggs, separated
⅓  cup Parmesan or Romano cheese
1  tablespoon ketchup

Prepare artichokes as directed in Boiled Artichokes (see index). Drain well. Lay artichokes on paper towels to absorb excess moisture. Place artichokes in one layer in a greased baking dish. Sprinkle with cream. Cover artichokes first with cheese slices and then with the ham. Follow recipe and preparation as directed in thick white sauce. Remove from heat. Beat egg yolks until light. Spoon little by little of the hot sauce into egg yolks, stirring constantly. Add egg mixture to the sauce, stirring constantly. Add grated cheese and ketchup, mix well to combine. Fold in stiffly beaten egg whites. Spoon over artichokes. Bake in a preheated 300°F (150°C) oven for 75 minutes. Serve immediately to prevent falling. Serves 8.

🌿🌿🌿

## BAKED LIMA BEANS
Φασόλια γίγαντες φούρνου

⅔  cup more or less olive oil
2  medium onions, finely chopped
4  cloves garlic, minced
4  ripe tomatoes, pressed through a food mill
2  tablespoons finely chopped parsley
Salt and pepper to taste
¼  teaspoon Cayenne pepper (optional)
½  teaspoon dry mustard
1  cup boiling water
20  ounces frozen lima beans

Saute onion in oil until onion is soft. Add garlic, tomato, parsley, salt, pepper, cayenne if desired, mustard and water. Bring to a boil. Add lima beans, stir, cook slowly for 30 minutes. Turn into a casserole and bake in a preheated 325°F (165°C) oven for approximately 60 minutes. As the liquid cooks away add more as needed. Serves 4-6.

🌿🌿🌿

## BRAISED LIMA BEANS
Φασόλια γίγαντες γιαχνὶ

⅔  cups more or less olive oil
1  medium onion, minced

4 ripe tomatoes pressed through a food mill or
    ½ cup tomato sauce
1 tablespoon minced parsley (optional)
Salt and pepper to taste
20 ounces frozen lima beans
1 cinnamon stick ½-inch long
1½ cups boiling water

Saute onion in oil until soft. Add tomato, parsley if desired, salt, pepper, cinnamon and water. Bring to a boil. Add lima beans, stir, cover and cook gently for 45 minutes or until beans are tender and sauce thickens. Add hot water as needed. Serve hot or cold. Serves 4.

# STRING BEANS WITH MUSHROOMS

Φασολάκια μὲ μανιτάρια

2 pounds string beans
1 pound fresh mushrooms, sliced
1 medium thinly sliced onion
1 clove garlic, chopped
1 can (16-ounces) whole tomatoes, chopped
2 tablespoons chopped parsley
½ cup olive oil
Salt and pepper to taste
1 cup water

Wash beans, string and snap. Cut into half or shorter pieces. Place all the ingredients in a saucepan. Cover and cook slowly for 90 minutes or until vegetables are tender. Serve hot or cold with feta cheese and fresh bread. Serves 4.

# SAUTEED STRING BEANS

Φασολάκια σωτὲ

2 pounds string beans
2 cups boiling water
Salt to taste
⅓ cup butter or margarine
½ cup slivered blanched almonds

Wash beans, string and snap. Cover with boiling water and cook slowly until tender. Add salt just before cooking is completed. Drain. Arrange in a serving dish. In a small frying pan saute almonds in butter. Add butter and almonds to beans and serve. Serves 6.

# STRING BEANS WITH TOMATOES
Φασολάκια λαδερὰ

2 pounds string beans
1 medium onion, thinly sliced
2 cloves garlic, sliced
3 medium ripe tomatoes, peeled, seeded and chopped
2 tablespoons chopped parsley
Salt and pepper to taste
½ cup or more olive oil
1½ cups water
2 medium potatoes, peeled and cut into quarters

Wash beans, string and snap. Cut into half or shorter pieces. Place all the ingredients except the potatoes in a saucepan. Cover and cook slowly for 30 minutes. Add potatoes and ½ cup boiling water, stir, cover and cook slowly for 60 minutes or until beans and potatoes are tender. Serve hot or cold with feta cheese and fresh bread. Serves 4.

# BROCCOLI AU GRATIN
Μπρόκολα ὁ γκρατὲν

2 heads or broccoli boiled (see index)
⅔ cup grated Parmesan or Romano cheese
2 cups medium white sauce (see index)
¼ teaspoon white pepper
2 beaten egg yolks

Prepare broccoli as directed in Boiled Broccoli. (Boil without salt). Drain well. Lay on paper towels to absorb excess moisture. Follow recipe and preparation as directed in medium white sauce. Spoon little by little of the hot sauce into egg yolks, stirring constantly. Add egg mixture to the sauce and cook over very low heat for 2-3 minutes, stirring constantly. Remove from heat. Add pepper and half of the cheese, stir well to combine. Place one layer of the cooked broccoli in a greased baking dish. Sprinkle with half of the remaining cheese, then spoon over half of the white sauce. Repeat with broccoli, cheese and the sauce. Bake in a preheated 350°F (180°C) oven for 30 minutes. Serve hot. Serves 6-8.

# BOILED BROCCOLI
Μπρόκολα βραστὰ

1 head of broccoli
1 quart boiling water
Salt to taste

Choose head that is bright green and crisp. Break the broccoli into flowerettes. Soak in cold water for 20 minutes. Rinse under cold running water. Insert carefully, stem end down in rapidly boiling water. The heads should not be submerged. Cover and boil for 20-30 minutes. Drain well. Serve with Maitre D Hotel sauce or Oil-Lemon Dressing A (see index). Serves 3-4.

✥✥✥✥

## CABBAGE AU GRATIN
### Λάχανο ὁ γκρατὲν

1 small head cabbage
3 quarts boiling water
2 tablespoons butter or margarine, melted
¼ teaspoon white pepper
2 cups medium white sauce (see index)
1 cup grated Kaseri or Swiss cheese
1 cup grated Parmesan or Romano cheese

Remove and discard outside leaves and core of cabbage. Cut into small pieces. Place in a colander and rinse under cold running water. Add cabbage to boiling water and boil uncovered until tender. Drain well. Add butter and pepper, toss well. Follow recipe and preparation as directed in medium white sauce. Remove from heat, add ¼ of the grated Parmesan cheese and pepper, stir well to combine. In a greased baking dish place a layer, half of the cabbage, then half of the grated Kaseri cheese and ¼ of the Parmesan cheese, cover with half of the white sauce, and continue with cabbage, cheese and sauce. Sprinkle the top with the remaining grated Parmesan cheese. Bake in a preheated 375°F (190°C) oven for 40 minutes. Serve hot. Serves 6-8.

✥✥✥✥

## CABBAGE RAGOUT
### Λάχανο γιαχνὶ

1 medium head cabbage
⅔ cup olive oil
1 cup minced onion
4 medium ripe tomatoes, pressed through a food mill
    or ½ cup tomato sauce
1 cinnamon stick ½-inch long
Salt and pepper to taste

Remove and discard outside leaves and core of cabbage. Cut into small pieces. Rinse well. Drop into boiling water and boil for 3 minutes. Strain well. Saute onion in oil until soft. Add tomato, cinnamon, salt and pepper. Cover and cook slowly for 10 minutes. Add cabbage, stir well. Cover and cook slowly for approximately 55 minutes or until cabbage is tender. Remove cinnamon stick and serve. Serves 6.

## MEAT STUFFED CABBAGE LEAVES
### Λαχανοντολμάδες

1 large savoy cabbage (napa) or 2 medium
⅓ cup butter or margarine
1 medium minced onion
½ pound lean ground pork
1½ pounds lean ground beef
½ cup converted rice
1 large ripe tomato, peeled, seeded and chopped or
    ¼ cup tomato paste
2 tablespoons minced parsley
Salt and pepper to taste
3 cups fresh beef stock or water
2 tablespoons corn starch
3 egg yolks
Juice of 1 lemon

Remove outside leaves of cabbage and cut around the stem and discard. Remove core as deeply as you can and discard. Leave whole. Plunge cabbage core-side down into boiling water and parboil for 10-12 minutes. Remove from water. Drain and cool; gently separate cabbage leaves one by one. Cut leaves in half, remove thick stems and reserve. Line bottom of a large Dutch oven with reserved thick stems to prevent stuffed cabbage from burning. Heat 2 tablespoons butter and saute onion until soft. Combine ground meat, onion, rice, tomato, parsley, salt and pepper. Mix thoroughly. Place 1 tablespoon of the stuffing on each of the half leaves. Fold base of leaf over filling, then fold in sides and wrap into a roll. Place rolls in layers close together seam-side-down. Add remaining butter and little salt. Place an inverted heavy plate on top of cabbage rolls. Add stock or water, cover. Cook slowly for approximately 60 minutes or until cabbage is tender. Arrange stuffed cabbage rolls on a serving platter. Keep warm. Drain stock from pot, add water or stock to make 2½ cups. Transfer stock to a small saucepan. Bring to a boil. Mix corn starch with ¼ cup cold water to a paste. Slowly add to the stock stirring constantly. Cook slowly for 5 minutes. Beat egg yolks with the lemon juice, gradually add some of the boiling sauce, stirring constantly. Add egg mixture to the sauce and cook over very low heat for 2-3 minutes, stirring constantly. Spoon sauce over stuffed cabbage rolls. Serve immediately. Serves 6-8.

✥✥✥✥

## RICE STUFFED CABBAGE LEAVES
### Λαχανοντολμάδες μὲ ρίζι

1 large savoy cabbage (napa) or 2 medium
¾ cup butter or margarine or more

1½ cups minced onion
2 cups converted rice
½ cup pine nuts or slivered blanched almonds
2 tablespoons minced parsley
Salt and pepper to taste
1 cup water
2 medium tomatoes, pressed through a food mill
4 cups fresh beef stock or water
1 cup milk or ½ cup milk and ½ cup cream
2 tablespoons corn starch
3 egg yolks
Juice of 1 lemon

Clean and prepare cabbage as directed in Meat Stuffed Cabbage Leaves (see index). Heat ½ cup butter and saute onion until soft. Rinse rice, add to the onion and saute for few minutes longer. Add tomato, water, parsley, salt and pepper. Stir and cover. Cook in medium heat for 10 minutes. Remove from heat. Place 1 tablespoon of the stuffing on each of the half leaves. Fold base of leaf over filling, then fold in sides and wrap into a roll. Place rolls in layers, close together seam-side-down. Add remaining butter and little salt. Place an inverted heavy plate on top of cabbage rolls. Add stock or water, cover, and cook slowly for approximately 60 minutes or until cabbage is tender. Gently arrange stuffed cabbage rolls on a serving platter. Drain stock from pot. Add water to make 2½ cups. Transfer stock to a small saucepan. Add milk or milk and cream if desired and bring to a boil. Mix corn starch with ¼ cup cold water to a paste. Slowly add to the stock stirring constantly. Cook slowly for 5 minutes. Beat egg yolks with the lemon juice. Gradually add some of the boiling sauce stirring constantly. Add egg mixture to the sauce and cook over very low heat for 2-3 minutes, stirring constantly. Spoon sauce over stuffed cabbage rolls and sprinkle toasted blanched almonds over. Serve immediately. Serves 6-8.

## SOUR CABBAGE
Λάχανο ξυνό

1 small head cabbage, finely shredded
2 teaspoons salt
¼ cup or more butter or margarine
¼ cup wine vinegar
¼ teaspoon pepper
1 teaspoon sugar

Sprinkle shredded cabbage with salt. In a saucepan place butter, when it is melted add vinegar, pepper and sugar. Bring to a boil. Add cabbage and stir well. Cover, reduce heat to medium-low and cook until cabbage is tender. Serve with steaks, eggs, fried meatballs, broiled chicken or hot dogs. Serves 4-6.

## SAUTEED CARROTS
Καρότα σωτέ

1 pound young carrots
1 quart boiling water
1½ teaspoons salt
⅓ cup or less butter, melted

Scrape and wash carrots. Leave whole or cut into slices crosswise or lengthwise. Boil for 30 minutes or until tender. Drain, add butter and serve. Serves 4-6.

## CAULIFLOWER AU GRATIN
Κουνουπίδι ὁ γκρατέν

1 large cauliflower
⅔ cup grated Kefalotyri or Parmesan cheese
2 cups medium white sauce (see index)
¼ teaspoon white pepper
2 beaten egg yolks

Prepare cauliflower as directed in Boiled Cauliflower (see index). Boil without salt. Drain well. Cut into flowerets. Lay on paper towels to absorb excess moisture. Follow recipe and preparation as directed in medium white sauce. Spoon little by little of the hot sauce into egg yolks, stirring constantly. Add egg mixture to the sauce and cook over very low heat for 2-3 minutes, stirring constantly. Remove from heat. Add half of the cheese and pepper, stir well to combine. Place one layer of the cooked cauliflower in a greased baking dish. Sprinkle with half the remaining cheese, then spoon over half the white sauce. Repeat with cauliflower, cheese and the sauce. Bake in a preheated 350°F (180°C) oven for 30 minutes. Serve hot. Serves 6-8.

## BOILED CAULIFLOWER
Κουνουπίδι βραστό

1 large cauliflower
2 quarts boiling water
1½ teaspoons salt
Oil-lemon dressing A (see index)

Remove the green leaves, cut off and discard thick stem and any bruised or dirty spots. Place it, top downward in a deep bowl of cold salted water and allow it to stay there about 40 minutes. Drain and rinse with cold water. Boil whole in boiling salted water, uncovered for 30-40 minutes or until tender. Lift out the cauliflower carefully and drain well. Separate into small flowerets. Serve with oil-lemon dressing. Serves 4-6.

## BRAISED CAULIFLOWER
### Κουνουπίδι γιαχνὶ

1 large cauliflower
1½ teaspoons salt
⅔ cup more or less olive oil or butter
½ cup minced onion
3 medium ripe tomatoes, pressed through a food mill
Salt and pepper to taste
1 cinnamon stick 1-inch long (optional)

Remove the green leaves, cut off and discard thick stem and any bruised or dirty spots from cauliflower. Cut into flowerets. Place flowerets in a deep bowl of cold salted water and allow them to stay there about 40 minutes. Drain and rinse with cold water. Drain. Saute onion in oil or butter until soft, add tomato, salt, pepper, cinnamon if desired and ½ cup water. Bring to a boil. Add flowerets, stir gently, cover and cook slowly for 45 minutes or until tender and sauce thickens. Serve hot or cold. Serves 4-5.

❦❦❦

## FRIED CAULIFLOWER
### Κουνουπίδι τηγανιτὸ

1 large cauliflower
1 beaten egg
¾ cup milk
¼ teaspoon salt
1 tablespoon olive oil
1 cup flour
1 teaspoon baking powder
⅛ teaspoon pepper
Oil for frying

Prepare cauliflower as directed in Boiled Cauliflower (see inndex). Cut into flowerets. Drain well. Lay on paper towels to absorb excess moisture. Combine all the ingredients except the oil for frying, and mix well with a whisk until smooth. Slip flowerets into the batter and fry in hot oil a few at a time until golden brown on all sides. Drain on absorbent paper and serve. Serves 4-6.

❦❦❦

## BAKED EGGPLANTS WITH CHEESE
### Μελιτζάνες μὲ τυρὶ στὸ φοῦρνο

4 pounds eggplants
Salt
1 cup flour
2 eggs, beaten with 2 tablespoons cold water
Oil or butter for frying
1 large finely chopped onion
1 clove garlic, minced
¼ cup butter or margarine
3 medium ripe tomatoes, peeled, seeded and chopped
1 tablespoon minced parsley
Salt and pepper to taste
1 pound Kaseri or Swiss cheese, cut into 1⅛-inch slices
⅔ cup grated Parmesan cheese
⅓ cup dried bread crumbs (see index)
3 tablespoons butter or margarine, melted

Remove stems of the eggplants and wash well. Peel and cut crosswise into ⅓-inch slices. Sprinkle with salt. Set aside for 30 minutes. Rinse and drain. Squeeze out excess moisture and pat dry. Dredge with flour. Shake off excess flour. Dip eggplant slices one at a time in egg and fry in hot oil on both sides until golden brown. Drain on paper towels. Saute onion and garlic in butter until soft. Add chopped tomatoes, parsley, salt and pepper, cover and simmer for 30 minutes. Place half the eggplant slices in a baking dish in one layer. Cover with half the cheese slices, then cover with half the tomato mixture. Sprinkle with half the grated cheese. Repeat with eggplant slices, cheese slices and tomato mixture. Sprinkle with remaining grated cheese. Top with buttered bread crumbs. Bake in a preheated 375°F (190°C) oven for 30 minutes. Serve immediately. Serves 4-6.

❦❦❦

## BAKED EGGPLANTS WITH FETA CHEESE
### Μελιτζάνες μὲ τυρὶ φέτα στὸ φοῦρνο

4 pounds eggplants
Salt
Oil for frying
1 can (28-ounces) whole tomatoes, finely chopped
1 large clove garlic, crushed
½ green bell pepper finely chopped
Pepper to your taste
2 tablespoons olive oil
1 pound feta cheese, crumbled

Remove stems of the eggplants and wash well. Peel and cut crosswise into ⅓-inch slices. Sprinkle with salt. Set aside for 30 minutes. Rinse and drain. squeeze out excess moisture and pat dry. Fry in hot oil on both sides until golden brown. Drain on paper towels. In a small saucepan combine chopped tomatos and liquid, garlic, green pepper, pepper and oil. Bring to a boil, reduce heat and simmer for 30 minutes. Place eggplant slices in a 9x13x3-inch baking dish in layers. Cover with tomato sauce. Sprinkle with feta cheese. Press cheese with a spoon into the sauce. Bake in a preheated 375°F (190°C) oven for 30 minutes. Serve hot. Serves 4-6.

# BAKED IMAN BAILDI EGGPLANT A
Μελιτζάνες ἱμὰμ μπαΐλντὶ στὸ φοῦρνο

**10 narrow eggplants, 5-inches long (Chinese or Italian)**
**Salt**
**Olive oil for frying**
**3 large onions, thinly sliced**
**½ cup or more olive oil**
**4 cloves garlic, thinly sliced**
**4 large ripe tomatoes, peeled, seeded and chopped or 1 can (20-ounces) whole tomatoes chopped**
**½ cup chopped parsley**
**Salt and pepper to taste**

Remove stems, wash well and dry eggplants. Make a deep slit from one end to the other lengthwise. Sprinkle the slit with salt. Let stand for 30 minutes. Rinse and drain. Saute eggplants in oil on medium heat on all sides covered, until soft. Place in a baking dish slit-side-up. Set aside. Saute onion with oil until soft. Add garlic, tomatoes, parsley, salt and pepper, cover and cook for 20 minutes. Fill the mixture into the slits in each eggplant. Spoon the rest on top. Cover and bake in a preheated 350°F (180°C) oven for 30-45 minutes. Serve hot or cold. Serves 5-6.

⚜⚜⚜

# BAKED IMAN BAILDI EGGPLANTS B
Μελιτζάνες ἱμὰμ μπαΐλντὶ στὸ φοῦρνο

**4 large round eggplants, about 5-6 pounds**
**3 large onions, thinly sliced**
**1 cup or more olive oil**
**5 large ripe tomatoes, peeled, seeded and chopped or 1 can (29-ounces) whole tomatoes, chopped**
**4 cloves garlic or less, thinly sliced**
**½ cup chopped parsley or less**
**Salt and pepper to taste**

Remove stems of the eggplants and wash well. Cut crosswise into ½-inch slices. Sprinkle with salt. Set aside for 30 minutes. Rinse and drain. Squeeze out excess moisture. Combine all the ingredients together and mix well. In a deep greased casserole place one layer (one third) of the sliced eggplants. Cover with (one third) of the onion-tomato mixture. Repeat with eggplants, onion-tomato mixture. Cover and bake in a preheated 350°F (180°C) oven for 90 minutes. Serve hot or cold. Serve with feta cheese and fresh bread. Serves4-8.

# BREADED EGGPLANTS
Μελιτζάνες πανὲ

**3 eggplants (round), about 3 pounds**
**1 cup flour**
**2 eggs, beaten with 2 tablespoons cold water**
**1½ cups dried bread crumbs (see index)**
**⅓ cup grated Parmesan or Romano cheese**
**Salt**
**Oil or clarified butter or margarine (see index) for frying**

Remove stems of the eggplants and wash well. Peel and cut crosswise into ⅓-inch slices. Sprinkle with salt. Set aside for 30 minutes. Rinse and drain. Squeeze out excess moisture and pat dry. Combine bread crumbs and cheese, mix well. Dredge eggplant slices with flour, shake off excess. Dip one at a time in egg and then into bread mixture until completely covered. Fry in hot oil if desired, on both sides until golden brown. Drain on paper towels. Serve hot with Garlic Sauce or Cucumber and Yogurt Dip if desired (see index). Serves 4- 8.

⚜⚜⚜

# FRIED EGGPLANTS
Μελιτζάνες τηγανιτὲς

**3 pounds round eggplants**
**Salt**
**1½ cups flour**
**Olive or salad oil for frying**

Remove stems of the eggplants and wash well. Cut crosswise into ⅓-inch slices. Sprinkle with salt. Set aside for 30 minutes. Rinse and drain. Squeeze out excess moisture and pat dry. Dredge eggplant slices with flour. Shake off excess flour. Dip slices one at a time in cold water. Fry in hot oil on both sides until golden brown. Drain on paper towels. Serve hot or cold with Garlic Sauce or Cucumber and Yogurt Dip if desired (see index). Serves 6.

⚜⚜⚜

# EGGPLANT "LITTLE SHOES"
Μελιτζάνες παπουτσάκια

**12 narrow eggplants 4-5 inches long (Chinese or Italian**
**Salt**
**Olive oil for frying**
**1 tablespoon butter, margarine or olive oil**
**1½ pounds lean ground beef**
**½ pound lean ground lamb**
**1 cup minced onion**
**½ cup dry white wine**

79

1 can (16-ounces) whole tomatoes, pressed through
    a food mill
1 tablespoon minced parsley
Salt and pepper to taste
2 beaten eggs
2 tablespoons grated Parmesan or Romano cheese
1½ cups medium white sauce (see index)
1 egg plus 1 egg yolk, beaten
½ cup grated Parmesan or Romano cheese

Remove stems of the eggplants and rinse well. Make a deep slit from one end to the other lengthwise. Sprinkle the slit with salt and leave for 30 minutes. Rinse and drain. Saute in oil, on medium heat, covered, until soft on all sides. Place eggplants in a baking dish, slit-side up. With 2 spoons push eggplant from the slit out to shape a shoe and make a hollow for the filling. In a saucepan heat butter if desired and saute onion and meat. Add wine and saute few minutes longer. Add tomato, 1 cup water, salt and pepper. Cook slowly 30-45 minutes, or until liquid evaporates. Remove from heat. Add bread crumbs, 3 tablespoons grated cheese, parsley and beaten eggs. Stir well. Stuff eggplants. Prepare white sauce as directed. Spoon little by little of the hot sauce into eggs, stirring constantly. Add egg mixture to the sauce and cook over very low heat for 2-3 minutes, stirring constantly. Place 1 tablespoon sauce on each little shoe to cover the meat. Sprinkle with grated cheese. Bake in a preheated 350°F (180°C) oven for 30 minutes or until golden brown. Serve hot. Serves 6.

# EGGPLANT MOUSAKA
Μελιτζάνες μουσακά

6 pounds round eggplants, about 4 large
Salt
Olive oil for frying
1½ pounds lean ground beef
½ pound lean ground lamb
1 cup minced onion
1 tablespoon butter, margarine or olive oil
½ cup dry white wine
1 can (16-ounces) whole tomatoes, chopped or
    pressed through a food mill
Salt and pepper to taste
1 cinnamon stick ½-inch long
1 tablespoon minced parsley
2 beaten eggs
2 tablespoons dry bread crumbs (see index)
2 tablespoons grated Parmesan or Romano cheese
5 cups medium white sauce (see index)
4 large beaten eggs
¾ cup Parmesan cheese

Remove stems of the eggplants and rinse well. Peel and cut into ½-inch slices, crosswise. Sprinkle with salt and leave for 30 minutes. Rinse and drain. Squeeze out excess moisture and dry on paper towels. Heat ½ cup oil and fry eggplant slices lightly on both sides; add more oil if needed. Lay on absorbent paper to drain. Saute onion and meat in butter if desired. Add wine and saute few minutes longer. Add tomato, ½ cup water, salt and pepper. Cover; cook slowly for 45 minutes. Remove from heat. Add bread crumbs, 3 tablespoons grated cheese, parsley and beaten eggs. Stir well to combine. Let stand. Prepare medium white sauce as directed. Spoon little by little of the hot sauce into eggs, stirring constantly. Add egg mixture to the sauce and cook over very low heat for 2-3 minutes, stirring constantly. Add ½ cup grated cheese and stir well to combine. Place in a 14x12x3 inch greased baking pan, half of the eggplant slices in a layer. Cover with meat mixture; add the remaining eggplant slices. Pour white sauce to cover the eggplants and spread evenly. Sprinkle with remaining grated cheese. Bake in a preheated 350°F (180°C) oven for 45 minutes or until golden. Let stand for 20 minutes to cool before cutting. Cut into squares to serve. Serves 12 as a first course or 6 as a main course.

# EGGPLANT SOUFFLE
Μελιτζάνες σουφλέ

2 eggplants about 2½ pounds or 1 large
1¼ cups cream
1 tablespoon melted butter
1 tablespoon minced onion (optional)
3 large beaten eggs
⅔ cup grated Parmesan cheese
⅔ cup grated Kaseri cheese or Swiss
⅔ cup dried bread crumbs (see index)
1 teaspoon baking powder
Salt and pepper to taste
Pinch nutmeg to taste (optional)

Remove stems of the eggplants and wash well. Puncture with a fork to prevent it from exploding while it bakes. Place in a baking pan and bake for 60 minutes or until soft to the touch. While hot remove skin. Cut into pieces and process in a food processor. In a large bowl combine eggplant puree and the rest of the ingredients except 3 tablespoons of the bread crumbs and mix well. Pour into a greased baking souffle dish and sprinkle with the remaining bread crumbs. Dot with butter and bake in a preheated 350°F (180°C) oven for 60 minutes. Serve at once to prevent falling. Serves 4-6.

80

## MEAT STUFFED GRAPEVINE LEAVES
Ντολμαδάκια αὐγολέμονο

1 jar (16-ounces) grape leaves
1 pound lean ground beef
½ pound lean ground lamb
½ cup converted rice
1 medium finely chopped onion
Salt and pepper to taste
2 tablespoons finely chopped fresh dill or ½
    teaspoon dried
1 tablespoon finely chopped fresh mint or ¼ teaspoon
    dried crushed
¼ cup butter or margarine
2 cups beef stock or water
2 tablespoons corn starch
3 egg yolks
Juice of 1 lemon or more

Rinse grape leaves thoroughly. Plunge grape leaves one by one into boiling water, few at a time and boil for 2 minutes. Rinse and drain. Cut off stems from leaves and reserve. Pick out few hard leaves. Line a Dutch oven with reserved stems and hard leaves. Combine heat, rice, onion, salt, pepper, dill and mint. Mix thoroughly. Place 1 teaspoon filling on underside of each grape leaf. Fold base of leaf over filling, then fold in sides and wrap into a roll. Place rolls in layers close together, seam-side-down. Add butter and juice of half lemon. Place an inverted heavy plate on top of stuffed grape leaves. Add water or stock. Cover, cook slowly for approximately 45-55 minutes, or until grape leaves are tender. Let stand for 15 minutes. Gently remove from pot and arrange into a serving platter. Drain stock from pot, add water to make 2 cups. Transfer stock to a small saucepan, bring to a boil. Mix corn starch with ¼ cup cold water to a paste. Slowly add to the stock, stirring constantly. Cook slowly for 5 minutes. Beat egg yolks with the remaining lemon juice, gradually add some of the boiling stock, stirring vigorously. Add egg mixture to the stock and cook over very low heat for 2-3 minutes, stirring constantly. Do not boil. Spoon sauce over stuffed grape leaves. Serve immediately. Serves 6-10.

## BRAISED LEEKS WITH RICE
Πράσα γιαχνὶ μὲ ρίζι

5 medium leeks
½ cup butter, margarine or olive oil
1 can (8-ounces) whole tomatoes chopped
Salt and pepper to taste
½ cup converted rice
2 cups water

Clean and wash leeks well. Chop 1-inch long and rinse again in a strainer under cold running water. Drain well. Saute leeks with butter if desired until soft. Add chopped tomatoes, salt, pepper and 2 cups water. Bring to a boil, reduce heat and cook slowly for 15 minutes. Rinse rice and add to the leeks, stir, cover and cook slowly until the liquid has been absorbed, about 20 minutes. Serve hot. Serves 4.

## BRAISED LEEKS WITH CRACKED WHEAT
Πράσα γιαχνὶ μὲ μπλουγούρι

Substitute cracked wheat for the rice.
Follow recipe and preparation as directed in Braised Leeks with rice (see index). Bring to a boil, reduce heat and cook gently stirring frequently until the liquid has been absorbed, about 30 minutes. Serve hot. Serves 4.

## BRAISED OKRA
Μπάμιες γιαχνὶ

2 pounds fresh okra or 3 packages frozen
½ cup wine vinegar
1 tablespoon salt
1 large minced onion
¾ cup or less olive oil
3 large ripe tomatoes, peeled, seeded and chopped
    or 1 can (16-ounces) whole tomatoes, chopped
1 tablespoon more or less minced parsley
Salt and pepper to taste

If okra is fresh, wash well and remove the stems very carefully. Place in one layer in a cookie sheet. Sprinkle with vinegar and 1 tablespoon salt, let stand under the sun if possible for 1 hour. Rinse the okra well. Drain. Set aside. Saute onion in oil until onion is soft. Add tomatoes, parsley, salt and pepper. Cover and simmer for 15 minutes. Add okra to the sauce neatly. Cover and simmer for approximately 30-45 minutes depending on size of okra until tender. Do not overcook. Occasionally shake the pot but do not stir. Serve hot or cold. Serves 4-6.

## PEAS WITH MUSHROOMS
᾽Αρακὰ μὲ μανιτάρια

1 bag (20-ounces) frozen peas
1 jar (16-ounces) mushrooms, sliced
½ cup or less olive oil
8 chopped scallions

2 tablespoons fresh dill, minced or ¾ teaspoon dried
Salt and pepper
Juice of half or more lemon

Saute scallions in oil until soft. Add peas, dill, salt, pepper and ½ cup water, stir. Cover and cook slowly for 20 minutes. Add mushrooms with the liquid and lemon juice, cover and cook slowly for 10 minutes or until tender. Serve hot or cold. Serves 6.

## SAUTEED PEAS
'Αρακὰς σωτὲ

1 bag (20-ounces) frozen peas
2 cups water
1 teaspoon salt
½ teaspoon sugar (optional)
⅓ cup or less butter or margarine, melted

Bring water to a boil. Add salt, sugar and peas. Cook for 20 minutes or until tender. Drain. Place in a serving bowl and add melted butter if desired, toss well. Serves 6.

## PEAS WITH TOMATO
'Αρακὰς μὲ ντομάτα

1 bunch scallions chopped
½ cup oil
1 can (8-ounces) whole tomatoes, chopped
1 tablespoon fresh chopped dill or ½ teaspoon dried
1 bag (20-ounces) frozen peas
Salt and pepper to taste
½ cup water

Saute scallions in oil until soft. Add chopped tomatoes, dill, salt, pepper and water. Stir, cover and cook slowly for 15 minutes. Add peas and stir. Cover and cook slowly for 30 minutes or until tender. Serve hot or cold. Serves 4.

## BAKED MEAT STUFFED PEPPERS
Πιπεριὲς γεμιστὲς μὲ κυμὰ

12 medium bell peppers
1 medium onion, minced
1 pound lean ground beef
½ pound lean ground pork
½ cup more or less olive oil
2 cloves garlic, minced (optional)
⅓ cup dry white wine
1 can (29- ounces) whole tomatoes, or 6 medium ripe pressed through a food mill
⅔ cup converted rice

1 tablespoon minced parsley
Salt and pepper to taste

Saute onion and ground meat with 3 tablespoons oil, add garlic if desired and saute few minutes longer. Add wine, 1 cup of the tomato puree, and bring to a boil. Add rice, cook for 5 minutes. Add parsley, salt and pepper. Set aside to cool. Rinse and dry peppers. Cut tops off peppers and reserve; remove inner fibers and seeds, poke in a few places with a fork. Fill peppers with meat mixture and cover them with reserved covers. Place them in a deep baking casserole. Add remaining tomato and the remaining oil. Cover. Bake in a preheated 350°F (180°C) oven for approximately 60 minutes or until peppers are tender. Serve hot. Serves 6.

## BAKED POTATOES
Πατάτες ψητὲς

6 medium smooth potatoes
6 tablespoons or more butter

Scrub and wash potatoes. Poke them in a few places with a fork. Place them on the rack in a preheated 400°F (205°C) oven and bake for 60 minutes, or until tender. When ready, break the skin to keep them from being soggy and serve with butter. Serves 6.

## STUFFED BAKED POTATOES
Γεμιστὲς πατάτες ψητὲς

6 medium smooth potatoes
⅓ cup milk or cream
⅓ cup butter
1 beaten egg
¼ cup grated Parmesan or Romano cheese
Salt and pepper to taste
3 bacon strips, fried and crushed

Scrub and wash potatoes. Place them on the rack in a preheated 400°F (205°C) oven and bake for 60 minutes or until tender. Remove from oven and cut a very thin slice off the top of the potatoes. Scoop out the inside, being careful not to break the shell. Mash very thoroughly, add butter, egg, cheese, salt and pepper. Beat adding milk a little at a time until the potatoes are light, add bacon and mix well. Pile the mixture back into the shells. Do not smooth down the top. Place the stuffed potatoes into a pan stuffed-side-up. Bake in a preheated 400°F (205°C) oven until lightly browned. Serve immediately. Serves 6.

## BOILED POTATOES
### Πατάτες βραστὲς

**6 medium potatoes**
**1 quart boiling water**
**1 teaspoon salt or more**
**Oil-lemon dressing A or B (see index)**

Scrub and wash potatoes. Drop them in boiling water and cook until tender when pierced with a fork. When done, drain. They may be peeled quickly before they cool. Cut into cubes and serve with oil-lemon dressing. Serves 4.

## BRAISED POTATOES
### Πατάτες γιαχνὶ

**12 medium potatoes, peeled and cut into fourths**
**1 large minced onion**
**2 cloves garlic, minced (optional)**
**¾ cup more or less olive oil or butter**
**3 large ripe tomatoes, pressed through a food mill or peeled, seeded and chopped**
**Salt and pepper to taste**
**1½ tablespoons minced parsley**
**3 cups water or fresh stock (beef or chicken)**

Saute onion in oil or butter until soft. Add garlic if desired and saute few minutes longer. Add tomatoes, parsley, salt, potatoes, pepper and water. Cover and bring to a boil; reduce heat and simmer for 60 minutes or until tender. Serve hot. Serves 6.

## FRENCH FRIED POTATOES
### Πατάτες τηγανιτὲς

**4 large potatoes**
**4 cups oil for frying**
**Salt**

Peel and wash potatoes. Cut into ¼-inch slices. Heat oil in a deep pot in high heat. Add potatoes and stir well. Reduce heat to medium-high heat and fry until golden, stirring occasionally. Drain on absorbent paper. Place in a uncovered dish and serve hot. Serves 4-5.
Note: Save oil for next use.

## MASHED POTATOES
### Πατάτες πουρὲ

**6 medium potatoes**

**⅓ cup more or less butter**
**¼ cup hot milk or cream**
**White pepper to taste**

Boil potatoes as directed in Boiling Potatoes (see index). Mash the hot potatoes with the mixer. Add butter and pepper and mix adding hot milk a little at a time until the potatoes are light. Serve hot. Serves 4-6.

## POTATOES AU GRATIN A
### Πατάτες ὁ γκρατὲν

**6 medium potatoes about 3 pounds, peeled and cut into very thin slices or sliced in a food processor**
**8 tablespoons butter or margarine**
**7 tablespoons flour**
**6 cups milk**
**1 cup grated Parmesan or Romano cheese**
**Salt and pepper to taste**

Prepare sauce with butter, flour and milk as directed in Thin White Sauce (see index). Remove from heat. Add cheese and seasoning, stir well to combine. Place in a greased baking-casserole a layer of the potatoes. Spoon a portion of the white sauce over each layer. Repeat and continue until required amount is used. Bake in a preheated 350°F (180°C) oven for approximately 90 minutes or until potatoes are tender when pierced with a fork. Serve hot from the baking casserole. Serves 6-8.

## POTATOES AU GRATIN B
### Πατάτες ὁ γκρατὲν

**4 medium potatoes, about 1½ pounds**
**5 tablespoons butter or margarine**
**5 tablespoons flour**
**3 cups milk**
**½ cup grated Parmesan or Romano cheese**
**Salt and pepper to taste**
**2 beaten eggs**

Peel and wash potatoes. Boil as directed in Boiled Potatoes (see index). Cut potatoes into very small cubes. Let stand. Prepare sauce. Melt butter over medium heat, blend in flour until smooth, using a whisk. Gradually add milk, stirring constantly until mixture is thick and smooth. Cook 3 minutes longer; add seasoning and blend. Remove from heat. Spoon little by little of the hot sauce into eggs, stirring constantly. Add egg mixture to the sauce and cook over very low heat for 2-3 minutes, stirring constantly. Remove from heat. Add ⅓ cup grated cheese and stir well to combine. Combine cubed potatoes and sauce, mix well. Turn into greased baking casserole. Sprinkle with remaining cheese and bake in a preheated 350° F (180°C) oven for 35 minutes. Serve hot. Serves 4-5.

## POTATOES MOUSAKE A
Πατάτες μουσακὰ

10 medium potatoes, about 4 pounds
1½ pounds lean ground beef
½ pound lean ground lamb or pork
1 cup minced onion
3 tablespoons butter or olive oil
½ cup dry white wine
1 can (16-ounces) whole tomatoes chopped or pressed
        through a food mill
Salt and pepper to taste
1 cinnamon stick ½-inch long (optional)
1 tablespoon minced parsley (optional)
5 cups medium white sauce (see index)
4 large beaten eggs
1 cup grated Parmesan or Romano cheese

Saute onion in butter or oil until soft. Add ground meat and brown, breaking up clumps as it browns. Add wine and saute few minutes longer. Add tomato, ½ cup water, salt, pepper, cinnamon and parsley if desired. Stir, cover and cook slowly for 40-45 minutes. Remove from heat. Let stand. While meat sauce simmers, prepare potatoes. Peel and wash them. Cut into slices ½-inch thick. Fry in hot oil until golden. Lay on absorbent paper to drain. Place in a 14x12x3-inch greased baking pan half of the potatoes in a layer. Sprinkle with ¼ cup grated cheese. Cover with meat sauce. Then cover with the remaining fried potatoes. Prepare white sauce as directed. Spoon little by little of the hot sauce into eggs, stirring constantly. Add egg mixture to the sauce and cook over very low heat for 2-3 minutes, stirring constantly. Remove from heat. Add ½ cup grated cheese and stir well to combine. Spoon sauce over potatoes to cover them and spread evenly. Sprinkle with the remaining grated cheese. Bake in a preheated 350°F (180°C) oven for 45 minutes or until golden. Let stand for 20 minutes to cool before cutting. Cut into squares to serve. Serves 6 as a main course or 12 as a first course.

**Variation:**

## POTATOES MOUSAKA B
Πατάτες μουσακὰ

1 recipe for the Potatoes Mousaka A (see index). Follow recipe and preparation for the meat sauce as directed. While meat sauce is simmering prepare potatoes. Peel and wash them. Boil in boiling salted water for 15 minutes. Drain well and slice into ¼-inch slices. Place in a 14x12x3-inch greased baking pan half of the potatoes in a layer. Brush with melted butter and sprinkle with ¼ cup grated cheese. Cover with meat sauce. Then cover with the remaining sliced potatoes, brushing with melted butter. Prepare white sauce as directed, and bake as directed in Potatoes Mousaka A.

## POTATO PATTIES
Πατατοκεφτέδες

4 cups mashed potatoes
⅔ cup grated Parmesan or Romano cheese
1 tablespoon minced parsley
Salt and pepper to taste
2 egg yolks
1 tablespoon dried bread crumbs (see index)
Flour for dredging
Oil for frying

In a mixing bowl combine all the ingredients except flour and oil. Mix thoroughly. Cover and chill for 60 minutes or more. Shape into round patties, rather thick. Roll them in flour, shake off excess flour and flatten them. Fry in hot oil until golden brown on both sides. Serve hot. Serves 6-8.

## POTATO SOUFFLE A
Πατάτες σουφλὲ

5 cups hot mashed potatoes
3 tablespoons butter
¾ cup warm milk
1½ cups grated Kaseri or Swiss cheese
4 egg yolks, beaten until very light
4 egg whites, stiffly beaten
Salt and white pepper to taste

In a large mixing bowl, combine mashed potatoes, butter, milk, cheese, pepper, salt and egg yolks, mix on medium speed for 3 minutes. Fold in the egg whites. Pile the souffle in a well greased souffle dish. Set in a pan containing hot water and bake in a preheated 375°F (190°C) oven for 30 minutes. Serve at once to prevent falling. Serve with roast meat. Serves 6.

## POTATO SOUFFLE B
Πατάτες σουφλὲ

4 tablespoons butter
4 tablespoons flour
1½ cups hot milk

2 cups hot mashed potatoes
½ pound grated sharp cheese or Kaseri
6 egg yolks, beaten until very light
6 egg white, stiffly beaten
Salt and white pepper to taste

Melt butter over medium heat, blend in flour until smooth using a whisk. Gradually add milk, stirring constantly until mixture is thick and smooth. Add seasoning, cheese and mashed potatoes. Heat until cheese is melted. Add beaten egg yolks, mix well. Pour into souffle beaten egg whites and fold well. Bake in a 3-quart baking souffle dish in a preheated 300°F (150°C) oven for 75 minutes. Serve at once to prevent falling. Serves 6.

✻ ✻ ✻ ✻

# SPINACH CHEESE CASSEROLE
## Πατάτες μὲ τυρὶ στὸ φοῦρνο

4 packages (10-ounces) each frozen cut leaf spinach thawed), well drained and chopped or 3 pounds fresh
1 bunch chopped scallions
¼ cup olive oil, butter or margarine
4 large beaten eggs
½ pound feta cheese, crumbled
½ pound ricotta cheese
1 package (7-ounces) farmer's cheese
2 tablespoons minced fresh dill or ½ teaspoon dried
2 tablespoons minced fresh parsley
Salt and pepper to taste

Prepare spinach if it is fresh as directed in Spinach Pitta A (see index). Saute onions in oil if desired until tender but not brown. In a large bowl combine spinach, eggs, cheese, dill, parsley and seasoning, mix thoroughly. Spoon into a well greased casserole and spread evenly. Bake in a preheated 350°F (180°C) oven for 45 minutes covered. Let stand 10 minutes Serve with meat and vegetables. Serves 6-8.

✻ ✻ ✻ ✻

# SPINACH MOUSAKA
## Σπανάκι μουσακὰ

2 pounds fresh spinach or 3 packages (10-ounces) each frozen, cut leaf spinach (thawed), well drained and chopped
2 tablespoons butter or margarine
1 pound lean ground beef
½ cup minced onion
2 tablespoons butter or olive oil
⅓ cup dry white wine
½ cup tomato sauce
Salt and pepper to taste

3 cups medium white sauce (see index)
3 large beaten eggs
½ cup Kefalotyri or Parmesan cheese

Prepare spinach if it is fresh as directed in Spinach Pitta A (see index). Let stand. Saute onion in butter or oil until soft. Add ground meat and brown breaking up clumps as it browns. Add tomato, ½ cup water, salt and pepper, stir, cover and cook slowly for 45 minutes or until all the liquids absorb. Let stand. Prepare white sauce as directed. Spoon little by little of the hot sauce into eggs, stirring constantly. Add egg mixture to the sauce and cook over very low heat for 2-3 minutes stirring constantly. Add ⅓ cup grated cheese and stir well. Melt butter and saute spinach. Place spinach in a 12x11x3-inch greased baking dish. Cover with meat sauce. Spoon white sauce to cover the meat and spread evenly. Sprinkle with the remaining grated cheese. Bake in a preheated 350°F (180°C) oven for 45 minutes. Let stand for 15 minutes to cool. Cut into squares to serve. Serves 4-6 as a main course or 8-10 as a first course.

✻ ✻ ✻ ✻

# SPINACH WITH RICE
## Σπανακόριζο

1 pound fresh spinach or 3 packages (10-ounces) each frozen cut leaf spinach (thawed), well drained and chopped
½ cup more or less olive oil
1 bunch scallions, chopped
2 tablespoons fresh chopped dill or ½ teaspoon dried
Salt and pepper to taste
¼ cup tomato sauce
1½ cups boiling water
½ cup converted rice
Juice of ½ or more lemon

Prepare spinach if it is fresh as directed in Spinach Pitta A (see index). Saute scallions in oil until soft. Add spinach, stir well and saute few minutes longer. Add water, tomato, dill, salt and pepper. Cover and cook slowly for 15 minutes. Pick over rice and rinse well. Sprinkle rice on top of spinach and push it down with a spoon until it is covered with the liquid, do not stir. Cover and simmer for 20 minutes. Remove from heat, add lemon juice, stir well to combine and serve. Serve with feta cheese and fresh bread or with meat if desired. Serves 4-6.

✻ ✻ ✻ ✻

# SAUTEED SPINACH
## Σπανάκι σωτὲ

2 pounds fresh spinach or 3 packages (10-ounces

each) frozen cut leaf spinach (thawed), well
drained and chopped
½ cup finely chopped onion
⅓ cup more or less butter, margarine or olive oil
1 tablespoon fresh chopped dill or ⅓ teaspoon dried
Salt and pepper to taste
Juice of ½ lemon

Prepare spinach if it is fresh as directed in Spinach
Pitta A (see index). Saute onion in butter or oil until
tender. Add spinach, stir well and saute few minutes
longer. Add ½ cup boiling water, dill, salt and
pepper. Cover and cook slowly for 20 minutes or until
tender. Remove from heat, add lemon juice, stir to
combine and serve with steaks, roast beef, chicken,
veal or pork. Serves 4-6.

## SPINACH SOUFFLE
### Σπανάκι σουφλὲ

2 pounds fresh spinach or 3 packages (10-ounces
each) frozen cut leaf spinach (thawed), well
drained and chopped
¼ cup finely chopped onion
2 tablespoons butter or margarine
2 cups Thick White Sauce (see index)
6 egg yolks, beaten until very light
6 egg whites, stiffly beaten
Salt and pepper to taste
¾ cup grated Kaseri, Kefalotyri or Parmesan cheese

Prepare spinach if it is fresh as directed in Spinach
Pitta (see index). Saute onion in butter if desired until
soft. Let stand. Prepare thick white sauce as directed.
When sauce is cool add beaten egg yolks and stir.
Add spinach, cheese and onion to the sauce, stir well
to combine. Add egg whites and fold. Spoon souffle
into ungreased souffle dish and bake in a preheated
325°F (165°C) oven for 60 minutes. Serve at once to
prevent falling. Serves 8.

## MEAT STUFFED TOMATOES
### Ντομάτες γεμιστὲς μὲ κυμὰ

12-14 medium round red tomatoes
1 pound lean ground beef
½ pound lean ground pork or lamb
½ cup or more olive oil
½ cup finely chopped onion
⅔ cup converted rice
½ cup dry white wine
Salt and pepper to taste
Some sugar (optional)
6 medium potatoes, peeled and cut into fourths

½ cup fine dried bread crumbs (see index)

Wash and dry tomatoes. Cut off the tops of the
tomatoes and reserve. Scoop out pulp and sprinkle
cavities with a little sugar if desired. Set aside. Press
pulp through a food mill and reserve. Heat 2 tablespoons oil and saute onion and meat, breaking up
clumps as it browns. Add wine, rice, salt, pepper
and saute few minutes longer. Add ½ cup pureed
tomato pulp, cover and cook slowly for 5 minutes.
Fill tomatoes with meat mixture, cover them with
reserved covers and place in a deep baking dish.
Season potatoes with salt and pepper. Arrange potatoes between the tomatoes. Spoon remaining oil over
tomatoes and sprinkle with bread crumbs. Add 1½
cups from the pureed tomato pulp and 1 teaspoon
sugar if desired. Bake in a preheated 375°F (190°C)
oven for 1½ hours. Serve hot. Serves 6.

## RICE STUFFED TOMATOES
### Ντομάτες γεμιστὲς μὲ ρίζι

12 medium round tomatoes
Some sugar (optional)
1 cup minced onion
3 cloves garlic, minced
1 cup or more olive oil
1 cup rice
1 small zucchini, grated
1 very small eggplant, grated
2 tablespoons minced parsley
1 tablespoon fresh minced mint
6 medium potatoes, peeled and cut into fourths
½ cup fine dried bread crumbs (see index)
Salt and pepper to taste

Wash and dry tomatoes. Cut off the tops of the
tomatoes and reserve. Scoop out pulp and sprinkle
cavity with a little sugar if desired. Set aside. Chop
the large pulp pieces, the rest of the tomato press
through a food mill and reserve. Saute onion with
½ cup oil until soft. Add garlic and saute few
minutes longer. Add grated zucchini, grated eggplant,
tomato, salt and pepper, stir and cook slowly for 5
minutes. Add 1 cup boiling water, rice and stir, cover
and cook slowly for 5 minutes. Remove from heat,
add parsley and mint. Fill tomatoes with rice mixture,
cover them with reserved covers and place them in a
deep baking pan. Season potatoes with salt and pepper. Arrange potatoes between the tomatoes. Spoon
remaining oil over tomatoes and sprinkle with bread
crumbs. Pour reserved pureed tomato and 1 teaspoon
sugar if desired. Bake in a preheated 375°F (190°C)
oven for 1½ hours. Serve hot or cold. Serves 6.

## STUFFED TOMATOES WITH RICE SALAD
Ντομάτες γεμιστὲς μὲ ρίζι σαλάτα

**12 medium red round tomatoes**
**1 recipe Rice Salad (see index)**

Wash and dry tomatoes. Cut off the bottom of the tomatoes and discard. Scoop out pulp and save for other use. Turn up-side-down to drain. Follow recipe and preparation as directed in Rice Salad. Fill tomatoes with rice salad mixture. Sprinkle with grated Parmesan cheese and bake in a preheated 450°F (230°C) oven for 15 minutes. Serve immediately. Serves 6-12.

## MEAT STUFFED VEGETABLES
Λαχανικὰ γεμιστὰ μὲ κυμὰ

**3 small eggplants (4-inches long)**
**6 medium red round tomatoes**
**3 medium green bell peppers**
**3 zucchini (5-inches long and 2-inches thick)**
**Sugar (optional)**
**½ cup olive oil**
**1 cup finely chopped onion**
**1½ pounds lean ground beef**
**½ pound lean ground lamb or pork**
**¾ cup converted rice**
**Salt and pepper to taste**
**½ cup dry white wine (optional)**
**½ cup fine dried bread crumbs (see index)**
**6 medium potatoes, peeled and cut into fourths**

Wash and dry vegetables. Slice off the tops of the eggplants. Scoop out the inside to within ½-inch of skin, poke a few places with a fork. Sprinkle cavities with salt and set aside. Slice tops from tomatoes and reserve; scoop out pulp and sprinkle cavities with a little sugar if desired. Set aside. Press pulp through a food mill and reserve. Cut tops off peppers and reserve; remove inner fibers and seeds, poke in a few places with a fork. Scrape some of the zucchini skin off with an apple corer, scoop pulp off and sprinkle a little salt, set aside. Heat 3 tablespoons oil and saute onion and meat, breaking up clumps as it browns. Add rice, salt and pepper, saute few minutes longer. Add wine if desired and 1 cup pureed tomato pulp. Cover and cook slowly for 5 minutes. Fill vegetables with meat mixture, cover them with reserved covers and place in a deep baking pan. Season potatoes with salt and pepper; arrange between the vegetables. Spoon remaining oil over vegetables. Sprinkle tomatoes with bread crumbs. Pour remaining pureed tomato pulp and 1 cup water into the pan and a little sugar if desired. Bake in a preheated 375°F (190°C) oven for 1½ hours or until vegetables are tender. Serve hot. Serves 6-8.

## RICE STUFFED VEGETABLES
Λαχανικὰ γεμιστὰ μὲ ρίζι

**6 medium red round tomatoes**
**Sugar (optional)**
**3 medium green bell peppers**
**3 zucchini (4-inches long and 2-inches thick)**
**1 cup minced onion**
**3 cloves garlic, minced**
**1 very small eggplant, peeled and grated**
**1 cup or more olive oil**
**2 large red ripe tomatoes, chopped**
**1¼ cups converted rice**
**2 tablespoons minced parsley**
**1 tablespoon minced mint**
**6 medium potatoes, peeled and cut into fourths**
**¼ cup fine dried bread crumbs (see index)**

Wash and dry tomatoes, cut off the tops of the tomatoes and reserve. Scoop out pulp and sprinkle cavities with a little sugar if desired. Set aside. Chop the large pulp pieces and the rest of the tomato, press through a food mill and reserve. Rinse and dry the peppers. Cut tops off peppers and reserve; remove inner fibers and seeds, poke in a few places with a fork. Set aside. Trim ends from zucchini and wash. With an apple corer, scoop pulp from zucchini, chop and reserve. Saute onion with ⅔ cup olive oil until soft, add garlic and saute a few minutes longer. Add chopped zucchini, pulp, grated eggplant, tomato, salt and pepper, stir and cook slowly for 5 minutes. Add 1 cup boiling water, rice and stir, cover and cook slowly for 2 minutes. Remove from heat, add parsley and mint. Fill vegetables with rice mixture, cover them with reserved covers and place in a deep baking pan. Season potatoes with salt and pepper. Arrange potatoes between the vegetables. Spoon remaining oil over tomatoes and sprinkle with bread crumbs. Pour reserved pureed tomato, 1 teaspoon sugar if desired and 1 cup water. Bake in a preheated 400°F (205°C) oven for 1½ hours or until vegetables are tender. Serve hot or cold. Serves 6-8.

## ZUCCHINI AU GRATIN
Κολοκυθάκια ὀ γκρατὲν

**3 pounds small zucchini**
**1 cup minced onion**
**½ cup butter or margarine**
**2½ cups soft bread crumbs (see index)**

3 beaten eggs
Salt and pepper to taste
1 tablespoon minced parsley
1 tablespoon minced fresh dill
1½ cups Kefalotyri, Parmesan or Romano cheese, grated
3 cups medium white sauce (see index)
3 beaten eggs

Trim ends from zucchini and wash them well. Boil in boiling salted water for 10 minutes. Drain well and slice into ¼-inch slices lengthwise. Lay them on paper towels to absorb excess moisture. Saute onion in butter until it is soft. Add bread crumbs, salt, pepper, parsley and dill. Saute for 2 minutes longer. Remove from heat. Add half of the cheese and 2 eggs, mix well to combine. In a well greased baking dish, place a layer of half of the sliced zucchini, cover with the onion-bread mixture. Finish with zucchini. Prepare white sauce as directed. Spoon little by little of the hot sauce into eggs stirring constantly. Add egg mixture to the sauce and cook over very low heat for 2 minutes, stirring constantly. Remove from heat. Add ½ cup from the remaining cheese and stir well. Spoon white sauce over zucchini and spread evenly to cover. Sprinkle with the remaining grated cheese. Bake in a preheated 350°F (180°C) oven for 45 minutes or until golden. Serve hot. Serves 6-8.

## BAKED ZUCCHINI WITH TOMATO SAUCE
Κολοκυθάκια μὲ ντομάτα φούρνου

4 pounds small zucchini, cut into thin slices
1 medium minced onion
½ cup more or less butter or olive oil
1 can (16-ounces) whole tomatoes finely chopped
Salt and pepper to taste
2 tablespoons chopped parsley
1 cup grated Kefalotyri, Parmesan or Romano cheese

Saute onion in butter if desired until soft. Add tomato, salt, pepper and ½ cup water. Cover and cook slowly for 10 minutes. In a well greased baking dish place half of the sliced zucchini in a layer. Cover with half of the tomato sauce and sprinkle with half of the grated cheese. Then cover with the remaining sliced zucchini, then tomato sauce and sprinkle with the grated cheese. Add bits of butter, cover and bake in a preheated 350°F (180°C) oven for 60 minutes, uncover and bake 30 minutes longer. Serves 6.

## FRIED ZUCCHINI
Κολοκυθάκια τηγανιτὰ

2 pounds medium zucchini
1½ cups flour
Olive or salad oil for frying
Garlic Sauce A or B (see index) or
Cucumber and Yogurt Dip (see index)

Trim ends from zucchini and wash well. Cut into ¼-inch slices. Sprinkle with salt. Dredge zucchini slices with flour. Shake off excess flour. Fry in hot oil on both sides, until golden brown. Drain on paper towels. Serve hot with garlic sauce or cucumber and yogurt dip if desired. Serves 4.

## ZUCCHINI PATTIES
Κολοκυθοκεφτέδες

3 pounds medium zucchini
½ cup boiling water
½ cup minced onion
¼ cup butter or margarine
3 beaten eggs
1½ cups grated Kefalotyri or Parmesan cheese
1 cup dried bread crumbs (see index)
Pepper to taste
2 tablespoons minced parsley
2 cups flour for dredging
Olive or salad oil for frying

Trim ends from zucchini and wash well. Cut into 1-inch cubes. Place zucchini cubes and ½ cup boiling water in a pot and cook slowly until tender, or if you have a steamer, steam until tender. Drain in a strainer very well and press to remove excess liquid. Saute onion in butter if desired until soft. Combine zucchini, onion,, eggs, cheese, bread crumbs, pepper and parsley, mix thoroughly. Add salt if needed. Cover and chill for 1 hour. Shape in round patties rather thick and dredge in flour. Pat to remove excess flour. Heat oil and fry zucchini patties until golden on both sides. Serve hot. Serves 8-10.

## ZUCCHINI "LITTLE SHOES"
Κολοκυθάκια «παπουτσάκια»

1 pound lean ground beef
¼ cup minced onion
¼ cup butter or margarine
3 tablespoons dry white wine
⅓ cup tomato sauce
Salt and pepper to taste
1 tablespoon parsley, chopped

1 tablespoon dried bread crumbs (see index)
1 large beaten egg
1 cup medium white sauce (see index)
1 large beaten egg
½ cup grated Kefalotyri or Parmesan cheese
6 medium zucchini (5-inches long)
1 cup fresh beef or chicken stock

Saute onion in butter if desired until soft. Add ground meat and brown, breaking up clumps as it browns. Add wine and saute a few minutes longer. Add tomato, salt, pepper, parsley and ½ cup water, stir. Cover and cook slowly for 45 minutes or until liquid evaporates. Remove from heat. Add 1 tablespoon bread crumbs, 2 tablespoons grated cheese, 1 beaten egg and stir well to combine it. Let stand. While meat sauce is simmering prepare zucchini. Trim ends from zucchini and wash them well. Boil in boiling salted water for 10 minutes. Drain well and cut into half lengthwise. Remove the pulp from the zucchini being careful to keep the little shoe in tact. In a greased baking dish place zucchini, stuff with meat sauce and smooth the surface. Prepare white sauce as directed. Spoon little by little of the hot sauce into egg stirring constantly. Add egg mixture to the sauce and cook over very low heat for 2-3 minutes stirring constantly. Remove from heat. Add 5 tablespoons grated cheese and stir well. Place 1 tablespoon sauce on each little shoe to cover the meat. Sprinkle with grated cheese, add stock to the pan and bake in a preheated 350°F (180°C) oven for 60 minutes. Serve hot. Serves 6 as a main dish or 12 as a side dish.

## MEAT STUFFED ZUCCHINI AVGOLEMONO
Κολοκυθάκια γεμιστὰ αὐγολέμονο

8 medium zucchini (5-inches long)
1 pound lean ground beef
¼ cup minced onion
¼ cup butter or margarine
1 medium ripe tomato, peeled, seeded and finely chopped
1 tablespoon minced parsley (optional)
⅓ cup converted rice
3 tablespoons dry white wine
Salt and pepper to taste
2 cups fresh beef stock or water
½ cup cream
3 tablespoons corn starch
3 egg yolks
Juice of 1 lemon

Trim ends from zucchini, wash them and with an apple corer scoop pulp from zucchini. Saute onion in butter until soft. In a large bowl combine ground meat, onion, chopped tomato, parsley if desired, rice, wine, salt, pepper and mix well. Stuff zucchini shells with meat mixture. Arrange stuffed zucchini in a Dutch oven. Add stock or water, cover and cook slowly for 60 minutes. Remove from heat. Let stand uncovered for 15 minutes. Gently arrange stuffed zucchini on a platter, keep warm. Drain stock from pot. Add water to make 2 cups. Transfer stock to a small saucepan. Bring to a boil. Mix corn starch with the cold cream to a paste. Slowly add to the stock, stirring constantly. Cook slowly for 5 minutes. Beat egg yolks with the lemon juice, gradually add some of the boiling sauce stirring vigorously. Add egg mixture to the sauce and cook over very low heat for 2-3 minutes stirring constantly. Spoon over stuffed zucchini. Serve immediately. Serves 4.

## ZUCCHINI MOUSAKA
Κολοκυθάκια μουσακὰ

4 pounds small zucchini
½ cup dried bread crumbs (see index)
½ cup melted butter, margarine or olive oil
1 cup minced onion
3 tablespoons butter or olive oil
1½ pounds lean ground beef
½ pound lean ground lamb
1 can (16-ounces) whole tomatoes, finely chopped
1 tablespoon finely chopped parsley
Salt and pepper to taste
2 beaten eggs
5 cups medium white sauce (see index)
4 large beaten eggs
1 cup grated Kefalotyri or Parmesan cheese

Trim ends from zucchini and wash them well. Cut into ¼-inch slices. Sprinkle with salt. Saute in hot butter if desired on both sides. Drain on paper towels. Set aside. Saute onion in butter if desired until soft. Add ground meat and brown, breaking up clumps as it browns. Add wine and saute few minutes longer. Add tomato, salt, pepper, parsley and stir, cover and cook slowly for 45min utes or until liquid evaporates. Remove from heat. Add the 2 eggs and stir well. Let stand. Sprinkle bread crumbs in a 14x12x3-inch greased baking dish. Place half of the zucchini in a layer. Sprinkle with 2 tablespoons grated cheese. Cover with meat sauce. Then cover with remaining sliced zucchini. Sprinkle with 2 tablespoons grated cheese. Prepare white sauce as directed. Spoon little by little of the hot sauce into eggs, stirring constantly. Add egg mixture to the sauce and cook over very low heat for 2-3 minutes stirring constantly. Remove from heat. Add ½ cup grated cheese and stir well to combine. Pour sauce over zucchini and spread evenly to cover. Sprinkle with the remaining grated cheese. Bake in a preheated 350°F (180°C) oven for 45 minutes. Let stand for 20 minutes to cool before cutting. Cut into squares to serve. Serves 6 as a main dish or 12 as a side dish.

# CHEESE AND EGGS

## CHEESE BOATS
Πεϊνιρλὶ

1 package active dry yeast
½ cup warm water
1 tablespoon sugar
1 teaspoon salt
2 tablespoons butter or margarine
¾ cup scalding milk
3½ cups all-purpose unbleached flour, sifted (about)
1 pound grated Kaseri cheese or 8 ounces Kaseri and 8 ounces Swiss cheese

Dissolve yeast in ¼ cup warm water. Cover, let stand 5 minutes. Add sugar, salt and butter if desired to milk and cool to warm. Place milk in a mixing bowl, add dissolved yeast and the flour. Beat well to make a soft dough. Turn out dough on floured board and knead until smooth and elastic. Place in greased bowl turning to greased top. Cover, let rise in warm place free from draft until doubled in bulk, about 60 minutes. Punch down dough and knead for a few minutes. Divide dough into four round balls. Cover, let rest for 10 minutes. Roll out each ball into 12x4-inch long and ⅓-inch thick. Sprinkle with ½ cup grated cheese. Bring edges lengthwise of each strip together, enclosing filling; pinch all edges together to seal, except the middle to form a boat. Place in a greased baking sheet. Repeat procedure with the remaining ingredients to make other boats. Cover; let rise in warm place free from draft until doubled in bulk, about 45 minutes. Bake in a preheated 375°F (190°C) oven for 15 minutes or until lightly golden. Serve hot. Serves 6.

## CHEESE SOUFFLE
Σουφλὲ μὲ τυρὶ

2 cups Thick White Sauce (no salt) (see index)

7 large eggs, separated
¼ teaspoon white pepper
2 cups grated Kaseri or any other sharp cheese

Follow recipe and preparation as directed in Thick White Sauce. Add pepper and cheese, heat until cheese is melted. Add beaten egg yolks. Cool. Fold into stiffly beaten egg whites. Pour in an ungreased souffle dish. Bake in a preheated 300°F (150°C) oven for approximately 75 minutes. Serve immediately to prevent falling. Serves 8.

## CHEESE AND SPINACH SOUFFLE
Σουφλὲ μὲ τυρὶ καὶ σπανάκι

2 pounds fresh spinach or 2 packages (10-ounces each) frozen cut leaf spinach (thawed), well drained and chopped
1 tablespoon finely chopped onion
2 cups Thick White Sauce (see index)
6 egg yolks, beaten until very light
6 egg whites, stiffly beaten
Salt and pepper to taste
2 cups grated cheese, preferably Kaseri

Follow recipe and preparation as directed in Thick White Sauce. Add grated cheese, onion, salt and pepper to white sauce and heat until cheese is melted. Prepare spinach if fresh as directed in Spinach Pitta A (see index). Add spinach and stir well to combine. When sauce is cool add egg yolks and mix well, to combine. Fold in stiffly beaten egg whites. Pour souffle into a buttered souffle dish, place in a pan of hot water and bake in a preheated 350°F (180°C) oven for 60 minutes. Serve immediately to prevent falling. Serves 8.

## CHEESE AND HAM TART
Τάρτα μὲ τυρὶ καὶ ζαμπὸν

½ recipe Homemade Pastry A (see index)
4 beaten eggs
4 slices boiled ham, cut into strips
¾ cup shredded Kaseri cheese
¾ cup shredded Swiss cheese
¾ cup cream
¾ cup milk
Salt and pepper to taste

Follow recipe and preparation as directed in Home-made Pastry. Roll out on floured board to desired size. Line the pie pan with the dough. In a bowl combine beaten eggs, ham, cheese, cream, milk and seasonings. Mix well and pour into the pie crust. Bake in a preheated 350°F (180°C) oven for 30 minutes. Serve immediately. Serves 4.

## CHEESE AND SPINACH TART
Τάρτα μὲ τυρὶ καὶ σπανάκι

½ recipe Homemade Pastry A (see index)
2 tablespoons butter or margarine
1 package (10-ounces) frozen cut leaf spinach (thawed), well drained and chopped
⅛ teaspoon dried dill
Pepper to taste
4 beaten eggs
½ cup cream
4 ounces feta cheese, crumbled or farmer's cheese
2 tablespoons grated Parmesan cheese
1 tablespoon minced onion

Follow recipe and preparation as directed in Home-made Pastry. Roll out on floured board to desired size. Line the pie pan with the dough. Heat butter and saute chopped spinach; cover and simmer for 15 minutes. In a bowl combine dill, pepper, eggs, cream, cheese and mix well. Add spinach to the egg mixture, mix well and pour into the pie crust. Bake in a pre-heated 350°F (180°C) oven for 30 minutes. Serve immediately. Serves 4.

## HOW TO BOIL EGGS
Αὐγὰ βραστὰ

**Soft Boiled Eggs:**
Place eggs in a saucepan, add cold water to cover them. Bring water to a boil. Reduce heat and boil for 2 minutes.
**Hard Boiled Eggs:**
Follow preparation as directed in Soft Boiled Eggs, increase cooking time from 2 minutes to 10 minutes or more depending on the size.

## EGG SALAD
Αὐγὰ σαλάτα

4 hard boiled eggs, cut into thin slices
½ cup cooked peas
1 tablespoon minced onion
2 slices boiled ham, cut into cubes
½ cup mayonnaise
¼ teaspoon mustard
Salt and pepper to taste

Combine all ingredients in a large bowl and toss gently. Make a bed of lettuce in a serving platter and place the salad. Serves 4.

## EGGS WITH TOMATOES AND PEPPERS
Αὐγὰ μὲ ντομάτες καὶ πιπεριὲς

1 small finely chopped onion
¼ cup olive oil or butter
4 large ripe tomatoes, peeled, seeded and chopped
1 large green bell pepper, chopped
Salt and pepper to taste
6 large well beaten eggs
3 tablespoons grated Parmesan cheese

Saute onion with oil if desired until soft. Add chopped pepper and saute a few minutes longer.. Add chopped tomatoes, salt and pepper. Simmer for 30 minutes. Add eggs and cheese and cook slowly stirring constantly, until the eggs thicken. Serve immediately. Serves 3.

## EGGS WITH TOMATOES
Αὐγὰ μὲ ντομάτες

1 small finely chopped onion (optional)
¼ cup olive oil or butter
4 large ripe tomatoes, peeled, seeded and chopped
Salt and pepper to taste
6 large beaten eggs
3 tablespoons grated cheese

Saute onion with oil or butter if desired until soft. Add chopped tomatoes, salt and pepper. Simmer for 30 minutes. Add eggs and cheese, cook slowly, stirring constantly until the eggs thicken. Serve immediately. Serves 3.

## CHEESE OMELETTE
'Ομελέττα μὲ τυρὶ

¼ cup butter or margarine
8 large eggs
½ cup grated Kaseri cheese
¼ cup grated Parmesan cheese
½ cup grated Swiss cheese
½ cup cream or milk
Salt and pepper to taste

Beat the eggs fast enough to mix the whites and yolks, add cream, salt, pepper and cheese. Mix well to combine. Heat butter or margarine in a large pan. Pour egg mixture into the pan. Shake the pan so that all the egg mixture spreads out. As the mixture cooks on the bottom and sides, gently lift the edges of the omelette with a flexible spatula so that the egg on top run under the sides. You must work quickly and carefully. Cook ½ minute longer. Gently turn omelette up-side-down and cook for ½ minute longer. Serve immediately. Serves 4.
Note: Individual omelettes may be cooked in a small frying pan.

## CHEESE AND HAM OMELETTE
'Ομελέττα μὲ ζαμπὸν καὶ τυρὶ

2 large eggs
3 tablespoons cream or milk
Pepper to taste
1 tablespoon butter or margarine
1 slice boiled ham, cut into cubes
½ cup grated Kaseri cheese

Beat the eggs just enough to mix the whites and yolks, add cream and pepper. Mix well. Heat butter in a pan. Pour egg mixture into the pan. Shake the pan so that all the egg mixture spreads out. Sprinkle grated cheese and ham over the omelette while it is cooking. As the mixture cooks on the bottom and sides, gently lift the edge of the omelette with a flexible spatula so that the egg on top runs under the sides. You must work quickly and carefully. While the eggs are still soft, but slightly thickened, fold over and cook for 2 minutes. Serve immediately. Serves 1.

## POTATO OMELETTE
'Ομελέττα μὲ πατάτες

1 large potato, french fried (see index)
1 tablespoon butter or margarine
2 large eggs
3 tablespoons cream
3 tablespoons grated Parmesan cheese
Salt and pepper to taste

Follow preparation as directed in French Fried Potatoes. Beat the eggs just enough to mix the whites and yolks, add cream, cheese, salt and pepper. Mix well to combine. Heat butter in a pan. Place french fries into the pan and pour egg mixture on top. Shake the pan so that all the egg mixture spreads out. As the mixture cooks on the bottom and sides, gently lift the edge of the omelette with a flexible spatula so that the egg on top runs under the sides. You must work quickly and carefully. Cook ½ minute longer. Gently turn omelette up-side-down and cook for ½ minute longer. Serve immediately. Serves 1.

## SPINACH OMELETTE
'Ομελέττα μὲ σπανάκι

3 tablespoons butter or margarine
1 package (10-ounces) frozen cut leaf spinach
    (thawed), well drained and chopped
1 teaspoon chopped fresh dill or ⅛ teaspoon dried
Salt and pepper to taste
4 eggs
¼ cup cream
4 ounces feta cheese
2 tablespoons grated Parmesan cheese

Heat 1 tablespoon butter in a pan. Add chopped spinach, salt, pepper and dill, cover and cook slowly until tender, about 15 minutes and absorb all its liquid. Beat eggs just enough to mix the whites and yolks, add cream, salt, pepper, crumbled feta and Parmesan cheese. Mix well to combine. Heat 1 tablespoon butter in a pan. Pour half of the egg mixture into the pan. Shake the pan so that all the egg mixture spreads out. As the mixture cooks on the bottom and sides gently life the edge of the omelette with a flexible spatula, so that the egg on top runs under the sides. You must work quickly and carefully. While the eggs are still soft, but slightly thickened, scatter half of the spinach over the center of the omelette. Fold over. Cook for 2 minutes. Repeat procedure with the remaining ingredients to make the other omelette. Serve immediately. Srves 2.

## ZUCCHINI OMELETTE
'Ομελέττα μὲ κολοκυθάκια

¼ cup butter or margarine
1 pound small zucchini, trimmed and cut into thin
    slices
Salt and pepper to taste
2 teaspoons finely chopped parsley
4 large eggs, well beaten with
¼ cup grated Parmesan cheese and

**3 tablespoons cream**

Saute zucchini slices with butter for a few minutes. Add salt, pepper and parsley, cover and cook slowly until tender and absorb all its liquid. Pour egg mixture on top of the zucchini slices. Shake the pan so that all the egg mixture spreads out. As the mixture cooks on the bottom and sides, gently lift the edge of the omelette with a flexible spatula so that the egg on top runs under the sides. You must work quickly and carefully. Cook ½ minute longer. Gently turn omelette up-side-down and cook for ½ minute longer. Serve immediately. Serves 2.

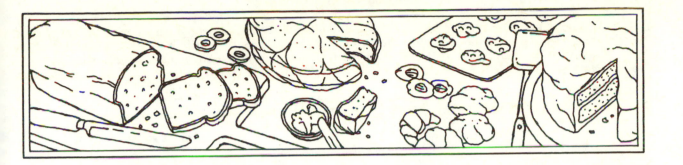

# BREADS, CAKES, COOKIES

## WHITE BREAD A
### Ψωμὶ ἄσπρο

2½  cups warm water
2  packages active dry yeast
1  cup scalding milk
2  tablespoons sugar
¼  cup butter or margarine
4  teaspoons salt
2  tablespoons wine vinegar
12  cups all-purpose or unbleached flour, sifted
1  egg white, beaten with 1 teaspoon water
3  teaspoons sesame seed

Dissolve yeast in ½ cup warm water. Cover, let stand 5 minutes. Add sugar, butter if desired and salt to milk and cool to warm. Place milk in a mixing bowl and dissolve yeast and 4 cups flour. Beat well. Add enough flour to make a soft dough. Turn out dough on floured board and knead until smooth and elastic. Place in greased bowl turning to greased top. Cover; let rise in warm place free from draft until doubled in bulk, about 60-70 minutes. Punch down dough and knead for a few minutes. Divide into three round balls, cover and let rest 10 minutes. Shape into loaves and place in greased 9x5x3-inch bread pans. Cover; let rise in warm place until doubled in bulk, about 45-55 minutes. Brush with egg white and sprinkle with sesame seed. Let stay 5 minutes to allow the egg to dry. Bake in a preheated 350°F 180°C) oven for 30 minutes. Remove from pans immediately and cool on wire racks. Makes 3 loaves.

## WHITE BREAD B
### Ψωμὶ ἄσπρο

1¼  cups warm water
2  packages active dry yeast

2¼  cups scalding milk
4  tablespoons sugar
4  teaspoons salt
½  cup butter or margarine
2  tablespoons wine vinegar
12  cups all-purpose or unbleached flour, sifted
1  egg white, beaten with 1 teaspoon water
3  teaspoons sesame seed

Follow preparation as directed in White Bread A (see index).  Makes 3 loaves.

## RICH WHITE BREAD
### Ψωμὶ ἄσπρο πολυτελείας

½  cup warm water
2  packages active dry yeast
3½  cups scalding milk
½  cup sugar
2  teaspoons salt
¾  cup butter or margarine
¼  teaspoon crushed masticha
12  cups all-purpose or unbleached flour, sifted
1  egg, beaten with 1 teaspoon water
2  tablespoons sesame seed

Follow preparation as directed in White Bread A (see index). Shape as desired. Place in greased pans and let rise until doubled in bulk. Brush with beaten egg. Let stand for 5 minutes to allow the egg to dry. Bake in a preheated 325°F 165°C) oven for approximately 45 minutes. Remove from pans immediately and cool on wire racks. Makes 3 loaves.

Variation:

## WHITE ROLLS
### Ψωμάκια

**1 recipe of Rich White Bread (see index)**

Follow recipe and preparation as directed. Punch down dough. Divide dough into half and shape as Crescent Rolls or Lucky Clovers.

**Crescent Rolls:**

Roll out one half of the dough on a floured surface ¼-inch thick and cut into triangles. Brush with melted butter or margarine. Roll each triangle beginning at the base. Place in greased baking sheets, with point underneath curving ends toward each other. Cover and let rise in warm place until doubled in bulk. Brush with beaten egg and sprinkle with sesame seed if desired. Let stand for 5 minutes to allow the egg to dry. Bake in a preheated 425°F (220°C) oven for 12 minutes or until done. Remove from the baking sheets and cool on wire racks. Makes 30-36.

**Lucky Clovers:**

Divide one half of the dough into 24 equal pieces. Form into balls, place in greased muffin pans. With scissors cut each ball in half, then into quarters, cutting through almost to bottom of rolls. Cover and let rise in warm place until doubled in bulk. Brush with beaten egg and sprinkle with sesame seed if desired. Let stand for 5 minutes to allow the egg to dry. Bake in a preheated 425°F (220°C) oven for 12 minutes or until done. Remove from baking sheets and cool on wire racks. Makes 24.

## WHOLE WHEAT BREAD A
### Ψωμὶ σταρένιο

**2 packages active dry yeast**
**2 cups warm water**
**1½ cups scalding milk**
**¼ cup honey**
**¼ cup oil**
**4 teaspoons salt**
**2 tablespoons wine vinegar**
**6 cups stone ground whole wheat flour, sifted**
**5 cups unbleached flour, sifted**
**1 egg white, beaten with 1 teaspoon water**
**3 teaspoons sesame seed**

Dissolve yeast in ½ cup warm water. Let stand 5 minutes. Cool milk to warm. Place milk, honey, oil, salt, water, vinegar and dissolved yeast in a large mixing bowl. Add the whole wheat flour and beat well. Add enough white flour to make a soft dough. place remaining flour on board, turn out dough and knead until smooth and elastic. Place dough in a greased bowl, turning to grease top. Cover, let rise in warm place, free from draft until doubled in bulk, about 60-70 minutes. Punch down. Divide dough into thirds, round into balls. Cover and let rest 10 minutes.

Shape into loaves and place in greased 9x5x3-inch bread pans, cover; let rise in warm place until doubled in bulk, about 50-60 minutes. Brush with egg and sprinkle with sesame seed. Let stay 5 minutes to allow egg to dry. Bake in a preheated 350°F (180°C) oven for 30 minutes. Remove from pans immediately and cool on wire racks. Makes 3 loaves.

## WHOLE WHEAT BREAD B
### Ψωμὶ σταρένιο

**2 packages active dry yeast**
**2¼ cups warm water**
**1½ cups scalding milk**
**¼ cup honey**
**¼ cup oil**
**4 teaspoons salt**
**2 tablespoons wine vinegar**
**6 cups stone ground whole wheat flour, sifted**
**2 cups rolled oats**
**3-4 cups unbleached flour, sifted**
**1 egg white, beaten with 1 teaspoon water**
**3 teaspoons sesame seed**

Follow preparation as directed in Whole Wheat Bread A (see index). Makes 3 loaves.

## DRIED BREAD CRUMBS
### Φρυγανιὰ ἀλεσμένη

**1 loaf sliced white bread or homemade**

Place bread slices into a baking sheet. Toast in a preheated 325°F (165°C) oven until slightly golden. Turn the other side and toast again. Remove from oven and cool completely. Cut into small pieces and grind in blender until very fine. Store in a jar.

## SOFT BREAD CRUMBS
### Ψωμὶ ἀλεσμένο

Use one day-old firm white Italian bread. Remove the crust. Tear into chunks. Put the bread in the food processor or blender and make bread crumbs.

**Variation:**

## FLAT BREAD
### Λαγάνα

**1 recipe of White Bread A or B (see index)**

Follow recipe and preparation as directed in White Bread. Punch down dough and knead for few minutes. Divide into four or five round balls, cover and let rest for 10 minutes. Using a rolling pin, roll out one at a time on a floured board into an oval shape ½-inch thick. Place on greased baking sheets. Brush with egg white and generously sprinkle with seseame seed and press with the rolling pin to adhere. Then with fingertips poke dough starting from the top to the bottom. Cover, let rise in warm place until doubled in bulk. Bake in a preheated 400°F (205°C) oven for 15-20 minutes. Tear in pieces by hand and serve hot. Makes 4 laganes.

## PITA BREAD
Πίττα γιὰ σουβλάκια

2 packages active dry yeast
4 cups warm water
¼ cup olive oil
1 tablespoon wine vinegar
13 cups unbleached flour (about) sifted
4 teaspoons salt

In a bowl dissolve the yeast in the warm water. Add oil and vinegar into yeast mixture. Stir together flour and salt. Add 4 cups flour and beat well. Add enough flour to make a soft dough. Turn out dough on floured board and knead until smooth and elastic. Place in greased bowl turning to grease top. Cover, let rise in warm place free from draft until doubled in bulk, about 45 minutes. Punch down dough and knead for a few minutes. Divide dough into 24 pieces. With hands work pieces into very smooth balls. Place on a floured surface; cover and let rest 20 minutes. Using a rolling pin, roll out one at a time on a generously floured surface into a disk 8-inches in diameter. Place rounds on an ungreased baking sheet. Bake in a preheated 450°F (230°C) oven for 4 minutes or until dough is puffed and set. Turn pita rounds over with a spatula; bake about 3 minutes longer. Repeat with remaining dough, baking one batch before rolling and baking the next. Cool on wire racks. Store tightly wrapped in plastic bags in refrigerator for 15 days or you can freeze. Makes 24 pitas.

Note: Pita bread makes delicious pizza too. Before baking the pita, spread some pizza sauce (see index) and sprinkle with cheese. Bake in a preheated 400°F (205°C) oven for 10-15 minutes. Serve hot.

## BREAD FOR ARTOCLASIA A
Ψωμὶ ἀρτοκλασίας

5 packages active dry yeast
2½ cups warm water
3 cups scalding milk
1⅓ cups butter or margarine
1⅓ cups sugar
½ teaspoon crushed masticha or anise seed
20-22 cups unbleached flour, sifted
religious seal (sfragetha)

Dissolve yeast in warm water. Cover; let stand 5 minutes. Add sugar, butter if desired to milk and cool to warm. Place milk, dissolved yeast and 4 cups flour into a large mixing bowl. Beat well. Add enough flour to make a soft dough. Turn out dough on floured board and knead until smooth and elastic. Place in greased bowl, turning to grease top. Cover, let rise in warm place free from draft until doubled in bulk, about 75-90 minutes. Punch down dough and knead for a few minutes. Divide dough into five round balls, cover and let rest 10 minutes. Shape into round loaves and place in greased round pans. Make an impression with the seal (sfragetha). Cover, let rise in warm place until doubled in bulk, about 50-60 minutes. Brush with melted butter. Bake in a preheated 325°F (165°C) oven for approximately 45 minutes or until done. Remove from pans and cool on wire racks. When they are completely cold brush with rose water and sift on generously confectioners sugar. Makes 5 artous.

## BREAD FOR ARTOCLASIA B
Ψωμὶ ἀρτοκλασίας

4 packages active dry yeast
5 cups warm water
¾ cup oil
1 cup sugar
4 teaspoons salt
½ teaspoon crushed masticha or anise seed
20-22 cups unbleached flour, sifted
religious seal (sfragetha)

Follow preparation as directed in Bread for Artoclasia A (see index). Bake in a preheated 325°F (165°C) oven for approximately 45 minutes or until done. Remove from pans and cool on wire racks. When they are completely cold brush with rose water and sift on generously confectioner's sugar. Makes 5 artous.

## CHURCH BREAD
Πρόσφορον

1 package active dry yeast
1¾ cups warm water

**2 teaspoons salt**
**6 cups unbleached flour, sifted**
    **religious seal (sfragetha)**

Dissolve yeast in warm water. Cover, let stand 5 minutes. Add salt and 4 cups flour to the yeast. Beat well. Add enough flour to make a soft dough. Turn out dough on floured board and knead until smooth and elastic. Place in greased bowl, turning to greased top. Cover, let rise in warm place free from draft until doubled in bulk, about 60-75 minutes. Punch donw dough and knead for a few minutes. Shape into 1 round loaf. Place in a greased round 9-inch pan. Make an impression with the seal (sfragetha). Cover; let rise in warm place until doubled in bulk, about 45-55 minutes. Bake in a preheated 350°F (180°C) oven for 45 minutes or until done. Remove from pan, cool on wire rack. Makes 1 prosforon.

# WHEAT FOR MEMORIAL SERVICE
Κόλλυβα

**5 pounds whole wheat kernels**
**2 cups toasted sesame seed, crushed**
**2½ cups chopped walnuts**
**3 cups golden raisins**
**2 tablespoons or more cinnamon**
**Pomegranete seeds from 2 poms**
**¼ cup finely chopped parsley**
**2 cups finely ground zwieback**
**5 cups confectioner's sugar, sifted**
**½ cup silver candy balls**
**White candied Jordan almonds**
**Whole blanched almonds**
**1 large silver tray**
**Paper doilies**
**100 -150 small paper bags**

Pick over wheat, three times. Rinse well. Place into a large pot and fill with warm water. Let stand overnight. In the morning drain and fill again with warm water; let stand for 8 hours longer. Drain. Cover with warm water, bring to a boil, reduce heat and simmer for 3-4 hours or until wheat is tender. Add water as needed. Stir often to prevent sticking. Drain. Spread on white cloth towel to absorb excess moisture and cover with another towel. Let stand for few hours or overnight. Combine wheat, sesame seed, walnuts, raisins, cinnamon, pomegranete seeds and parsley and mix well to combine. Line the edges of the tray with paper doilies; let overhand. Gently fill the whole tray with the wheat mixture, shaping it with the palms of your hand into a mound so there will be a rise in the center. Cover wheat with zwieback crumbs, pressing down, using a piece of waxed paper the size of the tray. Sift confectioner's sugar over the crumbs. Gently press down with clean waxed paper the size of the tray to form a smooth compact top. Make a cross in the center of the tray using the silver balls. With the Jordan almonds decorate a border. Decorate the initials of the deceased with the whole almonds. Serves 100-150.

# CHRISTMAS BREAD
Χριστόψωμο

**½ cup warm water**
**2 packages active dry yeast**
**3½ cups scalding milk**
**¾ cup sugar**
**1 teaspoon salt**
**¾ cup butter or margarine**
**¼ teaspoon crushed masticha**
**12 cups all-purpose or unbleached flour (about) sifted**
**1 egg, beaten with 1 teaspoon water**
**2 tablespoons seseame seed**
**10 whole walnuts**

Dissolve yeast in ½ cup warm water. Cover; let stand 5 minutes. Add sugar, butter if desired and salt to milk and cool to warm. Place milk mixture in a large mixing bowl, add dissolved yeast and 4 cups flour. Beat well. Add masticha and enough flour to make a soft dough. Turn out dough on floured board and knead until smooth and elastic. Place in greased bowl turning to greased top. Cover; let rise in warm place free from draft until doubled in bulk, about 60-70 minutes. Punch down dough and knead for a few minutes. Divide into two large pieces and one small the size of an orange, cover, let rest 10 minutes. Shape into rounds and place in greased 10-inch baking round pans. With the small piece shape strips and make a cross on top of each loaf. Press a walnut in the middle of the cross and on each of the ends. Cover, let rise in warm place until doubled in bulk, about 60 minutes. Brush with egg and sprinklle with sesame seed. Let stand 5 minutes to allow the egg to dry. Bake in a preheated 325°F (165°C) oven for approximately 45 minutes. Makes 2 Hristopsoma.

# ATHENIAN RICH EASTER BRAIDS
Ἀθηναϊκὰ τσουρέκια πολυτελείας

**1½ cups scalding milk**
**7 ounces yeast cakes**
**10 eggs, at room temperature**
**3 cups sugar**
**¼ teaspoon salt**
**1½ tablespoons finely ground machlepi**

2 cups melted clarified unsalted butter (see index)
14 cups all-purpose or unbleached flour (about), sifted
1 egg beaten with 1 teaspoon water
½ cup chopped blanched walnuts
6-8 red eggs

Dissolve yeast in warm milk. In a large mixing bowl beat eggs, sugar and salt until eggs are thick and creamy. Add dissolved yeast, ground machlepi and 1 cup of the warm butter, beat with a whisk. Gradually stir in flour until dough is soft and smooth. Add more flour if needed. Add warm butter little by little greasing hands and bowl; knead until all the warm butter is used and dough is smooth. Cover and let rise in warm place free from draft until doubled in bulk, about 3 hours. Punch down dough and knead. Divide dough into 8 parts and round into balls. Cover, let rest 10 minutes. Divide every ball evenly into three parts. Roll each into a rope 20 inches long. Press ends together and braid loosely, press ends together and tuck under loaf. Place in baking pans lined with waxed paper and greased. Press one red egg in one side of each braid. Cover and let rise in warm place until doubled in bulk. Brush with beaten egg and sprinkle with chopped almonds. Let stand 10 minutes to allow the egg to dry. Bake in a preheated 350°F 180°C) oven for 15 minutes. Reduce heat to 325°F and bake for 15 minutes longer. Cover loosely with foil. Let stand 10 minutes. Gently remove from pans and cool on wire racks.

## ATHENIAN EASTER BRAIDS
Ἀθηναϊκὰ τσουρέκια

1 cup scalding milk
4 ounces yeast cakes
8 eggs at room temperature
1¾ cups sugar
¼ teaspoon salt
1 tablespoon finely ground machlepi, ¼ teaspoon crushed masticha or grated rind of one orange
1¼ cups melted clarified unsalted butter (see index)
12 cups all-purpose or unbleached flour (about) sifted
1 egg, beaten with 1 teaspoon water
½ cup chopped or whole blanched almonds
Some red eggs

Dissolve yeast in warm milk. In a large mixing bowl beat eggs, sugar and salt until thick and creamy. Add dissolved yeast, machlepi if desired and half of the butter. Gradually stir in flour until dough is soft and smooth. Add more flour if needed. Add warm butter little by little greasing hands and bowl; knead until all the butter is used and dough is smooth. Cover; let rise in warm place free from draft until

doubled in bulk, about 3 hours. Punch down dough and knead. Divide dough into 5-6 parts and round into balls. Cover, let rest 10 minutes. Divide every ball into three parts. Roll each into a rope 20-inches long. Press ends together and braid loosely by pressing ends together and tuck under loaf. Place in baking pans lined with waxed paper and greased. Press one red egg in one side of each braid. Cover and let rise in warm place until double in bulk. Brush with beaten egg and sprinkle with chopped almonds or arrange the whole almonds. Let stand 10 minutes to allow the egg to dry. Bake in a preheated 350°F (180°C) oven for 15 minutes. Reduce heat to 325°F and bake for 15 minutes longer covered loosely with foil. Let stand 10 minutes. Gently remove from pans and cool on wire racks.

## EASTER BRAIDS A
Τσουρέκια πασχαλινὰ

½ cup warm water
8 ounces yeast cakes
2 cups scalding milk
4½ cups sugar
10 eggs, at room temperature
1½ tablespoons finely ground machlepi
1¾ cups melted clarified unsalted butter (see index)
5 pounds all-purpose or unbleached flour (about) sifted with 4 teaspoons baking powder
1 egg beaten with 1 teaspoon water
½ cup chopped or whole blanched almonds
Some red eggs

Follow preparation as directed in Athenian Easter Braids (see index).

## EASTER BRAIDS B
Τσουρέκια πασχαλινὰ

⅓ cup warm water
8 ounces yeast cakes
1 cup scalding milk
3 cups sugar
¼ teaspoon salt
10 eggs, at room temperature
1 tablespoon finely ground machlepi
1¾ cups melted clarified unsalted butter (see index)
14 cups all-purpose or unbleached flour (about) sifted
1 egg, beaten with 1 teaspoon water
½ cup chopped or whole blanched almonds
Some red eggs

Follow preparation as directed in Athenian Easter Braids (see index).

# EASTER FRUIT NUT BREAD
Τσουρέκια φρούτου

1  cup scalding milk
6  ounces yeast cakes
1½  cups sugar
½  teaspoon salt
9  eggs, at room temperature
Grated rind of one orange and 1 lemon
¼  cup cognac
1½  cups melted clarified unsalted butter (see index)
10  cups all-purpose or unbleached flour (about) sifted
2  cups chopped mixed candied fruits (see index)
½  cup golden seedless raisins
1  cup chopped blanched almonds
1  egg, beaten with 1 teaspoon water
½  cup chopped blanched almonds

Dissolve yeast in warm milk. In a large mixing bowl beat eggs, sugar and salt until eggs are light and creamy. Add dissolved yeast, grated rind and ½ cup of the butter, mix well. Gradually stir in flour until dough is soft and sticky. Add more flour if needed. Add warm butter little by little greasing hands and bowl; knead bread until all the butter is used and dough is smooth. Wash fruits and raisins with cognac, drain well. Sprinkle with little flour, shake excess. Add fruits and almonds to the dough and knead well to combine. Cover, let rise in warm place free from draft until doubled in bulk, about 3 hours. Punch down dough and knead. Divide dough into 6 parts and round into balls. Cover and let rest 10 minutes. Shape into loaves and place in bread pans lined with waxed paper and greased. Cover, let rise in warm place until doubled in bulk. Brush with egg and sprinkle with chopped almonds. Let stand 10 minutes to allow the egg to dry. Bake in a preheated 350° F (180°C) oven for 15 minutes. Reduce heat to 325°F and bake 15 minutes longer. Cover loosely with foil. Let stand 5 minutes. Gently remove from pans and cool on wire racks.

# HOLIDAY BREAD
Τσουρέκια

3  cups scalding milk
6  yeast cakes
3  cups sugar
8  eggs
16  cups all-purpose flour
Grated rind of 2 oranges or 1 tablespoon crushed masticha
2  cups melted unsalted butter
1  egg, beaten with 1 tablespoon water
1  tablespoon sesame seeds (optional)

Dissollve yeast in warm milk, cover; let stand 5 minutes. In a large mixing bowl beat eggs, sugar and masticha if desired until eggs are frothy and sugar has dissolved. Add milk and beat. Gradually stir in flour until dough is soft and sticky. Add the butter little by little greasing hands and bowl and knead until all the butter is used and dough is smooth. Cover, let rise in warm place free from draft until doubled in bulk. Divide dough into four parts and round into balls; cover and let rest 10 minutes. Shape as desired. Place in greased baking pans. Cover, let rise in warm place until doubled in bulk. Brush with beaten eggs and sprinkle with sesame seeds if desired. Let stand 5 minutes to allow the egg to dry. Bake in a preheated 325°F (165°C) oven for approximately 45 minutes. Let stand 5 minutes. Gently remove from pans and cool on wire racks. Makes four Holiday breads.

Recipe from Mrs. John D. Mickles

# NEW YEAR'S BREAD
Βασιλόπιττα

¾  cup warm milk
5  ounces yeast cakes
1¾  cups sugar
½  teaspoon salt
8  eggs at room temperature
Grated rind of one orange or 1 tablespoon finely ground machlepi
1  cup melted clarified unsalted butter (see index)
10  cups unbleached flour (about) sifted
1  egg, beaten with 1 teaspoon water
Whole almonds, blanched

Dissolve yeast in warm milk, cover and let stand 5 minutes. In a large mixing bowl beat eggs, sugar and salt until eggs are frothy. Add dissolved yeast and grated rind if desired, beat with whisk until sugar has dissolved. Gradually stir in flour until dough is soft and sticky. Add warm butter little by little greasing hands and bowl; knead until all the butter is used and dough is smooth. Cover; let rise in warm place free from draft until doubled in bulk, about 4-5 hours. Punch down dough and knead. Divide dough into 3 parts and round into balls. Cover, let rest 10 minutes. Shape into round loaves and place each one into a greased 8-inch round pans lined with waxed paper. Cover; let rise in warm place until doubled in bulk. Brush with beaten egg and decorate with whole almonds in numbers to denote the New Year, pressing lightly. Let stand 5 minutes to allow the egg to dry. Bake in a preheated 325°F (165°C) oven for approximately 45 minutes. Let stand 5 minutes. Gently remove from pans and cool on wire racks. Makes three

Vasilopitas. After baking, a coin is inserted through a slit in the base. Cut and serve the Vasilopita, first to the family starting from the Virgin Mary, the father, the mother, the rest of the family and then the guests. The person who finds the coin will have luck in the New Year.

## RICH NEW YEAR'S BREAD
### Βασιλόπιττα πολυτελείας

1½  cups scalding milk
8  ounces active dry yeast
10  eggs, at room temperature
3  cups sugar
¼  teaspoon salt
1½  tablespoons finely ground machlepi
2  cups melted clarified unsalted butter (see index)
5  pounds unbleached flour, sifted
1  egg, beaten with 1 teaspoon water
Whole blanched almonds

Dissolve yeast in warm milk, cover and let stand 5 minutes. In a large mixing bowl beat eggs, sugar and salt until eggs are thick and creamy. Add dissolved yeast, ground machlepi and ½ cup of warm butter, beat with whisk. Gradually stir in flour until dough is soft and sticky.   Add warm butter, little by little greasing hands and bowl; knead until all the warm butter is used and dough is smooth. Cover and let rise in warm place free from draft until doubled in bulk, about 4-5 hours.  Punch down dough and knead. Divide dough into 5 parts and round into balls. Cover and let rest 10 minutes. Shape into loaves and place each one into a greased 8-inch round pans lined with waxed paper. Cover, let rise in warm place until doubled in bulk. Brush with beaten egg and decorate with whole almonds in numbers to denote the New Year, pressing lightly. Let stand 5 minutes to allow the egg to dry. Bake in a preheated 325°F (165°C) oven for approximately 45 minutes. Let stand 5 minutes. Gently remove from pans and cool on wire racks. Makes five Vasilopitas. After baking, a coin is inserted through a slit in the base. Cut and serve the Vasilopita, first to the family starting from the Virgin Mary, the father, the mother, the rest of the family and the guests. The person who finds the coin will have luck in the New Year.

## HONEY RAISIN BREAD
### Σταφιδόψωμο μελιοῦ

2  cups warm water
3  packages active dry yeast
1  cup fresh orange juice

½  cup oil
½  cup honey
½  cup sugar
½  teaspoon salt
1  teaspoon ground cinnamon
½  teaspoon ground cloves
12  cups unbleached flour, sifted
1½  cups golden seedless raisins
1  egg white, beaten with 1 teaspoon water

Dissolve yeast in warm water. Let stand 5 minutes. In a large mixing bowl combine dissolved yeast, orange juice, oil, honey, sugar, salt, cinnamon and clove, mix well. Add 4 cups flour, beat well. Add enough flour to make a soft dough. Add raisins and mix well. Place remaining flour on board. Turn out dough on floured board and knead until smooth and elastic. Place dough in greased bowl turning to grease top. Cover; let rise in warm place free from draft, until doubled in bulk, about 60 minutes. Punch down dough and knead. Divide dough into three round balls.   Cover and let rest 10 minutes.   Shape into loaves and place in greased 9x5x3-inch bread pans lined with waxed paper. Cover; let rise in warm place until doubled in bulk, about 50-60 minutes. Brush with egg white. Let stand 5 minutes to allow the egg to dry. Bake in a preheated 350°F (180°C) oven for 30 minutes. Gently remove from pans immediately and cool on wire racks. Makes 3 Honey Raisin Breads.

## RICH FRUIT NUT BREAD
### Σταφιδόψωμο πολυτελείας

3  packages active dry yeast
1  cup sugar
6  eggs, at room temperature
1¾  cups melted unsalted butter or margarine
Grated rind of 2 oranges or lemons
12  cups unbleached flour, sifted (about)
1  cup finely chopped blanched almonds
1½  cups chopped mixed candied fruits (see index)
2  cups seedless golden raisins
1  cup finely chopped walnuts
1  egg, beaten with 1 teaspoon water

Add sugar to milk, stir until it dissolves. Let cool to warm. Dissolves yeast in milk. Cover; let stand 5 minutes. Beat eggs well, add milk mixture, butter, orange rind if desired and beat well. Gradually stir in flour until dough is soft and sticky. Add fruits, raisins, almonds and walnuts. Mix well to combine. Turn out dough on floured board and knead until smooth and elastic. Place dough in greased bowl turning to grease top. Cover; let rise in warm place free from draft until doubled in bulk, about 60 minutes. Punch down dough and knead. Divide into four round balls, cover and let rest 10 minutes. Shape into loaves and place in greased 9x5x3-inch bread pans lined with waxed paper. Cover; let rise in warm place until doubled in bulk, about 60 minutes. Brush with egg. Let stand 5 minutes to allow the egg to dry. Bake in a preheated 325°F (165°C) oven for approximately 45 minutes. Gently remove from pans immediately and cool on wire racks. Makes 4 loaves.

✠✠✠✠

# PLAIN RAISIN BREAD
### Σταφιδόψωμο

2 packages active dry yeast
1¼ cups warm water
2 cups scalding milk
½ cup melted butter or margarine
½ teaspoon salt
1 cup sugar
12 cups unbleached flour, sifted
2 cups golden seedless raisins
1 egg white, beaten with 1 teaspoon water

Dissolve yeast in warm water. Cover; let stand 5 minutes. Add butter, salt and sugar to milk and cool to warm. Place milk in a mixing bowl, add dissolved yeast and 4 cups flour. Beat well. Add enough flour to make a soft dough. Add raisins and mix well. Turn out dough on floured board and knead until smooth and elastic. Place in greased bowl turning to grease top. Cover; let rise in warm place free from draft until doubled in bulk, about 60-70 minutes. Punch down dough and knead for a few minutes. Divide into three round balls,, cover and let rest for 10 minutes. Shape into loaves and place in greased 9x5x3-inch bread pans. Cover; let rise in warm place until doubled in bulk, about 45-60 minutes. Brush with egg white, let stay 5 minutes to allow the egg to dry. Bake in a preheated 350°F (180°C) oven for 30 minutes. Remove from pans immediately and cool on wire racks. Makes 3 Plain Raisin Breads.

✠✠✠✠

# RICH RAISIN BREAD
### Σταφιδόψωμο

¼ cup scalding milk
1½ packages active dry yeast
4 eggs, at room temperature
½ cup sugar
Grated rind of 1 orange
5 cups unbleached flour, sifted
⅓ cup melted unsalted butter or margarine
1 cup golden seedless raisins

1 egg white, beaten with 1 teaspoon water

Cool milk to warm. Dissolve yeast in milk, cover; let stand 5 minutes. In a large mixing bowl, beat eggs, sugar and orange rind until sugar has dissolved. Add milk and beat. Gradually stir in flour until dough is soft and sticky. Add raisins and mix well. Add butter little by little greasing hands and bowl and knead until all the butter is used and dough is smooth. Cover; let rise in warm place free from draft until doubled in bulk, about 2 hours. Divide dough into two parts and round into balls. Cover; let rest 10 minutes. Shape into loaves and place each one into a greased pan. Cover; let rise in warm place until doubled in bulk. Brush with beaten egg white. Let stand 5 minutes to allow the egg to dry. Bake in a preheated 325°F (165°C) oven for approximately 45 minutes. Let stand 5 minutes. Gently remove from pans and cool on wire racks. Makes 2 loaves.

✠✠✠✠

# PUMPKIN SPICE BREAD
### Ψωμὶ κολοκύθας

1½ cups scalding milk
2 packages active dry yeast
½ cup orange juice, at room temperature
Grated rind of one orange
1 teaspoon salt
¾ cup honey
½ cup melted butter or margarine
2 cups cooked, pureed pumpkin
11 cups unbleached flour, sifted with
1 teaspoon cinnamon and
1 teaspoon pumpkin pie spice
1 egg white, beaten with 1 teaspoon water
3 teaspoons sesame seeds (optional)

Dissolve yeast in warm milk. Cover, let stand 5 minutes. In a large mixing bowl add dissolved yeast, orange juice, rind, salt, melted butter, pureed pumpkin, honey and 2 cups of the flour; beat well. Add enough flour to make a soft dough. Turn out on floured board and knead until smooth and elastic. Place in greased bowl turning to greased top. Cover, let rise in warm place free from draft until doubled in bulk, about 60-70 minutes. Punch down dough and knead for a few minutes. Shape into loaves and place in greased 9x5x3-inch bread pans. Cover, let rise in warm place until doubled in bulk, about 55 minutes. Brush with egg white and sprinkle with sesame seeds if desired. Let stay 5 minutes to allow the egg to dry. Bake in a preheated 350°F (180°C) oven for 30 minutes. Remove from pans immediately and cool on wire racks. Makes 3 loaves.

# ALMOND CAKE
### Κέϊκ ἀμυγδάλου

¾ cup unsalted butter or margarine, at room
   temperature
1¾ cups sugar
6 eggs, separated
1¾ cups unbleached flour
3 teaspoons baking powder
¼ teaspoon almond extract
1 teaspoon vanilla
1 cup chopped blanched almonds

Cream butter with sugar until light and fluffy. Add
eggs yolks one at a time beating thoroughly after each
one is added. Add vanilla and almond extract. Sift
flour and baking powder together. Gradually add
flour to the butter mixture beating until smooth
after each addition. Add almonds and mix thoroughly.
Fold in stiffly beaten egg whites. Pour into well
greased and floured tube pan. Bake in a preheated
350°F (180°C) oven for approximately 50 minutes or
until cake tester inserted in center comes out clean.
Cool 10 minutes. Remove from pan.

# ALMOND CHOCOLATE CAKE
### Κέϊκ ἀμυγδάλου μὲ σοκολάτα

½ cup cake flour
½ cup cocoa
5 eggs, separated
¾ cup plus 2 tablespoons sugar
2 tablespoons cognac
½ teaspoon vanilla
¼ teaspoon almond extract
6 ounces finely ground blanched almonds
6 tablespoons melted unsalted butter or margarine
2 tablespoons chopped almonds

Sift flour and cocoa together; set aside. Beat egg
yolks with sugar until creamy. Add cognac, vanilla
and almond extract and beat well. Fold in stiffly
beaten egg whites alternately with flour and cocoa
mixture. Add ground almonds and butter, fold well
to combine. Grease a tube pan and sprinkle with
chopped almonds, pour cake mixture into prepared
pan. Bake in a preheated 350°F (180°C) oven for
approximately 45 minutes. Remove from pan and
dust with confectioner's sugar or frosting.

# ALMOND CINNAMON CAKE
### 'Αμυγδαλόπιττα

5 eggs, separated

1½ cups sugar
¼ teaspoon almond extract
2 teaspoons baking powder
10 ounces finely ground almonds
½ cup Grille janet French crisp toast, finely ground
1 teaspoon cinnamon
2 cups heavy cream, whipped

Beat egg yolks with sugar until thick and creamy.
Add almond extract. Mix ground almonds, ground
toast, baking powder and cinnamon together. Gradually add almond mixture to egg mixture and mix well.
Fold in stiffly beaten egg whites. Pour into greased
and floured tube pan, and bake in a preheated 350°F
(180°C) oven for approximately 40 minutes. Cool,
slice and serve with whipping cream.

# ALMOND ORANGE CAKE
### 'Αμυγδαλόπιττα

4 eggs, separated
1½ cups sugar
1 cup finely ground blanched almonds
1 cup finely ground zwieback
¼ cup cognac
¼ teaspoon almond extract
Grated rind of ½ orange or lemon
2 teaspoons baking powder
2 tablespoons chopped blanched almonds
2 cups heavy cream, whipped

Beat egg yolks with sugar until thick and creamy. Add
almond extract. Combine ground walnuts, ground
zwieback and baking powder and mix well. Gradually
add almond mixture alternately with cognac. Add
orange rind if desired and mix well. Fold in stifly
beaten egg whites. Grease a tube pan and sprinkle
with chopped almonds, pour cake mixture into prepared pan. Bake in a preheated 350°F (180°C) oven
for approximately 45 minutes. Remove from pan and
cool in wire rack. Serve with whipped cream.

# ALMOND COGNAC CAKE
### Κέϊκ ἀμυγδάλου μὲ κονιὰκ

6 ounces finely ground blanched almonds
¾ cup plus 2 tablespoons sugar
2 tablespoons cognac
½ teaspoon vanilla
¼ teaspoon almond extract
5 eggs, separated
¾ cup cake flour, sifted
6 tablespoons melted unsalted butter or margarine

2 tablespoons chopped blanched almonds
Confectioner's sugar or frosting

Beat egg yolks with sugar until creamy. Add cognac, vanilla and almond extract and beat well. Fold in stiffly beaten egg whites alternately with flour and ground almonds. Add butter and fold well to combine. Grease a tube pan and sprinkle with chopped almonds. Pour mixture and bake in a preheated 350°F (180°C) oven for approximately 45 minutes. Remove from pan and dust with confectioner's sugar or frosting, or serve with whipped cream if desired.

## ALMOND VANILLA CAKE
Κέϊκ ἀμυγδάλου μὲ βανίλια

1 cup unsalted butter or margarine, at room temperature
2 cups sugar
5 large separated eggs
1 teaspoon vanilla
½ teaspoon almond extract
3½ cups unbleached flour
5 teaspoons baking powder
¾ cup milk
1 cup chopped blanched almonds

Cream butter and sugar until light and fluffy. Add egg yolks one at a time beating thoroughly after each one is added. Add vanilla and almond extract. Sift flour with baking powder together; add alternately with milk to creamed mixture beating until smooth after each addition. Add almonds and fold in stiffly beaten egg whites. Pour into well greased and floured 9-inch tube pan. Bake in a preheated 300°F (150°C) oven for 90 minutes or until cake tester inserted in center comes out clean. Cool 10 minutes. Remove from pan and cool on wire rack.

## ANGEL CAKE
Κέϊκ ἀγγέλων

1 cup unsalted butter or margarine, at room temperature
8 ounces confectioner's sugar, sifted
2½ cups cake flour
3 teaspoons baking powder
1 teaspoon vanilla
Grated rind of 1 orange (optional)
14 egg whites, stiffly beaten with pinch of salt

Cream butter with sugar until light and fluffy. Add vanilla and orange rind if desired. Sift flour with baking powder. Gradually add flour alternately with

beaten egg whites to butter mixture and fold. Pour into greased 9-inch tube pan. Bake in a preheated 350°F (180°C) oven for approximately 45 minutes.

## APPLE CAKE
Κέϊκ μήλου

½ cup butter or margarine, at room temperature (unsalted)
1¼ cups sugar
3 eggs, at room temperature
1 teaspoon vanilla
2 cups unbleached flour
1 teaspoon baking soda
¼ cup milk
4 tablespoons melted unsalted butter or margarine
4 apples, peeled and sliced
¼ cup sugar
1 teaspoon cinnamon
1 cup heavy cream, whipped

Cream butter and sugar until light and fluffy. Add eggs one at a time, beating thoroughly after each one is added. Add vanilla. Sift flour and soda together; add alternately with milk to creamed mixture, beating until smooth after each addition. Grease pan with the melted butter. Mix sugar and cinnamon together. Sprinkle apples well. Arrange apples in the pan; add remaining sugar and cinnamon mixture. Pour batter over apples. Bake in a preheated 350°F (180°C) oven for approximately 50 minutes. Remove from oven and place on wire rack to cool. When cool, remove from pan. Serve with whipped cream.

## APPLESAUCE SPICE CAKE
Κέϊκ μήλου μυρωδᾶτο

½ cup unsalted butter or margarine, at room temperature
2 cups sugar
3 eggs, at room temperature
2 cups unbleached flour
1 teaspoon baking soda
1 teaspoon baking powder
1 teaspoon cinnamon
½ teaspoon nutmeg
¼ teaspoon ground cloves
½ cup quick cooking oats
½ cup water
1½ cups thick unsweetened applesauce
1 cup seedless golden raisins
1 cup chopped walnuts

Cream butter and sugar until light and fluffy. Add

eggs one at a time beating thoroughlly after each one is added. Sift flour, baking powder, baking soda, cinnamon, nutmeg and cloves together. Gradually add flour mixture alternately with applesauce to creamed mixture beating thoroughly after each addition. Add oats and water and mix well. Add raisins and walnuts. Pour into a greased pan 7x10x3-inch. Bake in a preheated 350°F (180°C) oven for approximately 50 minutes. Cool 10 minutes. Remove from pan and dust with confectioner's sugar.

## APPLESAUCE CAKE
### Κέϊκ μήλου

½  cup unsalted butter or margarine, at room
       temperature
1  cup sugar
2  eggs, at room temperature
2  cups cake flour
1  teaspoon baking soda
1  teaspoon cinnamon
¼  teaspoon ground cloves
1  cup chopped walnuts
1  cup seedless golden raisins
1  cup thick unsweetened applesauce

Cream butter and sugar until light and fluffy. Add eggs one at a time beating thoroughly after each one is added. Sift flour, baking soda, cinnamon and cloves together. Gradually add flour mixture alternately with applesauce to creamed mixture, beating thoroughly after each addition. Add chopped walnuts and raisins and mix well. Pour into a greased pan 7x 10x3-inch. Bake in a preheated 350°F (180°C) oven for approximatelly 50 minutes. Cool and dust with confectioner's sugar. Cut when completely cold.

## CARROT WALNUT CAKE
### Κέϊκ καρότου

1⅓  cups oil
2  cups sugar
1  teaspoon vanilla
4  eggs, at room temperature
2  cups unbleached flour
1½  teaspoons baking soda
1  teaspoon baking powder
1½  teaspoons cinnamon
3  cups finely shredded carrots
1½  cups chopped walnuts
Confectioner's sugar for dusting

Blend oil and sugar in a large bowl. Add eggs one at a time beating well after each addition. Sift dry in-gredients together. Gradually add flour to oil mixture beating until smooth after each addition. Add shredded carrots and chopped walnuts and stir well to combine. Pour into greased tube pan. Bake in a preheated 325°F (165°C) oven for approximately 45 minutes. Cool 10 minutes. Remove from pan and dust with confectioner's sugar.

## CHEESE CAKE
### Κέϊκ τυριοῦ

6  eggs, separated
18  ounces cream cheese
1  cup sugar
1½  cups sour cream
3  tablespoons flour
2  tablespoons fresh lemon juice
1  teaspoon vanilla
½  cup or more apricot jam (see index)

Mix cream cheese and sugar until creamy. Add sour cream and blend well until light. Beat egg yolks until cream color; add to the cheese mixture and mix well. Add flour, lemon juice, vanilla and fold in stiffly beaten egg whites. Pour into 10-inch spring form and line bottoms with graham crackers. Bake in a pre-heated 325°F (165°C) oven for 60 minutes. Turn off heat, open oven door, let stand in oven for 60 minutes or longer. Remove from oven. Boil jam with 3 table-spoons water for 2 minutes on low heat. Pour over cheese cake.

## CHOCOLATE CAKE
### Κέϊκ σοκολάτας

½  cup unsalted butter or margarine, at room
       temperature
1½  cups sugar
3  eggs
1  teaspoon vanilla
1¾  cups unbleached flour
½  cup cocoa
¾  teaspoon baking soda
1½  teaspoons baking powder
2  tablespoons brandy
¾  cup milk

Cream butter and sugar until light and fluffy. Add eggs one at a time beating thoroughly after each one is added. Sift flour, baking soda, baking powder and cocoa together; add alternately with milk to creamed mixture beating until smooth after each addition. Add brandy, mix well. Pour into 2 well greased and floured baking pans. Bake in a preheated 350°F (180°C) oven for 45-55 minutes or until cake tester inserted in center comes out clean. Cool 10 minutes. Remove from pans. When they are cold cut each cake in half. Spread chocolate frosting (see index) to your desire between layers and on top. Makes 1 four layer cake.

## CHOCOLATE CHIP CAKE
Κέϊκ μὲ κοματάκια σοκολάτας

1 cup unsalted butter or margarine, at room
    temperature
1½ cups sugar
5 large eggs, separated
1 teaspoon vanilla
3 cups unbleached flour
½ teaspoon baking soda
2 teaspoons baking powder
¼ teaspoon salt
8 ounces semisweet chocolate chips
½ cup blanched and chopped almonds or walnuts

Cream butter and sugar until light and fluffy. Add egg yolks one at a time beating thoroughly after each one is added. Add vanilla. Sift flour, baking soda, baking powder and salt together. Gradually add flour mixture beating until smooth. Add chips and almonds if desired and fold in stiffly beaten egg whites. Pour into well greased and floured tube pan. Bake in a preheated 350°F (180°C) oven for approximately 45 minutes or until cake tester inserted in center comes out clean. Cool 10 minutes. Remove from pan and dust with confectioner's sugar.

## CHOCOLATE WALNUT CAKE
Κέϊκ σοκολάτας μὲ καρύδια

¾ cup unsalted butter or margarine, at room
    temperature
2 cups sugar
6 eggs, separated
1¾ cups unbleached flour
3 tablespoons baking powder
1 teaspoon vanilla
½ cup cocoa
1 cup chopped walnuts

Cream butter and sugar until light and fluffy. Add egg yolks one at a time beating thoroughly after each one is added. Add vanilla. Sift flour, baking powder and cocoa together. Gradually add flour to the creamed mixture beating until smooth after each addition. Add walnuts and mix thoroughly. Fold in stiffly beaten egg whites. Pour into well greased and floured tube pan. Bake in a preheated 350°F (180°C) oven for approximately 50 minutes or until cake

tester inserted in center comes out clean. Cool 10 minutes. Remove from pan and dust with confectioner's sugar.

## CHRISTMAS CAKE
Κέϊκ χριστουγεννιάτικο

1 cup unsalted butter or margarine, at room
    temperature
2 cups sugar
5 eggs
Grated rind of 1 orange
2½ cups unbleached flour
1 teaspoon baking soda
2 teaspoons baking powder
1 teaspoon cinnamon
½ teaspoon nutmeg
½ cup cognac or brandy
½ cup orange juice
½ cup blanched and chopped walnuts
¾ cup seedless golden raisins
¾ cup chopped mixed candied fruits (see index)

Cream butter and sugar until light and fluffy. Add eggs one at a time beating thoroughly after each one is added. Add orange rind. Sift dry ingredients together and mix with raisins and fruits. Add flour-fruit mixture alternately with orange juice and cognac and beat well to combine. Add almonds and walnuts. Pour into well greased and floured tube pan and bake in a preheated 325°F (165°C) oven for approximately 60 minutes or until cake tester inserted in center comes out clean. Cool 10 minutes, remove from pan. Cool on wire rack.

## ALMOND CORNMEAL CAKE WITH SYRUP
Κέϊκ ἀραποσίτου ἀμυγδάλου

2 cups unbleached flour
1 teaspoon baking soda
5 teaspoons baking powder
3 cups fine cornmeal
1 cup oil
½ cup sugar
2 cups fresh orange juice
½ cup cognac
Grated rind of 1 orange and 1 lemon
1 teaspoon vanilla
1 cup seedless golden raisins
1 cup choppd almonds (blanched)
SYRUP:
3½ cups sugar
3 cups water
½ teaspoon almond extract

Sift flour, cornmeal, baking powder and baking soda together. Cut in oil with a pastry blender. Add sugar, orange juice, cognac, orange and lemon rind and vanilla. Mix thoroughly. Add raisins and almonds, mix well. Pour into greased 13x9x3-inch baking pan. Bake in a preheated 350°F (180°C) oven for approximately 45 minutes. Let cool. Cut into square pieces. Combine syrup ingredients in a saucepan; bring to a boil and boil 5 minutes. Pour hot syrup over cold cake. Let stay until completely cold. Serve with whipped cream if desired.

## CORNMEAL CAKE
### Μπομπότα

¾ cup butter or margarine, melted
4 eggs, beaten
1½ cups milk
½ cup orange or apricot marmalade
¼ cup sugar
2 cups fine yellow cornmeal
2½ cups unbleached flour
½ teaspoon baking soda
5 teaspoons baking powder
1 cup seedless golden raisins
1 cup chopped walnuts or almonds

Sift cornmeal, flour, baking soda and baking powder together. Add milk, eggs, butter, marmalade and sugar to cornmeal mixture and mix well to combine. Add raisins and walnuts. Pour into greased 9x13x3-inch baking pan and bake in a preheated 350°F (180°C) oven for 45 minutes. Cut and remove from pan. Serve hot with butter.

Note: Spoon batter into greased muffin pans. Makes 24 muffins.

## ORANGE CORNMEAL CAKE WITH SYRUP
### Κέϊκ ἀραποσίτου πορτοκαλιοῦ

3 cups unbleached flour
2 cups fine yellow cornmeal
1¼ teaspoons baking soda
3 teaspoons baking powder
1⅓ cups milk
4 beaten eggs
½ cup sugar
1 teaspoon vanilla
1 cup melted butter or margarine
Juice and rind of 1 orange
1½ cups raisins
1½ cups chopped walnuts or almonds

**SYRUP:**
3½ cups sugar
3 cups water
1 tablespoon lemon juice

Sift dry ingredients together. Add the rest of the ingredients except the raisins and walnuts. Mix well to combine. Add raisins and walnuts if desired. Pour into greased 13x9x3-inch baking pan. Bake in a preheated 350°F (180°C) oven for 45 minutes. Cut cake into squares. Let cool. Combine syrup ingredients in a saucepan; bring to a boil, reduce heat and boil for 5 minutes. Spoon hot syrup over cool cake pieces. Let stay until completely cold. Serve with whipped cream if desired.

## FRUIT CAKE
### Κέϊκ φρούτου

1 cup unsalted butter or margarine, at room temperature
1 cup sugar
5 large eggs
1 teaspoon vanilla
2 tablespoons brandy or cognac
3 cups unbleached flour
5 teaspoons baking powder
1 teaspoon cinnamon
½ teaspoon nutmeg
¾ cup milk
1 cup chopped walnuts
1 cup chopped mixed candied friuts (see index)
1 cup seedless golden raisins

Cream butter with sugar until light and fluffy. Add egggs one at a time beating thoroughly after each one is added. Add brandy. Sift flour, baking powder, cinnamon and nutmeg together. Mix with fruits and nuts. Gradually add flour mixture to the butter mixture, beating until smooth after each addition. Pour into well greased and floured tube pan or 2 loaf pans and bake in a preheated 350°F (180°C) oven for approximately 60 minutes or until cake tester inserted in center comes out clean. Cool 10 minutes. Remove from pan. Cool on a wire rack.

## FRUIT NUT CAKE
### Κέϊκ φρούτου

1½ cups unsalted butter or margarine, at room temperature
2 cups sugar
12 eggs, separated
¼ cup cognac
3½ cups unbleached flour

5 teaspoons baking powder
1½ teaspoons cinnamon
½ teaspoon nutmeg
1 cup chopped walnuts
1 cup chopped mixed candied fruits (see index)
1 cup chopped blanched almonds
1 cup seedless golden raisins
1 egg beaten with 1 tablespoon water

Cream butter with sugar until light and fluffy. Add egg yolks one at a time beating thoroughly after each one is added. Add cognac. Sift dry ingredients together. Mix with fruits and nuts. Gradually add flour mixture to the butter mixture beating until smooth after each addition. Fold in stiffly beaten egg whites. Pour into well greased pans lined with greased waxed paper. Brush with beaten egg. Bake in a preheated 325°F (165°C) oven for approximately 45 minutes.

## FRUIT ORANGE CAKE
### Κέϊκ φρούτου

1 cup unsalted butter or margarine, at room
    temperature
2 cups sugar
4 large eggs, separated
Grated rind of 2 oranges
4½ cups unbleached flour
1 teaspoon baking soda
2 teaspoons baking powder
1 teaspoon cinnamon
1 cup chopped blanched almonds
1 cup chopped mixed candied fruits (see index)
1 cup seedless golden raisins
1 cup fresh orange juice
½ cup cognac or brandy

Cream butter with sugar until light and fluffy. Add egg yolks one at a time beating thoroughly after each one is added. Add orange rind. Sift dry ingredients together. Mix with fruits and nuts. Gradually add flour mixture alternately with orange juice and cognac to butter mixture beating until smooth after each addition. Fold in stiffly beaten egg whites. Pour into well greased and lined with waxed paper, 2 bread pans and bake in a preheated 350°F (180°C) oven for approximately 50 minutes or until cake tester inserted in center comes out clean. Cool 10 minutes. Remove from pans and cool on wire racks.

## HONEY CAKE
### Κέϊκ μελιοῦ

1 cup heavy cream

1 cup milk
¾ cup sugar
¾ cup honey
3¼ cups flour
5 teaspoons baking powder
1 teaspoon cinnamon
½ teaspoon nutmeg
1 cup chopped mixed candied fruits (see index)
1 cup chopped walnuts

Combine cream, milk, sugar and honey together and mix well. Sift dry ingredients together. Gradually add flour mixture to cream mixture beating until smooth after each addition. Add fruits and nuts and mix well to combine. Pour into well greased and floured tube pan. Bake in a preheated 350°F (180°C) oven for approximately 45 minutes or until cake tester inserted in center comes out clean. Cool 10 minutes. Remove from pan. Cool on wire rack.

## JAM CAKE
### Κέϊκ μαρμελάδας

1 cup unsalted butter or margarine, at room
    temperature
1 cup sugar
4 eggs, separated
1 cup apricot jam or any other kind you wish
4 cups unbleached flour
5 teaspoons baking powder
1 teaspoon cinnamon
1 cup milk
1 cup chopped walnuts

Cream butter with sugar until light and fluffy. Add egg yolks one at a time beating thoroughly after each one is added. Add jam. Sift dry ingredients together. Gradually add flour mixture alternately with milk to butter mixture beating until smooth after each addition. Add chopped walnuts. Fold in stiffly beaten egg whites. Pour into greased and floured tube pan. Bake in a preheated 350°F (180°C) oven for approximately 50 minutes or until cake tester inserted in center comes out clean. Cool 10 minutes. Remove from pan and dust with confectioner's sugar.

## LEMON CAKE
### Κέϊκ λεμονιοῦ

1 cup unsalted butter or margarine, at room
    temperature
1½ cups sugar
8 eggs, separated
1 teaspoon fresh lemon juice

1 teaspoon vanilla
Grated rind of 1 lemon
4 cups unbleached flour
5 teaspoons baking powder
SYRUP:
2½ cups sugar
2 cups water
1 teaspoon lemon juice

Cream butter with sugar until light and fluffy. Add egg yolks one at a time beating thoroughly after each one is added. Add vanilla, lemon rind and lemon juice. Sift flour and baking powder together. Gradually add flour to creamed mixture beating until smooth. Fold in stiffly beaten egg whites. Pour into a well greased and floured 9x13x3-inch baking pan. Bake in a preheated 350°F (180°C) oven for approximately 45 minutes or until cake tester inserted in center comes out clean. Cool. Combine syrup ingredients together in a saucepan and bring to a boil. Reduce heat to medium and boil for 5 minutes. Pour syrup over the cold cake. When it is cold and syrup is absorbed, cut into square pieces.

# LENTEN COCONUT CAKE
Κέϊκ νηστίσιμο μὲ καρύδα

¾ cup farina
1 cup unbleached flour
6 teaspoons baking powder
1 teaspoon cinnamon
1¼ cups sugar
1 cup oil
1⅓ cups water
Grated rind of 1 orange
¾ cup blanched chopped almonds
1 cup chopped walnuts
1¼ cups coconut

Sift dry ingredients together. Add sugar, oil, water, rind; stir until well blended. Add chopped almonds, chopped walnuts and coconut. Mix well to combine. Pour into greased and floured 8-inch tube pan. Bake in a preheated 350°F (180°C) oven for approximately 60 minutes. Cool 10 minutes. Remove from pan and dust with confectioner's sugar.

# LENTEN HONEY CAKE
Κέϊκ νηστίσιμο μελιοῦ

3 cups unbleached flour
6 teaspoons baking powder
1½ teaspoons cinnamon
1 cup oil

¾ cup sugar
½ cup honey
¾ cup fresh orange juice
Grated rind of 1 orange
1 cup seedless golden raisins

Sift flour with baking powder and cinnamon together in a mixing bowl. Add the oil, sugar, honey, orange juice and rind, mix well to combine. Add raisins and mix well. Pour into greased and floured 8-inch tube pan. Bake in a preheated 350°F (180°C) oven for approximately 60 minutes. Cool on wire rack for 10 minutes. Remove from pan and dust with confectioner's sugar.

# LENTEN ORANGE CAKE
Κέϊκ νηστίσιμο πορτοκαλιοῦ

4½ cups unbleached flour
4 teaspoons baking powder
½ teaspoon baking soda
1½ teaspoons cinnamon
¾ cup oil
2 cups sugar
1 cup milk
1 tablespoon cognac
1 cup fresh orange juice
Grated rind of 1 orange
1 cup seedless golden raisins
1 cup chopped walnuts

Sift dry ingredients together in a mixing bowl. Add the rest of the ingredients and stir until well blended. Pour into greased and floured 9-inch tube pan. Bake in a preheated 350°F (180°C) oven for approximately 60 minutes. Cool on wire rack for 10 minutes. Remove from pan and dust with confectioner's sugar.

# LENTEN SPICE CAKE
Κέϊκ νηστίσιμο

3¾ cups unbleached flour
1½ teaspoons baking soda
1 teaspoon cinnamon
¼ teaspoon ground clove
½ teaspoon ground nutmeg
1½ cups sugar
¾ cup oil
½ cup cognac
¾ cup water
½ cup fresh orange juice
Grated rind of 1 orange
1 cup seedless golden raisins
1½ cups chopped walnuts

Sift dry ingredients together in a mixing bowl. Add the rest of the ingredients and stir until well blended. Pour into greased and floured 8-inch tube pan. Bake in a preheated 350°F (180°C) oven for approximately 60 minutes. Cool on wire rack for 10 minutes. Remove from pan and dust with confectioner's sugar.

## MARBLE CAKE
### Κέϊκ μάρμπλ

1 cup unsalted butter or margarine, at room
    temperature
2 cups sugar
4 large eggs
1 teaspoon vanilla
3½ cups unbleached flour
4 teaspoons baking powder
¾ cup milk
1½ ounces sweet chocolate, melted

Cream butter with sugar until light and fluffy. Add eggs one at a time beating thoroughly after each one is added. Add vanilla. Sift flour and baking powder together; add alternately with milk to creamed mixture beating until smooth after each addition. To ⅓ of the batter add melted chocolate and blend thoroughly. Place by spoonfuls in a greased and floured 9-inch tube pan alternately light and dark mixtures. Bake in a preheated 350°F (180°C) oven for approximately 60 minutes. Cool 10 minutes. Remove from the pan and cool on wire rack.

## MUSLIN CAKE
### Κέϊκ μουσελὶν

1¼ cups unsalted butter or margarine, at room
    temperature
2½ cups sugar
4 eggs
Grated rind of 1 orange or lemon
1 teaspoon vanilla
Grated rind of 1orange or lemon
3 cups cake flour
¾ teaspoon baking soda
2½ teaspoons cream of tartar
1¼ cups milk

Cream butter with sugar until light and fluffy. Add eggs one at a time beating thoroughly after each one is added. Add vanilla and oragne rind. Sift dry in-ingredients together. Gradually add flour mixture alternately with milk, beating until smooth after each addition. Pour mixture into well greased and floured 8-inch tube pan. Bake in a preheated 350°F (180°C) oven for approximately 60 minutes. Cool on wire

rack for 10 minutes. Remove from pan onto serving platter and dust with confectioner's sugar.

## NEW YEARS CAKE WITH COGNAC
### Βασιλόπιττα μὲ κονιὰκ

1 cup unsalted butter or margarine, at room
    temperature
3½ cups sugar
12 eggs
7½ cups all-purpose flour
2 teaspoons cream of tartar
1½ tablespoons baking soda
¼ cup cognac
1 cup milk

Cream butter and sugar until light and fluffy. Add eggs one at a time beating thoroughly after each one is added. Sift dry ingredients together; add alternately with milk and cognac to creamed mixture beating until smooth after each addition. Pour into well greased baking pans and bake in a preheated 350°F (180°C) oven for approximately 60 minutes. After baking a coin is inserted through a slit in the base. Cut and serve the Vasilopita as directed in New Years Cake (see index).

Recipe from Mrs. John D. Mickles

## NEW YEAR'S CAKE
### Βασιλόπιττα

2 cups sugar
4 large eggs
4½ cups unbleached flour
6 teaspoons baking powder
1⅓ cups milk
¼ teaspoon ground masticha or 1 teaspoon vanilla

Cream butter with sugar until light and fluffy. Add eggs one at a time beating thoroughly after each one is added. Sift dry ingredients together; add alternately with milk and vanilla if desired to creamed mixture beating until smooth after each addition. Pour into well greased 10- inch baking pan and bake in a preheated 350°F (180°C) oven for approximately 60 minutes. After baking a coin is inserted through a slit in the base. Cut and serve Vasilopita, first to the family starting from the Virgin Mary, the father, the mother, the rest of the family and then the guests. The person who finds the coin will have luck in the New Year. Makes one Vasilopita.

# NEW YEAR'S ALMOND CAKE
### Βασιλόπιττα ἀμυγδάλου

1 cup unsalted butter or margarine, at room
    temperature
1⅔ cups sugar
6 large eggs, separated
Grated rind of 1 orange
½ cup milk
3½ cups unbleached flour
4 teaspoons baking powder
1 cup chopped blanched almonds

Cream butter with sugar until light and fluffy. Add
egg yolks one at a time beating thoroughly after each
one is added. Add grated rind. Sift flour with baking
powder together; add alternately with milk to creamed
mixture beating until smooth after each addition. Add
almonds and fold in stiffly beaten egg whites. Pour
into 11-inch baking pan lined with waxed paper and
bake in a preheated 350°F (180°C) oven for approximately 50 minutes or until cake tester inserted in
center comes out clean. Cool 10 minutes. Remove
from pan. Cool on wire rack. Cut and serve the
Vasilopita as directed in New Years Cake (see index).

# ONE-TWO-THREE CAKE
### Κέϊκ ἕνα-δύο-τρία

1 cup unsalted butter or margarine, at room
    temperature
1 cup sugar
4 eggs, separated
1 teaspoon vanilla
3 cups unbleached flour
1 teaspoon baking soda
1 cup plain yogurt
1 cup chopped blanched almonds
SYRUP:
2½ cups sugar
2 cups water
2 tablespoons fresh lemon juice

Cream butter with sugar until light and fluffy. Add
egg yolks one at a time beating thoroghly after each
one is added. Add vanilla. Sift flour and soda together; add alternately with yogurt to creamed mixture
beating until smooth each each addition. Add almonds.
Fold in stiffly beaten egg whites. Pour into well
greased 9x13x3-inch baking pan. Bake in a preheated
350°F (180°C) oven for approximately 45 minutes.
Remove from oven and cool. Cut into square pieces.
Combine syrup ingredients in a saucepan, bring to a
boil, reduce heat and boil for 5 minutes. Spoon syrup
over the cool cake. Cool completely before you serve.

# ORANGE CAKE
### Κέϊκ πορτοκαλιοῦ

1 cup unsalted butter or margarine, at room
    temperature
1⅓ cups sugar
5 large eggs, separated
4 cups unbleached flour
5 teaspoons baking powder
1 teaspoon vanilla
Grated rind of 1 orange
1½ cups fresh orange juice

Cream butter and sugar until light and fluffy. Add
egg yolks one at a time beating thoroughly after each
one is added. Add vanilla and orange rind. Sift flour
and baking powder together; add alternately with
orange juice to creamed mixture beating until smooth
after each addition. Fold in stiffly beaten egg whites.
Pour into a well greased and floured tube pan. Bake
in a preheated 350°F (180°C) oven for approximately
34 minutes, or until cake tester inserted in center
comes out clean. Coll 10 minutes. Remove from pan
and cool on wire rack.

# ALMOND PANTESPANI CAKE
### Παντεσπάνι μὲ ἀμύγδαλα

⅓ cup unsalted butter or margarine, at room
    temperature
1½ cups sugar
5 eggs
1 teaspoon vanilla
Grated rind of 1 orange or lemon
½ cup milk
2 cups cake flour
4 teaspoons baking powder
1½ cups finely chopped almonds

Cream butter until light and fluffy. Gradually add
sugar, beat well. Add eggs one at a time beating
thoroughly after each one is added. Add vanilla and
orange rind. Sift flour with baking powder together.
Gradually add flour alternately with milk, beating
until smooth after each addition. Add chopped
almonds and mix well. Pour mixture into well greased
and floured 8-inch tube pan. Bake in a preheated
350°F (180°C) oven for approximately 45 minutes.
Cool on wire rack for 10 minutes. Remove from pan
onto a serving platter and dust with confectioner's
sugar.

# PANTESPANI CAKE WITH SYRUP
### Παντεσπάνι μὲ σιρόπι

8 eggs, separated
1¼ cups sugar
1 teaspoon vanilla
2 cups unbleached flour
3 teaspoons baking powder
½ cup water
1 cup chopped blanched almonds
SYRUP:
2½ cups sugar
2½ cups water
1 tablespoon lemon juice
½ teaspoon almond extract

Beat egg yolks with sugar until thick and creamy. Add vanilla. Sift flour and baking powder together. Gradually add flour mixture alternately with water, to egg mixture and mix well. Add chopped almonds. Fold in stiffly beaten egg whites. Pour into a greased and floured 11x16x3-inch baking pan. Bake in a preheated 350°F (180°C) oven for approximately 45 minutes. Let cool. Combine syrup ingredients in a saucepan, bring to a boil, reduce heat and boil for 5 minutes. Spoon syrup over cool cake. Cover and let stay until completely cold.

# PLAIN PANTESPANI CAKE
Παντεσπάνι ἁπλὸ

6 eggs, separated
2 cups sugar
2 cups unbleached flour
1 teaspoon vanilla or grated rind of 1 lemon
2 teaspoons baking powder

Beat egg yolks with sugar until thick and creamy. Add vanilla. Sift flour and baking powder together. Gradually add flour mixture and mix well. Fold in stiffly beaten egg whites. Pour into a 14x10x3-inch baking pan lined with waxed paper. Bake in a preheated 350°F (180°C) oven for approximately 45 minutes. Cool. Turn up-side-down, remove waxed paper and cut into square pieces. Serve with ice cream or sweetened strawberries and top with whipped cream.

# PLAIN CAKE
Κέϊκ ἁπλὸ

¾ cup unsalted butter or margarine, at room temperature
1½ cups sugar
6 eggs, separated
1¾ cups unbleached flour
1 teaspoon vanilla
3 teaspoons baking powder

Grated rind of 1 lemon or orange
1 cup heavy cream, whipped (optional)

Cream butter with sugar until light and fluffy. Add egg yolks one at a time beating thoroughly after each one is added. Add vanilla and lemon rind if desired. Sift flour and baking powder together. Gradually add flour to the butter mixture beating until smooth after each addition. Fold in sitffly beaten egg whites. Pour into well greased pan lined with greased waxed paper. Bake in a preheated 350°F (180°C) oven for approximately 50 minutes or until cake tester inserted in center comes out clean. Cool, Remove from pan, remove and discard waxed paper. Cut and serve with whipped cream if desired.

# PUMPKIN NUT CAKE
Κέϊκ κολοκύθας

1 cup unsalted butter or margarine, at room temperature
2½ cups sugar
4 eggs
1 teaspoon vanilla
3 cups unbleached flour
1 teaspoon baking soda
1 teaspoon baking powder
1¼ teaspoons cinnamon
¾ teaspoon nutmeg
2 cups mashed cooked pumpkin
1 cup seedless golden raisins
1 cup chopped walnuts

Cream butter and sugar until light and fluffy. Add eggs one at a time beating thoroughly after each one is added. Add vanilla. Sift flour, baking soda, baking powder, cinnamon and nutmeg together. Gradually ad flour mixture alternately with mashed pumpkin beating until smooth after each addition. Add raisins and walnuts and mix thoroughly. Pour into greased and floured 8-inch baking tube pan. Bake in a preheated 350°F (180°C) oven for approximately 60 minutes. Cool 10 minutes. Remove from pan and cool on wire rack.

# RAISIN CAKE
Κέϊκ σταφίδας

½ cup sugar
¼ cup honey
¾ cup milk
4 beaten eggs
1 cup oil
4¼ cups cake flour
1 teaspoon baking soda

3 teaspoons baking powder
½ teaspoon nutmeg
1 teaspoon cinnamon
1 package (16-ounces) seedless golden raisins

Beat sugar, honey and milk together until sugar has dissolved. Add eggs and oil, beat until creamy. Sift dry ingredients together. Mix with raisins, add to the creamed mixture and mix thoroughly. Pour into greased and floured tube pan. Bake in a preheated 350°F (180°C) oven for approximately 50 minutes. Cool 10 minutes. Remove from pan, cool on wire rack.

## RAISIN WALNUT CAKE
### Κέϊκ μὲ σταφίδες καὶ καρύδια

1 cup unsalted butter or margarine, at room
    temperature
1½ cups sugar
5 large eggs
1 teaspoon vanilla
3 cups unbleached flour
5 teaspoons baking powder
1 teaspoon cinnamon
¾ cup milk
1 cup seedless golden raisins
1 cup chopped walnuts

Cream butter and sugar until light and fluffy. Add eggs one at a time beating thoroughly after each one is added. Sift dry ingredients together. Gradually add flour alternately with milk to creamed mixture beating until smooth after each addition. Add raisins and walnuts; mix well to combine. Pour into a well greased and floured tube pan. Bake in a preheated 350°F (180°C) oven for approximately 45 minutes or until cake tester inserted in center comes out clean. Cool 10 minutes. Remove from pan and dust with confectioner's sugar.

## PLAIN RAVANI
### Ραβανὶ ἀπλὸ

1 cup unsalted butter or margarine, at room
    temperature
2 cups sugar
6 eggs, separated
3½ cups unbleached flour
1 teaspoon baking soda
1 teaspoon cream of tartar
1 cup milk
3 tablespoons cognac

Cream butter with sugar until light and fluffy. Add egg yolks one at a time beating thoroughly after each one is added. Sift flour, baking soda and cream of tartar together. Gradually add flour mixture alternately with milk and cognac, beat until smooth after each addition. Fold in stiffly beaten egg whites. Pour into well greased 15x10x3-inch baking pan. Bake in a preheated 350°F (180°C) oven for approximately 45 minutes. Cool, cut into pieces and serve.

(Recipe from Mrs. John D. Mickles)

## SPONGE CAKE
### Κέϊκ σπόγγου

6 eggs
1 cup sugar
1½ cups unbleached flour
2 teaspoons baking powder
1 teaspoon vanilla
Gratd rind of 1 lemon
¼ cup melted unsalted butter or margarine

Combine eggs and sugar; beat thoroughly. Place over boiling water (double boiler) on low heat beating constantly until mixture is warm and sugar has dissolved. Remove from heat beating constantly until it is completely cold. Add lemon rind. Sift flour with baking powder together. Gradually add flour to egg mixture alternately with the melted cool butter. Bake in a preheated 350°F (180°C) oven for approximately 45 minutes.

## SAINT FANOUREO CAKE
### Πίττα ἁγίου Φανουρίου

1½ cups oil
1½ cups fresh orange juice
⅓ cup cognac
1½ cups sugar
Grated rind of 1½ oranges
6 cups unbleached flour
4 teaspoons baking powder
½ teaspoon baking soda
1½ teaspoons cinnamon
¼ teaspoon ground cloves
1 cup chopped walnuts
1 cup seedless golden raisins
½ cup sesame seed

In a mixing bowl combine oil, orange juice, cognac and sugar, beat well until sugar is dissolved; add orange rind. Sift dry ingredients together and mix with the raisins and walnuts. Gradually add flour mixture to the oil mixture and stir until well blended. Pour into a well greased and floured 10x15x3-inch baking pan; sprinkle with sesame seed and bake in a preheated 350°F (180°C) oven for approximately 60 minutes. Cool and cut into square pieces.

✠✠✠

## SAMALI
Σάμαλι

3½  cups semolina
4\teaspoons baking powder
1½  cups sugar
1 cup water
½ cup milk
1 teaspoon vanilla
1½  cups chopped blanched almonds
SYRUP:
3½  cups sugar
3½  cups water
Juice of ½ lemon
½ teaspoon almond extract

Sift semolina and baking powder together; add the rest of the ingredients except almonds. Mix thoroughly. Add almonds and mix well to combine. Pour into generously greased 9x13x3-inch baking pan. Spread evenly with wet spatula. Bake in a preheated 350°F (180°C) oven for 25 minutes. Remove from oven; cut into square pieces. Return to oven again and bake for 25 minutes longer. Combine syrup ingredients in a saucepan; bring to a boil, reduce heat and boil for 5 minutes. Pour hot syrup over hot cake. Cover, let stay until completely cold.

✠✠✠

## TAHINI CAKE
Κέϊκ μὲ ταχίνι

10  ounces tahini (crushed sesame seeds)
1 cup water
2 tablespoons cognac
½ cup fresh orange juice
2 tablespoons fresh lemon juice
2½  cups sugar
Grated rind of 1 orange
2½  cups unbleached flour
2 teaspoons baking soda
1⅔ cups farina
1 teaspoon cinnamon
¼ teaspoon ground cloves
¾ cup chopped walnuts
1 cup seedless golden raisins

In a mixing bowl combine tahini, water, cognac, orange and lemon juice and sugar. Beat until sugar is dissolved, add orange rind. Sift dry ingredients together, mix with raisins and walnuts. Gradually add flour mixture to the tahini mixture and stir until well blended. Pour into well greased and floured 10x15x 3-inch baking pan. Bake in a preheated 350°F (180°C) oven for approximately 60 minutes. Cool 10 minutes and dust with confectioner's sugar. Cut when cake is completely cold.

✠✠✠

## WALNUT CAKE
Καρυδόπιττα

½  cup unsalted butter or margarine, at room temperature
1¼  cups sugar
3 eggs
1½  cups unbleached flour
3 teaspoons baking powder
1 teaspoon cinnamon
¼ cup cognac
½ cup milk
1½  cups finely chopped walnuts
Grated rind of 1 orange

Cream butter with sugar until light and fluffy. Add eggs one at a time beating thoroughly after each one is added. Add orange rind. Sift flour, baking powder and cinnamon together; add alternately with milk and cognac to creamed mixture, beating until smooth after each addition. Add chopped walnuts and mix thoroughly. Pour into greased and floured 8-inch tube pan. Bake in a preheated 350°F (180°C) oven for approximately 55 minutes. Cool 10 minutes. Remove from pan and dust with confectioner's sugar. Cut when cake is completely cold. Serve with whipped cream if desired.

✠✠✠

## YOGURT CAKE
Γιαουρτόπιττα

1 cup unsalted butter or margarine, at room temperature
2¼  cups sugar
5 eggs, separated
1 teaspoon vanilla
4 cups unbleached flour
5 teaspoons baking powder
1½  cups plain yogurt

Cream butter with sugar until light and fluffy. Add egg yolks one at a time, beating thoroughly after each one is added. Add vanilla. Sift flour and baking powder together; add alternately with yogurt to creamed mixture, beating until smooth after each addition. Fold in stiffly beaten egg whites. Pour into a well greased and floured 8-inch baking tube pan. Bake in a preheated 350°F (180°C) oven for approximately 60 minutes. Cool 10 minutes. Remove from pan and dust with confectioner's sugar. Cut when cake it completely cold. Serve with ice cream if desired.

🍂 🍂 🍂 🍂

## YOGURT ALMOND CAKE
### Γιαουρτόπιττα μὲ ἀμύγδαλα

1 cup unsalted butter or margarine, at room
    temperature
2½ cups sugar
5 eggs,, separated
1 teaspoon vanilla
3⅔ cups unbleached flour
5 teaspoons baking powder
1½ cups plain yogurt
1 cup finely chopped blanched almonds

Cream butter with sugar until light and fluffy. Add egg yolks one at a time, beating thoroughly after each one is added. Add vanilla. Sift flour and baking powder together. Add alternately with yogurt to creamed mixture, beating until smooth after each addition. Add almonds and mix well. Fold in stiffly beaten egg whites. Pour into a well greased and floured 8-inch baking tube pan. Bake in a preheated 350°F (180°C) oven for approximately 60 minutes. Remove from pan and dust with confectioner's sugar. Cut when it is completely cold.

🍂 🍂 🍂 🍂

## YOGURT ORANGE CAKE
### Γιαουτόπιττα πορτοκαλιοῦ

1 cup unsalted butter or margarine, at room
    temperature
2 cups sugar
5 eggs, separated
3 cups unbleached flour
4 teaspoons baking powder
Grated rind of 2 oranges
1 cup plain yogurt
1 cup blanched finely chopped allmonds

Cream butter and sugar until light and fluffy. Add egg yolks one at at time, beating thoroughly after each one is added. Add orange rind. Sift flour and baking powder together; add alternately with yogurt to creamed mixture, beating until smooth after each addition. Add chopped almonds and mix well. Fold in stiffly beaten egg whites. Pour into a well greased and floured 8-inch tube pan. Bake in a preheated 350°F (180°C) oven for approximately 60 minutes. Cool 10 minutes. Remove from pan and cool on wire rack.

## YOGURT WALNUT CAKE
### Γιαουρτόπιττα μὲ καρύδια

1 cup unsalted butter or margarine, at room
    temperature
1½ cups sugar
3 eggs, separated
1 teaspoon vanilla
2⅓ cups unbleached flour
1 teaspoon baking soda
1 cup plain yogurt
½ cup sugar
1 teaspoon cinnamon
1 cup finely chopped walnuts

Cream butter and sugar until light and fluffy. Add egg yolks one at a time beating thoroughly after each one is added. Add vanilla. Sift flour and soda together; add alternately with yogurt to creamed mixture beating until smooth after each addition. Fold in stiffly beaten egg whites. Spread one half of the mixture in a greased and floured 9x9x3-inch baking pan. Combine the last three ingredients together and sprinkle one half over the batter in the pan. Add the rest of the cake batter on top and sprinkle the remaining of the filling over the top. Bake in a preheated 350°F (180°C) oven for approximately 45 minutes. Cool, and cut into square pieces.

🍂 🍂 🍂 🍂

## ZUCCHINI NUT CAKE
### Κέϊκ μὲ κολοκύθι

1 cup oil
1¾ cups sugar
4 eggs
1 teaspoon vanilla
3 cups unbleached flour
2 teaspoons cinnamon
1 teaspoon baking soda
2 teaspoons baking powder
2 cups grated zucchini
1 cup seedless golden raisins
1 cup finely chopped walnuts

Combine oil, sugar, eggs and vanilla in a bowl and beat well. Sift flour, cinnamon, baking soda and baking powder together. Gradually add flour mixture alternately with grated zucchini and mix well. Mix in raisins and walnuts. Pour into greased and floured 8-inch tube pan or bread pan. Bake in a preheated 350°F (180°C) oven for approximately 55 minutes. Cool on wire rack.

## ALMOND COOKIES
### Μπισκότα ἀμυγδάλου

1  cup unsalted butter or margarine, at room
      temperature
1  cup sugar
1  egg and 1 egg yolk
¼  teaspoon almond extract
1  teaspoon vanilla
¾  cup ground blanched almonds
1¾  cups all-purpose flour
2  teaspoons baking powder

Cream butter and sugar until light and fluffy. Add
eggs one at a time, beating thoroughly after each one
is added.  Add almonds and vanilla extract.  Add
ground almonds and mix well to combine. Sift flour
and baking powder together.  Gradually add flour,
beating until smooth after each addition. Drop from
teaspoon onto greased baking sheet and bake in a
preheated 375°F (190°C) oven for 15 minutes. Makes
5 dozen.

## ALMOND MACAROONS
### Μακαροὺν ἀμυγδάλου

5  egg whites
1  teaspoon cream of tartar
2  cups sugar
2  cups whole blanched almonds
⅓  cup sifted cake flour
2  packages (3.5 ounces each) almond paste
½  teaspoon almond extract

In a blender or food processor grind almonds and
sugar together, a little at a time. Beat egg whites
with cream of tartar until stiff but not dry. In a large
mixing bowl work almond paste with a wooden spoon
until smooth. Add ground almond, almond extract
and flour, mix well. Fold in egg whites. Drop from
teaspoon onto baking sheets, lined with waxed paper.
Bake in a preheated 300°F (150°C) oven for approximately 20-30 minutes or until lightly golden. Remove
from paper while still warm.  If paper sticks to cookies,
moisten it on the underside. Makes 6 dozen.

## ALMOND LACE COOKIES
### Γαλέττες ἀμυγδάλου

3  tablespoons unsalted butter or margarine, at room
      temperature
1¾  cups sugar
5  egg whites, well beaten
1  teaspoon vanilla

½  teaspoon almond extract
1  cup unbleached flour
1  pacage (10-ounces) finely chopped blanched
      almonds

In a large bowl combine butter, sugar, egg whites,
vanilla and almond extract and mix well. Gradually
add flour. Add chopped almonds and mix well. Drop
from teaspoon 3 inches apart on greased and floured
baking sheet. Bake in a preheated 350°F (180°C)
oven for approximately 10-12 minutes.

## ALMOND WAFERS
### Γκοφρέτες ἀμυγδάλου

1½  cups finely ground blanched almonds
1½  cups sugar
4  egg whites, beaten
½  teaspoon almond extract
1  teaspoon vanilla
¼  cup cake flour, sifted

Combine all ingredients in a food processor and blend
until smooth.  Drop from a teaspoon onto lightly
greased baking sheets. Bake in a preheated 300°F
(150°C) oven for approximately 20 minutes or until
lightly golden.

## CHOCOLATE COOKIES
### Μπισκότας σοκολάτας

1  cup unsalted butter or margarine, at room
      temperature
2  cups sugar
2  eggs and 1 egg yolk
1  teaspoon vanilla
1  tablespoon cognac or brandy (optional)
4  ounces (squares) chocolate, melted, semi-sweet
3  cups all-purpose flour
1  teaspoon baking soda
1  cup milk
½  cup finely chopped walnuts

Cream butter and sugar until light and fluffy. Add
eggs one at a time, beating thoroughly after each one
is added. Add vanilla, cognac if desired and melted
chocolate. Sift flour with baking soda together. Gradually add flour, beating until smooth after each addition. Add chopped walnuts and mix well. Drop
from teaspoon onto greased baking sheets and bake
in a preheated 375°F (190°C) oven for approximately
15 minutes.  Makes about 6 dozen.

# COCONUT MACAROONS
### Μακαροὺν καρύδας

5 egg whites
1 teaspoon cream of tartar
1 cup sugar
1 teaspoon vanilla
4 cups shredded coconut
¼ cup corn starch
½ cup finely ground blanched almonds (optional)

Beat egg whites with cream of tartar until stiff and dry. Beat in sugar and vanilla. Add coconut, corn starch and almonds if desired and mix well. Drop from teaspoon onto baking sheets lined with waxed paper. Bake in a preheated 300°F (150°C) oven for approximately 30 minutes. Remove from waxed paper while still warm.

# FRUIT NUT ROLLED OAT COOKIES
### Μπισκότα φρούτου μὲ κουάκερ

1 cup unsalted butter or margarine, at room temperature
1 cup or more sugar
2 eggs
1 teaspoon vanilla
2 cups all-purpose flour
3 teaspoons baking powder
½ teaspoon baking soda
1 teaspoon cinnamon
⅔ cup milk mixed with 1 tablespoon lemon juice
1½ cups instant rolled oats
1 cup finely chopped walnuts or almonds
1 cup seedless golden raisins
¾ cup chopped dates

Cream butter and sugar until light and fluffy. Add eggs one at a time, beating thoroughly after each one is added. Add vanilla. Sift flour, baking powder, baking soda and cinnamon together. Gradually add flour mixture alternately with milk to creamed mixture, beating until smooth after each addition. Add rolled oats, nuts, raisins and chopped dates; mix thoroughly. Drop from teaspoon onto greased baking sheets and bake in a preheated 350°F (180°C) oven for approximately 15 minutes. Makes 4 dozen.

# HONEY FRUIT NUT COOKIES
### Μπισκότα μελιοῦ

1 cup unsalted butter or margarine, at room temperature
½ cup sugar
1 cup honey
4 eggs
4 cups all-purpose flour
4 teaspoons baking powder
1 teaspoon baking soda
1 teaspoon cinnamon
1 teaspoon pumpkin pie spice
½ cup milk
1½ cups finely chopped almonds or walnuts
1½ cups seedless golden raisins
1½ cups chopped mixed candied fruit (see index)

Cream butter and sugar until light and fluffy. Add eggs one at a time, beating thoroughly after each one is added. Sift dry ingredients together. Gradually add flour mixture alternately with milk to creamed mixture, beating until smooth after each addition. Add fruits and nuts and mix thoroughly. Drop from teaspoon onto greased baking sheets and bake in a preheated 375°F (190°C) oven for approximately 12-14 minutes. Makes 7 dozen.

# LADYFINGERS
### Μπισκότα σαβαγιὰρ

6 eggs, separated
⅛ teaspoon salt
1 cup sugar
1 teaspoon vanilla
1 cup cake flour, sifted with
1 teaspoon baking powder
Sugar

Beat egg whites with salt until stiff but not dry. Gradually add ½ cup sugar and beat well. Beat egg yolks until thick, gradually add remaining sugar and beat well. Fold into egg whites, then fold in vanilla and flour. Shape into 3-inch fingers on a baking sheet lined with waxed paper. Sprinkle with sugar and bake in a preheated 350°F (180°C) oven for approximately 12 minutes. Makes 3-4 dozen.

# MARINGUES
### Μπιζέδες

5 egg whites
½ teaspoon cream of tartar
1¼ cups sugar
3 teaspoons baking powder
1 teaspoon vanilla
1 cup finely chopped toasted almonds

Beat egg whites with cream of tartar until stiff but not dry. Sift sugar with baking powder together.

Gradually add sugar, beating until stiff after each addition. Fold in vanilla and chopped almonds. Heap in rounds or press through a pastry bag onto baking sheets lined with waxed paper. Bake in a preheated 250°F (120°C) oven for approximately 50 minutes. Remove immediately from waxed paper. Makes 4 dozen.

## NUT RAISIN ROCKS
### Βραχάκια

1  cup unsalted butter or margarine, at room
        temperature
1⅓  cups sugar
3  eggs, separated
1  teaspoon vanilla
2½  cups all-purpose flour
1  teaspoon baking soda
1  teaspoon cinnamon
¼  teaspoon cloves
½  cup milk
1  cup seedless golden raisins
1  cup finely chopped walnuts or almonds

Cream butter and sugar until light and fluffy. Add egg yolks one at a time, beating thoroughly after each one is added. Add vanilla. Sift dry ingredients together. Gradually add flour mixture alternately with milk, beating until smooth after each addition. Add raisins and chopped nuts. Fold in stiffly beaten egg whites. Drop from teaspoon onto greased baking sheets and bake in a preheated 350°F (180°C) oven for approximately 15 minutes. Makes 4 dozen.

## ORANGE COOKIES
### Μπισκότα πορτοκαλιοῦ

1  cup unsalted butter or margarine, at room
        temperature
2¾  cups sugar
2  eggs
Grated rind of 1 orange
3  cups all-purpose flour
1  teaspoon baking soda
½  cup plain yogurt
¼  cup orange juice
1  cup finely chopped blanched almonds

Cream butter and sugar until light and fluffy. Add eggs one at a time,, beating thoroughly after each one is added. Add orange rind. Sift flour and baking soda together. Gradually add flour alternately with yogurt and orange juice to creamed mixture, beating until smooth after each addition. Add chopped almonds and mix thoroughly. Drop from teaspoon onto greased

baking sheets. Bake in a preheated 350°F (180°C) oven for approximately 15 minutes. Makes 5 dozen.

## ROLLED OAT MACAROONS
### Μακαροὺν μὲ κουάκερ

5  egg whites
1  teaspoon cream of tartar
1  cup sugar
3  tablespoons unsalted butter, melted
1½  cups sugar
5  egg yolks
4  cups instant rolled oats
¼  cup sifted cake flour
½  teaspoon baking soda
1  teaspoon baking powder
1  teaspoon cinnamon
1  teaspoon vanilla
1  cup finely chopped walnuts or almonds

Beat egg whites with cream of tartar until stiff but not dry. Beat in sugar and vanilla. In a large mixing bowl combine the nine last ingredients and mix well. Fold in egg whites. Drop from teaspoon onto baking sheets lined with waxed paper. Bake in a preheated 350°F (180°C) oven for approximately 12 minutes. Remove from paper while still hot.

## YOGURT SPICE COOKIES
### Μπισκότα μυρωδάτα μὲ γιαούρτι

½  cup unsalted butter or margarine, at room
        temperature
1¾  cups sugar
2  eggs
1  teaspoon vanilla
3  cups all-purpose flour
1  teaspoon baking soda
1  teaspoon cinnamon
½  teaspoon nutmeg
¼  teaspoon cloves
¾  cup plain yogurt
½  cup finely chopped walnuts

Cream butter and sugar until light and fluffy. Add eggs one at a time, beating thoroughly after each one is added. Add vanilla. Sift dry ingrediennts together. Gradually add flour mixture alternately with yogurt to creamed mixture, beating until smooth after each addition. Add chopped walnuts and mix thoroughly. Drop from teaspoon onto greased baking sheets and bake in a preheated 350°F (180°C) oven for approximately 13 minutes. Makes 4 dozen.

## ALMOND COOKIES
### Μπισκότα ἀμυγδάλου

1 package (10-ounces) blanched almonds, finely
    ground
2 cups sugar
3 egg whites, beaten
1 teaspoon vanilla
½ teaspoon almond extract
Some maraschino cherries
Some whole blanched almonds, split lengthwise
    into halves, to garnish top

Combine five first ingredients together, mix until mixture becomes thick but not stiff, if stiff add some egg white. Mold with cookie press onto baking sheets lined with waxed paper. Press a cherry or almond in centers. Bake in a preheated 300°F (150°C) oven for approximately 20 minutes or until lightly golden.

## ALMOND BUTTER COOKIES
### Μπισκότα βουτύρου μὲ ἀμύγδαλα

1 cup unsalted butter or margarine, at room
    temperature
1 cup sugar
1 egg
1 teaspoon vanilla
½ teaspoon almond extract
2½ cups cake flour
2 teaspoons baking powder
1 egg white, beaten with 1 teaspoon water
½ cup finely chopped blanched almonds

Cream butter and sugar until light and fluffy. Add egg, vanilla and almond extract, beating thoroughly. Sift flour and baking powder together. Gradually add flour to creamed mixture, beating until smooth after each addition. Mold with cookie press onto ungreased baking sheets. Brush cookies with egg white and sprinkle with chopped almonds. Bake in a preheated 400°F (205°C) oven for approximately 12 minutes.

## FILLED ALMOND
## CHOCOLATE COOKIES
### Μπισκότα ἀμυγδάλου σοκολάτας γεμιστὰ

1 package (10 -ounces) blanched almonds, finely
    ground
1⅓ cups sugar
5 eggs, beaten
5 tablespoons sifted cocoa
2 tablespoons cognac

1 teaspoon vanilla
1 cup more or less apricot jam
Sliced almonds

Combine six first ingredients and mix until mixture becomes thick but not stiff. Mold with cookie press 2-inch long onto greased and floured baking sheets and arrange with sliced almonds. Bake in a preheated 400°F (205°C) oven for approximately 10 minutes. Cool. Spread with apricot jam one cookie and top with another.

## FILLED ALMOND MACAROONS
### Μακαροὺν ἀμυγδάλου γεμιστὰ

2 packages (10-ounces each) blanched almonds,
    finely ground
4¾ cups sugar
8 egg whites, beaten
1½ teaspoons vanilla
1 teaspoon almond extract
1 cup more or less apricot jam or your desire

Combine five first ingredients and mix until they become thick but not stiff. If stiff beat in another egg white. Drop from teaspoon or press through a cookie press onto baking sheets lined with waxed paper. Bake in a preheated 300°F (150°C) oven for approximately 25-35 minutes or until lightly golden. Cool. Spread with apricot jam on one macaroon and top with another.

## BUTTER COOKIES
### Μπισκότα βουτύρου

1½ cups unsalted butter or margarine, at room
    temperature
1½ cups sugar
1 teaspoon vanilla
5 eggs
4 cups cake flour
5 teaspoons baking powder

Cream butter and sugar until light and fluffy. Add vanilla and eggs one at a time, beating thoroughly after each one is added. Sift flour and baking powder together. Gradually add flour, beating until smooth after each addition. Mold with cookie press onto greased baking sheets. Bake in a preheated 400°F (205°C) oven for approximately 10 minutes. Cool. Spread with jam on one cookie and top with another if desired.

119

# COCONUT COOKIES
### Μπισκότα καρύδας

1 package (16-ounces) coconut, finely ground
1 cup sugar
10 egg whites, beaten
1 teaspoon vanilla
Some whole blanched almonds, split lengthwise
    into halves to garnish top

Combine four first ingredients and mix well until mixture becomes thick but not stiff. If it is stiff beat in another egg white. Mold with the cookie press onto baking sheets lined with waxed paper. Press an almond in centers. Bake in a preheated 300°F (150°C) oven for approximately 20 minutes or until lightly golden.

# VANILLA COOKIES
### Γλῶσσες

1 cup unsalted butter or margarine, at room
    temperature
1 cup sugar
4 egg whites, well beaten
1 teaspoon vanilla
1½ cups cake flour
1 teaspoon baking powder

Cream butter and sugar until light and fluffy. Add beaten egg whites and vanilla beating thoroughly. Sift flour with baking powder together. Gradually add flour to creamed mixture, beating until smooth after each addition. Mold with cookie press onto greased baking sheets lined with waxed paper. Bake in a preheated 400°F (205°C) oven for approximately 7 minutes. Serve with ice cream.

# REFRIGERATOR SLICED COOKIES
### Μπισκότα ψυγίου

**STANDARD COOKIES:**
1 cup unsalted butter or margarine, at room
    temperature
2 cups sugar
2 eggs
1 teaspoon vanilla
3¼ cups all-purpose flour
4 teaspoons baking powder

Cream butter and sugar until light and fluffy. Add eggs one at a time, beating thoroughly after each one is added. Add vanilla. Sift flour and baking powder together. Gradually add flour, beating until smooth after each addition. Divide dough into four portions. Shape each piece of dough into a roll. Chill. When firm slice very thin and bake in a preheated 375°F 190°C) oven for approximately 12 minutes. Makes 5 dozen.

**Variations:**

**ALMOND**
Add 1 cup finely chopped blanched almonds and ½ teaspoon almond extract to standard cookies. Follow preparation as directed.

**CHOCOLATE**
Add 4 ounces (squares) chocolate, melted to standard cookies. Follow preparation as directed.

**COCONUT**
Add 1½ cups coconut and ¼ cup milk to standard cookies. Follow preparation as directed.

**WALNUT**
Add 1 cup finely chopped walnuts to standard cookies. Follow preparation as directed.

# SMALL ALMOND COOKIES
### Μικρὰ μπισκότα ἀμυγδάλου

1 cup unsalted butter or margarine, at room
    temperature
1⅓ cups sugar
¼ cup evaporated milk
1 teaspoon fresh lemon juice
2 egg yolks
¼ teaspoon almond extract
½ cup finely ground blanched almonds
2¾ cups all-purpose flour (about)
½ teaspoon baking soda

Cream butter and sugar until light and fluffy. Add egg yolks one at a time, beating thoroughly. Add milk, lemon juice, almond extract and ground almonds; mix well. Sift flour and baking soda together. Gradually add flour, beating until smooth after each addition. Add more flour to make a soft dough. Divide dough into four portions. Shape each piece of dough into a 1x8-inch roll. Chill for 60 minutes. When firm, slice very thin and bake in a preheated 375°F (190°C) oven for approximately 12 minutes.

# ANISE COOKIES
### Μπισκότα γλυκανίσου

½ cup fine oil

¾ cup sugar
¾ teaspoon cinnamon
¾ teaspoon anise extract
⅓ cup orange juice
2 eggs
4 cups all-purpose flour
1 teaspoon baking soda
2 teaspoons baking powder
1 egg white, beaten with 1 teaspoon water
Sesame seed

In a mixing bowl combine oil, sugar, cinnamon, anise extract and orange juice. Beat until sugar has dissolved. Add eggs one at a time, and beat well. Sift flour and baking soda and baking powder together. Gradually add flour, beating until smooth after each addition. Divide dough into four portions. Shape each piece of dough into a roll. Chill. When firm slice very thin. Brush with beaten egg white and sprinkle with sesame seed. Bake in a preheated 375°F (190°C) oven for approximately 12 minutes. Makes 6 dozen.

## ANISE ALMOND COOKIES
Μπισκότα γλυκανίσου μὲ ἀμύγδαλα

1 cup unsalted butter or margarine, at room
      temperature
1 cup sugar
2 eggs and 1 egg yolk
1 teaspoon anise extract
1 teaspoon vanilla
3¾ cups all-purpose flour
1 teaspoon baking soda
2 teaspoons baking powder
1 cup finely chopped blanched almonds
1 egg white, beaten with 1 teaspoon water

Cream butter and sugar until light and fluffy. Add eggs one at a time, beating thoroughly after each one is added. Add anise extract and vanilla. Sift flour, baking soda and baking powder together. Gradually add flour, beating until smooth after each addition. Add chopped almonds and mix well. Divide dough into four portions. Shape each piece of dough into a roll. Chill. When firm slice very thin. Brush with beaten egg white. Bake in a preheated 375°F (190°C) oven for approximately 12 minutes. Makes 5 dozen.

## ALMOND BARS
Ραβδὶ ἀμυγδάλου

4 eggs, separated
1¼ cups sugar
1 teaspoon vanilla

½ teaspoon almond extract
Grated rind of ½ orange
1¼ cups all-purpose flour
1 teaspoon baking powder
1¼ cups whole blanched almonds

Beat egg yollks with sugar until thick and creamy. Add vanilla, almond extract and orange rind. Sift flour and baking powder together. Gradually add flour and whole almonds. Fold in stiffly beaten egg whites. Spread into 10x15x2-inch greased and floured baking sheet. Bake in a preheated 350°F (180°C) oven for 30 minutes. Slice into ½-inch thick and 3-inch long bars. Place into a large baking sheet. Return to a preheated 300°F (150°C) oven and bake for 15 minutes or until lightly golden.

## ALMOND JAM BARS
Ραβδὶ ἀμυγδάλου μὲ μαρμελάδα

¾ cup unsalted butter or margarine, at room
      temperature
¾ cup sugar
2 eggs, beaten
1½ cups cake flour, sifted
1 cup apricot jam
4 eggs
1 cup sugar
⅓ cup cake flour, sifted with
1 teaspoon baking powder
½ teaspoon almond extract
2 cups chopped blanched almonds
4 teaspoons melted butter or margarine, unsalted
½ cup pine nuts
1 tablespoon rosewater

Cream butter and sugar until light. Add one egg at a time, beating thoroughly. Gradually add flour, beating until smooth after each addition. Spread in a very thin layer in 10½x15x2-inch greased baking pan. Spread jam over crust. Beat eggs with sugar until light and thick. Beat in almond extract. Add chopped almonds, flour and butter; blend well to combine. Spread over jam. Sprinkle with pine nuts. Bake in a preheated 350°F (180°C) oven for approximately 45-55 minutes. Remove from oven and sprinkle with rosewater. Cool and cut into bars.

Recipe from Mrs. John D. Mickles

## CHOCOLATE BARS A
Ραβδὶ σοκολάτας

½ cup unsalted butter or margarine, at room
      temperature

1¾ cups sugar
4 eggs, separated
1 teaspoon vanilla
1¾ cups all-purpose flour
2 teaspoons baking powder
¼ cup cocoa
½ cup milk
1½ cups finely chopped walnuts
Chocolate frosting (see index)

Cream butter and sugar until light and fluffy. Add egg yolks one at a time, beating thoroughly after each one is added. Add vanilla. Sift dry ingredients together. Gradually add flour mixture alternately with milk to creamed mixture, beating until smooth after each addition. Mix in chopped nuts and spread into well greased baking sheet. Bake in a preheated 350°F (180°C) oven for approximately 25 miutes. Frost with chocolate frosting. Cool thoroughly and cut into bars.

❦ ❦ ❦ ❦

## CHOCOLATE BARS B
Ραβδὶ σοκολάτας

1 cup unsalted butter or margarine, at room
    temperature
3 cups sugar
6 eggs
2 teaspoons vanilla
¼ cup honey
3 cups all-purpose flour
3 teaspoons baking powder
¾ cup cocoa
¾ cup milk
2 cups chopped walnuts
Chocolate frosting (see index)

Cream butter and sugar until light and fluffy. Add eggs one at a time, beating thoroughly after each one is added. Add honey and vanilla and continue creaming. Sift dry ingredients together. Gradually add flour mixture alternately with milk to butter mixture, beating until smooth after each addition. Mix in chopped walnuts and spread into well greased baking sheet. Bake in a preheated 350°F (180°C) oven for approximately 20 minutes. Frost with chocolate frosting. Cool thoroughly and cut into bars.

❦ ❦ ❦ ❦

## COCONUT JAM BARS
Ραβδὶ καρύδας μὲ μαρμελάδα

¾ cup unsalted butter or margarine, at room
    temperature
¾ cup sugar
2 egg whites, stiffly beaten

1½ cups cake flour, sifted
1 cup apricot jam
4 eggs and 2 egg yolks
1¼ cups sugar
4 tablespoons cake flour, sifted with
1 teaspoon baking powder
1 tablespoon rosewater
½ teaspoon almond extract
2 cups coconut
4 tablespoons melted unsalted butter or margarine
1 cup chopped blanched almonds

Cream butter and sugar until light and fluffy. Gradually add flour. Fold in stiffly beaten egg whites. Spread in very thin layer in 10½x15x2-inch baking dish. Bake in a preheated 350°F (180°C) oven for approximately 10 minutes. Cool for 5 minutes. Spread jam over baked crust. Beat eggs and egg yolks with sugar until light. Beat in rosewater and almond extract. Add coconut, flour, baking powder and melted butter and blend well. Spread over jam. Sprinkle with chopped almonds. Return to oven and bake for 25 minutes longer. Cool and cut into bars.

❦ ❦ ❦ ❦

## FRUIT NUT BARS
Ραβδὶ φρούτου

¾ cup unsalted butter or margarine, at room
    temperature
1 cup sugar
5 eggs, separated
1 teaspoon vanilla
½ teaspoon vanilla extract
¼ cup cream
2¼ cups cake flour
3 teaspoons baking powder
¾ cup chopped mixed candied fruits (see index) or
    chopped dates
1 cup seedless golden raisins
1 cup chopped blanched almonds
1 cup chopped walnuts

Cream butter and sugar until light and fluffy. Add egg yolks one at a time, beating thoroughly after each one is added. Add vanilla and almond extract. Sift flour and baking powder together. Gradually add flour alternately with milk to creamed mixture, beating until smooth after each addition. Add fruits and nuts and mix thoroughly. Fold in stiffly beaten egg whites. Spread onto well greased and floured 13x9x 2-inch baking sheet. Bake in a preheated 350°F (180°C) oven for approximately 25 minutes. Cool thoroughly and cut into bars.

# ALMOND BISCUITS
Μπισκότα ἀμυγδάλου

**1 cup unsalted butter or margarine, at room temperature**
**1½ cups sugar**
**4 eggs**
**1 teaspoon vanilla**
**¼ teaspoon almond extract**
**1 cup finely chopped blanched almonds**
**3 cups all-purpose flour**
**4 teaspoons baking powder**
**½ cup plain yogurt**
**1 egg, beaten**

Cream butter and sugar until light and fluffy. Add eggs one at a time, beating thoroughly after each one is added. Add vanilla, almond extract and chopped almonds; mix thoroughly. Sift flour and baking powder together. Gradually add flour mixture alternately with yogurt, beating until smooth after each addition to make a soft dough. Roll out a portion of dough about ⅛-inch thick on waxed paper and cut into rounds or squares. Place into greased baking sheet. Brush biscuits with beaten egg. Bake in a preheated 375°F (190°C) oven for approximatelly 18 minutes.

# FILLED ALMOND BISCUITS
Μπισκότα ἀμυγδάλου γεμιστὰ

**3 cups all-purpose flour, sifted with**
**2 teaspoons baking powder**
**1¼ cups sugar**
**Grated rind of 1 orange**
**1½ cups finely ground almonds**
**¾ cup unsalted butter or margarine, cut into cubes**
**2 eggs, beaten**
**½ cup orange marmalade**
**1 egg, beaten with 1 teaspoon water**

Combine first six ingredients in a food processor, (steel blade). Blend until crumbly. Add eggs and blend until the dough forms a ball. If the dough seems too soft add a tablespoon or so more of the flour and mix until incorporated. Roll out half of the dough about ⅛-inch thick on waxed paper and cut into rounds with a cookie cutter. Place rounds onto baking sheet lined with waxed paper. Spread on little marmalade; set aside. Roll out the other half of dough and cut with a doughnut cutter and place on top of the orange marmalade. Brush with beaten egg. Let stay 5 minutes to alow the egg to dry. Bake in a preheated 350°F (180°C) oven for approximately 12-15 minutes.

# FROSTED CHRISTMAS BISCUITS
Μπισκότα χριστουγεννιάτικα μὲ γλάσο

**1 cup unsalted butter or margarine, at room temperature**
**1½ cups sugar**
**2 eggs and 1 egg yolk**
**1 teaspoon vanilla**
**4 cups all-purpose flour (about)**
**4 teaspoons baking powder**

Cream butter and sugar until light and fluffy. Add eggs one at a time, beating thoroughly after each one is added. Add vanilla. Sift flour and baking powder together. Gradually add flour mixture beating until smooth after each addition to make a soft dough. Roll out a portion of dough about ⅛-inch thick on waxed paper and cut with Christmas cutters. Place onto baking sheets and bake in a preheated 375°F (190°C) oven for approximately 15-20 minutes. Cool. Frost as you desire. (See index for frostings).

# FILLED COGNAC BISCUITS
Μπισκότα μὲ κονιὰκ γεμιστὰ

**1 cup unsalted butter or margarine, at room temperature**
**2 cups or less sugar**
**3 eggs**
**1½ teaspoons vanilla**
**¼ cup cognac**
**4 cups all-purpose flour**
**4 teaspoons baking powder**
**1 cup jam or marmalade as you desire**

Cream butter and sugar until light and fluffy. Add eggs one at a time, beating thoroughlly after each one is added. Add vanilla and cognac, mix well. Sift flour and baking powder together. Gradually add flour mixture, beating until smooth after each addition to make a soft dough. Roll out a portion of dough about ⅛-inch thick on waxed paper and cut into rounds or squares. Place onto baking sheets and bake in a preheated 350°F (180°C) oven for approximately 12 minutes. Cool. Spread with jam on one biscuit and top with another.

# GINGER BISCUITS
Μπισκότα πιπερόριζας

**1½ cups unsalted butter or margarine, at room temperature**
**1½ cups sugar**
**2 eggs**
**½ cup honey**

4 cups all-purpose flour
1½ teaspoons baking soda
2 teaspoons ginger
2 teaspoons cinnamon

Cream butter and sugar until light and fluffy. Add eggs one at a time, beating thoroughly after each one is added. Add honey and mix well. Sift dry ingredients together. Gradually add flour mixture, beating until smooth after each addition to make a soft dough. Roll out a portion of dough about ¼-inch thick on waxed paper and cut into rounds. Place onto baking sheets lined with waxed paper. Bake in a preheated 375°F (190°C) oven for approximately 15 minutes.

## MOLASSES COOKIES
### Μουστοκούλουρα

1 cup fine quality oil
1 cup molasses
1 cup sugar
¼ cup cognac
1 egg
2 tablespoons warm water
8 cups all-purpose flour (about)
1¼ teaspoons cinnamon
½ teaspoon nutmeg
⅛ teaspoon cloves
1½ teaspoons baking soda
4 teaspoons baking powder

Combine first six ingredients in a large bowl, beat well. Sift dry ingredients together. Gradually add flour mixture and mix thoroughly. Roll out about ¼-inch in thickness on floured board, cut into rounds and bake in a preheated 400°F (205°C) oven for approximately 15 minutes.

## COCONUT BISCUITS
### Μπισκότα καρύδας

4 cups coconut (about), unsweetened
1 can sweetened condensed milk
1 teaspoon vanilla
Whole blanched almonds

Combine all the ingredients together, mix well to make a soft dough. Add more coconut if needed. Break off pieces of dough the size of a walnut and shape into balls. Press a whole almond into the center of each ball of coconut. Place into baking sheets lined with waxed paper. Bake in a preheated 375°F (190°C) oven for approximately 10 minutes or until lightly golden. Remove from sheet while hot.

## ANISETTE COOKIES
### Κουλουράκια μαστίχας

10 cups all-purpose flour (about)
2 teaspoons baking soda and 4 teaspoons baking
    powder
2 teaspoons cream of tartar
⅔ cup fine quality oil
2 cups anisette liqueur
1½ cups sugar

Sift dry ingredients together in a large mixing bowl. Add oil, anisette and sugar. Knead all the ingredients together into a soft dough. Add more flour if needed. Break off pieces of dough the size of a walnut, roll into a long cord and shape into twists. Place onto greased baking sheets. Bake in a preheated 375°F (190°C) oven for approximately 15 minutes or until golden.

## BUTTER COOKIES
### Κουλουράκια βουτύρου

1 cup unsalted butter or margarine, at room
    temperature
1¼ cups sugar
2 eggs
1 teaspoon vanilla
3½ cups all-purpose flour (about)
4 teaspoons baking powder
1 egg, beaten with 1 teaspoon water

Cream butter and sugar together until light and fluffy. Add eggs one at a time, beating thoroughly after each one is added. Sift flour and baking powder together. Gradually add flour, beating until smooth after each addition to make a soft dough. Add more flour if needed. Break off pieces of dough the size of a walnut, roll into a long cord and shape into twists or rings. Place on greased baking sheets. Brush lightly with beaten egg. Let stay 5 minutes to all the egg to dry. Bake in a preheated 375°F (190°C) oven for approximately 15 minutes or until golden.

## COGNAC COOKIES
### Κουλουράκια μὲ κονιὰκ

1 cup unsalted butter or margarine, at room
    temperature
2 cups sugar
6 eggs
2 teaspoons vanilla
6 cups all-purpose flour (about)
1 teaspoon baking soda

3 teaspoons baking powder
¼ cup cognac
1 egg, beaten with 1 teaspoon water
Sesame seed

Cream butter and sugar together until light and fluffy. Add eggs one at a time, beating thoroughly after each one is added. Add vanilla. Sift dry ingredients together. Gradually add flour alternately with cognac, beating until smooth after each addition to make a soft dough. Add more flour if needed. Break off pieces of dough the size of a walnut; roll into a long cord and shape into rings or twists. Place onto greased baking sheets. Brush lightly with beaten egg and sprinkle with sesame seed. Let stay 5 minutes to allow the egg to dry. Bake in a preheated 375°F (190°C) oven for approximately 15 minutes or until golden.

## CHOCOLATE COOKIES
### Κουλουράκια σοκολάτας

1½ cups sugar
4 eggs
⅓ cup melted butter or margarine (unsalted)
¼ cup milk
1 teaspoon vanilla
2 tablespoons cognac
5 cups cake flour (about)
1 teaspoon baking soda
3 teaspoons baking powder
⅓ cup cocoa
1 egg, beaten with 1 teaspoon water

Combine first 4 ingredients in a large mixing bowl and beat well. Add vanilla and cognac. Sift flour, baking soda and baking powder and cocoa together. Gradually add flour mixture, beating until smooth after each addition to make a soft dough. Add more flour if needed. Break off pieces of dough the size of a walnut, roll into a long cord and shape into wreaths. Place onto baking sheets (greased. Brush with beaten egg. Let stay 5 minutes to allow the egg to dry. Bake in a preheated 375°F (190°C) oven for approximately 12 minutes.

## FRUIT NUT COOKIES
### Κουλουράκια φρούτου

¾ cup sugar
¾ cup melted butter or margarine (unsalted)
¼ cup milk
2 eggs
1 teaspoon vanilla
1 cup ground orange preserve, drained or your desire

½ cup finely chopped almonds
4½ cups cake flour (about)
1 teaspoon baking soda
2 teaspoons baking powder
1 egg, beaten with 1 teaspoon water

Combine first 5 ingredients in a large mixing bowl and beat well. Add preserve of your desire and chopped almonds, mix well. Sift dry ingredients together. Gradually add flour, beating until smooth after each addition to make a soft dough. Add more flour if needed. Break off pieces of dough the size of a walnut, roll into a long cord and shape into rings or twists. Place into greased baking sheets. Brush lightly with beaten egg. Let stay 5 minutes to allow the egg to dry. Bake in a preheated 350°F (180°C) oven for approximately 18 minutes or until golden.

## HONEY NUT COOKIES
### Κουλουράκια μελιοῦ

¾ cup melted unsalted butter or margarine
⅔ cup milk
1½ cups sugar
½ cup honey
4 eggs
Grated rind of 1 orange
1 cup finely chopped walnuts
8 cups all-purpose flour
1 cup corn starch
2 teaspoons baking soda
5 teaspoons baking powder
1½ teaspoons cinnamon
2 eggs, beaten with 1 tablespoon water

Combine first 5 ingredients in a large mixing bowl and beat well. Add rind and chopped walnuts, mix well. Sift dry ingredients together. Gradually add flour,, beating until smooth after each addition to make a soft dough. Add more flour if needed. Break off pieces of dough the size of a walnut, roll into a long cord and shape into wreaths or twists. Place onto greased baking sheets. Brush with beaten eggs. Let stay 5 minutes to allow the egg to dry. Bake in a preheated 375°F (190°C) oven for approximately 18 minutes or until golden.

## MASTICHA COOKIES
### Κουλουράκια μαστίχας

1 cup unsalted butter or margarine, at room
      temperature
2½ cups sugar
3 eggs, separated

¼ cup cognac
⅔ teaspoon crushed masticha
8 cups all-purpose flour (about)
1 teaspoon baking soda
5 teaspoons baking powder
¾ cup evaporated milk
2 eggs, beaten with 1 tablespoon water

Cream butter and sugar until light and fluffy. Add egg yolks one at a time, beating thoroughly after each one is added. Add crushed mastica, stiffly beaten egg whites and cognac; mix thoroughly. Sift dry ingredients together. Gradually add flour mixture alternately with milk, beating until smooth after each addition to make a soft dough. Add more flour if needed. Break off pieces of dough the size of a walnut; roll into a long cord and shape into twists. Place onto greased baking sheets. Brush lightly with beaten eggs. Let stay 5 minutes to allow the egg to dry. Bake in a preheated 375°F (190°C) oven for approximately 15 minutes or until golden.

## MILK COOKIES
Κουλουράκια γάλακτος

10 cups all- purpose flour (about)
2 teaspoons baking soda
4 teaspoons baking powder
8 eggs, beaten
2¾ cups sugar
1½ cups milk
¾ cup melted unsalted butter or margarine
Grated rind of 1 lemon or more
2 tablespoons fresh lemon juice
2 eggs, beaten with 1 tablespoon water

Sift flour, baking soda and baking powder together in a large mixing bowl. Add beaten eggs and sugar, mix well. Add milk, butter, grated rind and lemon juice. Knead all the ingredients together into a soft dough. Add more flour if needed. Break off pieces of dough the size of a walnut; roll into a long cord and shape into twists. Place onto greased baking sheets. Brush lightly with beaten eggs. Let stay 5 minutes to allow the egg to dry. Bake in a preheated 375°F (190°C) oven for approximately 18 minutes or until golden.

## OUZO COOKIES
Κουλουράκια ούζου

1½ cups ouzo
1½ cups sugar
¾ cup fine oil
9 cups all-purpose flour (about)

2 teaspoons baking soda
3 teaspoons baking powder

Combine first 3 ingredients in a large mixing bowl and beat well. Sift flour with baking soda and baking powder together. Gradually add flour, beating until smooth after each addition to make a soft dough. Add more flour if needed. Break off pieces of dough the size of a walnut, roll into a long cord and shape into twists. Place onto greased baking sheets. Bake in a preheated 375°F (180°C) oven for approximately 18 minutes or until golden.

## ORANGE COOKIES
Κουλουράκια πορτοκαλιού

1½ cups unsalted butter or margarine, at room temperature
2 cups sugar
4 eggs
Grated rind of 1 orange
8 cups all -purpose flour (about)
1½ teaspoons baking soda
4 teaspoons baking powder
½ cup fresh orange juice
1 egg, beaten with 1 teaspoon water

Cream butter and sugar together until light and fluffy. Add eggs one at a time, beating thoroughly after each one is added. Add orange rind. Sift flour, baking soda and baking powder together. Gradually add flour mixture, alternately with orange juice, beating until smooth after each addition to make a soft dough. Add more flour if needed. Break off pieces of dough the size of a walnut, roll into a long cord and shape into twists, rings or wreaths. Place onto greased baking sheets. Brush lightly with beaten egg. Let stay 5 minutes to allow the egg to dry. Bake in a preheated 375°F (190°C) oven for approximately 18 minutes or until golden.

## PLAIN COOKIES
Κουλουράκια ἁπλὰ

1 cup unsalted butter or margarine, at room temperature
1¾ cups sugar
5 eggs
Grated rind of 1 orange
5 cups all-purpose flour (about)
1 teaspoon baking soda
3 teaspoons baking powder
1 egg, beaten with 1 teaspoon water

Cream butter and sugar together until light and fluffy. Add eggs one at a time, beating thoroughly after each one is added. Add grated rind. Sift flour, baking soda and baking powder together. Gradually add flour mixture, beating until smooth after each addition to make a soft dough. Add more flour if needed Break off pieces of dough the size of a walnut, roll into a long cord and shape into twists. Place onto greased baking sheets. Brush lightly with beaten egg. Let stay 5 minutes to allow the egg to dry. Bake in a preheated 375°F (190°C) oven for approximately 18 minutes or until golden.

## SESAME COOKIES
### Κουλουράκια σουσαμιοῦ

2 cups sugar
1 cup milk
4 eggs
½ cup melted unsalted butter or margarine
1½ teaspoons vanilla
9 cups all-purpose flour (about)
2 teaspoons baking soda
4 teaspoons baking powder
2 egg whites, beaten with 1 tablespoon water
1 cup or more sesame seed

Combine first 5 ingredients in a large mixing bowl and beat well. Sift flour, baking soda and baking powder together. Gradually add flour mixture, beating until smooth after each addition to make a soft dough. Add more flour if needed. Break off pieces of dough the size of a walnut and form into cylinders. Dip in beaten egg whites and roll them lightly in sesame seed. Place on greased baking sheets. Bake in a preheated 375°F (190°C) oven for approximately 18 minutes or until golden.

## SMYRNA COOKIES
### Κουλουράκια σμυρνέϊκα

9 cups all-purpose flour (about)
6 teaspoons baking powder
2⅓ cups unsalted butter, at room temperature
2 cups sugar
2 eggs, slightly beaten
½ teaspoon salt
2 teaspoons vanilla
¾ cup fresh orange juice, mixed with
⅓ cup cognac
2 egg yolks beaten with 1 teaspoon water

Sift flour and baking powder together in a large mix-

ing bowl. Add butter and cut with a pastry blender. Form a hole in the center and into it add sugar, beaten eggs, salt, vanilla and orange juice mixed with cognac. Knead all the ingredients together into a soft dough. Add more flour if needed. Break off pieces of the dough the size of a walnut, roll into a long cord and shape innto spirals. Place on greased baking sheets. Brush lightly with beaten egg. Let stay 5 minutes to allow the egg to dry. Bake in a preheated 375°F (190°C) oven for approximately 18 minutes or until golden.

## SMYRNA ORANGE COOKIES
### Κουλουράκια σμυρνέϊκα

5 cups all-purpose flour (about)
4 teaspoons baking powder
1 cup unsalted butter, at room temperature
1¼ cups sugar
⅓ cup milk
1 tablespoon honey
¼ teaspoon salt
2 eggs, slightly beaten
Grated rind of 1 orange
2 egg yolks beaten with 1 teaspoon water
Follow preparation as directed in Smyrna Cookies (see index).

## SPICE COOKIES
### Κουλουράκια μυρωδάτα

½ cup fine quality oil
1 cup unsalted butter, at room temperature
1½ cups sugar
Grated rind of 1 orange
½ cup cognac
5 cups all-purpose flour (about)
1 teaspoon baking soda
2 teaspoons baking powder
1 teaspoon cinnamon
¼ teaspoon cloves
1 cup fresh orange juice
1-2 egg whites, beaten with 1 teaspoon water
Sesame seeds

Cream butter, oil and sugar together until light and creamy. Add grated rind and cognac. Sift dry ingredients together. Gradually add flour mixture alternately with orange juice, beating until smooth after each addition to make a soft dough. Add more flour if needed. Break off pieces of dough the size of a walnut, form into cylinders. Place on greased baking sheets. Brush with beaten egg whites and sprinkle with sesame seeds. Let stay 5 minutes to allow the egg to dry. Bake in a preheated 375°F (190°C) oven for approximately 19 minutes or until golden brown.

⚜ ⚜ ⚜

# WINE COOKIES
## Κουλουράκια κρασιοῦ

1 cup fine quality oil
1 cup sugar
1 cup mavrodaphbe (Greek wine)
1 teaspoon baking soda
3 teaspoons baking powder
4½ cups all-purpose flour (about)
1 egg, beaten with 1 teaspoon water
Sesame seeds

Into a blender container put oil, sugar and wine. Cover. Blend for 5 minutes. Sift dry ingredients together into a large mixing bowl. Form a hole in the center and pour into it the oil mixture. Knead all the ingredients together into a soft dough. Add more flour if needed. Break off pieces of dough the size of a walnut, form into cylinders. Place on greased baking sheets. Brush with egg white and sprinkle with sesame seeds. Let stay 5 minutes to allow the egg to dry. Bake in a preheated 375°F (190°C) oven for approximately 18 minutes or until golden brown.

⚜ ⚜ ⚜

# YOGURT COOKIES
## Κουλουράκια μὲ γιαούρτι

1 cup unsalted butter or margarine, at room
    temperature
2 cups sugar
4 eggs
2 teaspoons vanilla
7 cups all-purpose flour (about)
2 teaspoons baking soda
1½ cups plain yogurt
1 egg, beaten with 1 teaspoon water

Cream butter and sugar together until light and fluffy. Add eggs one at a time, beating thoroughly after each one is added. Add vanilla. Sift dry ingredients together. Gradually add flour alternately with yogurt, beating until smooth after each addition to make a soft dough. Add more flour if needed. Break off pieces of dough the size of a walnut, roll into a long cord and shape into twists, rings or wreaths. Place on greased baking sheets. Brush lightly with beaten egg. Let stay 5 minutes to allow the egg to dry. Bake in a preheated 375°F (190°C) oven for approximately 18 minutes or until golden brown.

# ANISE RUSKS
## Παξιμαδάκια γλυκανίσου

1 cup fine quality oil
1½ cups sugar
1 teaspoon cinnamon
2 eggs and 2 egg yolks
1½ teaspoons anise extract
½ cup fresh orange juice
6 cups all-purpose flour (about)
1½ teaspoons baking soda
3 teaspoons baking powder
1 egg, beaten with 1 teaspoon water
Sesame seeds

Combine first 3 ingredients in a large mixing bowl and beat well. Add eggs and egg yolks one at a time, beating thoroughly after each one is added. Add anise extract and orange juice. Sift flour, baking soda and baking powder together. Gradually add flour, beating until smooth after each addition to make a soft dough. Add more flour if needed. Divide dough into 6 parts. Shape into long flat loaves about 2-inches wide and ¾-inch thick. Place on greased baking sheets 1½-inches apart. Brush them with beaten egg and sprinkle with sesame seed. Let stay 5 minutes to allow egg to dry. Bake in a preheated 375°F (190°C) oven for 20 minutes. Remove from oven, cut diagonally into ½-inch slices and separate. Return to oven; toast for 10-15 minutes.

⚜ ⚜ ⚜

# BUTTER RUSKS
## Παξιμαδάκια βουτύρου

10 cups all-purpose flour (about)
2 teaspoons baking soda
6 teaspoons baking powder
2½ cups melted unsalted butter or margarine
4 eggs, well beaten
3 cups sugar
2½ cups milk
2 teaspoons vanilla
1 egg,, beaten with 1 teaspoon water

Sift flour, baking soda and baking powder together in a large mixing bowl. Add melted butter and mix well with your hands. Add beaten eggs, sugar, milk and vanilla, beating until smooth to make a soft dough. Add more flour if needed. Divide dough into 8 parts. Shape into long flat loaves about 2-inches wide and ¾-inch thick. Place on greased baking sheets 1½-inches apart. Brush with beaten egg. Let stand 5 minutes to allow the egg to dry. Bake in a preheated 375°F (190°C) oven for 20 minutes. Remove from oven; cut diagonallly into ½-inch slices and separate. Return to oven and toast for 10-15 minutes.

✠✠✠✠

# CHOCOLATE RUSKS
Παξιμαδάκια σοκολάτας

1 cup fine quality oil
1½ cups sugar
3 eggs
1 teaspoon vanilla
2 tablespoons cognac
1 cup finely chopped walnuts
5 cups all-purpose flour (about)
1 teaspoon baking soda
4 teaspoons baking powder
¼ cup cocoa
1 egg, beaten with 1 teaspoon water

Combine oil and sugar in a large mixing bowl and beat well. Add eggs one at a time, beating thoroughly after each one is added. Add vanilla, cognac and chopped walnuts and mix well. Sift dry ingredients together. Gradually add flour mixture, beating until smooth after each addition to make a soft dough. Add more flour if needed. Divide dough into 6 parts. Shape into long flat loaves 2-inches wide and ¾-inch thick. Place on greased baking sheets 1½-inches apart. Brush with beaten egg. Let stay 5 minutes to allow the egg to dry. Bake in a preheated 350°F (180°C) oven for 20 minutes. Remove from oven; cut diagonally into ½-inch slices and separate. Return to oven and toast for 10-15 minutes.

✠✠✠✠

# CINNAMON-SUGAR RUSKS
Παξιμαδάκια κανέλλας

1 cup unsalted butter, room temperature
1 cup fine quality oil
1½ cups sugar
4 eggs
1 cup finely chopped walnuts
6 cups all-purpose flour (about)
4 teaspoons baking powder
1¼ teaspoons baking soda
1 teaspoon cinnamon
¼ teaspoon cloves
2 egg whites, beaten with 1 tablespoon water
½ cup sugar, mixed with
1 teaspoon cinnamon

Cream butter, oil and sugar until light and creamy. Add eggs one at a time, beating thoroughly after each one is added. Add walnuts. Sift flour with the dry ingredients together. Gradually add flour mixture, beating until smooth after each addition to make a

soft dough. Add more flour if needed. Divide dough into 6 parts. Shape into long flat loaves about 2-inches wide and ¾-inch thick. Place on greased baking sheets 1½-inches apart. Brush with beaten egg white and generously sprinkle with cinnamon-sugar mixture. Bake in a preheated 350°F (180°C) oven for 20 minutes. Remove from oven; cut diagonally into ½-inch slices and separate. Return to oven and toast for 10-15 minutes.

✠✠✠✠

# FRUIT NUT RUSKS
Παξιμαδάκια φρούτου

1½ cups unsalted butter or margarine, at room temperature
1½ cups sugar
4 eggs
1 teaspoon vanilla
1 cup seedless golden raisins
1 cup finely chopped almonds or walnuts
6 cups all-purpose flour (about)
1¼ teaspoons baking soda
4 teaspoons baking powder
1 egg, beaten with 1 teaspoon water

Cream butter and sugar until light and fluffy. Add eggs one at a time, beating thoroughly after each one is added. Add vanilla, raisins and almonds if desired, mix well. Sift dry ingredients together. Gradually add flour, beating until smooth after each addition to make a soft dough. Add more flour if needed. Divide dough into 5 parts. Shape into long flat loaves about 2-inches wide and ¾-inch thick. Place on greased baking sheets 1½-inches apart. Brush with beaten egg. Let stand 5 minutes to allow the egg to dry. Bake in a preheated 375°F (190°C) oven for 20 minutes. Remove from oven; cut diagonally into ½-inch slices and separate. Return to oven and toast for 10-15 minutes.

✠✠✠✠

# MILK RUSKS
Παξιμαδάκια γάλακτος

1½ cups unsalted butter or margarine, at room temperature
2½ cups sugar
6 eggs
2 teaspoons vanilla
10 cups all-purpose flour (about)
2 teaspoons baking soda
4 teaspoons baking powder
1 cup milk
1 egg, beaten with 1 teaspoon water
Sesame seed

Cream butter and sugar until light and fluffy. Add eggs one at a time, beating thoroughly after each one is added. Add vanilla. Sift dry ingredients together. Gradually add flour, beating until smooth after each addition to make a soft dough. Add more flour if needed. Divide dough into 7-8 parts. Shape into long flat loaves about 2-inches wide and ¾-inch thick. Place on greased baking sheets 1½-inches apart. Brush with beaten egg. Sprinkle with sesame seed. Let stay 5 minutes to allow the egg to dry. Bake in a preheated 375°F (190°C) oven for 20 minutes. Remove from oven; cut diagonally into ½-inch slices and separate. Return to oven and toast for 10-15 minutes.

## ORANGE RUSKS
### Παξιμαδάκια πορτοκαλιοῦ

1  cup fine quality oil
1½  cups sugar
5  eggs, well beaten
2  teaspoons vanilla
Grated rind of 1 orange
5  cups all-purpose flour (about)
1  teaspoon baking soda
3  teaspoons baking powder
1  egg, beaten with 1 teaspoon water
Sesame seed

Combine oil and sugar in a large mixing bowl and beat well. Add beaten eggs, vanilla and rind, mix well. Sift dry ingredients together. Gradually add flour mixture, beating until smooth after each addition to make a soft, slightly sticky dough. Add more flour if needed. Chill for 2 hours. Divide dough into 4 parts. Shape into long flat loaves about 2-inches wide and ¾-inch thick. Place on greased baking sheets 1½-inches apart. Brush with beaten egg and sprinkle with sesame seed. Let stay 5 minutes to allow the egg to dry. Bake in a preheated 375°F (190°C) oven for 20 minutes. Remove from oven; cut diagonally into ½-inch slices and separate. Return to oven and toast for 10-15 minutes.

## OUZO RUSKS
### Παξιμαδάκια οὔζου

1  cup unsalted butter or margarine, at room
        temperature
⅓  cup shortening
1½  cups sugar
6  eggs
1  teaspoon vanilla
Grated rind of half orange or lemon
⅓  cup Ouzo (Greek liqueur)

6  cups all-purpose flour
1¼  teaspoons baking soda
3  teaspoons baking powder
1  egg, beaten with 1 teaspoon water

Cream butter, shortening and sugar together until light and fluffy. Add eggs one at a time, beating thoroughly after each one is added. Add vanilla, rind and ouzo; mix well to combine. Sift dry ingredients together. Gradually add flour mixture, beating until smooth after each addition to make a soft dough. Add more flour if needed. Divide dough into 5 parts. Shape into long flat loaves about 2-inches wide and ¾-inch thick. Place on greased baking sheets 1½-inches apart. Brush lightly with beaten egg. Let stay 5 minutes to allow the egg to dry. Bake in a preheated 375°F (190°C) oven for 20 minutes. Remove from oven; cut diagonally into ½-inch slices and separate. Return to oven and toast for 10-15 minutes.

## PLAIN RUSKS
### Παξιμαδάκια ἁπλὰ

1  cup unsalted butter or margarine, at room
        temperature
2  tablespoons fine quality oil
1½  cups sugar
3  eggs
1  teaspoon vanilla
4½  cups all-purpose flour (about)
1  teaspoon baking soda
3  teaspoons baking powder
1  egg, beaten with 1 teaspoon water
Sesame seed

Cream butter, oil and sugar until light and fluffy. Add eggs one at a time, beating thoroughly after each one is added. Add vanilla. Sift dry ingredients together. Gradually add flour, beating until smooth after each addition to make a soft dough. Add more flour if needed. Divide dough into 4 parts. Shape into long flat loaves about 2-inches wide and ¾-inch thick. Place on greased baking sheets 1½-inches apart. Brush with beaten egg. Let stay 5 minutes to allow the egg to dry. Bake in a preheated 375°F (190°C) oven for 20 minutes. Remove from oven; cut diagonally into ½-inch slices and separate. Return to oven and toast for 10-15 minutes.

## SPICE RUSKS
### Παξιμαδάκια μυρωδάτα

1½  cups fine quality oil
½  cup unsalted butter, at room temperature

1 cup orange juice
1¾ cups sugar
½ cup cognac
Grated rind of 1 orange
Grated rind of 1 lemon
8½ cups all-purpose flour (about)
2 teaspoons baking soda
2 teaspoons baking powder
2 teaspoons cinnamon
½ teaspoon cloves
2 egg whites, beaten with 1 tablespoon water
Sesame seed

Combine oil, butter, orange juice, sugar and cognac together in a large mixing bowl and beat well. Add grated rind. Sift dry ingredients together. Gradually add flour mixture, beating until smooth after each addition to make a soft dough. Add more flour if neded. Divide dough into 6-7 parts. Shape into long flat loaves about 2-inches wide and ¾-inch thick. Place on greased baking sheets 1½-inches apart. Brush with beaten egg whites and generously sprinkle with sesame seed. Let stay 5 minutes to allow the eggs to dry. Bake in a preheated 375°F (190°C) oven for 20 minutes. Remove from oven; cut diagonally into ½-inch slices and separate. Return to oven and toast for 10-15 minutes.

❦❦❦❦

# VANILLA RUSKS
Παξιμαδάκια βανίλιας

1 cup unsalted butter at room temperature
⅓ cup shortening
2 cups sugar
6 eggs, separated
2 teaspoons vanilla
Grated rind of half lemon
6 cups all-purpose flour (about)
1½ teaspoons baking soda
4 teaspoons baking powder
1 egg, beaten with 1 teaspoon water
Sesame seed

Cream butter, shortening and sugar until light and fluffy. Add egg yolks one at a time, beating thoroughly after each one is added. Add vanilla and grated rind. Add stiffly beaten egg whites. Sift dry ingredients together. Gradually add flour, beating until smooth after each addition to make a soft dough. Add more flour if needed. Divide dough into 5 parts. Shape into long flat loaves about 2-inches wide and ¾-inch thick. Place on greased baking sheets 1½-inches apart. Brush with beaten egg. Let stay 5 minutes to allow the egg to dry. Bake in a preheated 375°F 190°C) oven for 20 minutes. Remove from oven;

cut diagonally into ½-inch slices and separate. Return to oven and toast for 10-15 minutes.

❦❦❦❦

Recipe from Mrs. John D. Mickles

# ALMOND BUTTER CHRISTMAS COOKIES A
Κουραμπιέδες ἀμυγδάλου

2½ cups clarified unsalted butter, at room temperature (see index)
1 cup confectioner's sugar, sifted
3 egg yolks
3 tablespoons cognac
1 cup finely chopped toasted blanched almonds
6½ cups cake flour, sifted with
4 teaspoons baking powder
Rosewater
Confectioner's sugar

Cream butter with an electric beater for 30 minutes. Add sifted sugar and beat well. Add egg yolks one at a time, beating thoroughly; add cognac and almonds and beat well. Gradually add flour and mix well with your hands until a soft dough. Add more flour if needed. Break off pieces of dough the size of a walnut and shape into half-moon or roll into balls and pinch tops twice making 4 indentions. Place on ungreased baking sheets. Bake in a preheated 350°F (180°C) oven for approximately 20 minutes or until lightly golden. Cool. Sprinkle with rosewater. Sift sugar over waxed paper. Gently remove cookies and place on the sugar. Sift more sugar on tops and sides. Remove to a serving platter. Sift more sugar until they are generously covered.

❦❦❦❦

# ALMOND BUTTER CHRISTMAS COOKIES B
Κουραμπιέδες ἀμυγδάλου

2 cups clarified unsalted butter, at room temperature (see index)
⅔ cup confectioner's sugar, sifted
2 egg yolks
¼ cup fresh orange juice
2 tablespoons cognac
1 teaspoon vanilla
½ teaspoon almond extract
1 cup finely chopped toasted blanched almonds
4½ cups cake flour (about), sifted with
4 teaspoons baking powder
Rosewater
Confectioner's sugar

Follow preparation as directed in Almond Butter Christmas Cookies.

⚜⚜⚜

# PECAN BUTTER CHRISTMAS COOKIES
### Κουραμπιέδες μὲ καρύδια

2 cups clarified butter (unsalted), at room
   temperature (see index)
½ cup confectioner's sugar
2 egg yolks
1 teaspoon vanilla
¼ cup orange juice
2 tablespoons cognac
¾ cup finely chopped pecans
6 cups cake flour (about), sifted with
4 teaspoons baking powder
Rosewater
Confectioner's sugar

Follow preparation as directed in Almond Butter Christmas Cookies A.

⚜⚜⚜

# HONEY CHRISTMAS COOKIES A
### Μελομακάρονα ἢ φοινίκια

2 cups fine quality oil
1 cup unsalted butter, at room temperature
¾ cup fresh orange juice
1 cup sugar
½ cup cognac
2½ teaspoons cinnamon
2 eggs, beaten
10 cups all-purpose flour (about)
1¼ teaspoons baking soda
5 teaspoons baking powder
SYRUP:
3 cups honey
2 cups sugar
2½ cups water
TOPPING:
2 cups or more finely chopped walnuts

Into blender container combine first 6 ingredients; cover and blend for 6 minutes. Sift dry ingredients together into a large mixing bowl. Form a hole in the center and pour into it the oil mixture and beaten eggs. Mix well. Knead into a soft dough. Add more flour if needed. Break off pieces of dough the size of a large walnut. Shape into ovals 2-inches long and press them lightly with the tips of your fingers on a cheese grinder. Place on ungreased baking sheets. Bake in a preheated 375°F (190°C) oven for ap-

proximately 20 minutes. Cool for 1 hour. Combine syrup ingredients in a saucepan. Bring to a boil. Reduce heat to medium and boil for 5 minutes. Skim th froth. Pour hot syrup over cookies. Cover with a larger baking pan or foil. After 1 hour turn them over, cover, let stay until cool. Remove carefully and drain. Place into layers on a serving platter and sprinkle with chopped walnuts.

⚜⚜⚜

# HONEY CHRISTMAS COOKIES B
### Μελομακάρονα ἢ φοινίκια

3 cups fine quality oil
1½ cups sugar
¾ cup cognac
¾ cup fresh orange juice
2½ teaspoons cinnamon
1 cup finely chopped walnuts (optional)
9 cups all-purpose flour (about)
1½ cups fine semolina
2 teaspoons baking soda
4 teaspoons baking powder
SYRUP:
3 cups honey
2 cups sugar
2½ cups water
TOPPING:
2 cups or more finely chopped walnuts

Follow preparation as directed in Honey Christmas Cookies A (see index).

⚜⚜⚜

# HONEY CHRISTMAS COOKIES C
### Μελομακάρονα ἢ φοινίκια

1 cup fine quality oil
1 cup unsalted butter, at room temperature
1 cup fresh orange juice
¾ cup sugar
⅓ cup cognac
2 teaspoons cinnamon
2 tablespoons honey
2 egg yolks
6 cups all-purpose flour (about)
1 teaspoon baking soda
4 teaspoons baking powder
SYRUP:
3 cups honey
2 cups sugar
2½ cups water
TOPPING:
2 cups or more finely chopped walnuts

Follow preparation as directed in Honey Christmas Cookies A (see index).

# DESSERTS, BEVERAGES, CANDIES, PRESERVES

## ALMOND DELIGHTS
### 'Εργολάβοι

**4 cups blanched almonds**
**2 cups sugar**
**2 envelopes sugar vanilla**
**1 teaspoon almond extract**
**3-4 egg whites, beaten**
**1¼ cups chopped sliced almonds**

In a food processor grind almonds and sugar together one cup at a time until almonds are very fine. Add vanilla, almond extract and egg whites, mix until the mixture is smooth and stiff. Break off pieces of the mixture the size of a large walnut and shape into oval (with your finger) thick cookie and roll in chopped almonds. Place them on baking sheet lined with waxed paper. Bake in a preheated 325°F (165°C) oven for approximately 20 minutes or until lightly golden. Remove from paper while still warm. If paper sticks to cookies, moisten it on the underside. Makes 4 dozen.

## ALMOND DELIGHTS HYDRAS STYLE

### 'Αμυγδαλωτὰ "Υδρας

**2 cups blanched almonds**
**¾ cup sugar**
**¼ cup fine semolina**
**3 egg whites, beaten**
**1 tablespoon rosewater**
**½ teaspoon almond extract**
**Rosewater**
**Confectioner's sugar**

In a food processor grind almonds and sugar together until almonds are very fine. Add semolina, egg whites,

rosewater and almond extract, mix until the mixture is stiff and smooth. Break off pieces of the mixture the size of a walnut and shape into balls or pears. Place cookies onto baking sheets lined with waxed paper. Bake in a preheated 350°F (180°C) oven for approximately 18 minutes or until lightly golden. Remove from paper while still warm. If paper sticks to cookies, moisten it on the underside. Sprinkle with rosewater. Sift confectioner's sugar over waxed paper. Place cookies on the sugar. Sift more sugar to cover well. When cool, gently remove to a serving platter.

## LENTEN ALMOND DELIGHTS HYDRAS STYLE

### 'Αμυγδαλωτὰ νηστήσιμα "Υδρας

**2 cups blanched almonds**
**¾ cup sugar**
**¼ cup fine semolina**
**½ teaspoon almond extract**
**2 tablespoons water**
**Rosewater**
**Confectioner's sugar**
**Whole cloves**

In a food processor grind almonds and sugar until almonds are very fine. Add semolina, almond extract and water, mix well. Gradually add rosewater to make a stiff smooth mixture. Break off pieces of the mixture the size of a walnut and shape into pears and stick a clove in the top. Place almond delights onto baking sheets lined with waxed paper. Bake in a preheated 300°F (150°C) oven for approximately 18 minutes or until lightly golden. Remove from paper while still warm. If paper sticks to cookies, moisten it on the underside. Sprinkle with rosewater. Sift confectioner's sugar over waxed paper. Place cookies on the sugar. Sift more sugar to cover well. When cool gently remove to a serving platter.

## PUFF PASTRY A
### Ζύμη γιὰ σοὺ

1 cup boiling water
½ cup unsalted butter
1 cup all-purpose flour, sifted
4 eggs, at room temperature

Add butter to boiling water and bring to a boil. Reduce heat. Add flour all at once and stir vigorously with a wooden spoon until mixture forms ball around spoon, leaving pan clean. Remove from heat. Add one egg at a time, beating thoroughly after each one is added. Continue beating until mixture is thick and smooth. In this form it is ready to use as you desire.

## PUFF PASTRY B
### Ζύμη γιὰ σοὺ

1 cup boiling water
½ cup unsalted butter
1½ cups all-purpose flour, sifted
6 eggs, at room temperature

Follow preparation as directed in Puff Pastry A.

## CREAM PUFFS
### Σοὺ ἀ λὰ κρέμ

**FOR THE SHELLS:**
1 recipe Puff Pastry A or B (see index)

**VANILLA CREAM FILLING:**
3 cups millk
1 cup sugar
¼ teaspoon salt
4 tablespoons flour
3 tablespoons corn starch
4 egg yolks
2 tablespoons unsalted butter
1 teaspoon vanilla
1 cup heavy cream, whipped

**CARAMEL TOPPING:**
¾ cup sugar
3 tablespoons water
½ cup chopped or sliced blanched almonds or pistachio nuts

Prepare shells as directed. Shape on greased baking sheets, using 1 teaspoon or 1 tablespoon of pastry for one puff (depending on the size you desire). Bake in a preheated 450°F (230°C) oven for 20 minutes. Reduce heat to 350°F (180°C) oven and bake 30 minutes longer. Cool. Make slit on one side of each puff and fill with cool cream filling.

Prepare cream filling. Scald 2½ cups milk. Combine sugar, salt, flour, corn starch, egg yolk and remaining milk mix well using a whisk. Gradually stir in scalding milk and cook slowly on top of double boiler, whisking constantly until mixture thickens. Cover and cook for 5 minutes. Remove from heat. Add butter and vanilla. Cover to prevent a skin from forming. Chill. Fold in whipped cream. Prepare caramel topping. Put sugar and water into a small heavy pan, stir and cook slowly until light brown, being careful not to scorch. Pour 1 tablespoon caramel on top of each puff and sprinkle with chopped nuts. Makes 1 dozen large or 3 dozen small puffs.

## CHOCOLATE CREAM PUFFS
### Τρούφφες

**FOR THE SHELLS:**
1 recipe Puff Pastry A or B (see index)

**CHOCOLATE CREAM FILLING:**
1 recipe Vanilla Cream Filling (see index for cream puffs)
2 ounces baker's sweet chocolate
2 cups chocolate sprinkles

Follow recipe and preparation as directed for Puff Pastry. Prepare vanilla cream filling as directed, add chocolate with the butter and stir well to melt. Cool. Fill shells with cool chocolate cream filling. Lightly spread the outside with some cream filling and cover with chocolate sprinkles. Chill. Makes 1 dozen large or 3 dozen small puffs.

## ECLAIRS
### Ἐκλαὶρ

**FOR THE SHELLS:**
1 recipe Puff Pastry A or B (see index)

**FOR THE FILLING:**
1 recipe Vanilla Cream Filling (see index for cream puffs)

**CHOCOLATE FROSTING:**
2 ounces baker's sweet chocolate
2 tablespoons unsalted butter or margarine
½ cup confectioner's sugar, sifted

**2 tablespoons water**
**½ teaspoon vanilla**

Follow recipe and preparation as directed for Puff Pastry. Shape puff pastry into strips ¾-inch wide and 3½-inches long into greased baking sheet. Bake in a preheated 450°F (230°C) oven for 20 minutes. Reduce heat to 350°F (180°C) oven and bake 30 minutes longer. When cool split. Prepare vanilla cream filling as directed. Fill eclairs with vanilla cream filling. Frost with chocolate frosting. Prepare chocolate frosting. Melt chocolate and butter over boiling water, stirring continuously. Remove from heat. Add confectioner's sugar, water and vanilla, stirring until the mixture is smooth and glossy. Frost eclairs when chocolate is still hot.

## CHOCOLATE NUT ROLLS WITH SYRUP

Ρολλὰ σοκολάτας μὲ σιρόπι

**FOR THE DOUGH:**
**1 cup scalding milk**
**1 yeast cake**
**½ cup sugar**
**¼ teaspoon salt**
**3 eggs**
**1 cup fine quality oil**
**5 cups all-purpose flour (about), sifted with**
**4 teaspoons baking powder**

**FOR THE FILLING:**
**1¼ cups finely chopped walnuts**
**½ cup sugar**
**3 tablespoons cocoa, sifted**
**1 teaspoon cinnamon**
**2 tablespoons cognac**

**FOR THE SYRUP:**
**4 cups sugar**
**2⅓ cups water**
**2 tablespoons fresh lemon juice**

Dissolve yeast in warm milk. In a large mixing bowl combine eggs, sugar, salt and oil. Beat well. Add milk mixture. Gradually stir in flour until dough is soft and smooth. Add more flour if needed. Cover; let rise in warm place free from draft until doubled in bulk. Divide dough into 4 parts. On lightly floured surface roll out the three of the parts, one at a time into sheets 17x4-inches, set aside. Mix the fourth part with chopped walnut, cocoa, cninamon, sugar and cognac. Roll into three cords 17-inches long. Place each cord on each roll-out sheet. Roll up like jelly roll. Cut into 1½-inch thick slices. Place into greased muffin pans or into small tart sheets, cut side up. Let rise until doubled in bulk. Bake in a preheated 350°F (180°C) oven for approximately 20 minutes. Remove from oven and cool. Combine syrup ingredients in a saucepan. Bring to a boil. Reduce heat to medium and boil for 5 minutes. Spoon hot syrup over chocolate rolls. Serve with whipped cream if desired.

## CINNAMON NUT ROLLS WITH SYRUP

Ρολλὰ κανέλλας μὲ σιρόπι

**FOR THE DOUGH:**
**½ cup scalding milk**
**1 yeast cake**
**4 eggs, at room temperature**
**¾ cup sugar**
**1½ teaspoons ground machlepi**
**½ cup melted unsalted butter or margarine**
**5 cups all-purpose flour (about), sifted**

**FOR THE FILLING:**
**1½ cups finely chopped walnuts or almonds**
**½ cup sugar**
**1½ teaspoons or more cinnamon**
**⅓ cup melted butter or margarine**

**FOR THE SYRUP:**
**4 cups sugar**
**2⅓ cups water**
**2 tablespoons fresh lemon juice**

Mix filling ingredients except the butter. Set aside. Dissolve yeast with warm milk. In a large mixing bowl beat eggs, sugar and machlepi until sugar has dissolved. Add milk mixture and melted butter, beat well. Gradually stir in flour until dough is soft and smooth. Add more flour if needed. Cover, let rise in warm place free from draft until doubled in bulk. Divide dough into halves. On lightly floured surface roll each half into sheet 14x10-inches. Brush with melted butter and sprinkle with the half of the filling mixture. Roll up like jelly roll. Cut into 1½-inch thick slices. Place onto greased baking sheets. Cover; let rise until doubled in bulk. Bake in a preheated 350°F (180°C) oven for approximately 20 minutes. While the rolls are baking prepare the syrup. In a saucepan combine syrup ingredients. Bring to a boil. Reduce heat to medium and boil for 5 minutes. Remove rolls from oven and spoon syrup over. Cool.

## SWEET CRESCENTS

Κρουσὰν

**FOR THE DOUGH:**

1 recipe Athenian Rich Easter Braids (see index)

FOR THE FILLING:
1 cup sugar
1½ cups coarsely chopped walnuts
1 teaspoon cinnamon
½ cup melted butter or margarine, unsalted
1 egg, beaten with 1 teaspoon water

FOR THE TOPPING:
2 cups sifted confectioner's sugar
2 tablespoons water
½ teaspoon vanilla

Follow recipe and preparation as directed in Athenian rich easter braids. Divide dough into three parts and round into balls. Cover; let rest 5 minutes. While dough is resting combine filling ingredients except beaten egg, mix well. Set aside. Using a rolling pin, roll out one part at a time on a floured surface into ¼-inch thick. Cut into triangles. Brush with melted butter and sprinkle with walnut mixture. Roll each triangle beginning at the base. Place on greased baking sheets, curving ends toward each other. Cover; let rise in warm place until doubled in bulk. Brush with beaten egg. Let stay 5 minutes to allow the egg to dry. Bake in a preheated 350°F (180°C) oven for approximately 15 minutes or until they are ready. While crescents are baking prepare frosting. In a small bowl combine confectioner's sugar, water and vanilla, mix well. Glaze crescent rolls when they are still hot.

NOTE: After crescents are baked, cool on racks without the glaze. Store in plastic bags and freeze. When you are ready to use, preheat oven to 450°F (230°C) oven. Place crescents in baking pan and cover with foil and bake for 30 minutes. Glaze and serve hot.

✘✘✘✘

# SMALL CAKES WITH SYRUP
Σαβαρὲν

FOR THE DOUGH:
½ cup scalding milk
1 yeast cake
½ cup sugar
¼ teaspoon salt
4 eggs, at room temperature
½ cup melted unsalted butter or margarine
Grated rind of ½ lemon
5 cups all-purpose flour (about), sifted

FOR THE SYRUP:
5 cups sugar
3 cups water
½ cup cognac
2 cups heavy cream, whipped

½ cup chopped pistachio nuts or blanched toasted almonds

Dissolve yeast in warm milk. In a large mixing bowl beat eggs, sugar, salt and lemon rind until sugar has dissolved. Add milk mixture and melted butter and beat well. Gradually stir in flour until dough is soft and smooth. Add more flour if needed. Cover; let rise in warm place free from draft until doubled in bulk. Divide dough into 30 equal pieces. Form into balls. Place in greased muffin pans or into small tart shells. Let rise until doubled in bulk. Bake in a preheated 350°F (180°C) oven for 15 minutes or until ready. Remove from pans and place on a serving platter. Combine syrup ingredients except cognac, cream and nuts. Bring to a boil, reduce heat to medium and boil for 5 minutes. Remove from heat and add cognac. Spoon syrup over savaren. Chill. Serve with whippepd cream and sprinkle with chopped nuts.

✘✘✘✘

# HONEY NUT TURNOVERS
Σκαλτσούνια

FOR THE DOUGH:
½ cup unsalted butter or margarine, at room temperature
¼ cup fine quality oil
½ cup sugar
1 tablespoon cognac
3 cups all-purpose flour, sifted with
1 teaspoon baking soda and
¼ teaspoon cinnamon

FOR THE FILLING:
1 package (8-ounces) finely chopped walnuts
3 tablespoons toasted sesame seeds
¼ teaspoon cinnamon
½ cup honey, and mix all together

FOR THE TOPPING:
Rosewater
Confectioner's sugar, sifted

Cream butter, oil and sugar together until light and fluffy. Add cognac. Gradually add flour mixture to butter, beating until smooth after each addition to make a soft dough. Add more flour if needed. Form dough into 3 balls. Roll out one ball at a time to ⅛-inch thickness. Cut dough into rounds 3-inches in diameter. Place one teaspoon of filling on each circle of dough. Dampen the edge of each circle of dough. Fold the dough over the filling to form a half-moon shape. Place turnovers on greased baking sheets. Bake in a preheated 350°F (180°C) oven for approximately 30 minutes. Remove from oven and sprinkle with rosewater. Sift confectioner's sugar over waxed paper. Remove turnovers and place on the sugar.

Sift more sugar on top and sides. When cool remove to a serving platter.

✄✄✄✄

# LENTEN NUT FRUIT TURNOVERS
### Σκαλτσούνια νηστήσιμα

**FOR THE DOUGH:**
**1 package (10-ounces) whole blanched almonds**
**⅓ cup sugar**
**⅓ cup and 1 tablespeoon cake flour, sifted with**
**¼ teaspoon cinnamon**
**4 tablespoons water**
**3 tablespoons cognac**
**⅓ cup orange juice**
**Grated rind of 1 orange**

**FOR THE FILLING:**
**1⅓ cups finely chopped walnuts**
**½ cup seedless golden raisins**
**¾ cup quince preserve (see index)**

**FOR THE TOPPING:**
**Rosewater**
**Confectioner's sugar**

Combine filling ingredients and mix well. Set aside. In a blender or food processor grind almonds and sugar together, a little at a time until almonds are very fine. Add the rest of the ingredients and mix until the dough if soft and smooth and begins to clean the sides of the bowl. If the dough appears to be too soft and 1 tablespoon or more flour. Form dough into two balls. Roll out one ball at a time to ⅛-inch thickness. Cut dough into rounds 3-inches in diameter. Place one teaspoon of filling on each circle of dough. Dampen the edge of each circle of dough. Fold the dough over the filling to form a half-moon shape. Place turnovers on greased baking sheets. Bake in a preheated 425°F (220°C) oven for approximately 10 minutes. Remove from oven and sprinkle with rosewater. Sift confectioner's sugar over waxed paper. Remove turnovers and place on the sugar. Sift more sugar on top and sides. When cool remove to a serving platter.

✄✄✄✄

# LENTEN NUT RAISIN TURNOVERS
### Σκαλτσούνια νηστήσιμα

**FOR THE DOUGH:**
**3 cups all-purpose flour, sifted with**
**2 teaspoons baking powder and**
**⅓ teaspoon cinnamon**
**2 tablespoons sugar**
**1¼ cups sesame tahini**
**1 tablespoon sesame oil**
**¼ cup lukewarm water**

**FOR THE FILLING:**
**½ cup chopped blanched almonds**
**½ cup chopped walnuts**
**½ cup seedless golden raisins**
**¾ cup apricot jam or your desire**

**FOR THE TOPPING:**
**¼ cup rosewater**
**Confectioner's sugar**

Combine filling ingredients and mix well. Set aside. Combine dough ingredients except water together and cut with a pastry cutter till mixture resembles coarse crums. Add water and gently toss with your fingers. Form dough into two balls. Roll out one at a time to ⅛-inch thick sheet. Cut dough into rounds 3-inches in diameter. Place one teaspoon of filling on each circle of dough. Dampen the edge of each circle. Fold the dough over the filling to form a half-moon shape. Place turnovers on ungreased baking sheets. Bake in a preheated 350°F (180°C) oven for approximately 30 minutes. Remove from oven and sprinkle with rosewater. Sift confectioner's sugar over waxed paper. Remove turnovers and place on the sugar. Sift more sugar on top and sides. When cool remove to a serving platter.

✄✄✄✄

# NUT TURNOVERS
### Σκαλτσούνια

**FOR THE DOUGH:**
**1 cup unsalted butter or margarine, at room**
    **temperature**
**1 cup fine quality oil**
**5 cups all-purpose flour (about)**
**1 teaspoon baking soda**
**3 teaspoons baking powder**
**⅓ teaspoon cinnamon**
**1 tablespoon cognac**
**Juice of ½ lemon**

**FOR THE FILLING:**
**1 cup finely chopped walnuts**
**1 cup finely chopped almonds**
**½ cup toasted sesame seeds, crushed**
**1 cup sugar**
**½ teaspoon cinnamon**

**FOR THE TOPPING:**
**Rosewater**
**Confectioner's sugar**

Combine filling ingredients together and mix well. Set aside. Cream butter, oil and sugar together until light and creamy. Sift dry ingredients together. Gradually add flour mixture to butter alternately with cognac and lemon juice, beating until smooth after each addition to make a stiff dough. Add more flour if needed. Form dough into 3 balls. Roll out one ball at a time to ⅛-inch thick. Cut dough into rounds 3-inches in diameter. Place one teaspoon of filling on each circle of dough. Dampen the edge of each circle. Fold the dough over the filling to form a half-moon shape. Place turnovers on greased baking sheets. Bake in a preheated 350°F (180°C) oven for approximately 30 minutes. Remove from oven and sprinkle with rosewater. Sift confectioner's sugar over waxed paper. Remove turnovers and place on the sugar. Sift more sugar on top and sides. When cool remove to a serving platter.

### ALMOND BAKLAVA
Μπακλαβὰς ἀμυγδάλου

3 cups finely chopped blanched almonds
⅓ cup sugar
⅓ cup finely ground Zwieback toast or dried bread
　　crumbs (see index)
1 teaspoon cinnamon
1½ cups melted clarified unsalted butter (see index)
1 pound Phyllo pastry, thawed

FOR THE SYRUP:
4 cups sugar
2 cups water
1 tablespoon fresh lemon juice
1 teaspoon almond extract
½ cup pistachio nuts, chopped (optional)

Combine chopped almonds, sugar, ground toast if desired and cinnamon together. Brush a 10x15x3-inch baking pan with melted butter. Lay two sheets of phyllo in the bottom of the pan, brush with butter, cover with two more sheets, brush again with butter, and repeat process until you have used 8 sheets. Then sprinkle evenly with ⅓ cup almond mixture, cover with two sheets, brush with the melted butter and sprinkle evenly with almond mixture. Repeat this process until all almond mixture is used. Then cover with the remaining sheets brushing every other one with melted butter. With a sharp knife cut the baklava into diamond shapes. Bake in a preheated 300°F (150°C) oven for 90 minutes. Cool. Combine syrup ingredients except almond extract and pistachio nuts. Bring to a boil, reduce heat to medium and boil for 10 minutes, add almond extract. Pour hot syrup over cool baklava. Sprinkle with pistachio nuts if desired. Cover until cool. Cut and serve.

**Variations:**

**ALMOND WALNUT BAKLAVA**
Substitute one half of the almonds with walnuts.
Follow recipe and preparation as directed in Almond

Baklava (see index). Reduce almond extract to ½ teaspoon.

### WALNUT BAKLAVA
Μπακλαβὰς καρυδιοῦ

Substitute walnuts for the almonds.
Follow recipe and preparation as directed in Almond Baklava (see index). Subtract almond extract from syrup.

### ALMOND FILLED FLUTES
Φλογέρες μὲ ἀμύγδαλα

2 cups finely chopped blanched almonds
¼ cup sugar
¼ cup finely ground Zwieback toast or dried bread
　　crumbs (see index)
1 teaspoon cinnamon
2 beaten eggs
1 pound Phyllo pastry (thawed)
1¼ cups melted clarified unsalted butter (see index)

FOR THE SYRUP:
3½ cups sugar
1¾ cups water
1 tablespoon fresh lemon juice
¾ teaspoon almond extract

Combine chopped almonds, sugar, ground toast if desired and cinnamon together. Add beaten eggs, mix well to combine. Cut phyllo sheets in half crosswise. Place strips on top of each other, cover with damp cloth to keep from drying while working. Take one strip at a time. Brush each strip with melted butter and fold in half crosswise. Place one tablespoon of filling at a narrow end of strip; turn sides in toward middle to enclose filling. Brush with butter and roll over lengthwise to other end to form a roll. Place in greased baking sheets. Repeat the filling rolling process. Generously brush each one with melted butter. Bake in a preheated 350°F (180°C) oven for 15-20 minutes or until golden. Cool, to lukewarm. Pierce them in 3-4 spots with a fork very gently so that they will absorb the syrup. Combine sugar, water and lemon juice in a saucepan, bring to a boil, reduce heat to medium and boil for 10 minutes. Add almond extract. Spoon hot syrup over floyieres. Cover, let cool.

**Variation:**

### WALNUT FILLED FLUTES
Φλογέρες μὲ καρύδια

Substitute walnuts for the almonds.

Follow recipe and preparation as directed in Almond Filled Flutes. Subtract almond extract from syrup.

# NUT PASTRY ROLLS
## Σαραΐλι

3 cups finely chopped blanched almonds or walnuts
⅓ cup sugar
1 teaspoon cinnamon
⅓ cup finely ground Zwieback toast or dried bread crumbs (see index)
1 pound Phyllo pastry (thawed)
1¼ cups melted clarified unsalted butter (see index)

**FOR THE SYRUP:**
3 cups sugar
2 cups water
1 tablespoon fresh lemon juice
1 teaspoon almond extract if you use almonds

Combine chopped almonds if desired, sugar, cinnamon and ground toast together. Brush one phyllo sheet with melted butter. Lay a second sheet on top, brush with butter and generously sprinkle with the almond mixture. Lay the third sheet on top, brush with butter and top with the fourth sheet, brush with butter and generously sprinkle with almond mixture. Carefully roll the sheets lengthwise. Gently place saraili into greased round baking pan. Repeat this process until all the almond mixture and phyllo sheets are used. Generously brush with the melted butter and cut each roll into 2 3-inch long pieces. Bake in a preheated 350°F (180°C) oven for approximately 20 minutes or until golden. Cool to lukewarm. Pierce them in 3-4 places with a fork so that they will absorb the syrup. Combine sugar, water and lemon juice in a saucepan, bring to a boil, reduce heat and boil for 10 minutes. Add almond extract if you used almonds. Spoon hot syrup over saraili. Cover, let cool.

# CREAM FILLED PASTRY A
## Γαλακτομπούρεκο

**FOR THE CREAM FILLING:**
8 egg yolks
1½ cups sugar
1 cup fine semolina
8 cups scalding milk
Rind of ½ lemon (optional)
2 tablespoons unsalted butter
1 teaspoon vanilla
¾ cup finely chopped blanched almonds (optional)
1 pound Phyllo pastry (thawed)
1 cup melted clarified unsalted butter (see index)

**FOR THE SYRUP:**
3½ cups sugar
1¼ cups water
2 tablespoons fresh lemon juice

Combine egg yolks and sugar in a saucepan, beat well using a whisk. Add semolina and mix well. Gradually add milk and lemon rind and cook slowly over medium-low heat stirring constantly until it thickens. Remove the lemon rind. Add vanilla, butter and almonds if desired, stir to mix it well. Cover and let cool. Brush a 11x17x3-inch baking pan with melted butter. Lay 12 of the phyllo sheets on the bottom of pan, one on top the other brushing each one with melted butter. The sheets will extend up the sides of the pan. Pour in the cream and spread evenly. Butter and fold overhanging sides and ends of phyllo sheets over the filling to enclose it. Lay the rest of the sheets over the top, brushing each one with melted butter. Score with a sharp knife into diamond shapes. Bake in a preheated 350°F (180°C) oven for approximately 45 minutes or until golden. Cool to warm. Combine syrup ingredients in a saucepan. Bring to a boil, reduce heat and boil for 10 minutes. Pour warm syrup over warm cream pastry. Let cool. Cut through the scored lines and serve.

# CREAM FILLED PASTRY B
## Μπουγάτσα

**FOR THE CREAM FILLING:**
6 cups milk
Rind of ½ lemon or orange (optional)
¾ cup fine semolina
4 eggs
2 cups sugar
1 teaspoons vanilla
1 tablespoon unsalted butter
10 Phyllo pastry (thawed)
½ cup melted clarified unsalted butter (see index)

**FOR THE TOPPING:**
1 cup confectioner's sugar, sifted with
1 teaspoon cinnamon

Boil the milk with the lemon rind if desired. Gradually add semolina stirring constantly using a whisk and cook over medium-low heat until it thickens. Remove from heat. Beat eggs with sugar well. Slowly add egg mixture to milk, stirring constantly over low heat until thick and smooth, add vanilla and butter. Let cool. Remove lemon rind. Brush a 10x15x3-inch baking pan with melted butter. Lay six of the phyllo sheets on the bottom of pan one on top of the other brushing each one with melted butter. The sheets will extend up the sides of the pan. Pour in the cream and spread evenly. Butter and fold overhanging sides and ends of phyllo sheets over the filling to enclose it. Lay the rest of the phyllo sheets over the top, brushing each one with melted butter. Fold in the overhanging sides brushing with melted butter. Score with sharp knife into diamond shapes. Bake in a preheated 350°F (180°C) oven for approximately 34 minutes or until golden. Remove from oven and sift confectioner's sugar mixture. Serve hot.

## CREAM FILLED FLUTES
Φλογέρες μὲ κρέμα

**1 recipe cream filling, from Cream Filling Pastry A (see index)**

**FOR THE SYRUP:**
**3 cups sugar**
**1½ cups water**
**1 tablespoon fresh lemon juice**

Follow recipe and preparation as directed.

Cut phyllo sheets in half crosswise. Place strips on top of each other, cover with damp cloth to keep from drying while working. Take one strip at a time. Brush each strip with melted butter and fold in half crosswise; place 1 tablespoon of filling at a narrow end of strip. Turn sides in toward middle to enclose filling. Brush with butter and roll over lengthwise to other end to form a roll. Place in a greased baking pan. Repeat the filling and rolling process. Generously brush each one with melted butter. Bake in a preheated 350°F (180°C) oven for approximately 20 miutes or until golden. Cool. Pierce them in 3-4 spots with a fork so they will absorb the syrup. Combine syrup ingredients in a saucepan. Bring to a boil, reduce heat and boil for 10 minutes. Spoon warm syrup over floyieres. Cover, let cool.

## COPENHAGEN PASTRY A
Κοπενχάγη

**9 eggs**
**1⅓ cups sugar**
**3 tablespoons cognac**
**2 cups ground almonds, finely chopped**
**1 cup finely ground Zwieback toast**
**3 teaspoons baking powder**
**1 teaspoon cinnamon**
**¼ teaspoon salt**
**1 pound Phyllo pastry (thawed)**
**1 cup melted clarified unsalted butter (see index)**
**FOR THE SYRUP:**

**4 cups sugar**
**2 cups water**
**2 tablespoons fresh lemon juice**
**1 teaspoon almond extract**

Beat eggs until frothy, add sugar and beat well until creamy and thick. Add cognac. Mix ground almonds, ground toast, baking powder, cinnamon and salt together. Gradually add to egg mixture, and mix well. Brush a 11x17x3-inch baking pan with melted butter. Lay on 10 of the phyllo sheets on the bottom of pan one on top of the other brushing each one with melted butter. The sheets will extend up the sides of the pan. Pour in the egg-almond mixture and spread evenly. Butter and fold overhanging sides and ends of phyllo sheets over the filling to enclose it. Lay the rest of the sheets over the top, brushing each one with melted butter. Score with sharp knife into diamonds. Bake in a preheated 350°F (180°C) oven for approximately 45 minutes or until golden. Cool. Combine syrup ingredients except almond extract in a saucepan. Bring to a boil, reduce heat and boil for 5 minutes. Pour hot syrup over pastry. Let cool. Cut through the scored lines.

## COPENHAGEN PASTRY B
Κοπενχάγη

**FOR THE CRUST:**
**1½ cups flour**
**1 teaspoon baking powder**
**¾ cup unsalted butter, at room temperature**
**¼ cup sugar**
**2 tablespoons cognac**
**1 egg, beaten**
**Grated rind of ½ orange**

**FOR THE FILLING:**
**½ cup apricot jam**
**¾ cup sugar**
**6 eggs, separated**
**3 tablespoons cognac**
**1½ cups finely ground almonds**
**1 cup finely ground Zwieback toast**
**3 teaspoons baking powder**
**1 teaspoon cinnamon**
**6 sheets of Phyllo pastry (thawed)**
**½ cup melted clarified unsalted butter (see index)**

**FOR THE SYRUP:**
**3 cups sugar**
**1⅔ cups water**
**2 tablespoons fresh lemon juice**
**½ teaspoon almond extract**

Sift flour with baking power together. Cut in butter to coarse crumbs. Add beaten egg, cognac and orange rind. Mix until mixture will hold together. Press

140

dough in bottom of a greased 13x9x3-inch baking pan and spread evenly. Bake in a preheated 400°F (205°C) oven for 6 minutes. Remove from heat. Spread jam over baked crush. Set aside. Beat egg yolks and sugar until thick and creamy, add cognac. Mix ground almonds, ground toast,, baking powder and cinnnamon together. Gradually add to egg mixture and mix well. Fold in stiffly beaten egg whites, Pour mixture over jam. Lay 6 phyllo sheets over egg-almond mixture, brushing each one with the melted butter. Score with sharp knife into diamond shapes. Bake in a preheated 350°F (180°C) oven for approximately 40 minutes or until golden. Cool to luke-warm. Combine syrup ingredients except almond extract in a saucepan. Bring to a boil, reduce heat and boil for 6 minutes. Pour hot syrup over pastry. Let cool. Cut through the scored lines.

☙☙☙

# APPLE FILLED PASTRY
## Μηλόπιττα

**FOR THE FILLING:**

**8 large apples, pared and thinly sliced**
**2 tablespoons fresh lemon juice**
**½ cup finely ground Zwieback toast or dried bread**
   **crumbs (see index)**
**½ teaspoon cinnamon**
**¾ cup sugar**
**1 cup chopped blanched almonds or walnuts**
**½ cup seedless golden raisins**
**1 pound phyllo pastry (thawed)**
**1 cup melted clarified unsalted butter (see index)**

**FOR THE SYRUP:**

**3 cups sugar**
**1½ cups water**
**1 tablespoon fresh lemon juice**
**1 1-inch cinnamon stick**

Mix dry ingredients together. Add sliced apples and lemon juice and mix well. Brush a 11x15x3-inch baking pan with butter. Lay 12 of the phyllo sheets on the bottom of the pan one on top of the other, brushing each one with the melted butter. The sheets will extend up the sides of the pan. Pour in the apple mixture and spread evenly. Butter and fold overhanging sides and ends of phyllo sheets over the top, brushing each one with the melted butter. Fold in the overhanging sides brushing well with melted butter. Score with a sharp knife into diamond shapes. Bake in a preheated 350°F (180°C) oven for approximately 45 minutes or until golden. Cool to lukewarm. Combine syrup ingredients in a saucepan. Bring to a boil, reduce heat to medium and boil for 10 miutes. Pour warm syrup over warm apple pastry. Let cool. Cut through scored lines.

# APPLE FILLED FLUTES
## Φλογέρες μὲ μήλα

**1 recipe Apple Filled Pastry (see index)**

Follow recipe and preparation as directed.

Cut phyllo sheets in half crosswise. Place strips on top of each other, cover with damp cloth to keep from drying while working. Take one strip at a time. Brush each strip with melted butter and fold in half crosswise. Place one tablespoon of filling at a narrow end of strip. Turn sides in toward middle to enclose filling. Brush with butter and roll lengthwise to other end to form a roll. Place in greased baking pan. Repeat the filling and rolling process. Generously brush each one with melted butter. Bake in a preheated 350°F (180°C) oven for approximately 20 minutes or until golden. Cool to lukewarm. Pierce them in 3-4 spots with a fork so that they will absorb the syrup. Combine syrup ingredients in a saucepan. Bring to a boil, reduce heat to medium and boil for 10 minutes. Spoon warm syrup over floyieres. Cover, let cool.

☙☙☙

# PUMPKIN NUT FILLED PASTRY
## Κολοκυθόπιττα

**FOR THE FILLING:**

**4 cups cooked and mashed fresh pumpkin**
**⅓ cup or more unsalted butter**
**½ cup finely ground Zwieback toast or dried bread**
   **crumbs (see index)**
**Grated rind of ½ orange**
**½ teaspoon cinnamon**
**1½ cups finely chopped walnuts**
**½ cup honey**
**1 cup sugar**
**1 pound Phyllo pastry (thawed)**
**1 cup melted clarified unsalted butter (see index)**
**1½ cups finely chopped blanched almonds**
**¼ cup finely ground Zwieback toast or dried bread**
   **crumbs (see index)**
**¼ cup sugar**
**¼ teaspoon cinnamon**

**FOR THE SYRUP:**

**1¼ cups sugar**
**¾ cup honey**
**1 cup water**

Wash the pumpkin and cut into large pieces. Peel and remove the seeds and the soft mesh surrounding them. Boil in 3 cups boiling water and 2 teaspoons salt until tender. Drain in a strainer very well and press to remove excess liquid. Mash and drain again. Melt butter in a medium saucepan. Add mashed pumpkin and saute for a few minutes, stirring constantly. Remove from heat; add ground toast if desired, grated rind, cinnamon, walnuts and honey and mix thoroughly. Set aside. Combine chopped almonds, ground toast if desired, sugar and cinnamon together. Brush a 11x15x3-inch baking pan with melted butter. Lay 6 of the phyllo sheets on the bottom of the pan one on top of the other brushing every one with melted butter. Then sprinkle evenly with almond mixture, cover with 2 sheets of phyllo, brush with butter and sprinkle with almond mixture.Repeat this process until you have used 14 sheets. The sheets will extend up the sides of the pan. Pour in the pumpkin mixture and spread evenly. Butter and fold overhanging sides and ends of sheets over the filling to enclose it. Lay the rest of the sheets over the top, brushing every one with melted butter and sprinkle with almond mixture. Fold in the overhanging sides brushing with melted butter. Score with sharp knife into diamond shapes. Bake in a preheated 350°F (180°C) oven for approximately 45 minutes or until golden. Cool to lukewarm. Combine syrup ingredients in a saucepan. Bring to a boil, reduce heat to medium and boil for 5 minutes. Pour hot syrup over lukewarm pumpkin pastry. Let cool. Cut through the scored lines.

# KATAIFI
### Καταΐφι

2½ cups finely chopped blanched almonds
⅓ cup sugar
⅓ cup finely ground Zwieback toast or dried bread crumbs (see index)
1 teaspoon cinnamon
4 tablespoons cognac
1 pound Kataifi shredded pastry (thawed)
1 cup melted clarified unsalted butter (see index)

**FOR THE SYRUP:**
4¼ cups sugar
2⅔ cups water
1 tablespoon fresh lemon juice
1 teaspoon almond extract

Combine first 4 ingredients together. Add cognac and mix well to combine. Gently separate kataifi pastry into three parts. Brush a 13x9x3-inch baking pan and lay one part of the Kataifi pastry. Sprinkle evenly with half of the almond mixture. Lay the second part of kataifi pastrry over almond mixture. Sprinkle with other half of the almond mixture. Sprinkle with the melted butter. Bake in a preheated 350°F (180°C) oven for approximately 45 minutes or until golden. Cool to lukewarm. Combine syrup ingredients except almond extract in a saucepan. Bring to a boil, reduce heat to medium and boil for 5 minutes,, add almond extract. Pour hot syrup onto

lukewarm kataifi. Cover and let cool. Cut into 2x2-inch squares or rectangles and serve.

# KATAIFI FROM IONNINA
### Καταΐφι Γιαννιώτικο

2½ cups finely chopped blanched almonds
⅓ cup sugar
⅓ cup finely ground Zwieback toast or dried bread crumbs (see index)
1 teaspoon cinnamon
4 tablespoons cognac
12 sheets Phyllo pastry (thawed)
1 pound kataifi shredded pastry (thawed)
1½ cups melted clarified unsalted butter (see index)

**FOR THE SYRUP:**
5½ cups sugar
3½ cups water
1 tablespoon fresh lemon juice
1 tablespoon almond extract

Combine first 4 ingredients together. Add cognac and mix well to combine. Brush a 10x15x3-inch baking pan with melted butter. Lay a sheet of phyllo in the bottom, brush with butter, cover with another sheet of phyllo, brush with butter, and repeat this process until you have used 6 sheets. Separate kataifi pastry into three parts. Lay one part of kataifi over phyllo sheets. Sprinkle with butter and spread evenly half of the almond mixture. Lay the second part of kataifi over almonds. Sprinkle with butter and spread evenly over the other half of almond mixture. Lay the third part of the kataifi over the almond and sprinkle with the melted butter. Cover kataifi with the remaining phyllo sheets brushing each with butter. Brush evenly the rest of the butter over the top sheet. score top six layers of sheets with a sharp knife into 2x2-inch squares or rectangles. Sprinkle with 2 tablespoons water. Bake in a preheated 350°F (180°C) oven for approximately 50 minutes or until golden. Cool to lukewarm. Cut through scored lines.Combine syrup ingredients except almond extract in a saucepan. Bring to a boil, reduce heat to a medium and boil for 5 minutes. Add almond extract. Pour hot syrup to lukewarm kataifi. Cover and let cool.

# CREAM FILLED KATAIFI
### Καταΐφι μὲ κρέμα

**FOR THE CREAM FILLING:**
8 egg yolks
1½ cups sugar
1 cup fine semolina

8 cups scalding milk
Rind of ½ lemon (optional)
1 teaspoon vanilla
2 tablespoons unsalted butter
¾ cup finely chopped blanched almonds (optional)
1 pound kataifi shredded pastry, thawed
1 cup melted clarified unsalted butter (see index)

FOR THE SYRUP:
3½ cups sugar
1¾ cups water
1 tablespoon fresh lemon juice

Combine egg yolks and sugar in a saucepan, beat well using a whisk. Add semolina and mix well. Gradually add milk and lemon rind, and cook slowly over medium-low heat, stirring constantly until it thickens. Remove the lemon rind. Add vanilla, butter and almonds if desired, stir to mix it well. Cover and let cool. Gently separate kataifi pastry into two parts. Brush a 10x15x3-inch baking pan and lay one part of the kataifi pastry. Sprinkle with half of the butter. Pour cream filling over and spread evenly. Lay the remaining kataifi pastry. Sprinkle with the remaining melted butter. Bake in a preheated 350°F (180°C) oven for approximately 45 minutes or until golden. Cool to lukewarm. Cut into pieces. Combine syrup ingredients in a saucepan. Bring to a boil and reduce heat to medium and boil five minutes. Pour hot syrup over kataifi. Cover and let cool.

# NUT FILLED KATAIFI ROLLS
### Ρολλὰ καταῖφι μὲ ἀμύγδαλα

2½ cups finely chopped blanched almonds
⅓ cup sugar
⅓ cup finely ground Zwieback toast or dried bread
    crumbs (see index)
1 teaspoon cinnamon
4 tablespoons cognac
2 beaten eggs
1 pound kataifi shredded pastry (thawed)
1 cup melted clarified unsalted butter (see index)

FOR THE SYRUP:
4¼ cups sugar
2⅔ cups water
1 tablespoon fresh lemon juice
1 teaspoon almond extract

Combine first 4 ingredients together. Add cognac and mix well to combine. Gently open the kataifi pastry. Divide into 24 equal parts, and lay them on a table. Cover with damp cloth to keep from drying while working. Work with one part at a time. Place one tablespoon from the almond mixture on one end.

Fold edges over to enclose the filling and roll up into a cylinder. Place rolls into greased baking pan. Repeat the filling and rolling process. Spoon melted butter over rolls to cover the top. Bake in a preheated 350°F (180°C) oven for approximately 45 minutes or until golden. Cool. Combine syrup ingredients except the almond extract in a saucepan, bring to a boil, reduce heat to medium and boil for 5 minutes. Add almond extract. Spoon hot syrup over kataifi rolls. Cover and let cool. Makes 24 kataifi rolls.

# CREAM FILLED KATAIFI ROLLS
### Ρολλὰ καταῖφι μὲ κρέμα

4 egg yolks
¾ cup sugar
½ cup fine semolina
4 cups scalding milk
Rind of ¼ lemon (optional)
1 teaspoon vanilla
1 tablespoon unsalted butter
1 pound kataifi shredded pastry, thawed
1 cup melted clarified unsalted butter (see index)

FOR THE SYRUP:
4½ cups sugar
2¾ cups water
1 tablespoon fresh lemon juice

Combine egg yolks and sugar in a saucepan, beat well using a whisk. Add semolina and mix well. Gradually add milk and lemon rind, cook slowly over medium-low heat stirring constantly until it thickens. Remove from heat, remove the lemon rind. Add vanilla and butter, stir to mix it well. Cover and let cool. Gently open the kataifi pastry and divide into 24 equal parts. Lay them on a table. Cover with damp cloth to keep from drying while working. Work with one part at a time. Place one tablespoon from the cream filling on one end. Fold edges over to enclose the filling and roll up into cylinders. Place rolls into a greased baking pan. Repeat the filling and rolling process. Spoon melted butter over rolls to cover the top. Bake in a preheated 350°F (180°C) oven for approximately 45 minutes or until golden. Remove from oven. Cool to lukewarm. Combine syrup ingredients in a saucepan, bring to a boil, reduce heat to medium and boil for 5 minutes. Spoon hot syrup over kataifi rolls. Cover and let cool. Makes 24 kataifi rolls.

# COCONUT CAKE WITH SYRUP A
### Κέϊκ καρύδας μὲ σιρόπι

1 cup unsalted butter or margarine, at room

temperature
1 cup sugar
5 eggs, separated
½ teaspoon vanilla
1½ cups all-purpose flour
2 teaspoons baking powder
2½ cups coconut
1 cup milk

**FOR THE SYRUP:**
2 cups sugar
2 cups water
1 teaspoon fresh lemon juice

Cream butter with sugar until light and fluffy. Add egg yolks one at a time beating thoroughly after each one is added. Add vanilla. Sift flour with baking powder together. Gradually add to the creamed mixture, alternately with milk, beating until smooth after each addition. Add 2 cups coconut and mix well. Fold in stiffly beaten egg whites. Pour into greased 13x9x3-inch baking pan and bake in a preheated 350°F (180°C) oven for approximately 45 minutes. Let cool. Combine syrup ingredients in a saucepan; bring to a boil, reduce meat to medium and boil for 5 minutes. Spoon hot syrup over cool cake. Sprinkle remaining coconut (½ cup) on top of cake. Cut and serve when it is completely cool.

# COCONUT CAKE WITH SYRUP B
### Κέϊκ καρύδας μὲ σιρόπι

1 cup unsalted butter or margarine, at room
temperature
1 cup sugar
4 eggs, separated
3½ cups all-purpose flour
4 teaspoons baking powder
1 teaspoon vanilla
1½ cups coconut
1 cup milk

**FOR THE SYRUP:**
2½ cups sugar
2½ cups water
1 tablespoon lemon juice (fresh)
Follow preparation as directed in Coconut Cake with Syrup A (see index).

# ALMOND FARINA CAKE WITH SYRUP
### Κέϊκ ἀμυγδάλου μὲ σιρόπι

5 eggs

1½ cups sugar
Grated rind of 1 orange
⅓ cup cognac
¾ cup all-purpose flour
¾ cup fine semolina
5 teaspoons baking powder
1½ cups ground blanched almonds

**FOR THE SYRUP:**
1½ cups sugar
1½ cups water
½ teaspoon almond extract

**FOR THE TOPPING:**
1½ cups heavy cream, whipped with
⅓ cup confectioner's sugar, sifted with
1 teaspoon vanilla

Beat eggs with sugar until thick and creamy. Add grated rind. Sift dry ingredients together. Gradually add flour mixture alternately with cognac to egg mixture. Add ground almonds and mix well. Pour into 10-inch spring form lined with waxed paper. Bake in a preheated 350°F (180°C) oven for approximately 45 minutes. Combine syrup ingredients in a saucepan, bring to a boil, reduce heat to medium and boil for 5 minutes. Spoon hot syrup over hot cake. Cover and let stay until completely cool. Cut and serve with whipped cream.

# FARINA CAKE WITH SYRUP
### Κέϊκ μὲ σιμιγδάλι

6 large eggs, separated
⅔ cup sugar
Grated rind of 1 orange
1 cup farina (fine semolina)
¼ cup all-purpose flour
3 teaspoons baking powder
½ teaspoon cinnamon
½ cup cognac
1 cup chopped blanched almonds

**FOR THE SYRUP:**
1¾ cups sugar
1¾ cups water
1 tablespoon fresh lemon juice
½ teaspoon almond extract

Beat egg yolks with sugar until thick and creamy. Sift dry ingredients together. Gradually add farina mixture alternately with cognac to egg mixture and mix well. Add chopped almonds. Fold in stiffly beaten egg whites. Pour into greased and floured 13x9x3-inch baking pan. Bake in a preheated 350°F (180°C) oven for approximately 45 minutes. Combine syrup ingredients except almond extract in a saucepan, bring to a boil, reduce heat and boil for 5 minutes. Pour hot syrup over hot cake, let stay until completely cool.

✗✗✗✗

# ALMOND BAKED HALVA RINAS
### Χαλβᾶς τῆς Ρήνας ἀμυγδάλου

1 ¼ cups unsalted butter or margarine, at room
     temperature
1½ cups sugar
7 eggs, separated
2½ cups fine semolina
4 teaspoons baking powder
2 teaspoons cinnamon or less
½ cup cognac
2¼ cups finely chopped blanched almonds

**FOR THE SYRUP:**
3½ cups sugar
3½ cups water
1 teaspoon almond extract
2 tablespoons fresh lemon juice

Cream butter with sugar until light and fluffy. Add egg yolks one at a time beating thoroughly after each one is added. Sift dry ingredients together. Gradually add alternately with cognac to creamed mixture, beating until smooth after each addition. Add chopped almonds and mix thoroughly. Pour into greased and floured 15x10x3-inch baking pan. Bake in a preheated 350°F (180°C) oven for approximately 45 minutes. While halva is baking prepare syrup. Combine syrup ingredients except almond extract in a saucepan, bring to a boil, reduce heat to medium and boil for 5 minutes. Remove halva from the oven and pour hot syrup over it. Cover halva with a larger baking sheet and let stay until completely cool. Cut into pieces and serve.

✗✗✗✗

# WALNUT BAKED HALVA RINAS
### Χαλβᾶς τῆς Ρήνας μὲ καρύδια

1 cup unsalted butter or margarine, at room
     temperature
1 cup sugar
5 eggs
2 cups fine semolina
4 teaspoons baking powder
1½ teaspoons or less cinnamon
½ cup orange juice
¼ cup cognac
1½ cups finely chopped walnuts

**FOR THE SYRUP:**
3 cups sugar

3 cups water
1 tablespoon fresh lemon juice
Follow preparation as directed in Almond Baked Halva Rinas (see index).

✗✗✗✗

# BAKED HALVA RINAS
### Χαλβᾶς τῆς Ρήνας

1 cup unsalted butter or margarine, at room
     temperature
½ cup sugar
4 eggs
2 cups fine semolina
½ cup all-purpose flour
4 teaspoons baking powder
1 teaspoon cinnamon
2 tablespoons cognac
1 cup milk
1¼ cups finely chopped blanched almonds

**FOR THE SYRUP:**
3½ cups sugar
3½ cups water
1 teaspoon fresh lemon juice
6 whole cloves
1 teaspoon almond extract

Cream butter with sugar until light and fluffy. Add eggs one at a time beating thoroughly after each one is added. Sift dry ingredients together. Gradually add alternately with milk to creamed mixture, beating until smooth after each addition. Add chopped almonds and mix thoroughly. Pour into well greased and floured 9x13x3-inch baking pan. Bake in a preheated 350F° (180°C) oven for 45 minutes. While halvas is baking prepare syrup. Combine syrup ingredients in a saucepan, bring to a boil, reduce heat to medium and boil for 5 minutes. Remove halva from the oven and pour hot syrup over it. Cover halva with a larger baking sheet and let stay until completely cool. Remove cloves and cut into pieces and serve.

✗✗✗✗

# BAKED HALVA RINAS
# WITH MILK SYRUP
### Χαλβᾶς τῆς Ρήνας μὲ σιρόπι γάλακτος

1 cup unsalted butter or margarine, at room
     temperature
1 cup sugar
5 eggs
3 cups fine semolina
1¼ teaspoons cinnamon
5 teaspoons baking powder

1¼   cups milk
1½   cups finely chopped blanched almonds

**FOR THE SYRUP:**
3½   cups sugar
3½   cups scalding milk
6   whole cloves
1   teaspoon almond extract

Follow preparation as directed in Baked Halva Rinas (see index). Combine sugar, milk and cloves, bring to a boil, reduce heat to medium and boil for 5 minutes. Pour hot syrup over hot halva. Cover with a larger baking sheet and let stay until completely cool. Remove cloves and cut into pieces and serve.

## BAKED YOGURT HALVA
### Χαλβᾶς φούρνου μὲ γιαούρτι

2   cups plain yogurt
1   cup sugar
3   cups fine semolina
½   cup flour
1   teaspoon baking soda
2   teaspoons baking powder
1½   teaspoons cinnamon
½   cup cognac
1½   cups finely chopped blanched almonds

**FOR THE SYRUP:**
3½   cups sugar
3½   cups water
6   whole cloves

Cream yogurt and sugar well. Sift dry ingredients together. Gradually add semolina mixture alternately with cognac. Add chopped almonds and mix thoroughly. Pour into well greased and floured 13x9x3-inch baking pan. Bake in a preheated 350°F (180°C) oven for approximately 45 minutes. While halvas is baking prepare syrup. Combine syrup ingredients in a saucepan, bring to a boil, reduce heat to medium and boil for 5 minutes. Remove cloves. Remove halva from the oven and spoon hot syrup over it. Cover halva with a larger baking sheet and let stay until completely cool. Cut into pieces and serve.

## HALVA WITH BUTTER
### Χαλβᾶς βουτύρου

4   cups water
2½   cups sugar
1   teaspoon cinnamon
1   cup unsalted butter or margarine
2   cups farina

1   cup slivered blanched almonds
½   cup pine nuts (optional)

In a saucepan combine water, sugar and cinnamon; bring to a boil, reduce heat to medium and boil for 5 minutes. Set aside. Melt butter in a four quart saucepan, add farina and almonds. Stir continuously with a wooden spoon on medium heat for 5 minutes, add pine nuts and continue cooking and stirring continuously until the farina turns to a golden color. Remove from heat. Slowly and carefully add the syrup to the farina mixture. Stir continuously over low heat until the halva becomes thick. Remove from heat, cover with a towel and let stand for 20 minutes. Stir. Turn halva into 10-cup mold. When partially cool, unmold onto a platter. Sprinkle with sugar and cinnamon if desired. Cut into pieces and serve. Serve hot or cold.

**Variation:**

## HALVA WITH OIL
### Χαλβᾶς λαδερὸς

Substitute ¾ cup fine quality oil for the butter. Follow recipe and preparation as directed in Halvas with Butter (see index).

## HALVA WITH HONEY
### Χαλβᾶς μὲ μέλι

¾   cup unsalted butter or margarine
1⅔   cups farina
21   ounces boiling hot honey
1½   cups scalding milk
1   teaspoon cinnamon

In a four quart saucepan melt butter and farina stirring continuously with a wooden spoon on medium heat until the farina turns to a golden color. Remove from heat. Slowly and carefully add hot honey, scalding milk and cinnamon to the farina mixture. Stir continuously over low heat until the halva becomes thick. Remove from heat, cover with a towel and let stand for 10 minutes. Turn the halva into 6-cup mold. When partially cool, unmold into a platter. Cut into pieces and serve.

Recipe from Mrs. John D. Mickles

## JELLY LOG
### Λόρμος

5   eggs

⅔ cup sugar
1 teaspoon vanilla
⅔ cup cake flour
1 teaspoon baking powder
1 cup apricot jam or any other kind you wish

Beat eggs with sugar until thick and has lemon color. Add vanilla. Sift flour with baking powder together. Fold into egg mixture. Pour into a jelly roll pan 13x17x1-inch lined with waxed paper. Bake in a pre-heated 400°F (205°C) oven for 15 minutes. Turn quickly onto waxed paper and trim sides. Wrap in waxed paper and cool. When cold unroll and spread with jam and roll again. Just before serving sprinkle with confectioner's sugar.

Variations:

WHIPPED CREAM LOG:
(Kormos Me Santigi)
Spread log with whipped cream instead of jam. Cover top of log with whipped cream and sprinkle with chopped toasted blanched almonds.

CHOCOLATE LOG:
(Kormos Sokolatas)
Spread with chocolate frosting instead of jam. Cover top of log with chocolate frosting and decorate with maraschino cherries. (See index for chocolate frosting.) Cover top of log with whipped cream and sprinkle with chopped toasted blanched almonds or chocolate sprinkles.

## ALMOND RAVANI
Ραβανὶ ἀμυγδάλου

1 cup unsalted butter or margarine, at room temperature
1 cup sugar
5 eggs, separated
Grated rind of 1 orange
1 cup farina
1 cup all-purpose flour
4 teaspoons baking powder
1 teaspoon vanilla
⅔ cup milk
1 cup blanched chopped almonds
2 cups heavy cream, whipped (optional)

FOR THE SYRUP:
2 cups sugar
2 cups water
1 tablespoon lemon juice
1 teaspoon almond extract

Cream butter with sugar until light and fluffy. Add egg yolks one at a time, beating thoroughly after each one is added. Add orange rind. Sift dry ingredients together. Gradually add flour mixture alternately with

milk, beating until smooth after each addition. Add almonds. Fold in stiffly beaten egg whites. Pour into well greased 13x9x3-inch baking pan. Bake in a pre-heated 350°F (180°C) oven for approximately 45 minutes. Combine syrup ingredients except almond extract. Bring to a boil, reduce heat to medium and boil for 5 minutes. Pour hot syrup over hot ravani. Let stay until completely cool. Cut and serve with whipped cream if desired.

## CINNAMON RAVANI
Ραβανὶ κανέλλας

½ cup unsalted butter or margarine, at room temperature
1 cup sugar
4 eggs, separated
¾ cup farina
1⅓ cups all-purpose flour
½ teaspoon baking soda
2 teaspoons baking powder
1 teaspoon vanilla
1 teaspoon cinnamon
¾ cup milk
1 cup chopped blanched almonds
1½ cups heavy cream, whipped (optional)

FOR THE SYRUP:
2 cups sugar
2 cups water
1 teaspoon fresh lemon juice
½ teaspoon almond extract

Follow preparation as directed in Almond Ravini (see index).

## FRUIT NUT RAVANI
Ραβανὶ φρούτου

7 eggs, separated
¾ cup sugar
1⅓ cups all-purpose flour
2 teaspoons baking powder
½ cup chopped mixed candied fruits (see index)
½ cup seedless golden raisins
½ cup chopped blanched almonds or walnuts
⅓ cup melted butter or margarine, unsalted

FOR THE SYRUP:
2½ cups sugar
2 cups water
1 teaspoon fresh lemon juice

Beat egg yolks with sugar until thick and has lemon color. Fold in stiffly beaten egg whites. Sift dry ingredients together. Gradually fold in egg mixture. Add fruits, nuts and melted butter. Stir gently with

DESSERTS, BEVERAGES, CANDIES, PRESERVES

a wooden spoon to combine. Pour into well greased 15x10x3-inch baking pan. Bake in a preheated 350°F (180°C) oven for approximately 45 minutes. Let cool. Combine syrup ingredients in a saucepan; bring to a boil, reduce heat to medium and boil for 5 minutes. Pour hot syrup over cool ravani. Serve when it is completely cool with whipped cream if desired.

❦❦❦

## RICE RAVANI
Ραβανὶ μὲ ρύζι

¾ cup unsalted butter or margarine, at room
   temperature
1½ cups sugar
8 eggs, separated
1¾ cups rice flour or cream of rice
1 teaspoon vanilla
2 teaspoons baking powder
1 cup blanched chopped almonds

**FOR THE SYRUP:**
2½ cups sugar
2½ cups water
½ teaspoon almond extract

Cream butter with sugar until light and fluffy. Add egg yolks one at a time, beating thoroughly after each one is added. Gradually add flour with baking powder alternately with stiffly beaten egg whites. Add vanilla and chopped almonds. Pour into well greased 15x 10x3-inch baking pan. Bake in a preheated 350°F (180°C) oven for approximately 45 minutes. Cool. Combine syrup ingredients in a saucepan, bring to a boil, reduce heat to medium and boil for 5 minutes. Pour hot syrup over cool ravani. Serve when it is completely cool.

❦❦❦

Recipe from Mrs. John D. Mickles

## VANILLA RAVANI
Ραβανὶ βανίλιας

8 eggs, separated
1 cup sugar
1½ teaspoons vanilla
2 cups all-purpose flour
4 teaspoons baking powder
½ cup water
1½ cups finely chopped blanched almonds
**FOR THE SYRUP:**
3 cups sugar
3 cups water
2 tablespoons lemon juice, fresh
1 teaspoon vanilla

Follow preparation as directed in Fruit Nut Ravani (see index).

❦❦❦

## WALNUT RAVANI
Ραβανὶ μὲ καρύδια

1 cup unsalted butter or margarine, at room
   temperature
1 cup sugar
5 eggs, separated
2 cups farina
1 cup all-purpose flour
5 teaspoons baking powder
1 teaspoon cinnamon
Grated rind of 1 orange
1 cup milk
1 cup finely chopped walnuts
1½ cups heavy cream, whipped

**FOR THE SYRUP:**
3½ cups sugar
3½ cups water
1 tablespoon fresh lemon juice

Cream butter with sugar until light and fluffy. Add egg yolks one at a time, beating thoroughly after each one is added. Add orange rind. Sift dry ingredients together. Gradually add farina mixture altlernately with milk, beating until smooth after each addition. Add walnuts. Fold in stiffly beaten egg whites. Pour into well greased 15x10x2-inch baking pan. Bake in a preheated 350°F (180°C) oven for approximately 45 minutes. Combine syrup ingredients in a saucepan, bring to a boil, reduce heat to medium and boil for 5 minutes. Pour hot syrup over hot ravani. Let stay until completely cool. Cut and serve with whipped cream.

❦❦❦

## WALNUT ALMOND CAKE WITH SYRUP
Καρυδόπιττα μὲ ἀμύγδαλο καὶ σιρόπι

6 eggs, separated
½ cup sugar
1 cup finely ground walnuts
1 cup finely ground almonds
1½ cups finely ground Zwieback toast
3 teaspoons baking powder
1½ teaspoons cinnamon
⅓ cup cognac

**FOR THE SYRUP:**
3 cups sugar
3 cups water
1 tablespoon fresh lemon juice

Beat egg yolks with sugar until thick and creamy. Mix ground walnuts, almonds, toast, baking powder and cinnamon together. Gradually add walnut mixture alternately with cognac and mix well. Fold in stiffly beaten egg whites. Pour into greased and floured 15x10x2-inch baking pan and bake in a preheated 350°F (180°C) oven for approximately 45 minutes. Let cool. Combine syrup ingredients in a saucepan; bring to a boil, reduce heat and boil for 5 minutes. Pour hot syrup over cold cake. Serve when it is completely cold with whipped cream if desired.

✕✕✕✕

# WALNUT CAKE WITH SYRUP
### Καρυδόπιττα μὲ σιρόπι

½ cup unsalted butter or margarine, at room temperature
½ cup sugar
5 eggs, separated
Grated rind of 1 orange
1½ cups finely ground Zwieback toast
1½ teaspoons baking powder
3 cups finely ground walnuts
1 teaspoon cinnamon
¼ cup cognac

**FOR THE SYRUP:**
2½ cups sugar
2½ cups water
1 tablespoon fresh lemon juice

Cream butter and sugar until light and fluffy. Add egg yolks one at a time, beating thoroughly after each one is added. Add orange rind. Combine dry ingredients together. Gradually add alternately with cognac to creamed mixture, beating until smooth after each addition. Fold in stiffly beaten egg whites. Pour into a well greased and floured 15x10x2-inch baking pan. Bake in a preheated 350°F (180°C) oven for approximately 45 minutes. Remove from oven, let cool. Combine syrup ingredients in a saucepan, bring to a boil, reduce heat and boil for 5 minutes. Pour hot syrup over karythopita. Serve when it is completely cold with whipped cream if desired.

✕✕✕✕

# WALNUT CHOCOLATE CAKE WITH SYRUP
### Καρυδόπιττα μὲ σοκολάτα καὶ σιρόπι

1 cup sugar
6 eggs, separated
1 can (8-ounces) finely ground walnuts
1 bag (7-ounces) finely ground Zwieback toast

1 teaspoon baking soda
1 teaspoon cinnamon
4 ounces melted chocolate
⅓ cup cognac
3 tablespoons fresh lemon juice
2 cups heavy cream, whipped (optional)

**FOR THE SYRUP:**
2½ cups sugar
2½ cups water
1 tablespoon fresh lemon juice
1 1-inch cinnamon stick

Beat egg yolks with sugar until thick and creamy. Combine dry ingredients together. Gradually add walnut mixture alternately with cognac and lemon juice and mix well. Add melted chocolate. Fold in stiffly beaten egg whites. Pour into greased and floured 15x10x2-inch baking pan. Bake in a preheated 350°F (180°C) oven for approximately 45 minutes. Let cool. Combine syrup ingredients in a saucepan, bring to a boil, reduce heat and boil for 5 minutes. Pour hot syrup over cool cake. Serve when it is completely cool with whipped cream if desired.

✕✕✕✕

# WALNUT CINNAMON CAKE WITH SYRUP
### Καρυδόπιττα μὲ σιρόπι

6 eggs
1 cup sugar
½ cup milk
2 tablespoons cognac
1 cup unsalted butter, at room temperature or margarine
2½ cups all-purpose flour
4 teaspoons baking powder
1¼ teaspoons cinnamon
1½ cups finely chopped walnuts

**FOR THE SYRUP:**
2 cups sugar
1½ cups water
2 tablespoons fresh lemon juice
1 cup heavy cream, whipped (optional)

Beat sugar, milk and cognac until sugar has dissolved. Add butter and beat well. Sift flour, baking powder and cinnamon together. Gradually add to egg mixture and mix thoroughly. Add chopped walnuts. Pour into greased and floured 10-inch baking pan. Bake in a preheated 350°F (180°C) oven for approximately 45 minutes. Let cool. Combine syrup ingredients in a saucepan, bring to a boil, reduce heat and boil for 5 minutes. Spoon hot syrup over cool cake. Let stay until completely cold. Serve with whipped cream if desired.

DESSERTS, BEVERAGES, CANDIES, PRESERVES

# WALNUT ORANGE CAKE
## WITH SYRUP
Καρυδόπιττα πορτοκαλιοῦ μὲ σιρόπι

6 eggs, separated
¾ cup sugar
1 cup finely ground walnuts
1 cup finely ground Zwieback toast
1 teaspoon cinnamon
1½ teaspoons baking powder
Grated rind of 1 orange
1 cup heavy cream, whipped

FOR THE SYRUP:
1½ cups sugar
1½ cups water
1 tablespoon fresh lemon juice

Beat egg yolks with sugar until thick and creamy. Combine dry ingredients together. Gradually add walnut mixture to creamed mixture, beating until smooth. Add orange rind. Fold in stiffly beaten egg whites. Pour into greased and floured 15x10x2-inch baking pan. Bake in a preheated 350°F (180°C) oven for approximately 45 minutes. Let cool. Combine syrup ingredients in a saucepan, bring to a boil, reduce heat and boil for 5 minutes. Spoon hot syrup over cool cake. When it is completely cold serve with whipped cream.

❦ ❦ ❦

# WALNUT VANILLA CAKE
## WITH SYRUP
Καρυδόπιττα μὲ σιρόπι

6 eggs, separated
9 teaspoons sugar
1 teaspoon vanilla
12 tablespoons finely chopped walnuts
9 tablespoons finely ground Zwieback toast
2 teaspoons baking powder
⅓ cup cognac

FOR THE SYRUP:
2 cups sugar
2 cups water
1 tablespoon fresh lemon juice

Beat egg yolks with sugar until thick and creamy. Add vanilla. Combine dry ingredients together. Gradually add dry ingredients alternately with cognac and mix well. Fold in stiffly beaten egg whites. Pour into greased and floured 15x10x2-inch baking pan. Bake in a preheated 350°F (180°C) oven for approximately 45 minutes. Let cool. Combine syrup ingredients in a saucepan; bring to a boil, reduce heat and boil for 5 minutes. Spoon hot syrup over cool

cake. When it is completely cold serve with whipped cream if desired.

❦ ❦ ❦

# YOGURT ALMOND CAKE
Γιαουρτόπιττα ἀμυγδάλου

1 cup plain yogurt
1 cup sugar
1 teaspoon vanilla
2 cups semolina
1 teaspoon baking soda
1 cup finely chopped blanched almonds
¾ cup milk

FOR THE SYRUP:
2½ cups sugar
2½ cups water
3 tablespoons cognac or brandy
1 1-inch cinnamon stick

Cream yogurt with sugar. Add vanilla. Sift dry ingredients together. Gradually add alternately with milk to yogurt mixture, beating until smooth. Add chopped almonds. Pour into generously greased 9x9x2-inch baking pan. Cover cake with waxed paper. Bake in a preheated 350°F (180°C) oven for 25 minutes. Remove waxed paper and bake 20 minutes longer. While cake is baking, combine syrup ingredients in a saucepan, bring to a boil, reduce heat to medium and boil for 5 minutes. Remove cake from oven and pour hot syrup over hot cake. When it is cold and syrup is absorbed, cut into square pieces.

❦ ❦ ❦

# YOGURT ALMOND RAISIN CAKE
Γιαουρτόπιττα μὲ ἀμύγδαλα καὶ σταφίδες

1 cup unsalted butter or margarine, at room temperature
1 cup sugar
4 large eggs, separated
Grated rind of 1 orange (optional)
1 teaspoon vanilla
4 cups all-purpose flour
1 teaspoon baking soda
3 teaspoons baking powder
1½ cups plain yogurt
1 cup seedless golden raisins
1 cup finely chopped blanched almonds

FOR THE SYRUP:
2 cups sugar
1½ cups orange juice
½ teaspoon almond extract

Cream butter with sugar until light and fluffy. Add egg yolks one at a time, beating thoroughly after each one is added. Add orange rind and vanilla. Sift dry ingredients together. Gradually add flour mixture alternately with yogurt to butter mixture, beating until smooth after each addition. Add raisins and chopped almonds. Fold in stiffly beaten egg whites. Pour into well greased and floured 13x9x2-inch baking pan. Bake in a preheated 350°F (180°C) oven for approximately 60 minutes. Combine sugar and orange juice and extract, stir until the sugar dissolves. Turn off oven. Remove cake and pour syrup over cake. Return cake to the oven and let stand for 30 minutes. Serve when cake is completely cold.

# ALMOND TART
Τάρτα ἀμυγδάλου

**FOR THE CRUST:**
2 cups flour
⅓ cup sugar
1 teaspoon baking powder
¾ cup unsalted butter
1 egg, beaten with
1 tablespoon rum and 1 tablespoon water

**FOR THE CREAM FILLING:**
4 tablespoons flour
2 tablespoons corn starch
½ cup sugar
3 egg yolks
½ cup milk
2 cups scalding milk
1 teaspoon vanilla
½ teaspoon almond extract
2 tablespoons unsalted butter
1½ cups whipped cream
½ cup chopped toasted blanched almonds

Sift dry ingredients together. Cut in butter with pastry blender. Add beaten egg with rum and water, mix until pastry will hold together. Roll out on waxed paper for 10-inch tart pan. Line greased tart pan with pastry. Line pastry shell with waxed paper and partially fill with beans, remove beans and paper after first 10 minutes of baking. Bake in a preheated 450°F (230°C) oven for approximately 15 minutes or until golden. Cool. Combine dry ingredients together, add egg yolks and ½ cup milk, mix well using a whisk. Gradually stir in scalding milk and cook slowly on top of a double boiler whisking constantly until mixture thickens. Cover and cook for 5 minutes. Remove from heat. Add butter, vanilla and almond extract. Cover to prevent a skin from forming. Chill. Pour over baked tart. Spoon whipped cream on top and sprinkle with chopped almonds. Chill.

# CHEESE TART
Τάρτα μυζίθρας

**FOR THE CRUST:**
2 cups flour
⅓ cup sugar
¼ teaspoon cinnamon
⅛ teaspoon salt
1 teaspoon baking powder
⅔ cup unsalted butter
1 egg, beaten
2 tablespoons cold water

**FOR THE CHEESE FILLING:**
4 eggs
1 cup sugar
1½ pounds unsalted mysithra or ricotta cheese
½ cup cream or milk
4 tablespoons flour
⅛ teaspoon salt
1 teaspoon vanilla
¼ teaspoon cinnamon
⅓ cup slivered blanched almonds

Sift dry ingredients together. Cut in butter with pastry blender. Add beaten egg, water using 1 tablespoon at a time until mixture will hold together. Roll out on waxed paper for 10-inch tart pan. Line greased tart pan with pastry. Beat eggs with sugar until light. Add cheese, cream, flour, salt, vanilla and cinnamon, mix well to combine. Press mixture through a food mill. Pour into pastry shell. Sprinkle with slivered almonds. Bake in a preheated 350°F (180°C) oven for approximately 60 minutes or until center is firm. Remove from oven and cool. Chill.

# CHOCOLATE TART
Τάρτα σοκολάτας

**FOR THE CRUST:**
1 recipe from Almond Tart (see index)

**FOR THE COCONUT CREAM FILLING:**
**FOR THE CHOCOLATE CREAM FILLING:**
4 tablespoon flour
2 tablespoons corn starch
½ cup sugar
3 egg yolks
½ cup milk
2 cups scalding milk
2 ounces sweet chocolate, cut in cubes
1 teaspoon vanilla
2 tablespoons unsalted butter
1½ cups whipped cream
Chocolate curls
Maraschino cherries

Prepare crust as directed. Combine dry ingredients together. Add egg yolks and ½ cup milk, mix well using a whisk. Gradually stir in scalding milk. Add chocolate cubes and cook slowly on top of a double boiler whisking constantly until mixture thickens. Cover and cook for 5 minutes. Add butter and vanilla, cover to prevent a skin from forming. Chill. Pour over baked tart. Spoon whipped cream on top and decorate with chocolate curls and cherries. Chill.

## COCONUT TART
Τάρτα καρύδας

FOR THE CRUST:
1 recipe from Almond Tart (see index)
4 tablespoons flour
2 tablespoons corn starch
⅓ cup sugar
3 egg yolks
½ cup milk
2 cups scalding milk
½ cup toasted coconut
1 teaspoon vanilla
2 tablespoons unsalted butter
1½ cups whipped cream
½ cup toasted coconut

Prepare crust as directed. Combine dry ingredients together. Add egg yolks and ½ cup milk, mix well using a whisk. Gradually stir in scalding milk and cook slowly on top of a double boiler, whisking constantly until mixture thickens. Add ½ cup coconut and mix well. Cover and cook for 5 minutes. Remove from heat. Add vanilla and butter. Cover to prevent a skin from forming. Chill. Pour over baked tart. Spoon whipped cream on top and sprinkle with toasted coconut. Chill.

## HONEY CHEESE TART
Μηλόπιττα

FOR THE CRUST:
2 cups flour
2 tablespoons sugar
⅛ teaspoon salt
1 teaspoon baking powder
⅔ cup unsalted butter
4-6 tablespoons cold water

FOR THE HONEY CHEESE FILLING:
4 eggs
½ cup sugar
1½ pounds unsalted myzithra or ricotta cheese
½ cup honey
½ cup cream or milk

4 tablespoons flour
1 teaspoon cinnamon
⅛ teaspoon salt
Grated rind of ½ lemon
⅓ cup slivered almonds

Sift dry ingredients together. Cut in butter with a pastry blender. Add water using 1 tablespoon at a time, until mixture will hold together. Roll out on waxed paper for 10-inch tart pan. Line greased tart pan with pastry. Beat eggs with sugar until light. Add cheese, honey, cream, flour, cinnamon, salt and rind, mix well to combine. Press mixture through a food mill. Pour into pastry shell. Sprinkle with slivered almonds. Bake in a preheated 350°F (180°C) oven for approximately 60 minutes or until center is firm. Remove from oven and cool. Chill and serve.

## JAM TART
Πάστα φλόρα

FOR THE CRUST:
3 cups flour
½ cup sugar
⅛ teaspoon salt
1½ teaspoons baking powder
1¼ cups unsalted butter
2 egg yolks, beaten with
¼ cup cognac

FOR THE FILLING:
1½ cups apricot jam (see index) or your desire
⅓ cup slivered blanched almonds

Sift dry ingredients together. Cut in butter with a pastry blender. Add beaten egg yolks with cognac and mix until pastry will hold together. Roll out ⅔ of the pastry on waxed paper for 10-inch tart pan. Line greased tart pan with pastry. Cover with marmalade or jam and sprinkle with almonds. Arrange strips of pastry over top in lattice design. Bake in a preheated 350°F (180°C) oven for approximately 45 minutes. Cool and serve.

## PEACH TART
Τάρτα γιαρμά

FOR THE CRUST AND FILLING:
Follow recipe and preparation as directed in Almond Tart (see index).

FOR THE TOPPING:
Sliced peach compote (see index) well drained or fresh
½ cup apricot jam
⅓ cup slivered toasted blanched almonds

Arrange chilled tart with sliced peaches. Boil jam with 3 tablespoons water for 2 minutes on low heat. Pour over peach tart and sprinkle with slivered almonds. Chill.

# STRAWBERRY TART
Τάρτα φράουλας

**FOR THE CRUST:**
**2 cups flour**
**⅓ cup sugar**
**1 teaspoon baking powder**
**¾ cup unsalted butter**
**2 egg yolks, beaten with**
**3 tablespoons cognac**

**FOR THE FILLING:**
**⅔ cup strawberry jam (see index)**
**¾ cup water**
**3½ teaspoons corn starch**
**1½ cups whipped cream**
**Small fresh strawberries, washed and well drained**
**⅓ cup chopped pistachio nuts**

Sift dry ingredients together. Cut in butter with pastry blender. Add beaten egg with cognac and mix until pastry will hold together. Roll out on waxed paper to a 10-inch tart pan. Line greased tart pan with pastry. Line pastry shell with waxed paper and partially fill with beans, remove beans and paper after first 10 minutes of cooking. Bake in a preheated 450°F (230°C) oven for approximately 15 minutes or until golden. Cool. Carefully remove from tart pan. Place on a flat serving platter. Mix jam with ½ cup water, bring to a boil on low heat; mix ¼ cup water with 3½ teaspoons corn starch. Slowly add to jam mixture stirring constantly until it thickens. Remove from heat. Cool. Spread on baked tart. Spread whipped cream over jam mixture and cover with fresh strawberries. Sprinkle with chopped pistachio nuts. Chill.

**Variation:**

## ALMOND TARTLETS A
Ταρτελέτες αμυγδάλου

**FOR THE CRUST AND FILLING:**
Follow recipe and preparation as directed in Almond Tarts (see index).

Line 12 or more greased tart pans with pastry. Prick and bake in a preheated 450°F (230°C) oven for 8-10 minutes or until golden. Gently remove from tart pans and cool. Fill baked tartlets with almond filling. Spoon whipped cream on top and sprinkle with chopped almonds. Chill.

# ALMOND TARTLETS B
Ταρτελέτες αμυγδάλου

**FOR THE CRUST:**
**1½ recipe. Follow recipe and preparation as directed in Almond Tart (see index)**

**FOR THE FILLING:**
**⅔ cup apricot jam**
**¾ cup water**
**3½ teaspoons cornstarch**
**⅔ cup unsalted butter, at room temperature**
**1 cup sugar**
**4 eggs**
**Grated rind of 1 orange**
**1½ cups finely ground blanched almonds**
**1 cup finely ground Zwieback toast**
**4 teaspoons baking powder**
**¼ cup cognac**
**1½ cups whipped cream**
**½ cup chopped toasted blanched almonds**

Line 24 greased tart pans with pastry. Mix jam with ½ cup water, bring to a boil on low heat, mix ¼ cup water with 3½ teaspoons corn starch. Slowly add to jam mixture stirring constantly until it thickens. Remove from heat. Pour on platter and cool. Spoon jam mixture on each tartlet. Set aside. Cream butter with sugar. Add eggs one at a time beating thoroughly after each one is added. Add orange rind. Mix ground almonds, toast and baking powder together. Add alternately with cognac to creamed mixture, beating until smooth after each addition. Fill tartlets with the mixture. Bake in a preheated 350°F (180°C) oven for approximately 25 minutes. Cool. Spoon whipped cream on top and sprinkle with chopped almonds. Chill.

**Variation:**

# CHOCOLATE TARTLETS
Ταρτελέτες σοκολάτας

**FOR THE CRUST AND FILLING:**
Follow recipe and preparation as directed in Chocolate Tarts (see index).

Line 12 or more greased tart pans with pastry. Prick and bake in a preheated 450°F (230°C) oven for 8-10 minutes or until golden. Gently remove from tart pans and cool. Fill baked tartlets with chocolate cream filling. Spoon whipped cream on top and sprinkle with chocolate curls. Place a cherry in the center on each tartlet and chill.

## COCONUT TARTLETS
### Ταρτελέτες καρύδας

**FOR THE CRUST AND FILLING:**
Follow recipe and preparation as directed in Coconut Tarts (see index).

Line 12 or more greased tart pans with pastry. Prick and bake in a preheated 450°F (230°C) oven for 8-10 minutes or until golden, Gently remove from tart pans and cool. Filled baked tartlets with coconut cream filling. Spoon whipped cream on top and sprinkle with toasted coconut. Chill.

Variation:

## FRUIT TARTLETS
### Ταρτελέτες φρούτου

**FOR THE CRUST:**
Follow recipe and preparation as directed in Honey Cheese Tars (see index).

**FOR THE FILLING:**
**Any fresh fruit you desire or**
**Any sweet preserve well drained you desire (see index) or**
**Any compote well drained you desire (see index) or**
**1½ cups whipped cream**
**½ cup chopped pistachio nuts or toasted blanched almonds**

Line 12 or more greased tart pans with pastry. Prick and bake in a preheated 450°F (230°C) oven for 8-10 minutes or until golden. Gently remove from tart pans and cool. Fill baked tartlets as you desire. Spoon whipped cream on top and sprinkle with chopped pistachio nuts if desired. Chill.

## HONEY CHEESE TARTLETS
### Μηλόπιττες

**FOR THE CRUST AND FILLING:**
Follow recipe and preparation as directed in Honey Cheese Tarts (see index).

Line 12 or more greased tart pans with pastry. Prick and fill with honey cheese mixture. Sprinkle with almonds. Bake in a preheated 450°F (230°C) oven for approximately 10 minutes. Reduce temperature to 325°F (165°C) oven and bake for 15 minutes longer or until center is firm. Cool.

## STRAWBERRY TARTLETS
### Ταρτελέτες φράουλας

**FOR THE CRUST AND FILLING:**
Follow recipe and preparation as directed in Strawberry Tarts (see index).

Line 12 or more greased tart pans with pastry. Prick and bake in a preheated 450°F (230°C) oven for 8-10 minutes or until golden. Gently remove from tart pans and cool. Cover with strawberry mixture. Spread with whipped cream over strawberry and cover with fresh strawberries. Sprinkle with chopped pistachio nuts. Chill.

## CAKE FOR TORTES
### Κέϊκ γιά τούρτες

**6 eggs**
**1¼ cups sugar**
**1 teaspoon vanilla**
**1½ cups all-purpose flour, sifted with**
**1½ teaspoons baking powder**

Beat eggs until frothy, add sugar and beat until thick. Add vanilla. Fold in flour. Pour into 10-11-inch spring form pan lined with waxed paper. Bake in a preheated 350°F (180°C) oven for approximately 30 minutes. Cool. Remove from pan. Turn cake upside-down on a flat dish, cover. The next day remove paper and split cake into four layers horizontally. Use as directed.

## CREAM FILLING FOR TORTES
### Κρέμα γιά τούρτες

**3 cups scalding milk**
**½ cup sugar**
**5 tablespoons flour**
**3 tablespoons corn starch**
**5 egg yolks, beaten with**
**1 cup milk**
**2 tablespoons unsalted butter**
**1 teaspoon vanilla**

Combine sugar, flour, corn starch and beaten egg yolks, beat well using whisk. Gradually stir in scalding milk and cook slowly on top of double broiler, whisking constantly until mixture thickens. Cover and cook for 5 minutes. Remove from heat. Add butter and vanilla, mix well to combine. Cover to prevent a skin from forming. Use as directed.

# ALMOND TORTE
Τούρτα ἀμυγδάλου

**FOR THE CAKE:**
5 eggs
1¼ cups sugar
1 teaspoon vanilla
⅓ cup cognac
¾ cup flour
¾ cup semolina
5 teaspoons baking powder
1½ cups finely ground blanched almonds

**FOR THE SYRUP:**
1⅓ cups sugar
1⅓ cups water
½ teaspoon almond extract

**FOR THE FILLING:**
1 recipe Cream Filling for Tortes (see index)

**FOR THE FROSTING:**
1½ cups heavy cream, whipped with
¼ cup confectioner's sugar, sifted and
½ teaspoon vanilla
⅓ cup sliced or chopped toasted blanched almonds
Maraschino cherries

Beat eggs with sugar until thick and creamy. Add vanilla. Sift dry ingredients together. Gradually add flour mixture alternately with cognac to egg mixture. Add ground almonds and mix well. Pour into 10-11-inch spring form pan lined with waxed paper. Bake in a preheated 350°F (180°C) oven for approximately 45 minutes. Cool. Remove from pan, turn cake upside-down on a flat dish, cover and let stay overnight. Split cake into three layers horizontally. Combine syrup ingredients in a saucepan, bring to a boil, reduce heat to medium and boil for 5 minutes. Spoon hot syrup over cool cake layers. Cover and let cool. Prepare cream filling. Follow recipe and preparation as directed in Cream Filling for Tortes (see index). Place one cake layer in a spring form pan, spread ⅓ of the cream filling. Place second cake layer over cream. Repeat layers. Cover and chill overnight. Gently remove the sides of the pan and place on a serving dish. Frost sides and top of torte with whipped cream as you desire. Sprinkle with chopped almonds and arrange cherries. Chill.

# ALMOND ORANGE TORTE
Τούρτα ἀμυγδάλου

**FOR THE CAKE:**
5 eggs, separated
1 cup sugar
grated rind of 1 orange

1¼ cups finely ground Zwieback toast
1¼ cups finely ground blanched almonds
3 teaspoons baking powder
¼ cup cognac

**FOR THE SYRUP:**
1¼ cups sugar
1¼ cups water
½ teaspoon almond extract

**FOR THE FILLING AND FROSTING:**
2 cups heavy cream, whipped with
½ cup confectioner's sugar, sifted and
1 teaspoon vanilla
1 cup or more chopped toasted blanched almonds
Orange preserved, thinly sliced (see index) or
Maraschino cherries

Beat egg yolks with sugar until thick and creamy. Add grated rind. Mix ground Zwieback, almonds and baking powder together. Gradually add almond mixture alternately with cognac and mix well. Fold in stiffly beaten egg whites. Pour into 10-11-inch spring form pan lined with waxed paper. Bake in a preheated 350°F (180°C) oven for 25-30 minutes. Let cool. Split cake in half horizontally. Combine syrup ingredients in a saucepan, bring to a boil, reduce heat to medium and boil for 5 minutes. Spoon hot syrup over cool cake layers. Cover and let cool overnight. Fill and frost torte with whipped cream. Sprinkle with chopped almonds and decorate with orange preserved slices or cherries. Chill overnight.

# BISCUIT TORTE
Τούρτα μπισκότου

2 packages (7-ounces each) Pettit Beurre Biscuites,
   break into very small pieces
1 cup unsalted butter, at room temperature
1½ cups confectioner's sugar, sifted
¼ cup cocoa, sifted
4 eggs, separated
1 teaspoon vanilla
2 tablespoons cognac
1 cup chopped toasted blanched almonds
2 cups heavy cream, whipped with
¼ cup confectioner's sugar, sifted and
1 teaspoon vanilla
1 cup sliced or chopped toasted blanched almonds
Maraschino cherries

Cream butter and 1 cup sugar until light and fluffy. Add egg yolks one at a time, beating thoroughly after each one is added. Add vanilla and cognac. Gradually add cocoa and mix well to combine. Add chopped almonds and biscuites. Beat egg whites with a pinch of salt until stiff, gradually add the remaining sugar and beat well. Fold in chocolate mixture. Add one cup whipped cream and fold. Place mixture into a 10-11 inch spring form, lined with plastic wrap. Cover and chill overnight. Remove from pan by turning upside-down on a serving dish. Frost sides and top with whipped cream and sprinkle sides and top with sliced almonds if desired. Decorate with maraschino cherries. Chill.

# CHOCOLATE TORTE
Τούρτα σοκολάτας

**FOR THE CAKE:**
1 recipe Cake for Tortes (see index), add
¼ cup sugar, and
½ cup cocoa

**FOR THE CHOCOLATE CREAM FILLING:**
1 cup unsalted butter, at room temperature
½ cup confectioner's sugar, sifted
6 eggs, separated
2 packages (4-ounces each) sweet chocolate, melted
    with
6 tablespoons warm water
2 tablespoons maraschino, cognac or rum liqueur
    (optional)
1 cup heavy cream, whipped
½ cup or more apple-pear marmalade (see index)

**FOR THE SYRUP:**
½ cup sugar, dissolved with
⅓ cup warm water
3 tablespoons maraschino, cognac or rum liqueur

**FOR THE CHOCOLATE GLAZE:**
¼ cup unsalted butter, at room temperature
1 package (4-ounces) sweet chocolate, chopped
3 tablespoons milk
1 cup confectioner's sugar, sifted
½ teaspoon vanilla
1 teaspoon fresh lemon juice

Follow recipe and preparation as directed in Cake for Tortes. Prepare chocolate filling. Cream butter and sugar until light and fluffy. Add egg yolks one at a time, beating thoroughly after each one is added. Add melted chocolate and maraschino if desired; mix well to combine. Chill. Beat egg whites with a pinch of salt until stiff but not dry. Fold in chocolate mixture. Add one cup whipped cream and fold. Place one cake layer in a spring form pan, brush with syrup and spread ⅓ of the cream filling. Place second cake layer over cream. Repeat layers; cover and chill overnight. Gently remove sides of the pan and place on a serving dish. Spread top and sides evenly with marmalade. Set aside. Prepare chocolate glaze. Melt butter on top of a double boiler, add

chopped chocolate, whisking constantly until chocolate has melted. Add milk and sugar and lemon juice whisking until it becomes syrupy. Remove from heat and slowly pour in the middle of the torte to cover top and sides. Chill. Decorate the base and top with whipped cream. Arrange cherries and chocolate curls. Chill.

# CHOCOLATE MOUSSE TORTE
Τούρτα μους σοκολάτας

1 recipe Cake for Tortes (see index)

**FOR THE CHOCOLATE CREAM FILLING:**
1 cup unsalted butter, at room temperature
½ cup confectioner's sugar, sifted
6 eggs, separated
2 packages (4-ounces each) sweet chocolate, melted
    with
6 tablespoons warm water
2 tablespoons maraschino or cognac liqueur (optional)
2 cups heavy cream, whipped with
½ cup confectioner's sugar, sifted and
1 teaspoon vanilla
Maraschino cherries
Chocolate curls

**FOR THE SYRUP:**
½ cup sugar
⅓ cup warm water
3 tablespoons maraschino or cognac liqueur (optional)

Cream butter and sugar until light and fluffy. Add egg yolks one at a time, beating thoroughly after each one is added. Add melted chocolate and liqueur if desired, mix well to combine. Chill. Beat egg whites with pinch of salt until stiff but not dry. Fold in chocolate mixture. Fold in 1 cup whipped cream. Place one cake layer in a spring form pan, brush with syrup and spread ⅓ of the cream filling. Place second cake layer over cream. Repeat layers; cover and chill overnight. Gently remove sides of the pan and place on a serving dish. Frost sides and top of torte with the remaining whipped cream and decorate the base and top with decorating tip as you desire. Arrange cherries and chocolate curls. Chill.

# MILK CHOCOLATE TORTE
Τούρτα σεράνο

**FOR THE CAKE:**
1 recipe Cake for Tortes (see index)

**FOR THE CHOCOLATE CREAM FILLING:**
2 cups heavy cream, whipped with

¼ cup confectioner's sugar, sifted and
1 teaspoon vanilla
5 eggs, separated
½ cup confectioner's sugar, sifted
2 packages (4-ounces each) sweet chocolate, melted with
4 tablespoons warm water
2 tablespoons maraschino or cognac liqueur (optional)

**FOR THE SYRUP:**
1 cup milk
¼ cup sugar
4 tablespoons maraschino or cognac liqueur (optional)
Pistachio nuts
Maraschino cherries

Beat egg yolks with sugar until thick and lemon colored. Add melted chocolate, vanilla and liqueur if desired, beat to combine. Fold in beaten egg whites and whipped cream (keep ½ cup for decoration). Stir milk, sugar and liqueur if desired to make the syrup, until sugar has dissolved. In a 10x4-inch round tupperware, place one cake layer, brush with syrup and spread ¼ of the cream filling. Place second cake layer over cream. Repeat layers; finish with cream filling. Cover and chill overnight. Use whipped cream to decorate with lattice design. Arrange cherries and pistachio nuts. Chill.

Note: If tupperware is not available use deep round pyrex dish.

## COFFEE TORTE
Τούρτα καφὲ

3 packages (7-ounces each) Pettit Beurre Biscuits
1 cup milk

**FOR THE COFFEE CREAM FILLING:**
1¼ cups unsalted butter, at room temperature
2 cups confectioner's sugar, sifted
6 egg yolks
1 teaspoon vanilla
1 package (4-ounces) chopped sweet chocolate melted with
2 tablespoons hot water and
2 tablespoons Nescafe or instant coffee
1½ cups milk
1 cup heavy cream, whipped with
¼ cup confectioner's sugar, sifted and
½ teaspoon vanilla
1 cup chopped toasted blanched almonds

Cream butter and sugar until light and fluffy. Add egg yolks one at a time, beating thoroughly after each one is added. Add vanilla. Gradually add melted chocolate and coffee. Mix well to combine. Fold in ½ cup whipped cream. Divide biscuits into four portions. Dip biscuits one at a time into milk and arrange on a serving dish. Spread with ¼ of the coffee cream filling and top with second fourth of the biscuits. Repeat layering with biscuits and filling, ending with fourth biscuit layer. Fold remaining coffee cream filling in whipped cream and frost sides and tops of torte. Sprinkle with toasted almonds. Chill overnight.

## HAZELNUT TORTE
Τούρτα μὲ φουντούκι

**FOR THE CAKE:**
¾ cup unsalted butter, at room temperature
1 cup sugar
4 eggs
1 teaspoon vanilla
1¾ cups flour, sifted with
4 teaspoons baking powder, and
¾ cup corn starch
¼ cup milk
1¼ cups unsalted finely ground blanched hazelnuts

**FOR THE CREAM FILLING:**
1 recipe Cream Filling for Tortes (see index)

**FOR THE FROSTING:**
1½ cups heavy cream, whipped with
¼ cup confectioner's sugar, sifted and
¾ teaspoon vanilla
1 cup chopped blanched toasted hazelnuts
Maraschino cherries

Cream butter and sugar until light and fluffy. Add eggs one at a time, beating thoroughly after each one is added. Add vanilla. Gradually add flour mixture alternately with milk, beating until smooth after each addition. Add ground hazelnuts and mix thoroughly. Pour mixture into well greased and floured 10-inch spring form pan. Bake in a preheated 350°F (180°C) oven for approximately 45 minutes. Cool. Remove from pan. Turn up-side-down on a flat dish. Cover. The next day split cake into three layers horizontally. Prepare cream filling. Follow recipe and preparation as directed. Place one cake layer in a spring form pan. Spread ⅓ of the cream filling. Place second cake layer over cream. Repeat layers; cover and chill overnight. Gently remove the sides of the pan and place on a serving dish. Frost sides and top of torte with whipped cream. Sprinkle sides and top with chopped hazelnuts. Decorate top with cherries. Chill.

## KATAIFI TORTE
Κανταΐφι σεράϊ

**FOR THE CRUST:**
1 pound kataifi shredded pastry (thawed)
1 cup melted clarified unsalted butter (see index)

**FOR THE SYRUP:**
2½ cups sugar
1⅔ cups water
1 tablespoon fresh lemon juice
½ teaspoon vanilla

**FOR THE CREAM FILLING:**
1 recipe Cream Filling for Tortes (see index)

**FOR THE FROSTING:**
1½ cups heavy cream, whipped with
¼ cup confectioner's sugar, sifted and
½ teaspoon vanilla
1 cup choppd toasted blanched almonds
Maraschino cherries

Gently separate kataifi pastry. Brush an 11-inch spring form pan with butter and lay kataifi pastry evenly. Sprinkle with the melted butter. Bake in a preheated 350°F (180°C) oven for approximately 30 minutes or until golden. Cool to lukewarm. Combine Syrup ingredients in a saucepan. Bring to a boil, reduce heat to medium and boil for 5 minutes. Spoon syrup over kataifi. Cover and let cool. Prepare cream filling. Follow recipe and preparation as directed in Cream Filling for Tortes. Gently remove crust from pan and place on a serving dish. Spoon cream filling over and spread evenly. Cover top with whipped cream and sprinkle with chopped almonds. Arrange cherries on top. Chill.

# NOUGAT TORTE
Τούρτα νουγκατίνα

**FOR THE CRUST:**
8 egg whites
1 cup sugar
2 cups finely ground almonds, skins on
5 tablespoons flour
1 teaspoon cinnamon

**FOR THE FILLING:**
1 recipe Cream Filling for Tortes (see index)

**FOR THE FROSTING:**
2 cups heavy cream, whipped with
⅓ cup confectioner's sugar, sifted and
1 teaspoon vanilla
1 cup chopped toasted blanched almonds
Maraschino cherries

Mix ground almonds, flour and cinnamon together. Beat egg whites with pinch of salt until stiff but not dry. Gradually add sugar, beat well. Gradually fold in almond mixture. Spoon into three greased and floured 10-11-inch round baking sheets and spread evenly. Bake in a preheated 350°F (180°C) oven for approximately 20 minutes or until lightly golden. Gently remove from sheets. Cool. Prepare cream filling. Follow recipe and preparation as directed. Place one crust in a spring form pan, spread ⅓ of the cream mixture. Place second crust over cream. Repeat layers. Cover and chill overnight. Gently remove the sides of the pan and place on a serving dish. Frost sides and top of torte with whipped cream. Sprinkle sides and top with chopped almonds and decorate top with cherries. Chill.

# ORANGE TORTE
Τούρτα πορτοκαλιοῦ

**FOR THE CAKE:**
1 recipe Cake for Tortes (see index)

**FOR THE CREAM FILLING:**
1 recipe Cream Filling for Tortes (see index)

**FOR THE SYRUP:**
½ cup orange marmalade
½ cup frozen concentrated orange juice (thawed)
3 tablespoons orange flavored liqueur

**FOR THE FROSTING:**
1½ cups heavy cream, whipped with
⅔ cup confectioner's sugar, sifted and
1 teaspoon vanilla
3 tablespoons cocoa, sifted
1 tablespoon water
½ cup chopped pistachio nuts or toasted blanched almonds

Follow recipe and preparation as directed in Cake for Tortes.

Follow recipe and preparation as directed in Cream Filling in Nougat Torte.

Combine syrup ingredients together. Place one cake layer in a spring form pan. Brush with orange mixture. Spoon ⅓ of the cream filling. Place second cake layer over cream filling. Repeat layers. Cover and chill overnight. Gently remove the sides of the pan. Place on a serving dish. Mix together cocoa and water to form a smooth paste, fold into remaining whipped cream. Frost sides and top of torte with whipped cream and decorate the base and top with pistachio nuts if desired. Chill.

# PINEAPPLE TORTE
Τούρτα ἀνανὰ

**FOR THE CAKE:**

1 recipe Cake for Tortes (see index)

**FOR THE CREAM FILLING:**
3 cups scalding milk
¾ cup sugar
10 tablespoons flour
3 eggs and 1 egg yolk, beaten with
⅓ cup milk
2 tablespoons unsalted butter
1 teaspoon vanilla
⅓ cup chopped toasted blanched almonds

**FOR THE FROSTING:**
2 cups heavy cream, whipped with
½ cup confectioner's sugar, and
1 teaspoon vanilla
1 can (20-ounces) sliced pineapple
Maraschino cherries

Prepare cake as directed in cake for tortes. Prepare cream filling. Combine sugar, flour and beaten eggs, beat well using a whisk. Gradually stir in scalding milk and cook slowly on top of a double boiler, whisking constantly until mixture thickens. Cover and cook for 5 minutes. Remove from heat. Add butter and vanilla, mix well to combine. Cover to prevent a skin from forming. Cool. Drain pineapple reserving syrup and 2 slices for decoration, chop the rest. Place one cake layer in a spring form pan. Brush with reserved syrup. Spoon ⅓ of the cream filling and sprinkle ⅓ of the chopped pineapple and chopped almonds. Place second cake layer over cream filling. Repeat layers. Cover and chill overnight. Gently remove the sides of the pan. Place on a serving dish. Frost sides and top of torte with whipped cream, decorate the base and top with decorating tip as you desire. Decorate with pineapple and cherries. Chill.

# PUMPKIN TORTE
Τούρτα κολοκύθας

**FOR THE CAKE:**
1 recipe Cake for Tortes (see index)

**FOR THE PUMPKIN CREAM FILLING:**
2 cups scalding milk
1 cup sugar
4 tablespoons flour
4 tablespoons corn starch
4 eggs, beaten with
½ cup cream
½ teaspoon cinnamon
½ teaspoon pumpkin pie spice
2 cups fresh cooked and mashed pumpkin
2 tablespoon unsalted butter

**FOR THE SYRUP:**

1 cup milk
¼ cup sugar

**FOR THE FROSTING:**
1½ cups heavy cream, whipped with
⅓ cup confectioner's sugar, sifted and
½ teaspoon vanilla
1¼ cups or more finely chopped walnuts

Follow recipe and preparation for the cake as directed. Prepare cream filling. Combine sugar, flour, corn starch and beaten eggs, beat well using a whisk. Gradually stir in scalding milk and cook slowly on top of a double boiler, whisking constantly until mixture thickens. Add mashed pumpkin and cinnamon, stir well to combine. Cover and cook for 5 minutes. Remove from heat. Add butter, mix well. Cover to prevent a skin from forming. Cool. Add ½ cup chopped walnuts, mix well. Dissolve sugar in milk. Place one cake layer in a spring form pan. Brush with milk mixture. Spoon ⅓ of the cream filling. Top with second cake layer. Repeat layers. Cover and chill overnight. Gently remove the sides of the pan. Place on a serving dish. Frost sides and top with whipped cream and sprinkle with chopped walnuts. Chill.

# STRAWBERRY TORTE
Τούρτα φράουλας

**FOR THE CAKE:**
1 recipe Cake for Tortes (see index)

**FOR THE CREAM FILLING:**
1 recipe Cream Filling from Pineapple Torte (see index)

**FOR THE SYRUP:**
1½ cups chopped fresh strawberries, mixed with
½ cup sugar and
⅓ cup or more rum and chill

**FOR THE FROSTING:**
2 cups heavy cream, whipped with
½ cup confectioner's sugar and
1 teaspoon vanilla
Whole strawberries

Follow recipe and preparation as directed in Cake for Tortes. Prepare cream filling by following recipe and preparation as directed in cream filling from Pineapple Torte. Place one cake layer in a spring form pan. Brush with strawberry-sugar liquid and sprinkle ⅓ of the chopped strawberries. Spoon ½ of the cream filling and spread evenly. Place second cake layer over cream filling. Repeat layers. Cover and chill overnight. Gently remove the sides of the pan. Place on a serving dish. Frost sides and top of torte with whipped cream and decorate the base and top with decorating tip as you desire. Decorate with whole or cut in half strawberries. Chill.

✲✲✲✲

## STRAWBERRY CHARLOTTE TORTE
Τούρτα σαρλότ φράουλας

4 envelopes unflavored gelatin
¼ cup cold water
3½ cups scalding milk
1 cup sugar
1 tablspoon corn starch
7 egg yolks, beaten with
½ cup milk
1½ cups heavy cream, whipped with
⅓ cup confectioner's sugar
Strawberry jam
4 tablespoons rum
1 recipe ladyfingers (see index)

Soak the gelatin in cold water until soft. Combine sugar, corn starch and beaten egg yolks, add milk, beat well using a whisk. Gradually stir in scalding milk and cook slowly on top of a double boiler, whisking constantly until mixture thickens. Stir the softened gelatin into the hot cream. When the gelatin has dissolved, remove from heat. Cool completely. Fold in whipped cream. Stand ladyfingers around sides of a 10-inch spring form pan. Line bottom with more ladyfingers. Mix ⅓ cup jam with rum and brush ladyfingers Pour the cream mixture into prepared pan. Cover cream with ladyfingers. Cover and chill overnight. Remove the sides of the pan leaving the bottom. Place torte on a serving dish. Boil ⅓ cup jam with 1 tablespoon rum for a few minutes. Spread top evenly with jam mixture and chill.

✲✲✲✲

## WHIPPED CREAM TORTE
Τούρτα σαντιγὶ

**FOR THE CAKE:**
¼ cup unsalted butter, at room temperature
1 cup sugar
5 eggs
1 teaspoon vanilla
½ cup milk
2 cups flour, sifted with
4 teaspoons baking powder
1¼ cups finely ground blanched almonds

**FOR THE FILLING AND FROSTING:**
18 cups apricot jam (see index)

¼ cup cognac
2½ cups heavy cream whipped with
½ cup confectioner's sugar, sifted and
1 teaspoon vanilla
Maraschino cherries

Cream butter until light and fluffy. Gradually add sugar,, beat well.. Add eggs one at a time, beating thoroughly after each one is added. Add vanilla. Gradually add flour alternately with milk, beating until smooth after each addition. Add ground almonds and mix thoroughly. Pour mixture into well greased and floured 10-inch spring form pan. Bake in a preheated 350°F (180°C) oven for approximately 45 minutes. Cool. Remove from pan. Turn cake up-side-down on a flat dish. Cover. The next day split cake into three layers horizontally. Dissolve jam with cognac. Place one cake layer on a serving dish. Brush with the apricot mixture and spread with ⅓ of the whipped cream. Cover with the second layer over cream. Repeat layers, finishing with whipped cream. Frost sides with whipped cream. Decorate the base and top of torte with whipped cream as you desire. Arrange cherries. Chill.

✲✲✲✲

## FRIED PUFFS WITH SYRUP
Σβίγγοι μὲ σιρόπι

2 cups boiling water
1 cup unsalted butter
1 teaspoon salt
Rind of ½ orange (optional)
2 cups flour, sifted
8 large eggs
4 cups fine quality oil for frying

**FOR THE SYRUP:**
1½ cups honey
1½ cups sugar
1 cup water
Cinnamon

Add butter, salt and orange rind if desired to boiling water and bring to a boil. Reduce heat and remove orange rind. Add flour all at once and stir vigorously until the dough becomes elastic and no longer sticks to the side of the pan. Remove from heat. When the dough has partially cooled, add eggs one at a time, beating until mixture is thick and smooth. Heat oil in a heavy saucepan, over medium heat until hot. With an oiled teaspoon drop the dough in teaspoonfuls into the hot oil. Puffs will float to the surface and become lightly golden. Remove them from the oil with a straining spoon and lay on absorbent paper to drain. Combine syrup ingredients in a saucepan. Bring to a boil for 5 minutes. Remove from heat and skim off the foam. Serve the puffs immediately with hot syrup and sprinkle with cinnamon.

## HONEY PUFFS A
### Λουκουμάδες

5 cups flour, sifted
2 tablespoons active dry yeast
2¼ cups warm water
1 teaspoon salt
4 cups fine quality oil for frying
Warm honey
Cinnamon

Place flour into a large bowl and make a well in the center of the flour. Dissolve yeast and salt in one cup of the warm water. Let stay 5 minutes. Add yeast mixture into the well and mix well with a whisk; slowly add warm water until it becomes a soft dough. Beat well. Cover and let stay in a warm place for 2 hours or until doubled in bulk and looks full of bubbles. Heat oil in a heavy saucepan over medium heat until hot. With a damp teaspoon drop the batter in teaspoonfuls into the hot oil. Puffs will float to the surface and become lightly golden. Remove from the oil with a straining spoon and lay on absorbent paper to drain. Serve immediately with warm honey and sprinkle with cinnamon.

## HONEY PUFFS B
### Λουκουμάδες

3 cups all-purpose flour, sifted with
5 teaspoons baking powder
¼ cup sugar
¼ cup melted butter
1¼ cups milk
2 eggs, beaten
4 cups fine quality oil for frying
Warm honey
Cinnamon

Combine first six ingredients and mix well with a whisk. Heat oil in a heavy saucepan over medium heat until hot. With a damp teaspoon drop the batter in teaspoonfuls into the hot oil. Puffs will float to the surface and become golden. Remove from the oil with a straining spoon and lay on absorbent paper to drain. Serve immediately with warm honey and sprinkle with cinnamon.

## HONEY PUFFS WITH YOGURT
### Λουκουμάδες μὲ γιαούρτι

2 cups all-purpose flour, sifted with
1½ teaspoons baking soda
1½ cups plain yogurt
4 cups fine quality oil for frying
Warm honey
Cinnamon

Combine flour, yogurt together, mix well with a whisk. Cover and let stay for one hour. Heat oil in a heavy saucepan over medium heat until hot. With a damp teaspoon drop the batter in teaspoonfuls into the hot oil. Puffs will float to the surface and become golden. Remove from the oil with a straining spoon and lay on absorbent paper to drain. Serve immediately with warm honey and sprinkle with cinnamon.

## HONEY FOLDS
### Δίπλες

8 eggs
1 teaspoon vanilla
2 tablespoons fresh lemon juice
6 cups all-purpose unbleached flour
1½ teaspoons baking powder
3 tablespoons melted butter
4 cups fine quality oil for frying
2 cups honey
⅓ cup water
Cinnamon
½ cup finely ground walnuts

Beat eggs until thick and light. Add vanilla. Sift flour with baking powder together. Gradually add flour to egg mixture alternately with lemon juice, beating until smooth. Add enough flour to make a soft dough. Gradually add melted butter and knead until smooth and elastic. Divide into three parts. With hands work each part into a very smooth ball. Place on a dish and cover with plastic wrap. Let stay for four hours or longer at room temperature. On floured surface roll out each part of dough into very thin sheet (phyllo). Cut into 6x3-inch strips. Pour oil into a deep three quart saucepan. Heat over a medium-low heat until hot. Drop strips one at a time in hot oil, press down and turn immediately. Gently roll up in hot oil; fry until slightly golden. Drain into a colander or lay them on absorbent paper. Boil honey with water for 5 minutes. Skim off the foam. Dip folds in honey one at a time. Sprinkle with cinnamon and walnuts.

Recipe from Mrs. Joanna Martys

# GREEK PANCAKES
Τηγανίτες

2 beaten eggs
¾ cup millk
¼ cup melted butter
¼ cup sugar
1½ cups flour, sifted with
3 teaspoons baking powder
Honey or marmalade

Combine first four ingredients together and mix well. Gradually add flour and beat until smooth. Drop by tablespoons on hot butter. When full of bubbles turn to brown other side. Serve with honey or marmalade.

# CHOCOLATE SOUFFLE
Σουφλὲ σοκολάτας

4 tablspoeons unsalted butter
4 tablespoons flour
2 ounces sweet chocolate, melted in
1¼ cups scalding milk
¼ cup sugar
1 teaspoon vanilla
4 eggs, separated

Melt butter over medium heat, blend in flour until smooth using a whisk. Gradually add milk whisking constantly until mixture is thick and smooth. Remove from heat. Beat egg yolks with sugar and vanilla until thick and creamy. Gradually add beaten egg yolks to cream mixture, mix thoroughly. Cool. Fold in stiffly beaten egg whites. Pour into lightly greased souffle dish. Set in pan of hot water and bake in a preheated 350°F (180°C) oven for approximately 55 minutes or until souffle is firm to the touch. Serve immediately.

# MOCHA SOUFFLE
Σουφλὲ μόκα

4 tablespoons unsalted butter
5 tablespoons flour
1½ tablespoons Nescafe, mix in
¾ cup hot water
½ cup heavy cream
⅓ cup sugar
4 eggs, separated

Follow preparation as directed in Chocolate Souffle (see index).

Variation:

# VANILLA SOUFFLE
Σουφλὲ βανίλιας

Subtract chocolate from Chocolate Souffle (see index). Follow recipe and preparation as directed.

# RICH CARAMEL CREAM
Κρέμα καραμελὲ πολυτελείας

1¼ cups sugar
4 tablespoons water
12 large eggs
1¼ cups sugar
⅛ teaspoon salt
1½ teaspoons vanilla
1½ cups heavy cream, mix with
6 cups scalding milk
1½ cups heavy cream, whipped
1 cup chopped blanched pistachio nuts

In a heavy small frying pan combine 1¼ cups sugar and 4 tablespoons water. Bring to a boil, reduce heat to medium-high, stirring constantly and cook until golden brown. Pour immediately into an eleven cup mold and before it hardens move the mold about so that the caramel will coat the sides. Let the caramel harden while you prepare the cream. Beat eggs with salt until frothy. Add sugar and vanilla and beat until thick and light. Gradually add milk. Pour into caramelized mold. Set in pan of hot water and bake in a preheated 300°F (165°C) oven for approximately 60 minutes or until firm. A knife blade run into the center of the cream will come out clean. Cool completely. Chill overnight. The next day unmold into a deep serving dish and serve with caramel syrup, whipped cream and sprinkle with pistachio nuts.

# CARAMEL CREAM
Κρέμα καραμελὲ

¾ cup sugar
3 tablespoons water
8 large eggs
¾ cup sugar
⅛ teaspoon salt
1 teaspoon vanilla
5 cups milk
1 cup heavy cream, whipped (optional)
½ cup chopped toasted blanched almonds

Follow preparation as directed in Rich Caramel Cream (see index).

## CARAMEL RICE PUDDING
### Ριζόγαλο καραμελὲ

¾ cup sugar
3 tablespoons water
4 cups milk
¼ cup rice
⅛ teaspoon salt
⅓ cup sugar
3 tablespoons corn starch
4 beaten eggs
1 teaspoon vanilla

In a heavy small frying pan combine ¾ cup sugar and 3 tablespoons water, bring to a boil, reduce heat to medium-high, stirring constantly and cook until golden brown. Pour immediately into 8-cup molds and before it hardens move the mold about so that the caramel will coat the sides. Let the caramel harden while you prepare the pudding. Bring the milk to a boil over medium heat. Pick over the rice and wash thoroughly, add to the milk, add salt. Cook slowly for 25 minutes, stirring occasionally. Dissolve corn starch with ½ cup milk and gradually add to rice mixture, stirring constantly, add sugar and cook for 20 minutes. Remove from heat. Beat eggs until thick and creamy. Add vanilla. Gradually add rice pudding, stirring constantly. Pour into caramelized mold. Set in pan of hot water and bake in a pre-heated 300° F (165°C) oven for approximately 60 minutes or until firm. A knife blade run into the center of the pudding will come out clean. Cool immediately. Chill overnight. The next day unmold into a deep serving dish. Serve with caramel syrup, whipped cream and sprinkle with chopped toasted almonds if desired.

## CREAMY RICE PUDDING
### Ριζόγαλο

¾ cup boiling water
½ cup rice
¼ teaspoon salt
7 cups milk
4 tablespoons corn starch
¾ cup sugar
Cinnamon

Pick over rice and wash thoroughly. Add rice and salt to boiling water, cook slowly until water has evaporated. Add milk, bring to a boil and cook slowly for 15 minutes, stirring occasionally. Dissolve corn starch with ¼ cup milk and gradually add to rice mixture, add sugar, stirring constantly; cook for 20 minutes. Remove from heat. Spoon into individual bowls and sprinkle with cinnamon. Chill.

## GRAPE PUDDING
### Μουσταλεβριὰ

6 cups unsweetened white grape juice (fresh if possible)
1 cup fine semolina
¾ cup or less sugar
Finely chopped walnuts
3 tablespoons sesame seeds, toasted and crushed
Cinnamon

Combine grape juice, sugar and semolina in a saucepan and mix well. Bring to a boil, reduce heat and cook slowly, stirring constantly until mixture thickens. Remove from heat. Pour into individual bowls. Cool. Sprinkle with walnuts, sesame seed and cinnamon. Chill.

## VANILLA CREAM
### Κρέμα βανίλιας

4 cups scalding milk
½ cup sugar
4 egg yolks
1 cup milk
9 tablespoons corn starch
2 teaspoons vanilla

Combine sugar and egg yolks, mix well. Dissolve corn starch with one cup milk. Add to the egg mixture. Gradually stir in scalding milk and cook slowly on top of double boiler, whisking constantly until mixture thickens. Remove from heat, add vanilla and pour into serving glass bowls. Chill.

Variations:

## CHOCOLATE CREAM
### Κρέμα σοκολάτας

Add 1,5 ounces chocolate and follow recipe and preparation as directed in Vanilla Cream (see index). Serve with whipped cream if desired.

## CINNAMON CREAM
### Κρέμα κανέλλας

Substitute vanilla with cinnamon. Follow recipe and preparation as directed in Vanilla Cream (see index). Pour into serving glass bowls and sprinkle with cinnamon.

# COCONUT CREAM
### Κρέμα καρύδας

Add ½ cup coconut flakes into egg mixture. Follow recipe and preparation as directed in Vanilla Cream (see index). Serve with whipped cream if desired.

※※※※

# CHOCOLATE MOUSSE
### Προφιντερὸλ

**3 egg whites, stiffly beaten**
**Pinch of salt**
**½ cup sugar**
**1 tablespoon water**
**2 ounces sweet chocolate,, melted with**
**1 tablespoon water**
**1 cup heavy cream, whipped**
**4-6 ladyfingers (see index) (optional)**
**4-6 tablespoons milk if you use ladyfingers**
**4-6 maraschino cherries**

Combine sugar and water together. Slowly bring to a boil, stirring constantly until sugar has dissolved. Remove from heat. Pour it slowly over the stiffly beaten egg whites and continue beating until it is cool. Chill. Combine egg mixture, chocolate and whipped cream, mix together. In each champagne glass put one ladyfinger if desired and sprinkle with 1 tablespoon milk and pour over chocolate mousse mixture. Decorate with a maraschino cherry. Chill.

※※※※

# MOCHA CREAM
### Κρέμα μόκα

**1 cup sugar**
**¼ cup cocoa, sifted**
**1 tablespoon Nescafe or instant coffee**
**5 tablespoons corn starch**
**4 egg yolks, beaten with**
**½ cup milk**
**3 cups scalding milk**
**1 teaspoon vanilla**
**1½ cups heavy cream, whipped with**
**1 teaspoon vanilla**
**Chocolate curls**

Combine sugar, cocoa, Nescafe if desired, corn starch and beaten egg yolks, beat well using a whisk. Gradually stir in scalding milk and cook slowly on top of a double boiler, whisking constantly until mixture thickens. Cover and cook for 5 minutes. Remove from heat. Add vanilla. Cool. Fold in 1½ cups whipped cream. Spoon into champagne glasses. Top with remaining whipped cream and chocolate curls. Chill.

# STRAWBERRY BAVARIAN CREAM
### Κρέμα μπαβαρουὰ φράουλας

**3 large eggs, separated**
**¼ cup sugar**
**2 cups milk**
**1 package (3-ounces) strawberry flavored gelatin**
**1 cup heavy cream, whipped with**
**¼ cup confectioner's sugar, sifted and**
**½ teaspoon vanilla**
**Fresh strawberries**

Combine egg yolks and half of the sugar, mix well. Gradually stir in milk and cook slowly on top of a double boiler, whisking constantly until mixture thickens. Add gelatin and stir well to combine. Remove from heat. Chill until almost set. Beat egg whites with a pinch of salt until stiff, gradually add the remaining sugar and beat well, fold in cream mixture. Add one cup whipped cream and fold. Pour into 6 cup lightly oiled mold. Chill until firm. Unmold on a serving dish and garnish with remaining whipped cream and strawberries.

※※※※

# TUTTI-FRUTTI BAVARIAN CREAM
### Κρέμα μπαβαρουὰ τούτι-φρούτι

**4 eggs, separated**
**¾ cup sugar**
**2⅔ cups milk**
**2 tablespoons unflavored gelatin, dissolved with**
**¼ cup water**
**⅓ cup chopped toasted blanched almonds**
**1 teaspoon vanilla**
**½ cup chopped mixed candied fruits (see index)**
**1½ cups heavy cream, whipped with**
**¼ cup confectioner's sugar, sifted and**
**½ teaspoon vanilla**
**Maraschino cherries**

Combine egg yolks and half of the sugar and mix well. Gradually stir in milk and cook slowly on top of double boiler, whisking constantly until mixture thickens. Add dissolved gelatin, vanilla and stir well to combine. Chill until almost set. Add chopped almonds and fruits, mix well. Beat egg whites with a pinch of salt until stiff, gradually add the remaining sugar and beat well. Fold in cream mixture. Add one cup whipped cream and fold. Pour into lightly oiled mold. Chill until firm. Unmold on a serving dish and decorate with remaining whipped cream and maraschino cherries. Chill.

# GREEK COFFEE
### Καφὲς ἑλληνικὸς

**VERY SWEET COFFEE:**

1 demitasse cup water (the size of ½ cup) . .
4 teaspoons sugar
2 teaspoons Greek coffee

Combine water and sugar in a small briki (small Greek coffee pot), let the water get warm, stirring until sugar has dissolved. Add coffee and stir well to blend. Remove from heat before the coffee boils and destroys the foam. Gently pour into demitasse cup. Serve with sweet preserve (see index) and glass of ice water. Serves 1.

**MEDIUM SWEET COFFEE:**

1 demitasse cup water
2 teaspoons sugar
2 teaspoons Greek coffee

Follow preparation as directed in Very Sweet Coffee. Serve as above.

**LIGHT SWEET COFFEE:**

1 demitasse cup water
1 teaspoon sugar
2 teaspoons Greek coffee

Follow preparation as directed in Very Sweet Coffee. Serve as above.

# SOUR CHERRY DRINK
### Βυσσινάδα

3 pounds ripe sour cherries, pitted
5 cups water
7 cups sugar
½ cup fresh lemon juice

Place cherries into a large pot and crush them with your hands as much as you can. Add water, bring to a boil, reduce heat and boil for 20 minutes. Cool. Press through a sieve. Return liquid to the pot, add sugar and bring to a boil, stir to dissolve the sugar; boil on medium heat to thicken into syrup. Add lemon juice, stir and remove from the heat. Cool. Place into clean dry bottles. Cover with a cork and store. To serve vyssinatha, place 1½-2 inches vyssinatha into a tall glass and fill with ice water, stir well and serve.

# APRICOT ICE
### Γρανίτα βερύκοκο

2 cups water

1½ cups sugar
⅓ cup fresh lemon juice
4 cups ripe apricots, mashed
2 cups fresh orange juice

Combine water and sugar in a large saucepan, bring to a boil, stir to dissolve the sugar and add lemon juice; boil for 5 minutes. Cool completely. Add mashed apricots and orange juice to syrup and mix well to combine. Pour into a plastic container. Freeze overnight. Scrape with a spoon and serve in tall glasses with a thick straw.

# CANTALOUPE ICE
### Γρανίτα πεπόνι

3 cups water
1¾ cups sugar
3 cups cantaloupe, mashed
⅓ cup fresh lemon juice
1 cup fresh orange juice

Combine water and sugar in a large saucepan, bring to a boil, stir to dissolve the sugar; boil for 5 minutes. Cool completely. Add mashed cantaloupe, lemon juice and orange juice to syrup and mix well to combine. Pour into a plastic container. Freeze overnight. Scrape with a spoon and serve in tall glasses with a thick straw.

# LEMON ICE
### Γρανίτα λεμόνι

7 cups water
4 cups sugar
Grated rind of two lemons (optional)
2 cups fresh lemon juice

Combine water, sugar and lemon rind if desired, in a large saucepan, bring to a boil, stir to dissolve the sugar; boil for 5 minutes. Cool completely. Add lemon juice to syrup and mix well. Pour into a plastic container. Freeze overnight. Scrape with a spoon and serve in tall glasses with a thick straw.

# ORANGE ICE
### Γρανίτα πορτοκάλι

4 cups water
3 cups sugar
Grated rind of one orange (optional)
3 cups fresh orange juice
¼ cup fresh lemon juice

Combine water, sugar and orange rind if desired in

a large saucepan, bring to a boil, stir to dissolve the sugar; boil for 5 minutes. Cool completely. Add orange and lemon juice to syrup and mix well. Pour into a plastic container. Freeze overnight. Scrape with a spoon and serve in tall glasses with a thick straw.

### PEACH ICE
Γρανίτα γιαρμά

4 cups water
2 cups sugar
4 cups peeled and mashed peaches, mixed with
⅓ cup fresh lemon juice, and
1 cup fresh orange juice

Combine water, sugar and bring to a boil, stir to dissolve the sugar; boil for 5 minutes. Cool completely. Add peach mixture to syrup and mix well to combine. Pour into a plastic container. Freeze overnight. Scrape with a spoon and serve in tall glasses with a thick straw.

### STRAWBERRY ICE
Γρανίτα φράουλα

4 cups water
2 cups sugar
4 cups strawberries, mashed
2 tablespoons fresh lemon juice

Combine water and sugar in a large saucepan, bring to a boil, stir to dissolve the sugar; boil for 5 minutes. Cool completely. Add mashed strawberries and lemon juice to syrup and mix well to combine. Pour into a plastic container. Freeze overnight. Scrape with a spoon and serve in tall glasses with a thick straw.

### APRICOT PRESERVE
Βερύκοκο γλυκό

4 pounds small apricots
2⅔ cups water
9 cups sugar
Juice of one lemon
1 cup or more whole blanched almonds
1 teaspoon almond extract

Gently remove the pit of each apricot. Place them into a large saucepan and cover with cold water. Bring to a boil and boil for 5 minutes. Pour off the water. Place fresh cold water. Drain well. Replace pit with the whole almonds. Combine water and sugar into a large saucepan, bring to a boil, stir to dissolve the sugar; boil for 5 minutes over medium heat. Add apricots and cook for 15 minutes. Remove from heat, skim the froth, cover and let stay for 24 hours. The next day cook again for 10 minutes. Add lemon juice and almond extract and cook until the syrup thickens and the fruit looks transparent. Spoon hot preserve into sterilized hot pint jars. Screw on hot lids. Let cool completely. Store in a cool dry place. Makes 7-8 pints.

### CHERRY PRESERVE
Κεράσι γλυκό

4 pounds large hard cherries
9 cups sugar
4 cups water
Juice of one lemon
1 cup slivered blanched almonds (optional)

Wash cherries in cold water. Remove the stems and pits gently so you don't crush the cherries. Place water and sugar in a large saucepan, bring to a boil, stir to dissolve the sugar; boil for 10 minutes over medium heat. Add cherries and cook for 5 minutes. Remove from heat, skim the froth, cover and let stay for 24 hours. The next day cook again for 10 minutes. Remove from heat, cover and let stay again for 24 hours. Add almonds and cook until the syrup thickens and fruit looks transparent. Add lemon juice and cook for a few minutes longer. Remove from heat and spoon hot preserve immediately into sterilized hot pint jars. Screw on hot lids. Let cool completely. Store in a cool dry place. Makes 4 pints.

### SOUR CHERRY PRESERVE
Βύσσινο γλυκό

4 pounds large hard sour cherries
10 cups sugar
2 cups water
Juice of one lemon

Wash sour cherries in cold water. Remove the stems and pits gently so you don't crush them. Combine sugar and water in a large saucepan, bring to a boil, stir to dissolve the sugar; boil for 5 minutes. Add sour cherries and cook for 30 minutes. Remove from heat, skim the froth, cover and let stay for 24 hours. The next day cook again until the syrup thicken. Add lemon juice and cook for a few minutes longer. Remove from heat and spoon hot preserve immediately into sterilized hot pint jars. Screw on hot lids. Let cool completely. Store in a cool dry place. Makes 4 pints.

## GRAPE PRESERVE
Σταφύλι γλυκὸ

4 pounds firm fat seedless white grapes
6 cups sugar
2 cups water
Juice of one lemon
1 cup slivered blanched almonds
1 teaspoon vanilla

Wash graps in cold water several times. Remove the stems and drain well. Combine sugar and water in a large saucepan, bring to a boil, stir to dissolve the sugar and boil for 5 minutes. Add grapes and cook for 10 minutes. Remove from heat and skim the froth. Let stay for 24 hours. The next day cook again for 15 minutes. Add lemon juice and slivered almonds and cook until the syrup thicken and fruit looks transparent. Add vanilla. Remove from heat and spoon hot preserve immediately into sterilized hot pint jars. Screw on hot lids. Let cool completely. Store in a cool dry place. Makes 4 pints.

## GRAPEFRUIT PRESERVE
Φράπα γλυκὸ

2 pounds rind from large, thick skinned grapefruits
   (about 8)
7 cups sugar
2½ cups water
Juice of one lemon

With vegetable peeler, peel the surface of each grape-fruit. Then with a sharp knife cut through the rind into 6 vertical sections. Gently remove the sections of rind and cut each one in half. Discard white membrane from each section of the rind. Place them in a large saucepan and cover with cold water. Place fresh cold water and boil again for 5 minutes. Repeat 2 more times. Drain. Return the rinds to the sauce-pan and cover with cold water, let stay for 2 hours. Drain well in a colander. Combine water and sugar in a large saucepan, bring to a boil, stir to dissolve the sugar; boil for 5 minutes over medium heat. Add rinds into the syrup and cook for 15 minutes. Remove from heat, skim the froth, cover and let stay for 24 hours. The next day cook again for 15 minutes, add lemon juice and cook until the syrup thickens and the fruit looks transparent. Remove from heat and spoon hot preserve immediately. Store in a cool dry place. Makes 3-4 pints.

## BITTER ORANGE PEEL PRESERVE
Νεράντζι γλυκὸ

3 pounds rind from large thick skinned bitter oranges
7 cups sugar
3 cups water
Juice of one lemon

With a vegetable peeler, peel the surface of each bitter orange. Then with a sharp knife cut through the the end into 4-5 vertical sections. Gently remove the sections of rind. Descard white membrane from each section of the rind. Roll up each orange section tight-ly passing a needle and thread through each roll. When 18 rolls are threaded tie ends together, form a wreath of rolls. Repeat with the remaining sections until you finish all. Place them into a large saucepan and cover with cold water. Bring to a boil and boil for 10 minutes. Pour off the water. Add fresh cold water and boil again for 5 minutes, repeat two more times. Drain. Return the wreaths to the saucepan and cover with cold water; let stay for 2 hours. Drain well in a colander. Remove the threads. Combine sugar and water in a large saucepan, bring to a boil, stir to dis-solve the sugar; boil for 5 minutes over medium heat. Add rolls into the syrup and cook for 15 minutes. Remove from heat, skim the froth, cover and let stay for 24 hours. The next day cook again for 15 minutes, and lemon juice and cook until the syrup thickens and the fruit looks transparent. Remove from heat and spoon hot preserve immediately into sterilized hot pint jars. Screw on hot lids. Let cool completely. Store in a cool dry place. Makes 4-5 pints.

Variation:

## ORANGE PEEL PRESERVE
Πορτοκάλι γλυκὸ

Substitute rind from large thick skinned oranges (about 16) for the Bitter Orange Preserve (see index).

Wash and scrub oranges. Don't peel them. Follow Wash and scrub oranges. Don't peel them. Follow preparation as directed in Bitter Oragne Preserve.

## WHOLE BITTER ORANGE PRESERVE
Νερατζάκι ὁλόκληρο γλυκὸ

3 pounds very small bitter oranges
9 cups sugar
4½ cups water
½ teaspoon green food color (optional)
1 cup or more slivered blanched almonds

Select fresh whole small (the size of a walnut) bitter oranges. Core them from the bottom and remove the

DESSERTS, BEVERAGES, CANDIES, PRESERVES

seeds by making a small hole in the center. Place into a large saucepan and cover with cold water, bring to a boil for 10 minutes. Pour off the water. Cover with warm water and boil again for 10 minutes. Repeat two more times. Drain. Return them to the saucepan and cover with cold water; let stay for 24 hours. Drain. Replace seeds with almonds. Combine water and sugar in a large saucepan, bring to a boil, stir to dissolve the sugar; boil for 5 minutes over medium heat. Add bitter oranges into the syrup and cook for 15 minutes. Add the green color if desired. Remove from heat, skim the froth, cover and let stay for 24 hours. The next day cook again for 15 minutes, add lemon juice and cook until the syrup thickens. Remove from heat and spoon hot preserve immediately into sterilized hot pint jars. Screw on hot lids. Let cool completely. Store in a cool dry place. Makes 5-7 pints.

❦ ❦ ❦ ❦

# PEAR PRESERVE
### Ἀχλάδι γλυκὸ

**4 pounds small not very ripe pears**
**Juice of two lemons**
**9 cups sugar**
**4 cups water**
**Juice of one lemon**
**Whole blanched almonds**

With a vegetable peeler, peel the surface of each pear. Then core them from the bottom and remove the seeds by making a small hole. Soak them in cold water with the juice of the two lemons. Drain. Replace seeds with almonds. Place the 4 cups water into a large saucepan, bring to a boil, add pears, cover, bring to a boil and cook for 10 minutes over medium heat. Add sugar and cook for 15 minutes. Gently stir to dissolve the sugar. Remove from heat, skim off the froth and let stay for 24 hours. The next day cook again for 10 minutes. Add lemon juice and cook until the syrup thickens and fruit looks transparent. Remove from heat and spoon hot preserve immediately into sterilized hot pint jars. Screw on hot lids. Let cool completely. Store in cool dry place. Makes 7-9 pints.

❦ ❦ ❦ ❦

# QUINCE PRESERVE
### Κυδώνι γλυκὸ

**5 pounds large ripe spotless quinces**
**10 cups sugar**
**5 cups water**
**Juice of one lemon**
**1 cup slivered blanched almonds**

**2 teaspoons vanilla**

Wash quinces well under cold running water. With a vegetable peeler, peel the surface of each quince and core it. Cut into thin slices and then into thin pieces the thickness of a toothpick, place in cold water to prevent discoloring. Cook peeling and cores in 4 cups of water for 45 minutes over medium heat. Strain the liquid. Measure liquid, add water to make 5 cups. Combine sugar and measure water into a large saucepan,, bring to a boil, stir to dissolve the sugar and boil for 5 minutes. Add quince and cook for 30 minutes over medium high heat. Skim off the froth. Add lemon juice and almonds and cook until the syrup thickens and the fruit looks transparent. Remove from heat and spoon hot preserve immediately into sterilized hot pint jars. Screw on hot lids. Let cool completely. Store in a cool dry place. Makes 5 pints.

❦ ❦ ❦ ❦

# STRAWBERRY PRESERVE
### Φράουλα γλυκὸ

**3 pounds ripe firm strawberries**
**7 cups sugar**
**Juice of one lemon**

Wash well and clean the stems gently to avoid crushing them. Drain. Place strawberries in a large bowl and sprinkle with the lemon juice. Let them stay for four hours. Place a colander into a large saucepan. Gently pour strawberries into the colander, cover and refrigerate overnight to drain. The next day place saucepan with the dripping liquid on the heat, add sugar and bring to a boil, stir to dissolve the sugar; boil until the syrup thickens. Add strawberries, bring to a boil and cook over medium high heat for 6 minutes. Remove from heat, skim off the froth. Cover with a cloth towel and let stay overnight. The next day gently remove strawberries from the syrup with a straining spoon. Bring syrup to a boil again and boil until it thickens more. Add strawberries to syrup and boil for 10 minutes or until syrup thickens. Remove from heat and spoon hot preserve immediately into sterilized hot pint jars. Screw on hot lids. Let cool completely. Store in a cool dry place. Makes 4 -5 pints.

❦ ❦ ❦ ❦

# APPLE PEAR JAM
### Μήλο καὶ ἀχλάδι μαρμελάδα

**2 pounds fully ripe tart apples**
**2 pounds fully ripe pears**
**2 cups water**
**9 cups sugar**
**Juice of one lemon**

Peel and core apples and pears. Slice into thin slices. Combine apples and pears into a very large saucepan, add water, bring to a boil and cook for 25 minutes over medium heat, stirring occasionally with a wooden spoon. Remove from heat and cool. Press through a food mill. Add sugar and cook for 20 minutes, stirring constantly to prevent burning, skim off the foam and continue cooking until the jam sets quickly if a portion is dropped on a cool plate. Add lemon juice and cook for 2 minutes longer. Remove from heat and spoon hot jam immediately into sterilized hot (6-ounce) jars. Screw on hot lids. Let cool completely. Store in a cool dry place. Makes 6 jars.

## APRICOT JAM
### Βερύκοκο μαρμελάδα

**4 pounds fully ripe apricots**
**1 cup water**
**8 cups sugar**
**Juice of one lemon**

Pit apricots and cut into small pieces. Combine apricots and water in a very large saucepan, bring to a boil and cook for 20 minutes over medium heat, stirring occasionally with a wooden spoon. Remove from heat and cool. Press through a food mill. Add sugar and cook for 20 minutes, stirring constantly to prevent burning, skim off the foam and continue cooking until the jam sets quickly if a portion is dropped on a cool plate. Add lemon juice and cook for 2 minutes longer. Remove from heat and spoon hot jam immediately into sterilized hot (6-ounce) jars. Screw on hot lids. Let cool completely. Store in a cool dry place. Makes 6 jars.

## APPLE JELLY
### Μῆλο πελτὲ

**4 pounds large ripe spotless red apples**
**Sugar**
**Water**

Wash apples and remove the stems and blossom ends. Cut in fourths. Cover with cold water and cook until tender. Pour apples into a cheese cloth bag and drain overnight. Measure an equal amount of sugar. Place liquid into a large saucepan, brig to a boil, stirring slowly. Boil rapidly until the jelling stage is reached. Skim off the foam. Remove from heat and spoon hot jelly immediately into sterilized hot (6-ounce) jars. Screw on hot lids. Let cool completely. Store in a cool dry place. Makes 4-5 jars.

## QUINCE JELLY
### Κυδώνι πελτὲ

**4 pounds large ripe spotless quinces**
**6⅔ cups sugar**
**Water**

Wash quinces well under cold running water. With a vegetable peeler, peel the surface of each quince and core it. Cut into slices and place into cold water with the juice of two lemons (to prevent discoloring). Drain. Place the peeling and cores into a cheese cloth bag and tie well. Place pulp and the bag into a very large saucepan, cover with cold water and cook until they are tender. Drain off the liquid (save pulp for quince jelly bars). Measure liquid, add more water to make 4 cups. Place liquid into the saucepan, bring to a boil. Gradually add sugar, stirring slowly. Boil rapidly until the jelling stage is reached. Skim off the foam. Remove from heat and spoon hot jelly immediately into sterilized hot (6-ounce) jars. Screw on hot lids. Let cool completely. Store in cool dry place. Makes 4-5 jars.

## MIXED FRUIT MARMALADE
### 'Ανάμικτα φρούτα μαρμελάδα

**3 large thick-skinned grapefruit**
**3 large thick-skinned lemons**
**3 large thick-skinned oranges**
**Water**
**Sugar**

With a vegetable peeler, peel the surface of grapefruits and lemons only. Place whole fruits in a large saucepan and cover with cold water, bring to a boil and cook for 5 minutes. Drain. Repeat twice. Cool. Slice and remove seeds. Press through a food mill, measure and add 3 times as much water, stir to combine. Let stay overnight. The next day bring to a boil and cook for 30 minutes over medium heat, stirring occasionally with a wooden spoon. Measure and add an equal measure of sugar. Bring to a boil and cook for 20 minutes, stirring constantly. Skim off the foam and continue cooking until the marmelade sets quickly if a portion is dropped on a cool plate. Remove from heat and spoon hot marmelade immediately into sterilized hot (6-ounce) jars. Screw on hot lids. Let cool completely. Store in cool dry place. Makes 8 jars (about).

## ORANGE MARMALADE
### Πορτοκάλι μαρμελάδα

10 large thick-skinned oranges
3 large thick-skinned lemons
Water
Sugar

With a vegetables peeler, peel the surface of lemons only. Then with a sharp knife remove the peel from fruits. Cover peel with water, bring to a boil and cook for 5 minutes. Drain. Repeat twice. Cool. Remove seeds from pulp and press with the peel through a food mill. Measure and add 3 times as much water. Let stay overnight. The next day bring to a boil and cook for 30 minutes over medium heat, stirring occasionally with a wooden spoon. Cool. Measure and add an equal measure of sugar, bring to a boil and cook for 20 minutes, stirring constantly. Skim off the foam and continue cooking until the marmelade sets quickly if a portion is dropped on a cool plate. Remove from heat and spoon hot marmelade immediately into sterilized hot (6-ounce) jars. Screw on hot lids. Let cool completely. Store in a cool dry place. Makes about 8 jars.

❦❦❦❦

# STRAWBERRY JAM
### Φράουλα μαρμελάδα

3 pounds ripe firm strawberries
7 cups sugar
Juice of one lemon

Wash well and clean the stems. Place strawberries into a large saucepan and crush them with your hand as much as you can. Bring to a boil, add sugar and cook over medium high heat for 20 minutes stirring constantly with a wooden spoon. Skim off the foam. Add lemon juice and continue cooking until the jam sets quickly if a portion is dropped on a cool plate. Remove from heat and spoon hot jam immediately into sterilized hot (6-ounce) jars. Screw on hot lids. Let cool completely. Store in a cool dry place. Makes 6 jars.

❦❦❦❦

# GRAPE JAM
### Σταφύλι μαρμελάδα

6 pounds concord grapes
6 cups sugar
¾ cup orange juice (fresh)
⅓ cup lemon juice

Wash grapes well and remove stems. Place grapes into a large saucepan and crush them with your hand as much as you can. Bring to a boil and cook for 20 minutes over medium heat, stirring occasionally with a wooden spoon. Cool. Press through a sieve.

Combine pulp, sugar and orange juice and cook for 20 minutes, stirring constantly. Skim off the foam. Add lemon juice and continue cooking until the jam set quickly if a portion is dropped on a cool plate. Remove from heat and spoon hot jam immediately into sterilized hot (6-ounce) jars. Screw on lids. Let cool completely. Store in a cool dry place. Makes 6 jars.

❦❦❦❦

# ALMOND FONDANT
### Φοντὰν ἀμυγδάλου

2 cups finely ground blanched almonds
½ recipe Vanilla Spoon Sweet (see index)
½ teaspoon almond extract
Small paper fondant cups

Combine all ingredients together and mix well. Shape each almond fondant into ball the size of a small walnut. Place them into paper cups. Makes 4-5 dozen.

❦❦❦❦

# COCONUT FONDANT
### Φοντὰν καρύδας

2 cups finely ground coconut
½ recipe Vanilla Spoon Sweet (see index)
½ teaspoon vanilla
Melted chocolate
Small paper fondant cups

Combine all ingredients together except the melted chocolate and mix well. Shape each coconut fondant into a ball the size of a small walnut. Dip them into melted chocolate. Let them dry and place into paper cups. Makes 4-5 dozen.

❦❦❦❦

# VANILLA SPOON SWEET
### Βανίλια γλυκὸ

4 cups sugar
2 cups boiling water
¼ cup cream of tartar
2 teaspoons vanilla or ⅛ teaspoon crushed masticha
    or ½ teaspoon almond extract if you desire

Place sugar, boiling water and cream of tartar into a saucepan, stirring constantly until the sugar is dissolved. Slowly bring to a boil over low heat. Cover and cook for three minutes. Remove the cover and continue to cook slowly without stirring to the soft-ball stage or until candy theremometer reaches 228°F. While cooking, keep the cover on part of the time so the steam can help to keep the crystals washed down. Remove from heat. Pour at once into a bowl dipped in cold water. Let the fondant stand until it is lukewarm. Stir vigorously with a wooden spoon until white and creamy. Add vanilla if desired and stir well to combine. Pour into a jar, cover tightly. Put a teaspoonful with vanilla sweet in a glass with ice water and serve.

## HONEY AND SESAME SEED BARS
### Παστέλι

1 cup honey
1 cup sugar
½ cup water
2 cups sesame seed
1 cup coarsely chopped walnuts or blanched almonds

Pick over sesame seed and toast in a frying pan until golden brown. Set aside. Combine honey, sugar and water in a heavy saucepan, bring to a boil, stirring constantly until syrup thickens or until candy thermometer reaches 255°F. Add sesame seed and walnuts if desired, stir well to combine. Remove from heat. Brush a 9x13-inch baking sheet with fine quality oil. Spread hot mixture evenly in the sheet. With a damp spatula smooth the surface. Let cool. Cut into small bars before it gets completely cool and hard.

## GREEK DELIGHTS
### Λουκούμια

3 tablespoons unflavored gelatin
½ cup cold water
2½ cups sugar
1 cup boiling water
3 tablespoons fresh lemon juice
1½ teaspoons vanilla or 1 tablespoon rosewater
1 cup chopped toasted blanched almonds, hazel nuts or coconut
Confectioner's sugar, sifted

Soften gelatin in cold water. Add sugar to boiling water, stir to dissolve. Slowly bring to a boil, add gelatin and simmer for 20 minutes. Remove from heat, add lemon juice, vanilla if desired and nuts you desire, mix well to combine. Pour into lightly oiled baking sheet. Chill until firm. When it is cold, loosen edges of sheet; turn out on a board lightly covered with confectioner's sugar. Cut into cubes and roll in confectioner's sugar. Store in a large jar.

## NOUGAT
### Μαντολάτο

1 cup confectioner's sugar, sifted
1 cup glucose
1 cup water
2½ cups sugar
6 egg whites, stiffly beaten
1½ teaspoons vanilla
3 cups warm toasted blanched almonds or hazel nuts

Combine confectioner's sugar, half of the glucose, half of the sugar and half of the water together and mix well. Slowly bring to a boil, stirring constantly until sugar has dissolved and boil until syrup thickens or until candy thermometer reaches 250°F (120°C). Remove syrup from heat and pour it slowly over the stiffly beaten egg whites and continue beating until it is cool. While beating, cook the remaining glucose, water and sugar until syrup thickens or until candy theremometer reaches 250°F (120°C). Remove syrup from heat and add it slowly over the egg mixture, beating while adding. Add vanilla and almonds if desired. Pour into lightly greased baking sheet and smooth over the surface. Let stand until completely cool. Cut into small pieces and wrap in waxed paper. Store in a tin box or glass jar.

## QUINCE JELLY BARS
### Κυδωνόπαστο

Use the pulp from quince jelly (see index). Press through a food mill. Measure, add an equal amount sugar. Place pulp and sugar into a heavy saucepan. Slowly bring to a boil and cook stirring constantly until the mixture no longer sticks to the sides of the pan. Remove from heat. Add 1½ teaspoons vanilla and 1 cup or more slivered toasted blanched almonds. Pour into lightly greased baking sheet and smooth over the surface. Cool completely. When it is cool, loosen edges of pan; turn out on a board lightly covered with crystalized sugar. Cut into small bars. Sprinkle with little cognac and roll in crystalized sugar. Allow to stand in the air until the surface loses all stickiness. Pack in layers in a tin box, using waxed paper between the layers.

## ORANGE FONDANT
### Φοντὰν πορτοκαλιοῦ

12 large oranges
3 cups chopped toasted blanched almonds
2⅔ cups sugar

**3 tablespoons water**
**1 tablespoon orange liqueur**
**1 teaspoon almond extract**
**Crystalized sugar**
**Small paper fondant cups**

Wash oranges and dry. Then with a sharp knife cut through the end into 4 vertical sections. Gently remove the sections of rind, (keep oranges for eating). Discard white membrane from each section of the rind. Place them into a large saucepan and cover with cold water  Bring to a boil and boil for 10 minutes. Pour off the water.  Place fresh cold water and boil again for 10 minutes; repeat one more time and cook until tender. Drain.  Return the rind to saucepan and cover with cold water, let stay 2 hours. Drain well.   Lay them on absorbent paper.   Press rind through a food mill. Combine rind, almonds, sugar, liqueur and almond extract together into a heavy saucepan and cook slowly, stirring constantly with a wooden spoon until the mixture no longer sticks to the side of the pan. Remove from heat. Cool. Shape

each orange fondant into a ball the size of a small walnut and roll in crystalized sugar. Place them into paper cups.  Makes about 6 dozen.

# CANDIED FRUITS
Φρουΐ γκλασὲ

Any kind of Spoon Sweet Preserve, drained well.
**SYRUP FOR CANDIED FRUIT:**
**3 cups sugar**
**1¼ cups water**

Combine sugar and water together, bring to a boil stirring constantly to dissolve the sugar and boil for 5 minutes. Add preserve pieces to the boiling syrup being careful not to have them crowded. Boil them for 3 minutes. Remove from syrup. Drain well. Roll in granulated sugar and allow them to dry well. Pack between sheets of waxed paper and place in a tin box or a glass jar or place each one into small paper fondant cups.

# MENUS FOR HOLIDAYS

## CHRISTMAS BRUNCH

Cocktail meatballs
Potato croquettes
Crackers
Cheese puffs
Spinach triangles
Canapes
Roasted peppers salad
Russian salad
Feta and Kaseri cheese
Fresh fruits
Christmas bread
Athenian rich Easter braids
Frosted Christmas biscuits
Almond butter Christmas cookies A
Honey Christmas cookies A
Coffee
   (See index for the recipes)

## CHRISTMAS DINNER

Appetizers
Turkey soup avgolemono
Roast stuffed turkey
Mashed potatoes
Gravy
Zucchini au gratin
Leek cheese pitta A or B
Salad
Christmas bread
Feta and Kaseri cheese
Fresh fruits
Chocolate torte
Coffee
   (See index for recipes)

## NEW YEAR'S BRUNCH

Canapes
Crackers
Meat Puffs
Cheese tiny pies with homemade pastry
Crab or lobster salad
Summer country salad
Cheese and artichoke souffle
Butternut squash pitta
Feta and Kaseri cheese
Fresh fruits
Rich New Year's bread
Almond baklava
Frosted Christmas biscuits
Coffee
   (See index for recipes)

## NEW YEAR'S DINNER

Appetizers
Meat stuffed artichokes
Chicken soup avgolemono
Roast stuffed suckling pig or roast pork
       with potatoes
Sour cabbage
Spinach pitta A
Tomato salad
Christmas bread
Feta and Kaseri cheese
Fresh fruits
Cream filled pastry A
Coffee
   (See indext for recipes)

## NIGHT AFTER RESURRECTION

Potato croquettes

Baton sale or crackers
Cheese tiny pies with homemade pastry
Easter soup
Fried lamb liver
Spring salad
Red eggs
Feta and Kaseri cheese
Fresh fruits
Athenian rich Easter braids
    (See index for the recipes)

## EASTER BRUNCH

Cucumber and yogurt dip
Deviled eggs
Cheese ham loaf
Ham log C
Crackers
Meat puffs
Tomato salad
Red eggs
Lamb liver with oregano or fried
        lamb liver
Cheese pitta
Feta and Kaseri cheese
Fresh fruits
Athenian rich Easter braids
Kataifi
Chocolate cream puffs
Coffee
    (See index for recipes)

## EASTER DINNER

Appetizers
Suckling lamb on a spit or baked
        stuffed suckling lamb
Red eggs
Roasted potatoes
Artichokes with peas
Scallion cheese pitta
Spring salad

Feta and Kaseri cheese
Fresh fruits
Athenian rich Easter braids
Nougat torte
Coffee
    (See index for recipes)

## THANKSGIVING BRUNCH

Codfish caviar spread
Carrots, celery sticks and small
        pieces of bread
Cocktail meatballs
Spinach triangles
Cheese tiny pies with homemade pastry
Meat salad mold
Rice au gratin
Zucchini salad
Rich white bread
Feta and Kaseri cheese
Fresh fruits
Pumpkin nut bread
Pumpkin nut cake
Coffee
    (See index for recipes)

## THANKSGIVING DINNER

Appetizers
Turkey soup avgolemono
Eggplant mousaka
Roast stuffed turkey
Mashed potatoes
Gravy
Sauteed string beans
Butternut and pumpkin pitta
Cabbage salad
White rolls
Feta and Kaseri cheese
Fresh fruits
Pumpkin torte
Coffee
    (See index for recipes)

*And I will serve you up a meal*
*Which shall be redolent*
*Of the Athenian breezes*

Athenaeus

# INDEX